MILLENNIUM LECTURES

"First we must dream, then we must believe, then it will happen"

The Clifford Chance

Millennium Lectures

The Coming Together of the Common Law
and the Civil Law

Edited by
BASIL S MARKESINIS

Sponsored by
Clifford Chance

Under the patronage of
The Lord Chancellor the
Rt Hon Lord Irvine of Lairg
the Lord Chief Justice of England and Wales
the Senior Law Lord
and the Master of the Rolls

·HART·
PUBLISHING
OXFORD – PORTLAND OREGON
2000

Hart Publishing
Oxford and Portland, Oregon

Published in North America (US and Canada) by
Hart Publishing c/o
International Specialized Book Services
5804 NE Hassalo Street
Portland, Oregon
97213-3644
USA

Distributed in the Netherlands, Belgium and Luxembourg by
Intersentia, Churchillaan 108
B2900 Schoten
Antwerpen
Belgium

Hart Publishing Ltd is a specialist legal publisher based in Oxford, England.
To order further copies of this book or to request a list of other
publications please write to:

Hart Publishing Ltd, Salter's Boatyard,
Folly Bridge, Abingdon Road, Oxford OX1 4LB
Telephone: +44 (0)1865 245533 or Fax: +44 (0)1865 794882
e-mail: mail@hartpub.co.uk

British Library Cataloguing in Publication Data
Data Available
ISBN 1 84113–068–0 (cloth)

Typeset in 10pt Sabon
by Hope Services (Abingdon) Ltd.
Printed in Great Britain on acid-free paper
by Bookcraft (Bath) Ltd,
Midsomer Norton, Somerset

Contents

vi *Contents*

List of Contributors

Professor Christian von Bar, is Professor of Private Law, Private International Law and Comparative Law in the University of Osnabrück and Director of that University's Institute of Private International and Comparative Law. He is also an Honorary Bencher of Gray's Inn.

The Rt Hon The Lord Bingham of Cornhill DCL, is the Lord Chief Justice of England and Wales and the Visitor of Balliol College, Oxford.

Keith Clark Esq, BCL, is Chairman of Clifford Chance.

Professor Walter van Gerven is a Member of the Royal Belgian and Dutch Academies. He was Advocate General at the Court of Justice of the European Communities and Professor at the University of Leuven, Belgium.

The Rt Hon Lord Goff of Chieveley PC, DCL, is a Fellow of the British Academy and High Steward of the University of Oxford.

Professor Dr Klaus Hopt is Professor of Commercial Law at the University of Hamburg and Co-Director of the Max-Planck Institute of Foreign and Comparative Law.

H.E. Dr Gil Carlos Rodriguez Iglesias is President of the Court of Justice of the European Communities, Luxembourg.

The Rt Hon the Lord Irvine of Lairg is Lord High Chancellor of Great Britain.

Madame Noëlle Lenoir is a Member of the *Conseil Constitutionnel* of France and an Honorary Bencher of Gray's Inn.

Professor Dr Jutta Limbach is President of the German Federal Constitutional Court.

Professor Basil Markesinis QC, DCL, D.Iur.h.c.mult. is Clifford Chance Professor of Comparative Law in the University of Oxford and a Fellow of Brasenose College. He also holds the Jamail Regents Chair of Law at the University of Texas at Austin. He is a Fellow of the British Academy and a Corresponding Member of the Academies of Athens, Belgium and The Netherlands.

Professor Cesare Mirabelli is President of the Italian Constitutional Court.

The Rt Hon the Lord Steyn is a Lord of Appeal in Ordinary.

H.E. Dr Luzius Wildhaber is President of the European Court of Human Rights, Strasbourg.

The Rt Hon the Lord Woolf of Barnes is Master of the Rolls and Visitor of University College London.

Introduction

KEITH CLARK, CHAIRMAN, CLIFFORD CHANCE

This conference comes at an opportune time: the start of a new millennium and a new phase in the European project. Yet, for many, the issues have become stale. *"As the European debate reaches fever pitch, it makes less and less sense. Pro-Europeans don't seem to know what their case is anymore...The sceptics want to repatriate power to national level and dismantle the EU . . . People don't want to be forced to choose between a federal superstate and a free trade area— neither will allow us to thrive in the next millennium."*

I quote from *Network Europe: A New Case For Europe* published by the Foreign Policy Centre, a British think-tank, to coincide with a conference we held in November last year. I said then that the time seemed ripe to stimulate new thinking about the future for Europe, and to map out some new roads for the European project. Clifford Chance supported that publication, and the November conference, and we are proud to be sponsoring this book and the conference at which the papers in it will be given and discussed.

Our role in this conference stems originally from our endowment of the Chair of Comparative Law held by Professor Basil Markesinis, out of which developed the Institute of European and Comparative Law at Oxford. We are delighted to be associated with the Institute's success and prestige and I pay particular tribute to Professor Markesinis's tremendous achievement in organising this conference. Supporting such endeavours is integral to Clifford Chance's vision to be the world's premier law firm. Let me explain why.

As many of you will know, the Clifford Chance of which I am chairman is a new firm which was born in January this year. The old Clifford Chance was originally the result of a merger in 1987 between two law firms in the City of London, the first UK merger of law firms on this scale. Our vision then was to be the pre-eminent law firm in Europe. As we approached our goal, we raised our sights higher. The result is the tri-partite merger between the British Clifford Chance, the German firm Pünder and the US firm Rogers & Wells. The merger cements our pre-eminence in Europe and equips us with in-depth capability in both English and New York law. Each of the three firms has built an international practice in its own right with offices in other jurisdictions, but together we are now uniquely well-placed to serve banks and companies across the global financial markets. The merger will enable us to achieve our goal of becoming a global, multi-cultural practice.

The new firm has a fresh vision, which touches on the subject-matter of this conference. We face challenges similar to those facing Europe. We have a shared vision of where we want to go and a shared awareness that our combined international efforts achieve far more than we could ever have done on a merely national basis.

This conference addresses some of the fundamental legal issues that underlie increasing convergence between the Anglo-Saxon and continental European legal systems.

As a former student of comparative law—I studied under Dr Otto Kahn-Freund in the 1960s—I have read these conference papers with great interest. Under his tutelage I analysed cases in France and England involving road accidents where compulsory insurance applied. The task that faced the courts in both countries was how to ensure that social justice was achieved so that the losses suffered by the injured could be most fairly spread amongst all motorists. What struck me was that the courts in both countries arrived at the same outcome but did so by different routes: the French courts through developing the law of causation; the English courts through developing the law of negligence—arriving at similar results despite different legal foundations.

I see the papers for this conference in a similar light. Each paper addresses a facet of the overriding question: how can common and civil law systems converge while allowing each to remain true to its foundations? For me, four themes stand out.

First, we must accept that there are fundamental differences between the legal system of England and Wales and those of continental European civil law systems. Lord Irvine warns that, while there is much scope for cross-fertilisation between civil and common law systems, the extent to which continental public law is able to take root in English domestic law is constrained by the constitutional framework within which English administrative law subsists. And, of course, the converse holds as well.

Second, there is, nevertheless, an increasing degree of cross-fertilisation between the civil and common law systems. Lord Bingham and Professor Markesinis point out that convergence between the legal systems of Europe is taking place, even if gradually and patchily. Lord Bingham warns the common lawyers of the fallacy of treating all civil law jurisdictions as the same. Professor Markesinis provides a useful analysis of the common law's debt to Europe. Christian Bar wittily returns the compliment by suggesting areas where the common law can have an impact on the development of a new collective European law.

Third, European human rights law is playing a critical role in bringing about constitutional change in the UK. Key issues here are the role of the judiciary and, in particular, the interpretative function of judges. Cesare Mirabelli analyses the concept of fundamental rights as the basis of a common European law. Gil

Carlos Rodríguez Iglesias describes the decisive role of the European Court of Justice in shaping the human rights of EU citizens. Luzius Wildhaber gives a first-hand review of the operation of the European Court of Human Rights. Lord Steyn analyses judicial approaches to interpretation. Noëlle Lenoir considers the task faced by the judge of a national court in interpreting international law, specifically the European Court of Justice and the European Court of Human Rights. Lord Woolf sets the changing role of the judiciary in the context of the evolution of English public law.

Finally, there is the development of 'economic law', reflecting the impact that government has on commercial life. W. Van Gerven sets European law in the context of the European Union, emphasising the extent to which commercial law is now part of economic law. The public and private sectors can no longer be isolated from each other. Klaus Hopt analyses the issues that concern the clients that a firm like Clifford Chance serves, in terms of capital market turf wars, corporate governance and judicial attitudes to the group corporate veil.

Turning to Lord Goff's closing paper, I particularly welcome what he says about "the development of the most extraordinary diversity and depth of culture that the world has ever known . . . We have today in Europe a whole range of legal cultures . . . We should be profoundly grateful for this diversity. We can learn more from these diverse systems than we could ever have derived from a single monolithic system."

GLOBALISATION

Lord Goff's words reflect our outlook at Clifford Chance. We are a genuinely multi-cultural firm. We seek to use the best forms of practice in each legal system, and combine them on a daily basis to deliver seamless solutions to our clients' problems. In this way we practise the law internationally across a large number of individual legal systems.

We are client driven. Operating all over the world, our clients face an increasingly complex and competitive environment. The world is becoming smaller all the time. The factors at work include deregulation, reduced barriers to entry, convergence of economies and technological advances, all of which enable business to view the world increasingly as a single market. Time zones and geographical barriers are no longer the obstacles they were. Economies of scale can be achieved through effective supply chain management and shared service centres, allowing a company to locate different parts of its operations in different markets according to relevant issues ranging from employment to tax. As we move from an industrial to a knowledge society, the Internet is accelerating these trends and rewriting the rules of business as it goes.

Yet the world is also becoming bigger. More markets are opening up all the time. Emerging sectors are attracting more investment than ever before. Third world economies are striving to industrialise, and often to leapfrog the traditional route to economic well-being. As the world becomes wealthier, so first world consumers are demanding to be treated as 'markets of one'. At the same time, as the world becomes more homogenised, individuals and nations want their heritage and culture to be respected.

These are the challenges that our clients face. Together, they can be termed 'globalisation'. The Foreign Policy Centre has summarised and defined globalisation in terms of an accumulation of links across the world's regions involving four distinct types of change:

- stretching social, political and economic activities across political frontiers, regions and continents;
- intensifying our dependence on each other as flows of trade, investment, finance, migration and culture increases;
- accelerating the world through new systems of communication that enable ideas, goods, information and capital to move quickly; and
- through the deeper impact that distant events have on our lives, with even the most local developments coming to have enormous global consequences, blurring the boundaries between domestic matters and global affairs.

Where businessmen and bankers go, lawyers are not far behind and often get there first. Lawyers help their clients manage risk, either by documenting transactions in a way that identifies and apportions risk between the commercial parties or, if a dispute has arisen, in advising the client on the optimal route to resolve that dispute, weighing up the risks of different strategies and their likely outcomes.

GLOBAL CONVERGENCE IN PRACTICE

The task of commercial lawyers like us is to ensure that our clients can successfully run their businesses on an international scale while minimising the burdens of compliance with local laws. Many of their transactions are complex, crossing borders and different legal systems. We structure, negotiate and document those transactions to provide the desired outcome in a predictable fashion by ensuring that the terms will be upheld by whichever courts are likely, in the event of a dispute, to have jurisdiction.

The drive towards the globalisation of legal practice has undoubtedly come from the world's capital markets. The trading empire created by Britain, superseded more recently by the economic dominance of the United States, made English and New York law the international *lex mercantilis*. Whatever the historical reasons, we common lawyers are fortunate that they have become so. English and New York law are regarded by many of our clients as virtually interchangeable. But it is not simply the law that has converged at this level.

The way in which transactions are carried out is also becoming homogenised. Global financial institutions—commercial banks, investment banks, pension funds, insurance companies and other investment vehicles—operate on a global stage and expect transactions to follow a similar course, wherever they are undertaken. For example, cross-border mergers and acquisitions are increasingly subject to New York or English law, simply because of the way in which such transactions are funded. The applicable law may or may not have a higher local content, but what is becoming standardised is the way in which such transactions are conducted. So a syndicated loan, a flotation, a bond issue, an international equity offering, a project financing and many other types of financial transaction are increasingly expected to follow an established track. These ways of doing business have tended, in general, to be developed in common law jurisdictions and cross-fertilised to civil law markets. The standardisation of such transactions drives down their costs.

To give an indication of the scale of activity, over the period from 1995 to 1998, the number of international equity issues increased by 130%, the number of European mergers and acquisitions by 119% and the number of international bond issues by 117% (according to figures compiled by the Bank for International Settlements and the OECD). This global financial market is one that Clifford Chance is designed to serve.

The ability to advise on such transactions requires a global capability and understanding, combined with local law expertise. We have lawyers who are expert in the law local to our clients, the locus of the transaction, and wherever it will be enforced. A typical example might be—and here I have a recent deal in mind—an aircraft financing, undertaken in our Frankfurt office by a German rechtsanwalt, to supply a German airline with aircraft funded by a German bank. All the documentation for this particular deal was in English and the transaction was governed by English law. Nowadays, this is not at all unusual in what would otherwise be a domestic transaction.

So it is that our daily work helps to drive convergence. Our lawyers are admitted in one or more local jurisdictions but advise on global transactions. The papers in this book echo our experience as practitioners. On the one hand, we see an inexorable trend towards convergence. On the other, we must remain mindful of profound jurisdictional differences.

This convergence is also being driven at a market level. Trade associations such as the International Securities and Derivatives Association have accelerated convergence by devising master agreements that banks can adopt for the trading of swaps, derivatives and other financial products. They are codifying practice in response to a multiplicity of sources of law, much as civil lawyers over the centuries codified law in response to the range of sources from courts and universities across Europe.

THE GLOBALISATION OF LEGAL PRACTICE

Where the capital markets lead, others follow. Companies that trade around the world look to protect their trade marks and copyrights. The applicable law varies from jurisdiction to jurisdiction, but companies increasingly want to manage the protection of their intellectual property rights around the world. Employment law varies from country to country, but corporate employment policy is increasingly centralised. Real estate is an area jealously guarded by local law but here, too, the role played by inward investment on the part of institutional investors, banks and multinational companies is promoting a standardisation of approach.

Over the last 30 years we have seen an explosion in global finance and international trade and increased competition for lawyers, as well as an explosion of publicity, and the rise of the corporate general counsel as the embodiment of the demanding client. Law firms have had to improve their management. They have had to invest in overseas offices and information technology. Legal practice is unrecognisable from the way it was 30 years ago.

The last bastion of local law lies in the courts. But any multinational faced with a major dispute increasingly plans its litigation strategy at headquarters. Our task is to advise multinationals at a strategic level on where best to defend or launch proceedings. A law firm cannot do this unless it is both local and global. Few have this aspiration and fewer still the capability.

One of the fascinating aspects of globalisation is the convergence between government and the private sector and the impact that each has on the other, something touched on in the European context by papers in this book. More and more clients need to conduct business in unfamiliar governmental and legal environments. Law firms based in Washington DC and Brussels were amongst the first to recognise the need to learn their way around the national and international corridors of political, official and regulatory power. We understand this: we were the first British firm to establish a public policy function in the early 1990s. As our clients operate on an increasingly global basis, so they must deal increasingly with the burdens of regulation, anticipate new legislation, and maintain a dialogue with government. In our experience, commercial lawyers are in discussion with government to a much greater extent than before. There is considerable scope for development of that dialogue, which is also a driver of convergence.

Let me put this into another context: the massive impact that information technology and the Internet are having on our world. We were retained by the US Federal Trade Commission to obtain injunctions in Antigua freezing bank accounts that held moneys solicited from investors through an illegal Internet pyramid scheme known as Fortuna Alliance. The task was to freeze those accounts at the moment that the FTC issued proceedings against the scheme organisers in Seattle—a moment too soon or late and the funds would have been sent electronically elsewhere. The FTC was successful and returned recovered funds to investors by way of the Internet. The case is a good illustration of what I mean by global issues. A total of 15,625 individuals in 71 countries made investments totalling $5.5 million. The spread of countries ranged alphabetically from Argentina to Zambia (one in each). There were over 8,000

Americans, 2,000 Australians, 500 Dutch and 100 UK investors. This is one aspect of a different kind of convergence, between computing, telecommunications and broadcasting that is, without doubt, altering the way business functions. The *Fortuna* case demonstrates the need for a global capability in this new business environment.

Information technology is critical to our own business. Information, knowledge and words are crucial to a global law firm. We have a document management system that allows any lawyer to access any document relevant to his or her current transaction, wherever that document has last been worked on within Clifford Chance worldwide, and to do so within seconds of the last person's input. We are developing intranets and harnessing the Internet. Next Law is an on-line service offered by Clifford Chance which provides comprehensive information, advice and compliance guidance about the impact of data protection laws in 30 jurisdictions around the world. The Internet allows us to collect material from other jurisdictions and marshall it to provide our clients with trans-jurisdictional advice. This allows us to undertake detailed comparative studies, weighing up the merits of different jurisdictions—for instance, to advise an international bank on where best to locate its operations to reduce the regulatory burden and the cost of capital.

THE IMPORTANCE OF CULTURES AND RELATIONSHIPS

In this new world, we believe that respect for different legal cultures and the strength of our internal and client relationships will be key.

The question of culture is critical. The Clifford Chance vision is to create a genuinely multi-cultural firm. For just as business has to be global and local, so the law firms that serve it must be both. Just as the world is becoming smaller yet larger, so global legal practice requires standardised approaches coupled with immersion in local law and culture.

Part of our vision is that we should operate at the highest levels, serving international investment banks, multinational companies and governments. We see as our peer group those who, in their role in commerce, finance or government, are at the forefront of global progress. As the world becomes both smaller and larger, so the people who will shape its future—government ministers, leading bankers, the chief executives of the world's largest companies, the officers of the multi-lateral agencies— will be increasingly cosmopolitan. The lawyers who wish to sit at their table will be the same: born in one part of the world, educated in another, living and working in another, at home in several languages and cultures. Our aim is to practise law in a new way, which will require a new type of lawyer: the type that governments, banks and businesses will wish to call upon for advice, and who will command their respect and friendship, for it is at this level that the most interesting and demanding legal work will arise.

In order to succeed in this, we will have to be more than a provider of legal advice: we will have to be able to operate at the highest levels and at the interface between commerce and government. Our lawyers will have to have broad horizons, beyond a preoccupation with transactions and advice.

If we are to maintain our ability to tackle the most demanding of transactions, and to help shape the law, we require intellectual input at the highest level. In Clifford Chance we now have support lawyers who specialise in maintaining and developing our know-how, lawyers who no longer handle transactions on a day-to-day basis but act as in-house counsel to those who do. The divide between practitioners and academics, more pronounced in common law than civil law jurisdictions, is narrowing, just as the constituent legal systems that will form a new European system of law are converging. Indeed, one of the lessons that common lawyers can learn from their civil law counterparts is the benefit of a symbiotic relationship between legal practice and academic institutions, between the practitioner and the jurist. Hence our support for this conference.

We are going further. We are creating our own Academy to help create the new type of lawyer I have mentioned, one who is at ease when dealing with the legal concepts of a number of jurisdictions, who is alert to the similarities and differences. The Academy is a critical component of our vision. It will be based in Amsterdam but, in keeping with the new information age in which we practise, will harness the latest technological and virtual advances to take from and deliver to any part of the globe in which we operate. The Academy is going to equip our common lawyers with sufficient understanding of civil law systems—and vice versa—to manage the delivery of transactions across a range of jurisdictions, knowing the issues to address and the obstacles to overcome.

As future generations of Clifford Chance lawyers pass through the Academy, they will absorb and impart in equal measure the culture of the firm and the local culture of the jurisdiction in which they originally qualified. Echoing Lord Goff, I believe that in terms of legal culture we all have much to learn from each other, and to adopt best practice wherever it occurs. So I hope that our Academy, bolstered by the relationship between practitioner and jurist that this conference represents, may in time become the foundation of the European Law School advocated by Lord Bingham in his paper.

FINAL THOUGHTS

I hope I have dispelled the notion that common lawyers think they are somehow leading the way in this world of change. We are not. A multicultural approach that takes the best from wherever it occurs is essential. But in many things we are driven by what happens in the US. I have before me a letter sent from the headquarters of an international oil company to its US subsidiary in 1916 in which the recipient—the president of the US company—is berated for his use of lawyers: *"It seems to me from your letter as if the lawyers are a kind of department to your business. Their idea that we should be inclined to give them a fixed fee is absurd. What astonishes me most is their proposal that you should make an arrangement by which one member of their firm should give practically his entire time to the conduct of our affairs. Although we have an enormous business here, we very rarely consult lawyers . . . whilst it seems to me that you employ them practically in every instance. Lawyers are not business people. However large a lawyer's experience may be, in the conduct of business he is absolutely useless. To ask a lawyer to draw up a contract for you is a most foolish thing to do, and this is bound to lead to trouble . . ."*

Such a letter could not be written now. We have seen huge changes in the cultures of business and law. In the nations of the West the law has been an enforcer of change and we are law-led societies. I believe that we can help to make a reality of a united Europe through a combination of the civil and common law. Hence the importance of this book and conference.

I hope I have succeeded in sharing with you our vision at Clifford Chance and how its strands interrelate: the local and the global, the civil and the common law, the real and the virtual, Europe and the world, the jurist and the practitioner, the transaction manager and the know-how officer, the law firm and the law school.

I and my partners enthusiastically support these developments and this conference. I know from these papers that you share my enthusiasm.

1

The Influence of Europe on Public Law in the United Kingdom

THE LORD CHANCELLOR, LORD IRVINE OF LAIRG

"BRITAIN IN EUROPE": EUROPEAN LAW IN BRITAIN

It gives me great pleasure to address this Conference. I should like to congratulate the University of Oxford, its Institute of European and Comparative Law and Professor Markesinis for organising this Conference and bringing together some of the finest legal minds in Europe.

The theme of the Conference—"Britain in Europe"—is an expression which should be read as affirming our perception of Britain's role, in the new Millennium, as an active participant in Europe, within both the European Union and the Council of Europe. In order for the United Kingdom to play such a role, European law must influence and—to some extent—infiltrate our national legal order. In this sense, "European law in Britain" is a necessarily and inevitable concomitant of "Britain in Europe". Although this phenomenon affects many branches of domestic law—as the contributions of other speakers today will demonstrate—I shall focus on the legal and constitutional implications of accommodating principles of European *public law* within the United Kingdom's legal framework.

There are two distinct (but related) aspects to this enquiry. First, how are principles of European public law to be given effect in Britain? How, in other words, does our constitution respond to the challenge of facilitating British membership of the European institutions? Secondly, once European law is thus received, what effect does it have on the future shape and direction of our system of public law?

THE LEGAL FACILITATION OF "BRITAIN IN EUROPE"

I shall begin by considering the constitutional methodology by which principles of European public law are accommodated within the British legal framework. The ultimate challenge in this field is to facilitate Britain's full participation in matters European while remaining faithful to the enduring principles of domestic constitutionalism which lie at the heart of our legal system. This challenge—which engages constitutional theory at its most fundamental level—arises in relation to Britain's membership of both the European Union and the Council of Europe. Let me take each in turn.

The British Constitution and the European Union

Central to the effective functioning of the European Union is the principle that European law should have uniform effect throughout all fifteen member states. As the Union expands, this will assume ever greater importance. National courts play a key role by seeking, wherever possible, to interpret national law consistently with Community law, thus ensuring that the latter takes effect throughout the Union.[1]

Occasionally, however, it is simply not feasible for a national court to construe domestic law in this way. As is well known, precisely this position was reached in the course of the *Factortame* litigation, in which the European Court of Justice held, and the British courts accepted, that in such situations domestic tribunals must be willing to set aside national legislation in order to secure effect for Community law.[2] In this way our courts have acquired a limited jurisdiction to review primary legislation and, to this extent, parliamentary sovereignty is curtailed so long as the United Kingdom remains part of the European Union. This, however, is to state the position in rather bald terms. In order properly to evaluate the constitutional implications of Community membership, it is essential to distinguish between what may be termed Parliament's *ultimate sovereignty* and its *contemporary sovereignty*.

Some commentators contend that the priority of Community law over national law can be rationalised so as to leave the theory of parliamentary supremacy in tact. Thus it is said that *Factortame* involved nothing more than the application of a rule of construction.[3] I do not share that view. It is elemental that rules of interpretation yield in the face of sufficiently clear contrary enactment.[4] The rule of construction which was supposedly applied in

---

[1] National courts do not, in fact, have any choice in this area. Community law directs that they must, by interpretative means, reconcile national and Community law whenever this is possible. This is known, in Community law, as the doctrine of indirect effect. See the decisions of the European Court of Justice in, inter alia, Case 14/83, *Von Colson* v. *Land Nordrhein-Westfalen* [1984] E.C.R. 1891; Case C-106/89, *Marleasing S.A.* v. *La Comercial Internacional de Alimentacion S.A.* [1990] E.C.R. I- 4135.

[2] *R.* v. *Secretary of State for Transport, ex parte Factortame Ltd. (No. 2)* [1991] 1 A.C. 603.

[3] See, *inter alios*, Sir John Laws, "Law and Democracy" [1995] P.L. 72, 89. This construction-based view derives some support from the speech of Lord Bridge in *R.* v. *Secretary of State for Transport, ex parte Factortame Ltd.* [1990] 2 A.C. 85, 140.

[4] Take, *e.g.*, the well-established rule of construction which holds that, when it legislates, Parliament is assumed not to intend to interfere with the right of the citizen to gain access to justice. The celebrated decision of the House of Lords in *Anisminic Ltd.* v. *Foreign Compensation Commission* [1969] 2 A.C. 147 demonstrates that this rule of interpretation will yield only in the face of extremely clear statutory provision. Nevertheless, as Laws J. explained in *R.* v. *Lord Chancellor,*

Factortame did not, however, yield: it prevailed over a legislative scheme which was acknowledged to be incompatible. It follows that, as Professor Wade remarks, *Factortame* constituted "much more than an exercise in construction".[5] It is therefore quite clear that, for so long as the United Kingdom is a member of the European Union, Parliament's competence is limited in the sense that it may not enact legislation which is incompatible with directly effective Community law. For this reason, it can be said that the contemporary sovereignty of Parliament has been curtailed.[6]

However, it is necessary to keep in mind the distinct concept of Parliament's ultimate sovereignty which—according to Professor Trevor Hartley—entails that "Community law will . . . prevail [over inconsistent national law] *unless Parliament clearly and expressly states in a future Act that the latter is to override Community law*",[7] a view which derives support from Lord Denning's judgment in *Macarthys* v. *Smith*.[8] On this approach, Parliament retains the theoretical capacity to derogate explicitly from Community law in exceptional circumstances. And, although not all commentators agree with this analysis,[9] it is universally accepted that Parliament, if it wished, could enact legislation to effect the withdrawal of the United Kingdom from the European Union, thereby restoring its absolute supremacy. In this sense, therefore, Parliament's ultimate sovereignty undoubtedly remains intact.

The importance of this point should not be underestimated. The survival of Parliament's ultimate supremacy, although a theoretical point in one sense, does have some tangible implications. It serves to emphasise that the limitation of Parliament's competence which EU membership involves does not render sovereignty a dead letter. Community membership does not, therefore, open the door to a more thoroughgoing theory of limited sovereignty embracing a whole series of higher order laws to which Parliament would be subject;[10] and this, in

ex parte Witham [1998] Q.B. 575, it is necessarily the case that the rule will yield if Parliament legislates to that effect with sufficient clarity. It follows from this that it would be futile—and quite meaningless—to seek judicial review of *legislation* (as opposed to judicial review of *executive action* carried out in purported reliance on a statutory authority) on the ground that it interfered with the constitutional right of access to the courts. Since that right is enshrined only in a rule of construction, it cannot prevail over contrary enactment. For further comment, see M.C. Elliott, "Reconciling Constitutional Rights and Constitutional Orthodoxy" [1997] C.L.J. 474.

    5 H.W.R. Wade, "Sovereignty—Revolution or Evolution?" (1996) 112 L.Q.R. 568, 570.
    6 See also *R.* v. *Secretary of State for Employment, ex parte Equal Opportunities Commission* [1995] 1 A.C. 1.
    7 T.C. Hartley, *The Foundations of European Community Law* (Oxford: Oxford University Press, 1998), 4th edn., p. 255 (emphasis added).
    8 *Macarthys Ltd.* v. *Smith* [1979] 3 All E.R. 325, 329.
    9 E.g. H.W.R. Wade, "Sovereignty—Revolution or Evolution?" (1996) 112 L.Q.R. 568, 570-571.
    10 A number of commentators have, in recent years, argued in favour of just such a thoroughgoing limitation of Parliament's legislative competence: see, *inter alios*, Sir Robin Cooke, "Fundamentals" [1988] N.Z.L.J. 158; Lord Woolf, "*Droit Public*—English Style" [1995] P.L. 57 (although *cf.* Lord Woolf, "Judicial Review—The Tensions Between the Executive and the Judiciary" (1998) 114 L.Q.R. 579); Sir John Laws, "Law and Democracy" [1995] P.L. 72 and "The Constitution: Morals and Rights" [1996] P.L. 622. My own views on this subject can be found in "Judges and Decision-Makers: The Theory and Practice of *Wednesbury* Review" [1996] P.L. 59. For

turn, impacts upon a range of public law issues—such as the constitutional basis of judicial review[11] and the proper role of the courts in public law proceedings[12]—which have been, and continue to be, profoundly influenced by the supremacy principle. The crucial point, therefore, is that while the theory of parliamentary sovereignty has unquestionably been modified by our membership of the European Union, it nevertheless remains a key constitutional foundation that continues to shape the public law superstructure which it supports.

The British Constitution and the European Convention on Human Rights

Let me turn, now, to the European Convention on Human Rights. Although states are not legally obliged to incorporate the Convention into national law,[13] the rights of the individual tend to be better protected when incorporation is effected.[14] This is particularly so in countries—like the United Kingdom—which do not possess domestic bills of rights. For this reason, incorporation of the Convention into our national law has long been overdue, and it gives me

a useful overview of this discourse, see R. Mullender, "Parliamentary Sovereignty, the Constitution, and the Judiciary" (1998) 49 N.I.L.Q. 138.

[11] For an explanation of how the principle of parliamentary sovereignty profoundly affects the way in which judicial review is justified in constitutional terms, see H.W.R. Wade and C.F. Forsyth, *Administrative Law* (Oxford: Oxford University Press, 1994), 7th edn., pp. 41-46; C.F. Forsyth, "Of Fig Leaves and Fairy Tales: The Ultra Vires Doctrine, the Sovereignty of Parliament and Judicial Review" [1996] C.L.J. 122; M.C. Elliott, "The Demise of Parliamentary Sovereignty? The Implications for Justifying Judicial Review" (1999) 115 L.Q.R. 119; M.C. Elliott, "The Ultra Vires Doctrine in a Constitutional Setting: Still the Central Principle of Administrative Law" [1999] C.L.J. 129. Opposing views are expressed by D. Oliver, "Is the Ultra Vires Rule the Basis of Judicial Review?" [1987] P.L. 543; Sir John Laws, "Law and Democracy" [1995] P.L. 72; Sir John Laws, "Illegality: The Problem of Jurisdiction" in M. Supperstone and J. Goudie (eds.), *Judicial Review* (London: Butterworths, 1997); P.P. Craig, "Ultra Vires and the Foundations of Judicial Review" [1998] C.L.J. 63.

[12] See below, section 3, and also my "Judges and Decision-Makers: The Theory and Practice of *Wednesbury* Review" [1996] P.L. 59.

[13] See, *e.g.*, *The Guardian and The Observer* v. *United Kingdom* (1991) Series A, vol. 216.

[14] A number of commentators have suggested that the courts, through the medium of the common law, *can* protect human rights adequately in the absence of incorporation: see, *inter alios*, Lord Browne-Wilkinson, "The Infiltration of a Bill of Rights" [1992] P.L. 397; Sir John Laws, "Is the High Court the Guardian of Fundamental Constitutional Rights?" [1993] P.L. 59; M. Hunt, *Using Human Rights Law in English Courts* (Oxford: Hart Publishing, 1997). These theories are not, however, supported by the practice of the courts. Notwithstanding that the courts subject decisions which engage fundamental rights to "the most anxious scrutiny" (*R.* v. *Secretary of State for the Home Department, ex parte Bugdaycay* [1987] A.C. 514, 531, *per* Lord Bridge), the courts, ultimately, have refused—for good constitutional reasons (on which see my 1998 National Heritage Lecture, "Constitutional Reform in the United Kingdom: British Solutions to Universal Problems" (Washington D.C., May 1998, publication forthcoming)—to depart from the *Wednesbury* standard of review. Incorporation, therefore, *will* mark the inception of a more rigorous system of rights protection, given that the emphasis will then shift, in human rights cases, from rationality to proportionality (on which see below and also my 1998 Tom Sargant Memorial Lecture, "The Development of Human Rights in Britain under an Incorporated Convention on Human Rights" [1998] P.L. 221). For further discussion see below, section 3.

great personal pleasure to be able to say that this situation will be remedied on 2 October, 2000, when the Act will be implemented.

I have already observed that one of the fundamental challenges posed by EU membership concerns the accommodation of Community law within the British constitutional framework. A comparable issue arises in relation to the European Convention—namely, how best to reconcile the need for an effective regime of rights protection with the constitutional structure of the United Kingdom?

The imperative of balancing these two objectives is central to the scheme of the new legislation. To this end, all public authorities will be placed under a wholly new obligation to respect human rights as they discharge their functions,[15] and the courts will be placed under a strong duty[16] to construe legislation, wherever possible, consistently with the Convention rights.[17] Crucially, however, when national legislation cannot be construed in this way, the judges will *not* be empowered to set aside parliamentary legislation.[18] Instead, the higher courts[19] will be permitted to declare that national law is incompatible with human rights.[20] This will trigger a fast-track procedure under which the Government may, subject to parliamentary approval, amend the offending legislation.[21] This scheme, it has been said, effects "an ingenious and successful reconciliation of the principles of parliamentary sovereignty and the need for effective domestic remedies".[22]

As with the impact of EU membership, however, it is important to recognise that, while the ultimate principle of legislative supremacy is emphatically preserved by our new human rights system, there will nevertheless—quite rightly— be implications of a more practical nature for the sovereignty doctrine. The balance which the Human Rights Act seeks to strike will be secured by maintaining the sovereignty principle, while changing the environment within which it is exercised. The new powers of the higher courts to issue declarations of incompatibility,[23] and the duty incumbent upon Ministers to draw Parliament's attention to the human rights implications of draft legislation,[24] will focus legislators' minds more clearly than ever before on fundamental rights issues.

---

[15] Human Rights Act 1998, s. 6(1).

[16] Lord Cooke, who, of course, has extensive knowledge of the New Zealand Bill of Rights Act 1990, has said that the interpretative obligation in the British draft legislation "is, if anything, slightly stronger than the New Zealand section. If it is scrupulously complied with, in a major field the common law approach to statutory interpretation will never be the same again; moreover, this will prove a powerful Bill indeed." See H.L. Deb., 3 Nov. 1997, col. 1273.

[17] Human Rights Act 1998, s. 3(1).

[18] Neither the courts' interpretative obligation nor the issue of a declaration of incompatibility under s. 4 shall affect "the validity, continuing operation or enforcement" of any primary legislation. See ss. 3(2)(b) and 4(6)(a).

[19] As defined in s. 4(5).

[20] See s. 4.

[21] See s. 10 and sch. 2.

[22] Lord Lester of Herne Hill, H.L. Deb., 18 November 1997, col. 521.

[23] See s. 10.

[24] See s. 17.

Consequently, while Parliament will unequivocally retain its sovereignty, it will be much less likely to use it in a manner that is insensitive to the values embodied in the Convention. What this will reduce to is a political doctrine of legislative self-restraint in deference to human rights considerations. The fundamental parameters represented by sovereignty theory will therefore remain, but the dynamics of the relationships between the courts, the executive and Parliament will, within those ultimate limits, subtly change. In this manner, an accommodation is once again reached between, on the one hand, embracing the influences which inevitably follow from Britain's participation in Europe and, on the other hand, adhering to the hallowed principles on which our constitution has—for over three hundred years—been founded.

THE LEGAL CONSEQUENCES OF "BRITAIN IN EUROPE"

I have concentrated, thus far, on how European influences are received into British law—how, in other words, "Britain in Europe" is facilitated at the level of constitutional theory. I now turn to the second issue which I identified in my opening remarks—the question of how European public law influences the development of specific principles of administrative law in Britain. It will quickly become apparent that these two implications of Britain's being "in Europe" are, in reality, two sides of the same coin, because the extent to which European influences may affect the development of English public law is ultimately a function of the constitutional framework within which that system of public law subsists. Let me illustrate this argument through two examples. I will turn, shortly, to the principle of proportionality. First, however, I wish to consider the doctrine of legitimate expectation.

The Doctrine of Legitimate Expectation

Introduction

That principle is well-established in the law of the European Union,[25] and our own courts have also embraced it, recognising its capacity both for protecting against arbitrary treatment and upholding the principle of legal certainty, both of which are central to the rule of law.[26] Thus it is now well established in English law that expectations can be protected procedurally by, for example, requiring consultation or a hearing before established practice is departed from. The European Court of Justice, however, has gone further, holding that the

---

[25] For an overview, see P.P. Craig, "Substantive Legitimate Expectations in Domestic and Community Law" [1996] C.L.J. 289, 304-310.

[26] On the inception of legitimate expectation as an established ground of review in English administrative law, see C.F. Forsyth, "The Provenance and Protection of Legitimate Expectations" [1988] C.L.J. 238.

expectation doctrine possesses a substantive, as well as a procedural, dimension.[27] The question whether English administrative law should follow suit has generated a good deal of controversy in our courts.

Three Models of Legitimate Expectation in English Law

Consideration of the domestic case law discloses three competing conceptions of legitimate expectation. The first holds that the expectations of individuals can only ever be protected by the provision of some form of procedural relief. Laws J. (now Laws L.J.) advocated this *procedural model* in the *Richmond* case, holding that "the law of legitimate expectation . . . only goes so far as to say that there may arise conditions in which, if policy is to be changed, a specific person or class of persons affected must first be notified and given the right to be heard".[28]

Secondly, there is the *rationality model*. This holds that legitimate expectation offers a largely—but not exclusively—procedural protection. On this view, individuals' expectations will normally be protected by means of a court order requiring a certain procedure to be followed before the competent agency decides whether or not its policy should be changed. This second model, however, recognises that a given policy change may, exceptionally, cause such extreme prejudice to citizens that altering the policy is not a step which is open to rational decision-makers. The courts may therefore intervene in a substantive manner—by preventing the policy change from taking place, or by requiring the policy not to be applied to the applicant—when the agency's decision to change its policy was, in the first place, *Wednesbury*[29] unreasonable. Precisely this approach was adopted by the Court of Appeal in *Hargreaves*.[30]

In the course of giving its judgment in that case, the Court of Appeal considered a third, *substantive model* of legitimate expectation. That approach had been advocated by Sedley J. (now Sedley L.J.) in *Hamble Fisheries*, who opined that it is "the court's duty to protect the interests of those individuals whose expectation of different treatment has a legitimacy which out-tops the policy choice which threatens to frustrate it".[31] On this view, it is for the court to balance the merits of the relevant policy against the value of the individual's expectation and, whenever the latter—*in the court's opinion*—outweighs the former, substantive relief may be granted in order to preclude departure from the policy.

---

[27] For discussion of the substantive legitimate expectation doctrine both in English and European law, see Craig, op. cit., n. 25.

[28] *R. v. Secretary of State for Transport, ex parte Richmond-upon-Thames London Borough Council* [1994] 1 W.L.R. 74, 93. See also *R. v. Secretary of State for the Home Department, ex parte Ruddock* [1987] 1 W.L.R. 1482.

[29] *Associated Provincial Picture Houses Ltd.* v. *Wednesbury Corporation* [1948] 1 K.B. 223.

[30] *R. v. Secretary of State for the Home Department, ex parte Hargreaves* [1997] 1 W.L.R. 906.

[31] *R. v. Ministry of Agriculture Fisheries and Food, ex parte Hamble (Offshore) Fisheries Ltd.* [1995] 2 All E.R. 714, 731.

Although this fully substantive conception of legitimate expectation was emphatically rejected by the Court of Appeal in *Hargreaves*, it has now resurfaced in the decision of a differently constituted Court of Appeal in *Coughlan*.[32] The respondent health authority in that case was seeking to implement a new policy with regard to the service provided to those in long term nursing care. However, adoption of the new policy would have involved the closure of the residential facility where the applicant was being cared for which, in turn, breached an earlier undertaking given to the applicant to the effect that she would be able to remain at that facility for the rest of her life. This undertaking, said the Court, gave rise to a legitimate expectation. The question, therefore, was how it ought to be protected.

Had the Court of Appeal followed its earlier decision in *Hargreaves*, it would have concluded that the applicant was entitled to be consulted, but that substantive relief could not issue unless the policy change was truly irrational. The Court, however, did not follow its earlier decision.[33] Instead, it held that when an individual holds a legitimate expectation, it is for the judiciary to balance the public interest in allowing public bodies to formulate new policies against the private interest of individuals who are, in some way, disadvantaged by policy changes. The Court could see no reason why the judiciary, rather than the public authority, should not ultimately determine whether the desirability of the new policy was sufficient to justify the frustration of the individual's expectation.[34]

It is strongly arguable that this conclusion is contrary to the fundamental principles on which our system of administrative law is founded and incompatible with the leading authorities. Let me explain why.

Legitimate expectation and constitutional theory

When a court protects an expectation by procedural means, this has a minimal impact on the administrative autonomy of the relevant authority. This is because the imposition of a procedural requirement merely constitutes a condition precedent to the proposed policy change, and does not attenuate the authority's ultimate freedom to alter its policy. This, in turn, means that proce-

---

[32] R. v. *North and East Devon Health Authority, ex parte Coughlan* (*The Times*, 20 July 1999).

[33] Lord Woolf M.R., giving the judgment of the Court of Appeal, explained that the *Coughlan* case involved an "abuse of power" which amounted to a "failure of substantive fairness". This distinguished it from cases—of which *Hargreaves* was presumably one—"where what is in issue is a conventional application of policy or exercise of discretion". It is, however, difficult to understand what the exact distinction between *Coughlan* and *Hargreaves* is supposed to be. Because terms such as "abuse of power" and "failure of substantive fairness" do not appear to bear any precise meaning, their use creates the impression of an *ex post facto* rationalisation of a judicial decision to intervene, rather than the deployment of principled criteria which determine the proper scope of review in such cases.

[34] "There is no suggestion in [the relevant case law] ... that the final arbiter of [the] justification [for departing from existing policy], rationality apart, is the decision-maker rather than the court," *per* Lord Woolf M.R.

dural protection of legitimate expectations carries with it no risk of the courts transgressing their proper constitutional bounds, since they are concerned with *how*, not *whether*, the policy is changed. Hence no constitutional difficulty is disclosed: the courts remain within their proper sphere, and the ultimate autonomy of public authorities is never placed in jeopardy.

The position is very different if expectations are protected substantively. The provision of substantive relief may well have the effect of preventing the agency in question from departing from its existing policy which, in turn, represents a significant reduction in the freedom which the public authority enjoys in formulating and implementing policy. Substantive enforcement also has important implications for the role of the court since, once judges begin to adjudicate on the content and substance of executive decisions, the risk arises that they may, in effect, take over the role of the decision-maker, so exceeding their proper constitutional function.[35] These are precisely the issues which the Court of Appeal overlooked in *Coughlan*, and it is for this reason that it is strongly arguable that the decision is inconsistent with well-established constitutional principle.

It is certainly not my view that the courts should never review public decision-making on substantive grounds. However, in light of the constitutional implications which I have outlined, it is essential that they exercise particular caution in this area. The real issue, therefore, is not whether expectations should *ever* be protected substantively, but, rather, the *circumstances* in which substantive relief should be issued.

The difficulty with the approach adopted in *Coughlan* is that it permits a court to prevent a change in policy whenever it disagrees with the public authority's evaluation of the case. Arguably this discloses a fundamental misconception of the relationship which obtains, within our constitutional framework, between Parliament, the administration and the judiciary. It is not the constitutional function of a court to decide what the policy of the executive ought to be, and whether that policy can be changed. That is properly a matter for the decision-making agency which Parliament has designated.

It is for precisely this reason that our courts have long held that the appropriate standard of review in cases which engage issues of substance is the

---

[35] In *Coughlan*, the Court of Appeal stated that "it is unimportant whether the unfairness [which affects an administrative decision] is analytically within or beyond the power conferred by law: on either view public law today reaches it". (The Court of Appeal attributed this view to Lord Scarman, on the basis of his speech in *R. v. Inland Revenue Commissioners, ex parte National Federation for Self-Employed and Small Businesses Ltd.* [1982] A.C. 617.) This, however, is fundamentally inconsistent with the orthodox position, affirmed by the decision of the House of Lords in *Boddington* v. *British Transport Police* [1988] 2 W.L.R. 639, according to which the ultra vires principle is the organising concept upon which the law of judicial review is founded. Once this is accepted, it becomes clear that judicial review is about identifying the precise location of the line which traces the perimeter of the competence which Parliament has conferred upon administrative agencies. Conceptualising administrative law in this way serves to emphasise the fact that the agency possesses a core of discretion with which the courts have no licence to interfere. It appears that the Court of Appeal's misconception, in *Coughlan*, of this foundational issue caused it to overlook the importance of drawing the limits of the supervisory jurisdiction in a manner which accords proper respect to the autonomy of executive decision-makers.

Wednesbury doctrine. By permitting judicial intervention only when the public authority has acted as no reasonable body could, the *Wednesbury* principle strikes the correct balance between judges and decision-makers. It reflects the constitutional philosophy on which our administrative law is founded, according to which it is the prerogative of the sovereign Parliament to choose upon whom decision-making power ought to be conferred, and that it is therefore unacceptable for the judicial branch to seize that power for itself.

The courts have accepted with striking consistency that—for these good constitutional reasons—*Wednesbury* traces the perimeter of their jurisdiction in matters of substance. Nowhere is this more readily apparent than in the field of human rights. Although British courts—it has been said—are "straining at the leash" to give greater effect to fundamental rights,[36] they have recognised that, pending legislative intervention, it would be constitutionally improper for them to depart from *Wednesbury* as their guiding principle in matters of substance.[37] One of the most surprising aspects of the *Coughlan* decision is that it departs from this well-established line of authority without attempting to justify that departure.

Let me offer a final thought on this subject before moving on. The public law jurisprudence of other European countries quite properly forms a rich source of inspiration for our own courts: the scope for cross-fertilisation is immense. Nevertheless, the extent to which principles of European public law can influence and take root in domestic law is ultimately constrained by the constitutional framework within which English administrative law subsists. That framework quite clearly indicates that the concept of substantive expectation, as it exists in national law, must be kept within carefully defined limits—and it is the constitutional duty of our courts to recognise that.

Proportionality

Let me now turn to doctrine of proportionality. In light of the important role which it occupies in the jurisprudence of the European Courts of Justice[38] and Human Rights,[39] I wish to examine the extent to which it has influenced—and ought to influence—English public law.

Introduction

A good starting point is the *Smith* case,[40] which involved a challenge to the government's policy (since suspended) that prohibited persons of homosexual

---

[36] M.J. Beloff and H. Mountfield, "Unconventional Behaviour: Judicial Uses of the European Convention in England and Wales" [1996] *European Human Rights Law Review* 467, 495.

[37] The attitude of the courts to the *Wednesbury* principle in the human rights context is discussed below, section 3.2.

[38] See, e.g., Case 120/78, *Cassis de Dijon* [1979] E.C.R. 649.

[39] See, e.g., *Sunday Times* v. *United Kingdom* (1979) 2 E.H.R.R. 245.

[40] [1996] Q.B. 517.

orientation from serving in the armed forces. This, said the applicants, consti-tuted a breach of Article 8 of the European Convention, which requires respect for an individual's private life. Having accepted that the applicants' human rights were engaged, Simon Brown L.J., in the Divisional Court, went on to con-sider whether there existed a compelling public interest which could justify that policy. He concluded that the arguments were finely balanced, but that, in his view, those seeking to condemn the policy had the stronger case.[41] Thus it appears that, had the courts used the proportionality test in *Smith*, they may well have concluded that the qualification placed on the applicants' rights was not proportionate to the aim being pursued. Indeed, this was the conclusion which the European Court reached when it adjudicated on this case last year.[42]

However, the domestic courts did not analyse the facts of *Smith* by reference to the proportionality principle. Instead, they held that the government's policy would be unlawful only if it could "properly be stigmatised as irrational".[43] Although Lord Bingham M.R. held that the greater the prima facie human rights infringement, "the more the court will require by way of justification before it is satisfied that the decision is reasonable [in the *Wednesbury* sense]",[44] it remains the case that, at the present time, English courts continue to evaluate the legality of decisions which engage human rights by reference to the ratio-nality test, not the proportionality principle.

Against this background, I should like to address two specific points. I will consider, in a moment, the likelihood of proportionality taking root as a general principle of English administrative law. First, however, let me focus on the domestic role of proportionality in the particular context of human rights.

Proportionality, English Law and Human Rights

It may, at first glance, seem odd that the English courts have refused to deploy the proportionality doctrine in human rights cases, particularly in light of the role which it plays at the European level. In order to understand why this posi-tion obtains, it is necessary to look to the constitutional framework within which our courts develop public law.

As I remarked earlier, the *Wednesbury* principle reflects a particular concep-tion of the respective constitutional roles of the judiciary and the executive, according to which primary responsibility for decision-making rests with pub-lic authorities acting under powers conferred by Parliament. While the courts serve a crucial function—by ensuring that public administration is conducted

---

[41] Ibid., at p. 533.

[42] *Lustig-Prean and Becket* v. *United Kingdom; Smith and Grady* v. *United Kingdom* (*The Times*, 11 October 1999).

[43] *Smith*, op. cit., at p. 540.

[44] Ibid., at p. 554, following the decision of the House of Lords in R. v. *Secretary of State for the Home Department, ex parte Brind* [1991] 1 A.C. 696, which - pending the entry into force of the Human Rights Act 1998 - remains the leading authority on the status of the European Convention in English law and on the standard of review which is to be applied in human rights cases.

according to law—their role is, ultimately, secondary. This means that a government decision cannot be overturned simply because a court disagrees with it.

There are three good reasons which explain why this is so. First, there exists a *constitutional imperative*: if Parliament confers decision-making power on a particular agency, the courts would frustrate Parliament's sovereign will if they arrogated that power to themselves. Secondly, there is the *pragmatic imperative*: the courts, particularly on substantive matters of policy, have considerably less expertise than the designated authority; it is, therefore, desirable that the authority itself should make such decisions because it is better equipped to do so. And, thirdly, there exists a *democratic imperative*: the electoral system operates as an important safeguard against misuse of public power by requiring many public authorities to submit themselves to the verdict of the electorate at periodic intervals. If this system of political accountability is to function, it is important that the decision-making role of those agencies is not usurped by the courts.

This is the constitutional philosophy which gives rise to the distinction between legality and merits, and which is given practical effect by *Wednesbury*, which permits judicial intervention on substantive grounds only when the court concludes that a decision is irrational.[45] In contrast, the proportionality principle would require the judiciary to make a far more detailed evaluation of the merits of public decisions which, in turn, would fundamentally change the nature of the relationship which obtains between judges and decision-makers. As Simon Brown L.J. commented in *Smith*, although British judges fully recognise that "the protection of human rights is . . . a matter with which the courts are particularly concerned and for which they have an undoubted responsibility", they nevertheless "owe a duty too to remain within their constitutional bounds and not trespass beyond them".[46]

It is true that English courts will begin to use the tool of proportionality in cases which affect fundamental rights once the Human Rights Act enters into force in October.[47] Crucially, however, they will do so because Parliament will

---

[45] The position is very different, of course, in relation to matters of procedure. It is open to the courts to impugn issues of decision-making procedure, and to require a better process to be followed, without first having to conclude that the original procedure followed by the agency was so defective that no reasonable agency would ever have adopted it. The *Wednesbury* doctrine therefore operates to confine the role of the reviewing court only in relation to matters of substance, not procedure. Space precludes detailed analysis of why this is so. However, the essential reasoning is captured well by J. Jowell, "Of Vires and Vacuums: The Constitutional Context of Judicial Review" [1999] P.L. 448, 451-452: "[T]he tenets of procedural fairness do not require a utilitarian evaluation of preferred outcomes. They are not based upon policy evaluations best suited to elected officials or their agents in a democracy . . . [I]t is not seriously contended that the imposition of procedural norms is beyond the constitutional capacity of judges, who aim thereby not to achieve any particular social or economic objective but to ensure only that the decision was fairly arrived at."

[46] [1996] Q.B. 517, 541.

[47] Although the Act does not explicitly refer to the principle of proportionality, it is clearly implicit in the scheme of the legislation that the courts will be permitted to make recourse to that doctrine. In particular, s. 2(1) directs that, when British courts and tribunals are dealing with issues which relate to the Convention, they must take into account (inter alia) the jurisprudence of the European Court of Human Rights which is, of course, imbued with the theory of proportionality.

have ordained that they should. In our constitutional system, the three branches of government are not equal and co-ordinate: Parliament is the senior partner, and Parliament alone is able to change the constitutional ground rules. This explains why, notwithstanding the considerable influence exerted by the principle of proportionality, English courts have, until now, been unable to embrace it in the domestic context. This, in turn, illustrates one of the fundamental themes of my address today: that, while European public law strongly influences the development of domestic law, the extent to which those influences may actually take root is ultimately determined by the constitutional context within which English administrative law is located.

Proportionality: A General Principle of English Public Law?

Let me address one final point. Once proportionality does come to be used by English courts in human rights cases, the critical question will become whether this will prompt a change in the standard of review, from rationality to proportionality, in *all* public law cases, whether or not they possess a human rights dimension.

Some writers urge that proportionality *should* be used as a general principle of administrative law,[48] arguing that it constitutes a more transparent and structured methodology than what has been termed the "blunt tool"[49] of *Wednesbury* unreasonableness. However, I do not share this view. The fact that proportionality will become an established ground of judicial review in cases brought under the Human Rights Act does not mean that it will become the appropriate standard of review in every public law case. This follows for two related reasons.

The courts have rightly refused to use the proportionality test until the Human Rights Act is activated. The entry into force of that Act will not, of course, have any bearing on the consequences which follow from applying the proportionality doctrine: it will remain the case that, in using proportionality as a ground of review, executive action will be subjected to considerably more rigorous scrutiny than it is, presently, on *Wednesbury* review. The effect of the Act, therefore, is not to change the implications of proportionality-based review but, rather, to ordain that the use of proportionality is constitutionally acceptable notwithstanding that it carries such implications. In this sense, the Act will form a warrant which will confer constitutional legitimacy on proportionality-based review. It is, however, perfectly clear from the Human Rights Act that this warrant extends only to cases which, in the first place, engage fundamental human

---

[48] See, inter alios, J. Jowell and A. Lester, "Proportionality: Neither Novel nor Dangerous" in J. Jowell and D. Oliver (eds.), *New Directions in Judicial Review* (London: Stevens, 1988); P.P. Craig, "The Impact of Community Law on Domestic Public Law" in P. Leyland and T. Woods (eds.), *Administrative Law Facing the Future: Old Constraints and New Horizons* (London: Blackstone Press, 1997).

[49] This term was used to describe the *Wednesbury* principle by Craig, op. cit., at p. 283.

rights. It follows that the considerations based on constitutional propriety which have, to date, rightly deterred English courts from embracing proportionality will continue to apply to cases which do not fall under the new human rights legislation: it is the Act which will justify the courts' shifting from rationality- to proportionality-based review, and it is therefore the Act which ought to determine the compass of the proportionality principle.

A second factor points towards the same conclusion. It is already well-established that judicial review does not constitute a monolithic standard of supervision. Rather, the intensity of review in any particular case is determined by its facts and context. For instance, the courts accept that it is appropriate to adopt a relatively deferential attitude to decisions concerning national economic policy.[50] In contrast, although they are, at present, ultimately constrained by the *Wednesbury* principle, the courts certainly subject executive action which engages human rights to much more thoroughgoing scrutiny. Thus it is possible to envisage a continuum along which cases of different types lie, ranging from those which attract only a modest degree of scrutiny, to human rights cases which lie at the other end of the spectrum and which are, quite properly, examined with great rigour. This recognises that the need for judicial review varies according to the context. Different levels of intervention—and tools of differing intensity—are therefore required at the various points which lie along the continuum. Fundamental rights possess a normative resonance which makes the incisive tool of proportionality an appropriate method by which to uphold them. Such a high degree of judicial intervention in the administrative process is not, however, appropriate in other contexts. It is for this reason that the intrusive device of proportionality should be confined to the special area of human rights, and should not be perceived as a panacea which constitutes a standard of review suitable for every case.

CONCLUSION

This Conference is extremely timely. We are presently living in a period of significant constitutional change in the United Kingdom, and those changes are occurring within a public law environment that is no longer purely domestic, but which, instead, embraces the rich seam of jurisprudence and public law scholarship which subsists within Europe. Just as British administrative law can—and, once our judges begin to interpret the European Convention, increasingly will—influence the development of European public law, so the European principles enrich national law. Through these processes of cross-fertilisation we begin to see the emergence of common principles of European public law which, in turn, helps to ensure that all European citizens benefit from certain benchmark standards as they interact with national and transnational public bodies.

[50] See, e.g., *Nottinghamshire County Council v. Secretary of State for the Environment* [1986] A.C. 240.

However, against this background of dynamic development, one challenge remains constant. I refer, of course, to the imperative of embracing the influences which arise from our full participation in Europe in a manner which is consistent with the principles on which our own constitution is founded. The need to balance these objectives is a recurrent theme in modern British public law. It is reflected in the idea that, although Parliament's contemporary sovereignty is limited by the European doctrine of primacy, its ultimate supremacy remains. That same ethos of balance lies at the heart of the Human Rights Act, which unequivocally recognises the sovereignty of Parliament, while substantially changing the environment within which that sovereignty will, in the future, be exercised. And it is also possible to discern—in the way that our courts develop specific principles of administrative law—a clear awareness of the need to reconcile European influences with constitutional principle. Hence (with one or two exceptions) the courts' recognition that, pending legislative intervention, the *Wednesbury* principle marks the proper standard of substantive review.

Our constitutional landscape is changing, and administrative law in Britain and Europe are growing closer together. This is a natural consequence of Britain's presence in Europe, and it is of great benefit to the citizen. British public law's embrace of European influences is therefore as inevitable as it is desirable—but these developments must not occur at the expense of ignoring the constitutional foundation on which domestic public law rests. These two objectives are not, however, mutually exclusive. Far from it. They represent the twin principles on which administrative in Britain must be based in the twenty-first century, and which will ensure the existence of a system of public law that accommodates both the uniqueness of Britain's constitution and its place within the European legal family.

2

A New Common Law for Europe

LORD BINGHAM

Nearly a quarter of a century has passed since the European University Institute in Florence held a colloquium to consider "New Perspectives for a Common Law of Europe". The published record of that colloquium,[1] to which scholars from a wide range of countries, inside the European Community and outside, contributed, provides an invaluable starting point from which to set out on any further review of "A New Common Law for Europe". The colloquium provided many insights which remain valid today.

Tempting though it may be to yearn for a golden age in the past when a *jus commune* prevailed throughout western Christendom, such yearning has a tenuous historical foundation:

> "With the exception of two short periods of our political history and the longer-lasting epoch when the Catholic church was at the height of her influence—during the later Middle Ages—Europe never had a common legislator or a common judicial system".[2]

In many parts of Europe local laws flourished, often in areas not coincident with modern national boundaries.[3] With the emergence of nation states further balkanisation of the law and legal systems was inevitable. Thus while the leading countries of continental Europe can be fairly said to derive their laws from Roman roots and may be grouped as falling within a civil law tradition, and England from an early date developed its own judge-made and largely indigenous common law, a law administered by royal justices throughout the country, the civil law as found in (say) France, Germany, Italy, Spain or The Netherlands is no more uniform than the common law as found in (say) England, the United States, Canada and Australia.[4] In the field of delict, Professor von Bar has indeed observed that

> ". . . the reconciliation of French and German law, rather than the integration of common law, poses the greatest problem for the approximation of laws within Europe".[5]

[1] Cappelletti (ed.), *New Perspectives for a Common Law of Europe* (1978).
[2] *Op. cit.* at 31: Coing, "European Common Law: Historical Foundations".
[3] *Ibid.*
[4] *Op. cit.* at 138: Kahn-Freund, "Common Law and Civil Law—Imaginary and Real Obstacles to Assimilation".
[5] *The Common European Law of Torts*, vol. 1 (1998), at 384, para. 368.

But since the states of western Europe have reached roughly the same stage of economic and social development, we find (unsurprisingly) the courts of these countries confronting very much the same problems, and while the legal rules used to solve the problems may be very different, the solutions are often very similar.[6] Deep and enduring differences nonetheless remain, the product of history and differing cultural assumptions. Sir Otto Kahn-Freund drew attention to differences in the method of legal reasoning and organised fact finding, in the outward form of legal rules, in legislative and judicial styles,[7] in the structure of the courts, the structure of both criminal and civil procedure, the role played by the judge and by the advocates at the trial of civil actions and criminal prosecutions, the nature and the law of evidence, the role of the trial jury,[8] the role of the courts as law making agencies, the style and interpretation of legislation and the dichotomy of methods of adjudication in matters of public law in continental Europe as compared with the United Kingdom.[9] Professor Schwarze has pointed out:

> "The recent political developments before and after Maastricht have in fact illustrated how much national constitutional law is regarded as an elementary expression of national identity. In this respect I may mention only some specific examples: the French understanding of *souverainete nationale*, the English idea of 'supremacy of Parliament' or the German concept of federalism".[10]

It is difficult to gainsay the force of these points. Two examples will suffice. It is, for instance, difficult for an English criminal lawyer to begin to understand the working of a system of criminal justice, such as the French, in which there is no such thing as a plea of guilty.[11] And, thinking of judicial style, it is hard to imagine a French judgment opening with the words:

> "It happened on April 19, 1964. It was bougainvillea time on the Côte d'Azur".[12]

These considerations have compelled acceptance that a common law of Europe cannot be achieved by a simple process of unification, harmonisation or transplantation. Sir Otto Kahn-Freund expressed a

> "conviction that to harmonise entire legal systems is, from the point of view of the political, economic and cultural future of Europe, a work of supererogation, and, moreover, the work perhaps more of a Sisyphus than of a Hercules".[13]

---

[6] Cappelletti (ed.), *New Perspectives for a Common Law of Europe*: Kahn-Freund, *op. cit* at 148; Jolowicz, "New Perspectives of a Common Law of Europe: Some Practical Aspects and the Case for Applied Comparative Law," at 243. Markesinis, "The Not so Dissimilar Tort and Delict" [1977] 93 *LQR* 78. Markesinis (ed.), *The Gradual Convergence*, at 31, "Learning from Europe and Learning in Europe" (1994).

[7] *Op. cit.*, at 138 and 155. See also Markesinis, *op cit.*, at 30.

[8] *Ibid.*, at 144.

[9] *Ibid.*, at 150.

[10] Schwarze, "Towards a Common European Public Law," *European Public Law*, vol. 1, issue 2, at 232 (1995).

[11] Spencer in *The Gradual Convergence*, "French and English Criminal Procedure", at 36.

[12] *Cf.* Lord Denning MR, *Hinz* v. *Berry* [1970] 2 QB 40 at 42.

[13] *Op. cit.*, at 142.

He thought it

"not only useless, but dangerous to extend attempts at harmonisation into fields in which legal differences reflect differences in political or social organisation or in cultural or social mores".[14]

Professor Markesinis has more recently described the idea of whole-hearted transplantation as "utopic at best, ludicrous at worst",[15] and Professor Kötz has made plain that he is "not an aficionado of immediate codification" of European private law.[16] Professor Basedow goes further: he suggests that the Community at present lacks the power to legislate comprehensively in the area of private law, its competence being limited to harmonisation of laws for the purposes of market integration.[17] One recalls that the law of the European Community was once, but some time ago and in language which now seems rather dated, described as "in substance a sophisticated body of International Economic Law".[18]

These cautionary reservations are a salutary warning, if such be needed, against any simplistic belief that the experience and tradition of centuries can be ignored or overridden or replaced by a common code or series of codes, or that the laws of the western European nations can within a short timescale be reduced to their highest common factor. The scholarly tradition of the civil law and the pragmatism of the common law would be at one in resisting so facile a solution. But while caution should guide, it should not obstruct our progress towards the goal very clearly recognised at the Florence colloquium in 1977. As Professor Cappelletti put it:

". . . no other area better than the law could epitomise the past and present history, the glories and decays, the hopes and the fears, and, above all, the present titanic challenge of Europe. Twenty-one countries—to count, quite artificially, only those in the 'West' from Iceland to Cyprus—each with a distinct legal system, represent an irrational, suicidal division within a modern world which demands larger and larger open areas of personal, cultural, commercial, labour and other exchanges. Harmonisation, co-ordination, interdependence are absolute needs of our time; and history is there to provide clear evidence that division is not an ineluctable fate, that indeed division is a relatively recent phenomenon in a Continent which, for centuries in past epochs, was characterised by a law common to most of its peoples".[19]

Professor Jolowicz took up the theme:

---

[14] *Op. cit.*, at 164.
[15] *The Gradual Convergence*, at 7.
[16] Kötz, "The Common Code of European Private Law: Third General Meeting, Trento 17–19 July 1997", *European Review of Private Law*, 5–549 at 550.
[17] Basedow, 1997, "A Common Contract Law for the Common Market", *Common Market Law Review* 33, 1169 at 1173, 1996.
[18] Schwarzenberger, "European Common Law" 1973, vol. 26: *Current Legal Problems* 114 at 119.
[19] Cappelletti, *New Perspectives for a Common Law of Europe*, "Introduction", at 1.

". . . should we not now seek the deliberate but gradual and piecemeal sacrifice, by the various nations of Europe, of some of their 'special usages' in order that the whole of Europe may enjoy the benefit of some common and uniform laws?"[20]

There has been an encouraging measure of agreement on the steps needed to transform this vision into reality. Professor Coing wrote:

"We should fight for an organization of academic training in the field of law at our law schools in Europe, which instead of dividing the lawyers in Europe, tries to further mutual understanding".[21]

This is an aim close to the heart of Professor Van Gerven:

"A dream which I would like to become true is the creation of a European Law School where general principles are taught which are common to the legal systems of Western Europe".[22]

Such an education will give a central role to scholarship in comparative law,[23] and Professor Kötz has suggested the way forward:

"One type of academic scholarship must be aiming at the production of textbooks, treatises and casebooks based on a decidedly non-national point of view, seeking to discuss their subjects in a way which by no means ignores the rules of national legal systems but treats them as merely local variations of a European theme which in principle is unitary . . . Another type of needed academic scholarship must be aimed at the development of rules that apply uniformly over the territories of the various European states, are detached from a particular legal system, and are intended to reflect the best solution offered by the laws of these states".[24]

If a changed approach to legal thinking and legal literature is the first stage, a changed approach to judicial decision-making is the second:

"The second element is a more systematic use and development, by judges and legal writers, of principles and concepts of law which are common to the legal systems of Western Europe and which are reflected, among others, in judicial decisions relating to European Community law and European human rights law rendered by national courts and by the Courts of Luxembourg and Strasbourg respectively".[25]

Among courts commended for their attention to comparative sources have been the Australian and German Constitutional Courts and the House of Lords.[26]

---

[20] Cappelletti, *New Perspectives for a Common Law of Europe*, "Introduction", at 1, Jolowicz, "*New Perspectives of a Common Law of Europe: Some Practical Aspects and the Case for Applied Comparative Law*," 237 at 238.

[21] Coing, *op. cit.*, at 44.

[22] Van Gerven, *The Common Law of Europe and the Future of Legal Education*, "Court Decisions, General Principles and Legal Concepts: Ingredients of a Common Law of Europe", at 339.

[23] *New Perspectives for a Common Law of Europe*: Cappelletti at 8, R Sacco, "Droit Commun de l'Europe, et Composantes du Droit", at 95.

[24] H. Kötz, *op.cit.*, at 550.

[25] Van Gerven, *op. cit.*, at 339.

[26] J. Schwarze, *op. cit.*, at 235

The search must however be for general principles.[27] And the approach should be pragmatic:

> "The line between what is to be and what can usefully be unified must . . . be drawn pragmatically and flexibly, not dogmatically or rigidly . . .[28]

> . . . those interested in the harmonisation of law in Europe should give serious consideration to the need for studying each rule and each institution not as a piece of legal history or dogmatic reasoning or organisational technique, but as the outcome of the social and political history and the social and political environment in which they grew and exist. The strength of Europe lies not only in its unity but also in its great diversity. This will, one hopes, be preserved, and it cannot fail to be reflected in the variety of its legal systems".[29]

It would greatly over-burden this paper, and as greatly over-tax the competence of the author, to attempt to assess the extent to which or identify the ways in which the ideas expressed at Florence in 1977 have borne fruit in the years since then. But no one could possibly doubt the judgment of Professor Markesinis that convergence between the legal systems of Europe is taking place, even if gradually and patchily.[30] Some of the manifestations of convergence are obvious and unambiguous, such as decisions of the ECJ which member states are bound to respect and international conventions which different states have contracted to observe, since in each case the object is to eliminate variations of response to facts which are legally indistinguishable from one state to another. Other manifestations are less obvious and perhaps more ambiguous, such as the suggested modification of the ECJ's approach to precedent and the handling of its previous case law,[31] or the English courts' approach to interpretation of domestic statutes,[32] or the approach to procedural matters.[33] But, since it is necessary to be selective, I propose to touch on four important areas in which the foundations of effective and enduring rapprochement have been laid, or effective and enduring rapprochement actually achieved.

First, the law of contract, and I draw attention to the *Principles of European Contract Law* prepared by The Commission on European Contract Law under the leadership of Professors Ole Lando and Hugh Beale.[34] The advantages of formulating common principles of contract law are persuasively spelled out: the

---

[27] *New Perspectives for a Common Law of Europe*: J. H. Merryman, "On the Convergence (and Divergence) of the Civil Law and the Common Law", 196 at 198.

[28] Kahn-Freund, *op. cit.*, at 147.

[29] *Ibid.*, at 168.

[30] *The Gradual Convergence*, at 30.

[31] Andenas (ed.), *English Public Law and the Common Law of Europe* (1998): A. Arnull, "Interpretation and Precedent in English and Community Law: Evidence of Cross-Fertilisation?", at 119, 121.

[32] Andenas and Jacobs (eds.), *European Community Law in the English Courts* (Oxford, 1998): J. F. Avery Jones, "Tax Law: Rules or Principles?", at 262.

[33] Werlauff, *Towards a Common European Procedural Law Part I*, *European Business Law Review*, Nov/Dec 1998.

[34] *Part I : Performance, Non-Performance and Remedies*, 1995.

facilitation of cross-border trade within Europe; the strengthening of the single European market, the creation of an infrastructure to guide Community legislators in the contractual field; the provision of guidelines for national courts and legislatures; the construction of a bridge between the civil law and the common law.[35] The purposes for which the principles are said to be designed are also persuasive: as a foundation for European legislation; as a code to which parties may choose to subject their contracts; as a nationally neutral and modern *lex mercatoria;* as a model for judicial and legislative development of contract law; as a basis for harmonisation.[36] This undertaking, scholarly, co-operative and voluntary, seems to me to provide a model of how a new common law for Europe may best be achieved, by way of consensus and not imposition, seeking to draw from each national law the principles judged to provide the soundest basis of an international code.

When one turns to the principles themselves, no one will find his own contract law faithfully reproduced. That, after all, is the essence of the exercise. Thus some English lawyers would resist Article 1. 106—Good Faith and Fair Dealing:

> "(1) In exercising his rights and performing his duties each party must act in accordance with good faith and fair dealing.
> (2) The parties may not exclude or limit this duty".[37]

It may be, as Professor Kötz has intriguingly suggested, that

> "Much of the doctrinal development of the contract law of a country depends on the types of contract litigated before the higher courts of that country".[38]

Whereas the leading English decisions have concerned commercial contracts (charter parties, carriage of goods, marine insurance), the courts in Australia and West Germany have, it seems, been more concerned with personal, non-commercial contracts, and this, if so, would go far to explain a difference of approach.[39] Be that as it may, many of the articles in the code would cause few qualms to the English lawyer. I take two examples almost at random:

> "Article 1. 108 Reasonableness
> Under these principles reasonableness is to be judged by what persons acting in good faith and in the same situation as the parties would consider to be reasonable. In particular, in assessing what is reasonable the nature and purpose of the contract, the circumstances of the case, and the usages and practices of the trades or professions involved should be taken into account".[40]

> "Article 2. 101 Determination or Price on Other Contractual Terms
> When the contract does not fix the price or the method of determining it, the parties

---

[35] *Part I : Performance, Non-Performance and Remedies*, 1995, "Introduction", at xv to xvii.
[36] *Ibid.*, at xvii to xix.
[37] *Op. cit.*, at 4, 53.
[38] H. Kötz, *op. cit.*, at 551.
[39] *Op. cit.*, at 551–2.
[40] *Ibid.*, at 4, 61.

are to be treated as having agreed on a reasonable price. The same rule applies to any other contractual term".[41]

The desirability of a common contract code to govern international trade seems to me obvious. Here, surely, is the basis of such a code.

Secondly I turn to the law of delict, a field dominated by Professor von Bar's majestic work on *The Common European Law of Torts*,[42] the product of what must be one of the most comprehensive comparative law exercises ever undertaken. Described by Lord Goff as "one of the most remarkable, and significant, books on comparative law ever to have seen the light of day",[43] this treatise examines in depth the codified laws of delict of continental Europe, the liability laws of Scandinavia and the common law of torts. Most striking, of course, to the English lawyer is the contrast between the short and general statements of principle in the continental codes,[44] and what Professor Van Gerven has described as the "pigeon-hole" approach of English law in this field.[45] Professor von Bar observes that

"A continental lawyer looking for the first time at the English law of torts would, in the way the latter is presented, be reminded of his own criminal law . . . Nowhere in the realm of criminal law is there a wide basic principle comparable to that which applies to civil law . . . So there are, whether necessarily or not, a large number of different specific crimes . . . In England this is true not only of criminal offences but also of torts, with the so-called nominal torts".[46]

The Professor's hope and aspiration that there should evolve (though not through imposition) a truly common European law of torts[47] must be brought a step closer by this exhaustive audit of how the law now stands in the countries of Western Europe. So it must by the production of comparative casebooks such as that edited by Professor Van Gerven on *Tort Law: Scope of Protection*.[48]

Professor Van Gerven had earlier urged the study of comparative law through the cases as the route to ultimate uniformity:

"Instead of comparing differences and resemblances between written laws, a more useful method of comparative law 'consists in comparing judicial decisions which have been rendered in various countries in respect of similar situations. Beginning with a comparison of such decisions from the point of view of the results arrived at and the grounds on which they are based, it is possible for the comparatist to compare underlying rules and doctrines'."[49]

[41] *Ibid.*, at 8, 69.
[42] Vol. 1, 1998.
[43] *Ibid.*, "Foreword", at xxi.
[44] *Ibid.*, at 13 *et passim*.
[45] Van Gerven, *Tort Law: Scope of Protection* (Oxford, 1998), at 3.
[46] Von Bar, *op. cit.*, at 281 para. 254.
[47] *Op. cit.*, "Foreword" by Lord Goff, at xxii.
[48] See footnote 45. (A greatly enlarged and revised new edition is forthcoming in 2000.)
[49] Van Gerven, *The Common Law of Europe and the Future of Legal Education*, "Court Decisions, General Principles and Legal Concepts: Ingredients of a Common Law of Europe", at 339.

The casebook facilitates exactly that exercise. It is just what the jurists gathered at Florence in 1977 hoped to see.

Thirdly, public law. There has undoubtedly been a pooling of thinking and experience. Thus British lawyers have been credited with exporting to the ECJ their law of legal professional privilege and the right to be heard.[50] But, in relation to the established European doctrines of proportionality and substantive legitimate expectation, the English courts have, in domestic matters, behaved like a nervous patient, willing to taste the medicine but hesitant to swallow it.[51] In the longer term, however, the trend must surely be towards ever closer assimilation between the rules which prevail in public law disputes in matters with a Community element and those which prevail in purely domestic matters. There is compelling extra-curial support for this view. With reference to the liability of public bodies for non-contractual damages, Professor Van Gerven has written:

> "It is indeed not desirable for the non-contractual liability of public bodies—be they Community institutions or national authorities (including the legislature proper)— and of individuals to be regulated differently in each Member State depending on whether the rule breached is a rule of Community law or a rule of domestic law".[52]

Dr Andenas has more recently echoed the same point, more generally:

> "It is not likely that judges will favour operating with one legal method, or one kind of review, or one set of remedies, and then a completely different one depending on rather arbitrary and unclear jurisdictional criteria: in one case *Wednesbury* unreasonableness, in the other proportionality and legitimate expectations, and the outcome depending on whether the administrative action is based on a Community law measure or not".[53]

This view of the way judges are likely to think is borne out by dicta of the judges themselves. In *Woolwich Building Society* v. *Inland Revenue Commissioners* [1993] AC 70 at 177, Lord Goff said:

> "I only comment that, at a time when Community law is becoming increasingly important, it would be strange if the right of the citizen to recover overpaid charges were to be more restricted under domestic law than it is under European Law".

A year later, in the seminal case of *M* v. *Home Office* [1994] 1 AC 377 at 422, concerned with the grant of injunctions against the Crown in the wake of *R* v.

---

[50] Andenas (ed.), *English Public Law and the Common Law of Europe* (Oxford, 1998): Fennelly, "Legal Interpretation—Towards Freedom of Movement of Principles", at 10–11, paras. 8, 9. Schwarze, "Tendencies Towards a Common Administrative Law in Europe", *European Law Review*, vol. 16 (1991) 3 at 9–11.

[51] *Ibid.*, Craig, "Substantive Legitimate Expectations and the Principles of Judicial Review", 23 at 49; de Burca, "Proportionality and Wednesbury Unreasonableness: The Influence of European Legal Concepts on UK Law". 53 at 59.

[52] Van Gerven, "Non-contractual Liability of Member States, Community Institutions and Individuals for Breaches of Community Law with a View to a Common Law for Europe", *MJ* 1 (1994) 6 at 39–40.

[53] Andenas, *English Public Law and the Common Law of Europe*: (Oxford, 1998), "Introduction", 1 at 3.

Secretary of State for Transport, Ex parte Factortame Ltd [1990] 2 AC 85, Lord Woolf observed:

> "It would be most regrettable if an approach which is inconsistent with that which exists in Community law should be allowed to persist if this is not strictly necessary".

It seems likely that, sooner or later, the twin-track approach to public law issues will give way to a single, perhaps somewhat different, track.

I have left to the end what is, I suggest, the most striking rapprochement of all: the acceptance throughout the Community of certain principles, almost limitless in their scope and fundamental in their nature: the rule of law, equality, non-discrimination, legal certainty, fairness and all the rights and freedoms protected by the ECHR. Advocate General Jacobs has described the right to equal treatment irrespective of nationality as one of over-arching significance,[54] and a moment's reflection reminds one how unattainable such a principle would have seemed half a century ago. It is not surprising that legal questions should loom large in the Community, since the Community is a legal artefact in a way in which most nation states are not. We are right to continue to worry away at the unnecessary divergences which continue to divide us. But the things which unite us are greater than the things which divide us. The dawning of the new millennium should, no doubt, act as a spur to further endeavour; but it is also an opportunity to reflect on the extraordinary progress already made during what, historically speaking, is "like an evening gone".

---

[54] Guild (ed.), *The Legal Framework and Social Consequences of Free Movements of Persons in the European Union* (1999): F. G. Jacobs, "Introduction", at 3.

3

Our Debt to Europe[1]:
Past, Present and Future

BASIL S. MARKESINIS

1. INTRODUCTORY REMARKS

On the 4th of February 1998 I attended a lecture given at the Travellers' Club by the Lord Chief Justice. Europe was the theme; and the effect that it was having on our law. The Chief Justice spoke forcefully, diplomatically, and with his usual clarity. I recall all this as clearly as I do the sceptical tone of the questions that were put to him when he finished. It was disturbing to note that the scepticism was prompted by the usual degree of misinformation. We were all, for instance, reminded of the (alleged) bad habit of our French neighbours to treat people as guilty until proven innocent! Such misinformation is permissible, though no less unattractive, if the audience, though educated, is not one specialised in legal matters (which was the case with most in the audience that night). Unfortunately, however, we also encounter it in the writings of some of our most learned judges and jurists. One, for instance, and names are really irrelevant for our purposes, told us many years ago that the advantage of having our contract law put in the form of a Code was that we would then be able to find all the relevant law very easily. Another, some years later, repeated the commonly held belief about the (apparently) errant ways of French criminal law. More recently, a very learned colleague referred to Germany being subject to the Napoleonic Code. The examples could, alas, be multiplied but this would serve no purpose. For my aim here is not to criticise the commission of errors

---

[1] I am, of course, using the term here in the typically British way to refer to the Continent of Europe. The impact that Continental—mainly German law—had on the development of the law in the USA is much better documented. From the considerable literature see: Herbst, *The German Historical School in American Scholarship; A Study in the transfer of Culture* (1965); Clark, "Tracing the Roots of American Legal Education—A Nineteenth-Century German Connection" 51 *RabelsZ* (1987), 313 ff.; Herget and Wallace "The German Free Law Movement as the Source of American Legal Realism" 73 *Va. L. Rev.* 399 (1987); Herman, "Llewellyn, the Civilian, Speculations on the Contribution of Continental Experience to the Uniform Commercial Code" 56 *Tul. L. Rev.* 125, 1161 (1982); Hoeflich, *Roman Law and Civil Law and the Development of Anglo-American Jurisprudence in the Nineteenth Century* (1997); Reimann (ed. and contr.), *The Reception of Continental Ideas in the Common Law World 1820–1920* (1993); Riesenfeld, "The Influence of German Legal Theory on American Law: The Heritage of Savigny and His Disciples" 37 *Am. J.Comp. L*, (1989).

for, as the saying goes, to err is human but to forgive divine. What I wish to attack is the arrogance and prejudice which, I think, lies behind critical statements about European law, especially when they form part—consciously or unconsciously—of the campaign about our position in Europe over the next hundred years and more. My own view as a scholar is that we have in law, as in so many other areas, more that unites us with Europe than separate us. I also share the views of colleagues such as Professor Reinhard Zimmermann (and others present here today) that we owe many intellectual debts to Europe. The wider realisation of these debts should, I think, help dispel persisting fears about the effects of growing integration with Europe and thus help us assume the kind of leading role that I think we deserve to play in the shaping of the next thousand years.

This aim I hope to achieve by presenting some thoughts under four headings. First, I would like to substantiate my claim about the existence of the intellectual debt. Because of lack of space I shall begin by focusing on our law of contract. Though this forms only one part of the law of obligations and an even smaller part of private law as a whole, it should, I think, be sufficient for my purposes. For in our contract law we were always taught that we find some of the clearest signs of the genius of the Common law. My own view, partly based on the learning of others who have looked at this topic before me, is that matters are not that clear cut and that greater modesty on our part might be called for. Then I would like to mention briefly a few reasons why the debt is there in the first place and speculate as to why it is nowadays so unacknowledged. I shall, next, return to a favourite theme of mine in order to show how this interaction between legal cultures can and should continue in the future. At this stage, however, I shall shift the emphasis from contract law to public law for I think that much of the future of comparative law lies in this branch of the law. In the final part of the paper I shall conclude with some very general thoughts about how we, in England, can contribute to this melting pot of ideas. Though standing on its own, the paper should thus be seen as part of my wider effort to contribute to the creation of a workable methodology of comparative law.[2]

2. CONTRACT LAW: OUR DEBT TO EUROPEAN JURISTIC REASONING

In his Francis Mann lecture[3] the Lord Chief Justice reminded us that in the 19th century the authority of Pothier[4] was, for a judge asked to decide a given legal

---

[2] My ideas on this can be found in a collection of essays recently published under the title *Foreign Law and Comparative Methodology: A Subject and a Thesis* (Oxford, 1997).

[3] "There is a World Elsewhere: The Changing Perspectives of English Law", (1992) 41 *ICLQ*, 513 at 528.

[4] Whose *Treatise on the Law of Obligations*, translated by William David Evans, appeared in 1806, four years after the first American edition saw the light of day. The original (French) edition first appeared between 1761 and 1764.

issue, the next best thing to an English decision to the point.[5] But appropriately, it was an eminent legal historian—Professor Brian Simpson[6]—and an equally learned German émigré—Professor Stefan Riesenfeld of the University of California at Berkeley School of Law[7]—who have reminded us of the even greater debt to a long line of German and Dutch jurists, ranging from Pufendorf, Grotius, Savigny and the other Pandectists of the 19th century. We thus see that the doctrine of offer and acceptance was, in the 19th century, superimposed on the earlier doctrine of consideration. And we now see it performing, in part at least, some of the requirements of consideration but also new functions generated by the emerging contracts concluded by correspondence. But that is not all. For the importation of the continental doctrine clarified in English minds the distinction—hitherto not always clear—between *promissio* and *pollititatio* which, however, in Continental doctrine was clearly perceived since at least the drafting of the Digest Title on *De Pollicitationibus*.[8] Sir Frederick Pollock, in the first edition of his *Principles of Contract*,[9] thus kindly obliges us by admitting freely that his use of the word "proposal"[10] corresponds to the German expression *Antrag*. His notion of "acceptance", required *inter alia* to turn the promise into a contract, is the counterpart of the German *Annahme*.

We can, for present purposes, ignore the doctrine of consideration largely because its comparative examination requires a chapter if not a book of its own. But we cannot ignore the fact that a strong case has been made that it be seen as a local version of the civilian *causa promissionis*. But we should note that the doctrine's subsequent accretions—such as that found in the infamous decision of *Foakes* v. *Beer*[11]—not only depart from the civilian tradition but are, in contemporary scholarship, also increasingly seen as creating troublesome anomalies requiring new devices and techniques to mitigate their unfair results.

But one of the by-products of consideration—the rigid adherence to the doctrine of privity—calls for a few brief comments. For here, again, we see English law departing from the civilian model which emerged form the Middle Ages onwards and, by the 19th century, both in Europe and the USA,[12] had come to recognise an ever-increasing number of exceptions allowing third parties to sue directly the promisor. Of course, English law progressively developed *ad hoc* solutions, statutory or judicial, to mitigate the rigours of the old doctrine. But despite growing calls for reform, it has remained attached to the doctrine. Traditional common lawyers, one suspects instinctively suspicious of civilian

---

[5] *Cox* v. *Troy* (1822) 5 B & All. 474,480; 106 E.R. 1264 (per Best J.)

[6] "Innovation in Nineteenth Century Contract Law" 91 *LQR* (1975) 247 ff.

[7] "The Impact of Roman Law on the Common Law System", (1985) 2, *Lesotho Law Journal*, 267 ff. Reinhard Zimmermann, "Belohnungsversprechen: 'pollicitatio', 'promise' oder 'offer'? *ZfRV* 1998, 138 ff.

[8] "Pactum est duorum consensus atque conventio, pollitatio vero offerentis solus promissium". D. 50.12.3.

[9] Pollock, *Principles of Contract* (1876), at 1, 4 and 5 and n. 1.

[10] In later editions replaced by the term "offer".

[11] (1884) 9 App. Cas. 605.

[12] Thus, see, *Lawrence* v. *Fox* 20 NY 268 (1859).

ideas, have comforted themselves that by hook or by crook the English practice avoided, in the end, the injustice that the English doctrine had the tendency to cause.[13] But by the 1990's a series of papers from the Law Commission,[14] came to advocate with increasing eloquence and resolution the need to abandon the doctrine. The fact that, more often than not, it seemed to pay more attention to Commonwealth innovations can only be expected. For the informed reader cannot fail to see that the move towards the (chronologically older) civilian—Germanic rather than French—doctrine is also notable. Some references in these Reports make it clear that this was, indeed, brought to the attention of the Commissioners; but a full extent of the acknowledgement of the debt has yet to come.

Professor Simpson's magnificent article makes clear to anyone who reads it that the debt to civilian doctrine extends to the areas of mistake, intention to create legal transactions, frustration, and much more. What, since the early part of this century we have come to call frustration, is in fact an interesting topic. For in Blackburn's famous judgment in *Taylor* v. *Caldwell*[15] we find a blend of a common law idea—the notion of an implied condition which very nearly prevailed in the interesting case of *Hall* v. *Wright*[16] decided only five years before *Caldwell*—but also the civilian doctrine which dictates that an *obligatio de certo corpore* is discharged if the object has perished.[17] Blackburn the judge was, in fact, able to use the research of Blackburn the writer who, twenty years earlier, had written his *Treatise on the Effect of the Contract of Sale on the Legal Rights of Property and Possession of Goods, Wares and Merchandises*.[18] In his elegant Hamlyn Lectures[19] the late C. H. S. Fifoot described this work as "an early essay in comparative law." For in his book Blackburn had made extensive use of Pothier's *Treatise on the Contract of Sale* as well as using Roman law. In fact, references to both systems appear in the *Taylor* judgment. And, ironically, they give the French writer the dubious and unusual distinction to have influenced (in part) the development of English law but having failed to impress his own law. For it is well known that French civil law[20] failed to adopt any notion akin to our doctrine of frustration.

Let me complete this brief *tour d'horizon* by adding one more example to show our debt to Continental legal thought. I derive some of my information from an unpublished piece written by Professor Bernard Rudden of my own

[13] Thus, see Professor Reynolds' remarks in "Privity of Contract" 113 (1997) *LQR*, 53.
[14] The one containing its definitive proposals being *Privity of Contract: Contracts for the benefit of Third Parties*, No. 242, 1996.
[15] (1863) 32 L.J.Q.B. 164.
[16] (1858) El. Bl. & El. 746, 765.
[17] D. 45. 1.
[18] Published in London in 1845. See, also, Reinhard Zimmermann, "Heard melodies are sweet, but those unheared are sweeter . . .". Condicio facita, implied condition und die Fortbildung des europäischen Vertragsrechts, AcP 193 (1993), 121 ff.
[19] *Judge and Jurist in the Reign of Victoria* (1959), at p.16. In his History of English Law, vol. XV (1965), 506, he informs us that Sir James Shaw Willes, another of the great mid-Victorian judges, had a sound knowledge of foreign law.
[20] The doctrine of *imprevison* is known only in public law.

University. It refers to what is often seen to be, especially by contemporary American authors, as a very "English rule": the rule (or rules) in *Hadley* v. *Baxendale*.[21] For many modern legal economists like to see in this litigation a typical example of law made at the time of nascent industrialisation. In this respect, the interpretation of Professor Richard Danzig of the Stanford law School, takes the biscuit for, writing in 1975 an avowedly historical article,[22] he maintained that: "*Hadley* v. *Baxendale* can usefully be analysed as a judicial invention in an age of industrial invention. . . . Arising squarely in the middle of the industrial revolution and directly in the midst of the 'Great Boom' of 1820–74, *Hadley* v. *Baxendale* was a product of those times. The case was shaped by the increasing sophistication of the economy and the law . . ." The truth could hardly be more different.

For we know that Counsel in that case had been citing Sedgwick *On Damages*[23] and Sedgwick was mainly relying on the *Code Civil*—arts. 1149–51—which are based on the writings of Pothier who, in turn, derived most of his ideas from Domat's work on Roman law and the *Coûtumes de Paris*.[24] Professor Rudden then makes a plausible case that these views can be traced back to Dumoulin's *Tractatus de Quod Interest*,[25] Cino da Pistoia's *Lectura super Codicem: ad C. 7 47*,[26] and from there back to a number of Justinianic texts.

The debt to civilian thought is thus, once again, there to be seen. Yet why have contemporary British contract lawyers, and some notable legal historians, so persistently refused to acknowledge their huge intellectual debt to continental legal thought? Professor John Baker, for instance, talks in his excellent text book of English law "flourish[ing] in *noble isolation* [sic] from Europe";[27] and that most learned of our contemporary contract lawyers, Sir Guenter Treitel, concealed his vast knowledge of Continental law until his forties when he started writing monographs on comparative contract law,[28] and then kept it rigorously apart from his Common law work. Indeed, at times we find more than this tendency to present English law as having an autonomous existence of its own. For we can even find eminent contract lawyers castigating those of their brothers who "with [a] penchant for self flagellation" over-criticise the Common law by presenting it as being inferior to the modern civilian sysems.[29]

---

[21] (1854) 9 Ex. 341.

[22] "*Hadley* v. *Baxendale*: A Study in the Industrialisation of the Law, IV *JLS* (1975) 249, 250 259. See, also, Judge Posner's remarks in *Economic Analysis of Law*, 3rd edn. (1986) # 4.9: "[B]y the famous case of *Hadley* v. *Baxendale* . . . incentives are created to allocate the risks in the most efficient manner".

[23] Sedgewick, *A Treatise on the Measure of Damages*, 1st edn. (1847).

[24] Donat, *Les lois civiles dans leur ordre naturel*, Book 1, tit. II, sale.

[25] Written in 1546.

[26] Written, probably, during the early part of the 14th century.

[27] Baker, *An Introduction to English Legal History*, 3rd edn. (1990), 35.

[28] And still keeps it totally out of his classic textbook.

[29] The truncated quotation comes from Professor Reynolds' comments in "Privity of Contract" 113 (1997) *LQR*, 53 where the learned author, while welcoming the proposals of the Law Commission to reform the doctrine for privity, argues that authors (presumably such as myself) underestimated the extent to which the common law mitigated its harshness in practice.

One is, therefore, inclined to agree with Professor Simpson's conclusion that "It has become the aim of a number of modern English legal writers to avoid incursions into both history and other legal traditions; English law is to be presented as capable of standing alone. But in this they conceal the historical origins of much of what they transmit as homespun law, just as they conceal, too, the historical source of the literary tradition in which they stand."[30] But when scholars take such introverted positions they not only distort history; they are also, one hopes inadvertently, providing ammunition to a political argument that is attempting to depict Europe as a divisive and, even, dangerous issue. The attitudes that Professor Simpson (and I along with him) regret, thus not only call for condemnation: they raise the question of what lies behind them?

3. THE REASONS FOR THE DEBT AND WHY WE ARE, NOWADAYS, TRYING TO CONCEAL IT

Such insularity was not, as already shown, always fashionable; and it was certainly not a position advocated by our intellectual élites. From about the second half of the eighteenth century judges were, if anything, unashamedly internationalist in spirit, learning, and, sometimes, background. Sir William Jones, whose *Essay on the Law of Bailments* published in 1781 may well be regarded as the first modern monograph on English contract law, was a classical scholar who drew openly on many systems including the Roman and the Hindu. Blackstone, as well, had had some civilian training; and it may be partly because of this that Lord Mansfield (unsuccessfully) proposed him for the Regius Chair at Oxford. Leone Levi was an Italian Jew; and we all know how much he did to reform commercial law through his overtly comparative works.[31] Benjamin was another Jew who, during the first half of his remarkable life, had benefited from an American civilian background. All this shows in his work on the *Sale of Goods*. William Markby's *Elements of Law Considered with Reference to Principles of General Jurisprudence*,[32] may now be forgotten. Yet, not only did it adopt Pandectist models; it was also very influential in its time. Maitland adored Germany, hardly lost an opportunity to express his admiration for its 19th century intellectual achievements, and by all accounts his idol—Gierke—reciprocated the admiration by describing him as a "genius".[33] Dicey, Pollock

---

[30] *Op. cit.*, n. 6, above at pp. 256–7.

[31] In his *International Commercial Law*, published in 1887 he thus had the courage (audacity) to consider the law of, among others, Austria, Belgium, England, Germany, Greece, Italy, the Netherlands, Portugal, Russia, Spain and Sweden. In his earlier *Manual of Mercantile Law of Great Britain and Ireland* (1854) his approach was, once again, comparative in style.

[32] Published in 1871 (and since 1986 available in microfiche).

[33] According to the distinguished émigré Professor Martin Wolff. The story is recounted by the late Professor Lawson in his "Doctrinal Writing: A Foreign Element in English Law" in *Ius Privatum Gentium—Festschrift für Max Rheinstein* (1969), vol. I, pp. 191 ff., n. 44.

and Anson—to whom we shall return later on—were, as the late Professor Lawson put it so felicitously, "members of the very remarkable Victorian intellectual aristocracy[34] and, as such, able to look at English law with some detachment from outside."[35] Indeed, it was political developments abroad, namely the creation of the Empire, that gave a great stimulus to such outward looking habits. Thus, the Victorian pre-occupation with India *forced* many of the jurists of that era to re-examine English law from without as well as from within as part of their effort to determine what could be used in their attempts to draw up legislation for that sub-continent.

The Second World War proved an unfortunate turning point. As I shall state further down, the inward trend can be traced back to the various scars that it left on the collective psyche. But before this trend became established, our country benefited from one last wave of émigrés. Thus the exodus from Germany, that gained momentum in the 1930's, ensured that the (mainly) central European and Jewish influence continued after the War thanks to the presence of (forced) émigrés like Martin Wolf, Sir Otto Kahn Freund, Kurt Lipstein, Francis Mann, Clive Schmithoff. or E. J. Cohn.[36] To this group we must add another, namely a brilliant group of Jewish students—like Zamir and Rubinstein—whose London Ph D. theses[37] gave a great impetus to the development of our administrative law. So why, despite this, did we progressively lapse into the state of insularity which I, for one, deplore? Before considering some possible explanations I would like to exclude one: a strange and sudden kind of collective amnesia that has led us to forget how inclined towards Europe were our intellectual élites of the 19th century.

I discard what I have called collective amnesia as a cause of the prevailing tendency to underplay our intellectual debt to Europe not because I have any particular faith in the broad reading of the current generation of lawyers: I do not. I exclude it, however, because I know that the European work of these past masters is well known, as it well ought to be, to our contemporary textbook writers. Thus, the material that has led distinguished legal historians such as

---

[34] On which see Lord Annan's "The Victorian Intellectual Aristocracy" in Plumb (ed.), *Studies in Social History: A Tribute to G. M. Trevelyan*, ch. 8.

[35] Lawson, "Doctrinal Writing: A Foreign Element in English Law" in *Ius Privatum Gentium—Festschrift für Max Rheinstein* (1969), vol. I, 191 at p. 210.

[36] I am not including here earlier émigrés such as Sir Hersch Lauterpacht, Professor Felix Jolowicz or Lassa Oppenheimer, who possessed all the manifold talents of the central European Jewish émigrés. The Germanic background of Sir Guenther Treitel must also be noted.

[37] Zamir, *The Declaratory Judgment* (1962) and Rubinstein, *Jurisdiction and Illegality* (1965). The influence that the Jewish-German emigrants had on American law is well documented. Thus, see, Stiefel and Mecklenburg, *Deutsche Juristen im amerikanischen Exil (1933–1955)* (1991) and, more recently, Lutter, Stiefel and Hoeflich (eds.), *Der Einfluss deutscher Emigranten auf die Rechtsentwicklung in den USA und in Deutschland. Vorträge und Referate des Bonner Symposium im September 1991* (1994). The role of the Jewish immigrants in England is not so well documented though, in addition to Professor Goodhart's book mentioned above see, also, Professor Lipstein's contribution in Carlebach, Hirschfeld, Newman, Paucker and Pulzer (eds.), *Second Chance. Two Centuries of German-Speaking Jews in the United Kingdom* (1991) 221 ff.

Professors Simpson and, before him, Maitland,[38] Fifoot[39] and Lawson[40] (from England), Berman[41] and Helmholz[42] (from the USA) and Wieacker[43] and Zimmermann[44] (from Germany), forms some of the most elegant writings of contemporary legal history. But this material is not just elegantly presented; it is unequivocal in emphasising the strong influence that European legal and philosophical ideas had on modern, English law. In his Hamlyn Lectures,[45] for instance, the late C. H. S. Fifoot made much of the fact that in his *Principles of Contract* Sir Frederick Pollock "sought . . . to examine the inter-play of law and equity, and [to] set the results not only against Roman, Continental and American models, but also against the Indian Contract Act." "Anson", he tells us further down, "was even more fervently than Pollock, the disciple of Savigny, and it was through the superior vision of the master that he hoped to irradiate the concepts of obligation and agreement and to correct the English astigmatism."[46] Indeed, one could go further and suggest that so pervasive was the influence of German philosophy and law on the intelligentsia of the 19th century that even those authors[47] who chose to attack German conceptualism—which

---

[38] His Introduction to Gierke's *Political Theories of the Middle Ages* is a sustained tribute to Savigny the Romanist and historian. Ironically, of course, Gierke was, in later life to be a severe critic of the Pandectists for over-emphasising Roman law and ignoring the Germanic elements in the law. But that is another matter!

[39] Who, for instance, in the first chapter of his masterly Hamlyn Lectures, *op. cit.*, n. 19, above, at 7–8: "The influence of Germany was not confined to history. It flowed through every branch of English culture . . . English law was not insulated from these currents of thought and opinion."

[40] "Doctrinal Writing: A Foreign Element in English Law", *Ius Privatum Gentium—Festschrift für Max Rheinstein* (1969) vol. I, pp. 191 ff.

[41] *The Formation of Western Legal Tradition* (1983), 39.

[42] *Canon Law and the Law of England* (1987); Continental Law and Common Law: Historical Strangers or Companions?" (1990) *Duke Law Journal*, 1207."

[43] "Foundations of European Legal Culture" 38 *The Am. J. Comp. L.*,1 (1990) and, more extensively, in his masterly *Privatrechtsgeschichte der Neuzeit* 2nd edn. (1967) *passim*.

[44] "Savigny's Legacy. Legal History, Comparative Law, and the Emergence of a European Legal Science" 112 (1996) *LQR*, 576, esp.587 ff.

[45] *Op. cit.*, n. 19, above, at 28.

[46] Yet, the 27th edition of his classic text book, so skilfully updated by Professor Beatson, not only ignores the European influence but starts its account with the following statement: "The principles of the *English* law of contract are almost entirely the creation of *English* courts . . .". The statement is correct if read together with the phrase that follows it: "and the legislature has, until recently, played a relatively small part in their development." Yet I have italicised the words "English" since, to an uninitiated reader they certainly conceal the European debt which Anson, among others, regarded as so great. But even the growing (and more recent) European influence is only grudgingly mentioned in one short para. on p. 18 of the text. The above, in my view, lend further credence to the complaints made by Professor Simpson, *op. cit.*, n. 6 above; but they do not give any clues as to what reasons may lie behind such attitudes.

[47] Such as Oliver Wendell Holmes in his celebrated monograph *The Common Law*. More recently, however, authors such as Professor Mathias Reimann have suggested that Holmes' real target was not the German Pandectists but his Harvard colleague, Christopher Columbus Langdell. For the latter believed, in a matter which reminds one of contemporary German legal doctrine, that abstract principles can be used to build a coherent and consistent legal system. See, "Holmes Common Law and German Legal Science" in Gordon (ed.), *The Legacy of Oliver Wendell Holmes Jr.* (1992), 72 ff. Writing in 1887—in vol. 3 of the *Law Quarterly Review*, 118, esp 123 ff.—Langdell, himself, stressed his eagerness to move the law curriculum of the Harvard Law School away from the English world and closer to the European model. Of course, both Langdell, and the even more

reached its peek at about this period—were, themselves, greatly influenced by Germanic ideas.[48]

So "ignorance" of these past debts is certainly not the reason for our current cultivation of insularity. The question that thus arises is this. If these debts are known, why are they being "hushed up" or, at the very least, seriously minimised? Could Professor Simpson be suggesting[49] some kind of deliberate historical revisionism? And if so, what may be the reasons behind it? Though it may be rather too drastic to read such a strong assertion in Professor Simpson's cautiously phrased sentences, the idea that he might at least be hinting at something like this does not strike me as being so preposterous. In exploring this idea further, one might well be advised to consider how the autochthonous lawyers may have (unintentionally) combined with the wave of post-World War Two (forced) émigrés to produce this result.

One explanation why some members of the latter group may have succumbed to this tendency seems fairly obvious. The temptation to present themselves as being more English than the English must have been considerable. After all, being a refugee in England is very different from being a refugee in the melting pot culture of the Americas; and that is why I think we find this "rejection of the past" more in the former country than in the latter. I am, myself, personally aware of examples—and names need not be mentioned here—that make such a thesis plausible. Having met and talked to many of these colleagues, and being an émigré, albeit a voluntary one myself, I am beginning to see why playing down the intellectual strengths of their Germanic origins seemed a small price to pay in exchange for joining the "spiritual ancestry"[50] of the host nation and thus achieving "recognition" in the country of choice.[51] We are, of course, here in the precarious domain of subjective interpretations of the personalities and characters of judges and jurists. Yet, whatever the dangers, the task of studying more carefully the backgrounds, philosophies, and temperaments of those

influential President of Harvard University Charles Eliot, had acquired a first hand knowledge of the European, mainly German, scene by spending time in Europe.

[48] Holmes exemplifies this phenomenon since his debt to, Savigny and, even, to that most Germanic of German philosophers Immanuel Kant, (in so far as both wish to draw a clear line between ethics and the law) is considerable. Yet Holmes rarely fully acknowledges these intellectual debts. Understandably, therefore, one specialist commentator observes that Holmes was "notorious for not giving credit to his intellectual forebears and for being petty in his insistence on the primacy of his own contributions." See, Touster, "Holmes a Hundred Years Ago: The Common Law and Legal Theory", *Hofstra L. Rev.* 10 (1982), 673 at 687. Jhering's attack on the tendencies of the early Pandectists to abstract and generalise to excess is forcefully stated in some of his later works such as *Scherz und Ernst in der Jurisprudenz* (1885, 4th edn. 1892), 341, 2 and *Besitzwille: Zugleich eine Kritik der herrschenden juristischen Methode* (1889) 283, 4. Many other examples can be given which suggest that Holmes was deliberately ignoring such comments in mounting his own attack against his real target.

[49] See text and n. 30, above.

[50] See Baade, "Time and Meaning. Notes on the Intertemporal Law of the Statutory Construction and Constitutional Interpretation" 43 *Am. J. Comp. L.* 319, at 341 (1995).

[51] One of them who, somehow, came to think that I might be asked to have hand in the drafting of his *Times* obituary asked me "to play down the fact that he was both German and Jewish." When I enquired, half in jest "what is then left?" he just smiled!

included in the more recent waves of immigration must, one day, be undertaken more systematically than it has hitherto been done. For, as the late C. H. S. Fifoot observed:[52] "Law . . . is made by men". Whatever the pitfalls, it is less misleading to adopt or adapt Carlyle's[53] creed and approach legal history through biography. English lawyers, of all men, should believe in the power of the great judge.[54] Incidentally, one need not fear that adopting an "heroic" approach to law would lead us into the kind of controversies which arose— erroneously it seems to me—from Carlyle's famous aphorism that, at bottom, all history is the "Biography of great men". For, as the most recent scholarship on his work shows, "The Carlylean hero does not create history out of titanic will, but rather responds to the monitions and the forces alive in his world."[55]

But what about the autochthonous jurists? Why did they, too, choose to under-play the common European ancestry? Once again, one can only advance some very tentative suggestions. I offer four for consideration.

First, it is widely said that the inhabitants of modern England have lost their self-confidence. Nothing is these days shielded from criticism: the Monarchy, Parliament, and the Courts. The tendency for self-flagellation, to borrow Professor Reynolds' expression, came mainly after the Second World War when, in the famous words of Dean Acheson, "Britain lost an Empire and went in search of a role". I find this a very revealing phrase. For not only many refused

---

[52]   Op. cit., n. 19, above, at 12. It is both intriguing and gratifying to note that such advice was, essentially, given also by the late Professor Max Rheinstein in one of his most famous essays "Die Rechtshonoratioren und ihr Einfluss auf Charakter und Funktionen der Rechtsordnungen" (1970) 34 RabelsZ, 1 ff. In our treatise The [German] Law of Contracts and Restitution, (1998), Professor Lorenz, Dr Dannemann and I have, on several occasions, (e.g. ch. 1 and 6) given instances of how the understanding (or, sometimes, misunderstanding) of the law by one influential jurist has deeply affected subsequent developments. Mommsen's "Die Unmöglichkeit der Leistung in ihrem Einfluss auf obligatorische Verhältnisse" in Beiträge zum Obligationenrecht, I (1853) is one such example.

[53]   His celebrated (but nowadays out of fashion) lectures on On Heroes, Hero-Worship, and the Heroic in History were delivered in May 1840 and were published in London a year later. Numerous inconclusive debates have taken place about the reasons why he excluded from his list certain "professions" or individuals (for instance, his beloved Goethe). It would thus be idle to speculate why he never included a chapter on "The Hero as Judge". Perhaps, one reason for such an omission is the fact that the giants of the Victorian era had still to come. From an earlier era, Lord Mansfield could, of course, have supplied a perfect model. But then one must remember that at the time when the lectures were being delivered, the courts were undoing the last remnants of the Mansfield revolution. Thus, see: Eastwood v. Kenyon (1840) 11 A & E 438, at p. 450. One must, therefore, hope that the omission will be made good by some other future writer.

[54]   And, on the basis of what has already been said, one should add the great jurist.

[55]   Thomas Carlyle "On Heroes, Hero-Worship, and the Heroic in History" (University of California Press, 1993), introduction by Michael K. Goldberg at p. lix. On the previous page, Professor Goldberg states that the "superior insights [of heroes], and their actions based on them, crystallise what is merely latent." To me, this comes very close to Professor Simpson's observations on p. 252 of his already-cited article, where he states. "The point is not that the common law of contract was simply a jungle of unrelated instances, though it is certainly not always easy to identify and formulate the doctrine that is latent in the sources . . . It is rather that there existed no literary tradition of expounding the law of contract in a form which invites the reader to proceed to the solution of problems by applying general principles of substantive law . . .". This, the great 19th century judges and jurists did; and, arguably, this represents their major contribution to the development of our contemporary law.

to give up what they had lost—remember, for instance, that the so-called "east of Suez" policy found strong advocates even among the most thoughtful in the Conservative party. The country, its leaders, and its lawyers became over-dependent on the so-called special relationship with the USA (or the Commonwealth) neglecting Europe's inexorable pull both on the economic and political field. But what I say is, I believe true, not only of politics and the world of finance. I think it applies with even greater force to law, legal education, and legal thinking. The community of language with the USA provides, in my view, only a partial reason for this Americano-mania which we find in many contemporary debates in our law.[56]

Loss of confidence and loss of a sense of direction usually leads to confusion; and such feelings, it seems to me, push people inwards.[57] The confidence of the Victorians, when we find the height of the pro-Europe intellectual movement is exemplified by the famous laconic phrase attributed to Sir George Jessel.[58] Lord Annan, in his elegant study of the Victorian "aristocracy of intellect", discusses and explains this phenomenon. He thus shows how its members "judged people by an exterior standard of . . . intellectual merit". "Because their own proud standards were assured they tolerated a wide variety of belief."[59] Going beyond England, I think a strong case can be made for the proposition that the more confident the civilisation the more willing it is to graft new shoots on its trunks to encourage richer and differentiated growth. Such confidence, apart from brief intervals, has been conspicuously absent for the better part of the second half of this century. And this lack of confidence is, I believe, one reason for England—and I am deliberately excluding Scotland from this exercise—being unwilling to open up to what we have nowadays convinced ourselves to be different if not alien. It is tempting to suggest that those living in the past are fighting to cling to *die Welt von gestern*, to borrow the title of Zweig's last (and tragic) work. Security, it would seem, comes for them by re-asserting their distinctiveness; and in this case it means putting as much "blue water"—literally and metaphorically—between themselves and "Europe." This attitude has been a key feature of internal party politics for the last ten years or more; and I do not think it is that improbable to argue that we can also find traces of the phenomenon in the work of the academic community. Indeed, some have allowed themselves such flights of (academic) fancy that have led them to discover parallels between the collapsed regimes of Eastern Europe and the emerging European Union![60]

[56] For instance in calls that we introduce some kind of *New York Times* v. *Sullivan* (376 US 254 (1964)) rule in our law of defamation instead of attempting to understand the more balanced German model.

[57] Re-reading Lord Bingham's Mann Lecture, op cit., n. 3, above, especially at p. 514, I find traces of the same idea.

[58] "I may be wrong, and often am, but I never doubt" In later times Jessel, apparently, disclaimed that he could have ever used the words "often wrong". But otherwise, he accepted the authenticity of the attribution. See Goodhart, *Five Jewish Lawyers of the Common Law* (1949), 70, n. 23.

[59] N. 34, above, at 250.

[60] "[As] the twentieth century . . . meanders to its end, we see the leaders of Western Europe adamant to create an insanely bureaucratic and multilingual ideological empire such as the nations

Secondly, I think we have progressively moved away from encouraging a wider culture. I made this the topic of my inaugural lecture in Oxford. So I need not come back to it again here.[61] The emphasis on the functional curriculum, that my colleague Professor Peter Birks has attacked so eloquently but alas, without success, is thus taking its toll. The "conversion courses" will not produce Pollock's and Maitland's what ever else they do. This, I think, is so obvious a point I need not labour it further.[62] Yet the neo-conservative theories that dominated our country in the 1980's have pushed both academic law and the system of administration of justice into thinking in terms of "returns", "market solutions", "cost-benefit analyses" which Lord Mustill, among others, has caustically—and rightly—condemned in a little noticed lecture.[63]

Thirdly, the sovereignty issue, which has been allowed to inhibit our relations with Europe to such an extent, has also taken its toll on the education system. For here, as in the rest of Europe, the triumph of the sovereign state in the 19th century made legal education inward looking. Rudolf von Jhering noted this phenomenon at its height when he remarked that ". . . legal science has been brought down to the plane of territorial jurisprudence" as "the scientific boundaries in law have been made coterminous to the political".[64] Thus, whereas the teaching of scientific subjects remained international and, nowadays have increasingly become more so, law has, with few exceptions and until at least the seventies, retained its local character. The tendency of our current textbooks to proclaim the "Englishness" of their subject matter fits well into this climate. Yet Jhering, though writing almost a century and a half ago was, once again right, in maintaining that "That nations do not lead an isolated existence but, like humans, have a common existence . . . [they] live in a world of constant contact and reciprocal influence, of give and take, of borrowing and giving: in a sentence a complex system of exchanges that embrace every side of human existence."[65] Every banker and economist has come to recognise the validity of this statement. Why are some lawyers still dragging their feet?

A final reason may be the following. When English lawyers turned to Roman law they already had a corpus of their own law but lacked the superior jurisprudential techniques and categories offered by the Roman law as developed by generations of Continental European jurists. In that sense, French and German law could be described as being not only older but also more developed than contemporary English law. One hundred and fifty years later the situation has changed. English law has grown in stature and sophistication; and the acquisi-

---

of Eastern Europe have just broken loose from . . .". Cane and Stapleton (eds.), *Essays in Honour of John Fleming* (Oxford, 1998); Weir, "The Staggering March of Negligence", 97.

[61] Author, "The Comparatist (or a Plea for a Broader Legal Education)", reprinted in *Foreign Law and Comparative Methodology: A Subject and a Thesis* (Oxford, 1997) 15 ff.

[62] Though Annan, again, n. 34 above at pp. 250–1, may prompt some sad comparisons with the decline of educational standards at home.

[63] "What do Judges Do?" *Särtryck Ur Juridisk Tidskrift* 1995–96 Nr 3 611, esp. 614 ff.

[64] Von Jhering, *Geist des römischen Rechts* (3rd edn., 1873), vol. I, pp. 11 and 15.

[65] *Ibid.*, at pp. 5 and 6.

tion of an academic component to the law, especially during the last one hundred years, has made up for the need to borrow from elsewhere.

Such arguments in my opinion confirm, unwillingly perhaps, the view that serious intellectual debts have *already* been incurred; but they do not undermine the thesis advanced here. For, at best, they only suggest that future borrowings are not likely to take the form they took in the 19th century. This approach, however, cannot deny the undeniable fact that a new form of Europeanisation is currently taking place thanks to a growing number of Directives, International Conventions, and the spreading influence of the case law of the two European courts in Luxembourg and in Strasbourg. Thus, it cannot be used as a reason for saying that no further borrowings are likely to happen. The give and take in law and other academic subjects never comes to an end. If anything, because people and ideas travel better than they used to, the trend will increase. Further down, I shall be arguing that in my view there remain some important areas, mainly of public law, where the European models still have much that is inspiring.

The problem of explaining the current, insular mode thus remains unanswered if one remains at a legal or purely rational level. To avoid such an intellectual impasse one has to go into politics to find an answer. But European politics provide not only part of the explanation for what has been happening thus far. European politics also provide strong clues as to what will happen in the future. Thus in "Europe" I find at least a partial palliative to the problems and objections that I have mentioned. But since trying to explain why this is so would turn this paper into a sociological rather than a legal essay I would like, instead, to concentrate my arguments on two specific points. The first will be a technical one: how best can we re-ignite the interest of our judges in foreign law in general and European law in particular? I shall discuss this in section four of this paper while retaining for section five my views about future borrowings and where and how they are likely to occur.

4. HOW CAN WE INCREASE INTELLECTUAL INTERACTION AND BORROWINGS?

The mental blocks towards foreign models are caused by understandable reaction towards events in Germany in the 1930's and 40's, chauvinism, prejudice, scepticism about the utility of foreign ideas, and concern about (lack of) time and space to make proper use of them. These are all, undoubtedly, major stumbling blocks; but in a shrinking world of increased economic inter-dependence they will all have to be overcome. In such a new and challenging environment, how does one proceed to make the best of other people's *ideas*? The italicised word is crucial; for my thesis has always been that it is the basic idea that should be studied and, if found attractive, transplanted. By contrast, the conceptual apparel in which it is clothed can be discarded or, at any rate, studied only when a mere technical command of the law is required. I can think of at least two ways of attempting this task. First, you get the interested parties to talk to one another in a *focused* context; then you present the ideas of one side to the other in a way that makes sense to the receiver of the "new" information. Dr. Dannemann and I once called this the need, first to "deconstruct" and then "reconstruct" German law.[66] It is something which comparative lawyers have not done enough up to now.

The Goff/von Bar Anglo-German judicial conferences of recent times have developed an attractive (but not exclusive) format for achieving the first aim. In fact, two judicial conferences have been held thus far; and a third one is being planned.[67] In my view, the second of these conferences scored more highly than the first. The reason is because the organisers chose to ask their high-powered participants to talk about a set of problems confronted in a number of carefully pre-selected decisions taken from both systems—the English and the German— and arising in similar factual contexts. The variety of issues raised in one of these cases I have, myself, discussed in a comparative piece dedicated to the memory of the late John Fleming.[68] Even a quick perusal of the material I have reproduced in that essay will convince the reader that this way of approaching foreign law rapidly reveals the actual differences and similarities that exist between the legal systems that are being compared. But it does more than that since the study of focused problems also provides a convenient springboard for broader examination of the foreign system. Thus, to give but one example from this particular topic, the greater generosity shown by the American decisions towards the child's wrongful birth claim can quickly be explained by reference to the German system's willingness to continue the parental obligation to maintain the child beyond the age of majority. This not only reveals a difference in the family law provisions of the two systems; it also shows how the answer to tort problems may, sometimes, be determined by the position adopted by a particular system in other parts of its law such as family or inheritance law. The comparison thus progresses from the obvious to the less obvious, from the particular to the more general, providing, *en passant*, the novice observer with broader and interesting information about the system that he is trying to understand. And all this is achieved quite painlessly by staying mostly on a factual plane and avoiding the confusion that comes with all efforts to explain each other's legal jargon. Incidentally, this moving from one part of the Code to another or, even, a different branch of the law, is an undeniable feature of German law which can reach great sophistication in that system. This is especially true in restitution kind of problems where the method of "paragraph chains" (*Paragraphenketten*) can reach great complexity and prove off-putting to an impatient English lawyer.

---

[66] "The Legacy of History on German Contract Law" *Essays for Roy Goode* (ed. Ross Cranston) (Oxford, 1997) pp. 1–28.

[67] The first of which was reported in (*RabelsZ*) 58 (1994) 421 ff.

[68] Cane and Stapleton (eds.), *The Law of Obligations: A Celebration of John Fleming* (Oxford, 1998). "Reading through a Foreign Judgment", ch. 10.

The above observations naturally lead to my second point, already hinted in the previous paragraph. One still has to show one's "native" colleagues that the *idea* found in a foreign system is worth copying; and discovering what the idea is and whether it works in practice may not always be easy given the differences in structure, concepts, and techniques that exist between different legal systems. It takes a special kind of training to disentangle the two; and that is where comparative lawyers can make their major contribution to the study of law. To make my point, I thus move from generalities to specifics. But since the ideas are complex and the material that supports them voluminous, I propose to subdivide the remainder of this section into four sub-sections. Thus, in the first I shall state the theoretical point I wish to discuss in this paper stressing, of course, that others can be subjected to a similar kind of analysis. In the second and third sub-sections I shall sketch the German and US approaches to my problem, placing most of the emphasis on the difficulties that obscure the substantive similarities. In the final sub-section I shall try to draw this material together in the form of some specific conclusions. In attempting the above, I am not unaware of the price one has to pay for compressing[69] such complex material into a small space. But, I believe this is a price worth paying if the exercise can lead to the development of a theory of comparative methodology that will be judge and practitioner-friendly.

4.1 The problem

As English courts come to grapple with the new Human Rights legislation I believe they will, sooner rather than later, be forced to realise that the traditional public/private law divide, until recently unknown in our system, is in fact breaking down in most systems. Thus, in Germany, where the public/private law divide has been an almost axiomatic feature of its law, this change has been noticed for at least fifty years now though, admittedly, there is considerable disagreement as to how German lawyers should cope with its consequences. In Germany, when it comes to human rights, this debate has come to be expressed by the shorthand phrase *mittelbare Drittwirkung der Grundrechte* (though often the protection in the private domain is achieved by other, not strictly speaking constitutional, means). Rendering the German notion into English as "the third party (*indirect*) effect of constitutional rights" makes the underlying idea marginally more intelligible but, at the same time, even less acceptable to a traditional Common lawyer. For we all know (and until recent times unquestionably accepted) that Human Rights were developed to protect individuals against intrusions by the state and that, therefore, they were designed to work in a "vertical" manner. Giving them a "horizontal" effect, so as to enable them

---

[69] In attempting this I have had the benefit of the advice of a number of American colleagues namely (in alphabetical order) Professors Hans Baade, Donald Kommers, and Douglas Laycock. All are gratefully thanked and, at the same time, absolved from the errors of my ways.

to regulate the relations between private entities as well, runs the risk of under-mining private autonomy on which our private law—especially the Common law—has for so long been based. "Privatising Human Rights"[70] thus poses seri-ous philosophical problems, especially for those who believe that the state should be interfering with individual autonomy as little as possible. Though this worry is, if anything, more forcefully reflected in the American legal literature, it is also found in the writings of many German jurists.[71] Yet, despite its signif-icance, this philosophical point need not be laboured in this paper. For it is obvi-ous that in its jurisprudential form this debate is unlikely to produce a conclusive answer to our problem since the legal answer, ultimately, will always be coloured by the observer's political views. More significantly, if we go down this path we are unlikely to discover whether the notion exists and works in countries other than Germany.

I thus start from the premise that a need for some kind of *Drittwirkung* approach will prove necessary even to our own system. For, as our doyen of public lawyers put it so eloquently, "it would, indeed, be a poor sort of 'incor-poration' which exempted private individuals and bodies from respecting the fundamental rights of their fellow-citizens and drove them back to Strasbourg . . . the very evil which 'incorporation' is supposed to remedy."[72] So the horizon-tality issue will arise and, in my view, it will be one of the more thorny ones that will confront our judges once the new legislation is in force. If I am right in this prediction, and I think time will prove me right, we must at least make the effort to understand German law, since it has accumulated much experience on this matter—an experience which, at present, we in England, simply do not have.[73] But even if we surmount the hurdle of understanding the German material, the adoption of some kind of *Drittwirkung* doctrine will still be hampered by the philosophical objections levelled against the doctrine. That is why I believe progress on this matter will be facilitated only if we present to our audiences fac-tual situations that have been litigated *both* in Germany and the USA that show that the notion, *in substance if not in form*, also exists and works in both systems. I thus propose to offer examples from two broad areas of human rights law—sex and race discrimination, and speech rights—in both instances

[70] The expression belongs to Andrew Clapham who until very recently, was one of the few British lawyers to address the problem of horizontality with much originality. Thus, see his "The Privatisation of Human Rights" (1996) 1 *EHRLR*, 20.

[71] Dürig in Maunz/Dürig, Grundgesetz Kommentar, Art. 1, Abs. III, Rdnr. 129–30. Criticism has thus been voiced at the increasing "constitutionalisation of such areas of private law as landlord and tenant, surety, and employment law. See: Zollner, "Regelungsspielräume im Schuldvertragsrecht, *AcP* 196 (1996), 1; Oeter, "Drittwirkung" der Grundrechte und die Autonomie des Privatrechts, *AöR* 119 (1994), 529. Roellecke, "Das Mietrecht des BVerfG", *NJW* 1992, 1649; Medicus, "Der Grundsatz der Verhältnismäßigkeit im Privatrecht" *AcP* 192 (1992), 35.

[72] Sir William Wade, "Human Rights and the Judiciary", Judicial Studies Board *Annual Lecture 1998*, 5.

[73] But which the Germans do. Thus, see: "Privacy, Freedom of Speech and the Horizontality of the Human Rights Bill" *1998 Wilberforce Lecture*, 115 (1999) *LQR*, 47 ff. See, also, "The Applicability of Human Rights as between Individuals under German Constitutional Law" (with Dr. Stefan Enchelmaier) in Markesinis (ed.), *Protecting Privacy* (1998), ch. 8.

emphasising the degree of protection offered to individuals in private, not state, contexts.

4.2 Sex (and race) discrimination

Once again, my main concern is the applicability of human rights law in the private work place.

During the last thirty years or so United States law has taken great strides towards protecting the human rights of individual in the private workplace and against powerful private actors.[74] This is obvious from the civil rights legislation that came into being in the mid-sixties and the way in which this has been progressively applied by the courts.[75] To be sure, the picture that emerges seems more complex than the one that one encounters in Germany. Thus, in the USA the source of the rules can be attributed both to statutory material[76] and judicial activism.[77] The available remedies also vary enormously depending upon the rule that is being used.[78] The method of adjudicating about complaints is anything but uniform. The resulting complexity is so great that even experts in the field may not be aware that a remedy may be available.[79] As if all this were not enough, the entire debate is strongly coloured by a clash between "right" and "left". In this clash the left typically argues that discrimination is still rampant and the courts making it hard to prove, while the right maintains with equal passion that discrimination is not in the employers' interest and that false claims are more common than real discrimination. To the above one must, finally, add the

[74] The (main) equality clause of the German Constitution of 1949 can be found in Art. 3, para. 3 of which declares that "No one may be prejudiced or favoured because of sex, ancestry, race, language, homeland and origin, faith or religious or political opinions. Persons may not be discriminated against because of their disability."

[75] Starting with Title VII of the Civil Rights Act of 1964, now codified as 42 USC § 2000. This declares it to be an "unlawful employment practice to fail or refuse to hire or to discharge any individual, or otherwise to discriminate against any individual . . . because of such individual's race, colour, religion, sex or national origin".

[76] For instance, see: The Age Discrimination in Employment Act, 29 USCA §§ 621 ff. The "Equal Pay" amendment to the Fair Labour Standards Act, 29 USCA § 206 (d). The Fair Housing Act, 42 USCA § 2000e–5. The National Labour Relations Act, s. 7 (which applies to almost all private sector employees), and multiple enactments in every state.

[77] E.g. by important decisions such as the (controversial) *Jones* v. *Alfred E. Mayer Co.*, 392 US 409 (1968) where the dissenters, essentially, objected with the court's interference with Congress' work in the Fair Housing Act. See, also, *Runyon* v. *McCrary* 427 US 160 (1976) where the court held that the reach of USC § 1981 extends to private relationships as well as those that involved the state. In its original version § 1981 proclaimed that "All persons within the jurisdiction of the US shall have the same right . . . to make and enforce contracts, . . . and to full and equal protection of all laws . . ."

[78] Thus under the original version of Tile VII complaints should go through the Equal Employment Opportunity Commission whereas with the passing of the Civil Right Act of 1991 judges and juries were authorised to award compensatory and punitive damages to victims of intentional sex and race discrimination. For more details see, *inter alia*, Livingston, "The Civil Rights Act 1991 and EEOC Enforcement" 23 *Stetson L. Rev.* 53 (1993).

[79] See the comments of Professor Estlund in "Free Speech and Due Process in the Workplace", 71 *Ind. L. J.* 101, 108 and n. 68 (1995).

debates about the respective merits of regulation versus deregulation and about the proper limits of the powers of a non-elected judiciary. The American judicial debate thus appears to be even more overtly politicised than the German.

For a foreign observer, be he English or German, such complexity is particularly daunting. Yet if we are to deal with foreign systems, as we increasingly will be called upon to do, we must at least attempt to find ways to de-mystify them and make them accessible to outside observers. This is not, as some academics have argued from their red brick towers,[80] a question of intellectual arrogance but of practical necessities. Transactions will be facilitated and, even, ideas will begin to travel more easily if and only if lawyers learn to look for the "corpus" of foreign law and are not put off by its differing apparel. We thus need urgently a methodology that can (a) help us set aside (without too much distortion) the differences in appearances and, when that is done, (b) help us show the strengths and weaknesses of the foreign system as well as the similarities it bears with our own. In our shrinking world, this will be needed even more in the future than it has been in the past.

A comparative study on how United States and German law have approached these problems leaves one in no doubt that both are striving for the same final goal. My belief is that both in the United States and Germany the dividing line between discriminatory private action and discriminatory state action has become blurred. On the whole, the consensus is that they are also reaching the overall goals with similar effect[81] though one could argue that American *statutory* protection goes further than the typical *constitutional* protection in at least two ways. For first, the Constitution protects only against deliberate discrimination whereas Title VII (and many other statutory rules that have flown from this key law) requires justification of apparently neutral rules that disproportionately exclude minorities, such as testing programmes. Secondly, statutory protection goes further in so far as the non-discrimination regime in the US has been largely generalised to cover such varied topics as age, pregnancy, handicap and sexual orientation,[82] some of which have yet to make an appearance on the German scene.[83] The above broad community of aims and results must not be allowed to

[80] For instance Professor Legrand "Are civilians educable?" 18 No. 2 *Legal Studies*, 216 at 227 n. 62 (1998).

[81] See the compact and, on the whole politically neutral presentation by Professor Currie in his excellent *The Constitution of the Federal Republic of Germany* (1994) 322 ff.

[82] Thus see: CT ST s.46a–81c; NJ ST 10; 2–1; 10; 5–12; 5–33; RI ST s.28–5–7; VT ST 21 s.495; WA ST T. 49. 60; WI ST 16.765; 111.31; (all including "sexual orientation" as a prohibited heading of discrimination). Some states have gone even further and, under the pressure of the smokers lobby, have prohibited discrimination for unlawful activities off the [employers'] premises". Thus, see, CO ST s. 24 34–205.5. In the light of such provisions one must entertain some doubts as to how convincing Professor Currie's claim is that "the list of suspect classifications is significantly longer in Germany than it is in the United States." *Op. cit.*, 324.

[83] Disability (*Behinderung*) was added to Art. 3 (3) of the Constitution in 1994. But the German legislator has thus far refused to include in art. 3 of the *Federal* Constitution—though see Art. 12.(2) of the Constitution of the State of Brandeburg of 1992—the notion of *sexuelle Identität* ("sexual orientation"). In its judgment of 17 February 1998, Case C-249/96, the Court of the European Communities, took the same view. It thus held that it was legal for an (English) employer to refuse

obscure differences of interpretative techniques since, methodologically speaking, German jurists seem to prefer a more holistic interpretation of their Constitution than their American counterparts do. In the German case law we thus find equality notions influencing the results of other disputes even though they allegedly bear a closer connection with different constitutional provisions.[84] Nor, secondly, should one fail to note that the United States has extended such protection in the domain of private relationships though it has done so (mainly) through specific federal[85] or state statutes that have proliferated after the Equal Rights legislation of the mid 1960's. Many of these "rights" go well beyond the normal ambit of constitutional protection though, admittedly, and for the reasons already alluded to, the improved protection has come about in a very Hegelian manner.[86] Thirdly, in Germany the catalyst for such protection seems to have been not *internal* political "unrest" (as is the case in the USA) but *external* influences, mainly[87] in the form of various European Community Directives that were then incorporated into domestic German law. Moreover, it

to extend travel concessions to the homosexual cohabitee of one of his workers, such travel concessions being available to the spouses or heterosexual partners of his workforce. The Court, however, conceded that after the Treaty of Amsterdam has come into force the Council may, under certain conditions, take appropriate action to eliminate discrimination based on sexual orientation. If (or when) Community law changes in this respect, German municipal law will then be forced to follow suit. The notion of equality, once again, will then have been extended not because of the wording of the national Constitution (or the decision of the national legislator) but because of developments on the international legal scene. See, in this context, the observation made in the following para. of the text, above.

[84] For illustrations see Professor Kommers' excellent *The Constitutional Jurisprudence of the Federal Republic of Germany* (2nd edn. 1997), esp. 289 ff.

[85] Mainly, it seems to me, by "exploiting" the "commerce clause" which enable Congress to prohibit all forms of discrimination having a substantial effect on interstate commerce. Since, the Supreme Court more or less seems to leave it to Congress to decide what interstate commerce is and how substantial the effect of discrimination is, the latter has the ability to reach nearly all forms of private discrimination. But Congress is *empowered* but *not constitutionally required* to pass such legislation; and here there may be a difference with German Constitutional law. Congress, of course, also has broad power under section 5 of the 14th Amendment to enact remedial legislation for discriminatory *state* activity. (I am grateful to Professor Kommers for reminding of these points.)

[86] *Patterson* v. *McLean Credit Union* 41 US 164 (1988) offers a good illustration of this for in that case a much more conservative court, adopting a hyper technical interpretation of § 1981 took the view that this provision, prohibiting discrimination and harassment, did not apply to post-formation discrimination. One suspects, however, that the real reason why they adopted such a narrow interpretation of the text was the court's (sincere) belief that the earlier decisions of *Jones* and *Runyon* were wrong. Be that as it may, the (still) Democratically controlled Congress then swung into action and, by passing the Civil Rights Act 1991, overruled *Patterson* by clarifying the words "make and enforce contracts" to include, performance, modification, and termination.

[87] But not exclusively, as the seminal Nocturnal Employment case (BVerfGE 85, 191) of 1992 shows. For in that case the Constitutional Court declared unconstitutional a statute that forbade the employment of women as blue-collar workers during the night allegedly on the grounds of protecting their health and safety. As Professor Kommers rightly points out "The old GDR [East Germany] had no such statute, and in the face of mass unemployment among East German women after reunification, it would have seemed callous to saddle these women with the added burden of a ban on nocturnal work." *Op. cit.*, n. 84, above. The European influence is, however, also obvious in the judgment since the Constitutional Court took note of a 1991 decision of the European Court of Justice invalidating a similar French prohibition. See: *The Republic* [France] v. *Alfred Stoeckel*, Case C–345/89.

is interesting to note that this *enlarged* (and European-inspired) protection against sex discrimination first appeared in the domain of private law relations and was only later extended by statute to cover public service employees.[88] To this interesting list of differences one must, however, add a notable similarity. Thus, in this area of human rights' law—race equality in particular[89]—neither system felt the need for a *Drittwirkung* type of doctrine even though both have reached the same conclusion: that protection against sex harassment should not depend upon the public or private status of the employer.[90]

But more than what has just been asserted emerges from this rich material. For the comparatively minded teacher can, if so inclined, draw even wider conclusions from these texts—rich, varied, and contradictory though they sometimes are. Thus, to return to my earlier point, starting from fairly narrow factual situations, he can show not only how two different systems have attempted to solve the problems they present. He can go further than that and also use the material to tell his students something about the interaction of the political and judicial process. Not content with describing this, he might even ask the more inquisitive of their students to consider how this political interaction is manifested in systems such as the English and the German where the judicial debates are more prone to concealing the political forces that influence these battles. This, incidentally, is the best place to bring into the discussion the debate about the continuing force of the theory of autonomy of the will and move the debate from the practical to the theoretical field. Finally, in advocating to English lawyers the possibility of giving a horizontal effect to their new Human Rights legislation, the comparatist can claim that the idea that human rights need to be

---

[88] See, for instance, The *Arbeitsrechtliches EG-Anpassungsgesetz*, BGBl (1980), 1308 (Fair Employment Act) extended in 1994 by the *Gesetz zur Durchsetzung der Gleichberechtigung von Frauen und Männern*, art. 1, sec. a BGBl I (1994), 1406. The (initial) limitation to private contracts was never very convincing. The "Female Fitter" decision of the Constitutional court—BverfGE 89, 276—decided on 16 November 1993 (and before the 1994 law altered § 613 a BGB) illustrates this point. There, a University Institute—in principle a public employer—wished to hire a fitter for a project which was financed by private funds. The method of financing and implementation of the project apparently brought the employment relationship within the domain of private law. The court found that the plaintiff—a female fitter—had been discriminated against. For first, she had been told that the post was physically too demanding for a woman and then, later, the employer had added the reason that the male fitter actually employed had superior experience to the woman candidate. The court was wary of arguments added ex post facto; and also expressed doubts about the validity of concerns connected with experience in jobs that were traditionally male dominated. This last type of criterion was bound to place women at a disadvantage. (See observations at 290 ff.) The applicant's complaint was thus successful.

[89] German law has, in contrast to that of the United States law, little case law to show in the domain of race inequality. Characteristically, however, in his *magnum opus*—Maunz/Dürig, *op. cit.* n. 71, above, Art. 1, Abs. III, Rdnr 133—Professor Dürig offers a *Drittwirkung* example of race discrimination: contract not to let an apartment to a Jew would be contrary to good morals and thus void. Cf. Cass. 3ème civ., 6 mars 1996, JCP 1996, éd. G, iv, 973 and JCP 1997, 22764 where the French court of cassation held that art. 8.1. of the European Convention of Human Rights could be used to set aside a clause in a private lease which prevented a tenant from allowing his close relatives to reside in the leased premises.

[90] This view is advanced by Hartwin Bungert, "Gleichberechtigung von Mann und Frau im amerikanischen und deutschen Verfassungsrecht" 89 *Zeitschrift für Vergleichende Rechtswissenschaft*, 441, 463 ff (1990).

protected against powerful entities (public or private) is neither as alien nor as dangerous as it may sound. For, if this brief survey demonstrates anything, it is surely that in *substance if not in form* many of these concerns, voiced in Germany since the Second World War, have come to be shared by both courts and academics in the most market oriented economy of the world: the USA.

4.3 Constitutional protection of speech in the workplace

In the previous sub-paragraph we noted that in the field of sex equality German and American law are not that different, at any rate in their results if not in their theories. The need to protect individual rights against private actors, especially employers, is strong in both systems. And, in a broad sort of way, it has taken the same kind of form—statutory interventions of different kinds supplemented by bold case law. But when we move to protection of speech rights in the private workplace we find in the United States a picture that is not only complex but also different. Yet we also encounter some case law developments which, though rejected (or qualified) by most State jurisdictions, show that methodologically the German solution is perfectly transplantable to the US. Indeed, a foreign observer would be justified in arguing that where American courts have used these techniques they have produced fairer results for the plaintiffs in question than the leading German case. So, once again, let us turn to specifics for here comparative methodology can be even more instructive in revealing how similar the two (apparently different) systems can be.

Thus, in both systems we find speech disputes that arose in a private employment relationship. In both instances, the plaintiff/employees indulged in a political activity, which did not meet with the approval of their (private) employer. Finally, in both the employers' attempt to dismiss the employees was countered by the argument that such an action would, in the final analysis, conflict with basic Human Rights enshrined in the Constitutions of the two countries. It was, precisely, this kind of factual setting that in Germany launched the expression *unmittelbare Dittwirkung* (*direct* third party effect)[91] in the sense that the Human Rights articles of the Constitution *directly* governed such disputes. Four years later, however, the Constitutional Court[92] adopted a more subtle variant propounding the view that Constitutional provisions had a "radiating effect" (*Ausstrahlungswirkung*) on private law, "influencing" rather than "directly governing" its relationships. Much ink has flowed in America[93] to show that—

---

[91] BArbGE 1, 185 (1954). The judgment of the Court, presided by Judge Hans-Carl Nipperdey, draws heavily on his earlier writings as an academic, notably his seminal "Gleicher Lohn der Frau für gleiche Leistung. Ein Beitrag zur Auslegung der Grundrechte" in *Recht der Arbeit* 1950, 121 ff. As is explained in what follows in the text the theory that now prevails allows the constitutional rules to have an indirect, over-arching effect on private law relations but denies to them any direct applicability.

[92] BVerfGE 7, 195 (1958).

[93] Professor Peter Quint has collected the references in his excellent "Free Speech and Private Law in German Constitutional Theory" 48 *Maryland L. Rev.* 247 (1989).

rightly or wrongly, this is not the point here—the parallel American doctrine of "state action", extended to its furthest reach in *Shelley* v. *Kraemer*,[94] is not as wide as the German doctrine of *Drittwirkung*.[95] Yet whatever may be the right answer, the fact remains that a few American courts have, in the context of the factual situation here examined, had little difficulty in adopting a *basic* stance which is very similar to the one found in Germany. What is interesting about this case law is that it allowed the constitutional law to penetrate the private law dispute not through the "state action" doctrine but through another amorphous notion, that of "public policy".

Novosel v. *Nationwide Insurance Company*[96] gives us the perfect illustration. In this case, the Court of Appeals of the Third Circuit took the view that the concern for rights of political expression, which animated First Amendment *public*[97] employee cases, was also applicable to *private* employees under Pennsylvania law.[98] The Court was thus able to state in distinctly Nipperdeian terms that "The protection of important political freedoms . . . goes well beyond the question whether the threat comes from state or private bodies."[99]

Other cases, which have followed this line of argument, could be quoted.[100] Yet it will suffice to mention but two since they relate to the right of privacy which is likely to cause most of the headaches when our new Human Rights legislation comes into force. Thus, in the Californian case of *Semore* v. *Pool*[101] the Court of Appeal of the Fourth District held that the right of privacy in the California Constitution prohibits a private employer from conducting arbitrary drug testing and that the dismissal of the employee for failing to submit to the

[94] 334 US, 1 (1948).

[95] But see *Sullivan* v. *Barnett*, 139 F. 3d 158 (3rd Cir. 1998), petition for cert. Pending No. 97–2000. That the problem is not going away can be seen in the discussion of Siegel, "The Constitution and Private Government: Toward the Recognition of Constitutional Rights in Private Residential Communities Fifty Years After *Marsh* v. *Alabama*" 6 *William and Mary Bill of Rights Law Journal*, 461 (1998).

[96] 721 F. 2d 894 (1983). The (predictably adverse) reactions to *Novosel* are discussed by Professor Perritt "The Future of Wrongful Dismissal Claims: Where does Employer Self-Interest Lie?" in 58 *U. Cin. L.Rev.* 397, esp. 402 ff. (1989) where the author describes the *Novosel* doctrine as "an important model for possible future expansion of the public policy tort into *a constitutionalization of private employment*." (Italics supplied.)

[97] Thus, to stick with the same State, see *Hunter* v. *Port Authority of Allegheny County* 419 A 2d. 631 (1980): Employer's right to dismiss employee of an "at-will employment" is circumscribed by requirements of public policy which may be derived directly from First Amendment of the US Constitution and sec. 7 of the Pennsylvania Constitution.

[98] In *Borse* v. *Piece Goods Shop, Inc.* 963 F. 2d 611 (1992) the Court refused to extend the *Novosel* ruling to a dismissal of an employee who refused to submit herself to urinalysis screening for drug use. Significantly, however, it refused to hold ". . . that a constitutional provision may never serve as a source of public policy in . . . wrongful discharge actions [taking place in a private workplace]." It is precisely this last point which brings the two systems closer together than they are commonly believed to be.

[99] *Ibid.* at p. 900.

[100] For instance: *Devlin* v. *North Shore Door Co.* 1995 WL 277, 110 (Ohio App. 8 Dist.): "Clear 'public policy' sufficient to justify an exception to the employment-at-will doctrine . . . may be discerned by the Ohio judiciary based on sources such as the Constitution of Ohio and the United States . . ."

[101] 217 Cal. App. 3rd 1087, 266 Cal. Rptr. 280 (1990).

proposed test violated the public policy of the state. The position was re-affirmed four years later by the (state) Supreme Court in *Hill* v. *National Collegiate Athletic Assn.*[102] where the court held that the privacy clause of article 1, section 2, of the State Constitution, "creates a right of action against private as well as government agencies."[103] Accordingly, when a private employee's contract is terminated on the grounds that he refused to take a random drug test, the employee may invoke the public policy exception to the "at-will termination" doctrine to assert a violation of his constitutional right of privacy.

The above discussion and the case law given in the notes reveals, once again, the lack of a solution that is uniformly acceptable to the fifty American jurisdictions. It also reveals that the wider *Novosel* doctrine—that the Constitutional texts can help shape the public policy exceptions to the doctrine that "at will contracts" can be terminated by the employer for any reason or no reason—has had a mixed reception. In particular, the drug testing cases, which seem to have shown the greater reluctance to use this technique, may in part be explicable by the general desire to fight the drug war with all means available setting aside what are seen as legalistic niceties. A more general explanation for rejecting the *Novosel* approach may be linked to the wider debate alluded to in the previous sub-section, concerning the desirability of taking such powers away from the legislator and giving them to the judiciary. But, in my view, the validity of my thesis remains unaffected by these attempts to keep the judicially created exceptions to the employment "at will" doctrine to a minimum. For what the *Novosel* case law shows is that that the *Drittwirkung* technique is not entirely inconceivable even in the United States in the sense that constitutional ideas can and do enter into the domain of a private law dispute. To be sure, in Germany this "revolution" came about through the use of some the quasi metaphysical concepts relied upon by the court in *Lüth* such as *Drittwirkung*, *Wechselwirkung*, *Ausstrahlungswirkung*, in combination with some of the most amorphous paragraphs found in the Civil Code. That in America the same result came about through the equally amorphous concept of public policy is, I submit, a matter of relative detail. What does, however, matter is the realisation that human rights are, nowadays, seriously threatened from powerful private entities as much as

---

[102] 7 Cal. 4th 1, 26 Cal. Rptr. 2d 834, 865 P. 2d 633 (1994). This has been followed in different contexts. See, for instance, *Pettus* v. *Cole* 49 Cal. App. 4th 402,57 Cal. Rptr. 2d 46. (Employee made prima facie showing that disclosure to employer of detailed medical information by psychiatrists in connection with request for disability leave violated his constitutional right to privacy as he had legally cognizable interest in preserving privacy of his medical history and psychological profile.)

[103] Once again, the generality of this statement is of especial significance for the wider comparative point that I am trying to make. One must, however, also note two further points. First, in n. 20 (p. 869) of the *Hill* judgment referred to in n. 102, above, the court expressed doubts as to the continued validity of the *Semore* ruling. Secondly, courts, as we already noted when mentioning the *Borse* judgment in n. 98, above, are reluctant to apply these principles in drug-testing cases. Thus, in *Jennings* v. *Minco Technology Labs Inc.* 765 SW 2d 497 (1989), a Texas court not only held that employers can require drug testing (and dismiss employees of "at will" contracts if they refuse to comply); it also slapped the employee with attorneys' fees for even raising the issue.

they are by State. A theory of horizontality of some kind is thus called for. How, precisely, we implement it must, however, be left to the techniques used by and the philosophies prevalent to each system that has to face this problem.

Finally, one must not bring this discussion to an end without noting that *Novosel* in the USA achieved what eluded the *Bundesarbeitsgericht* in Germany. For at the end of the day the latter court, despite its grandiloquent declarations, failed to come to the assistance of the employee who was dismissed simply because his political views differed from those of his employer. But then, perhaps we can come back to the point we made at the beginning of this section: the German case involved a communist sympathiser. This may give us as intriguing a clue as the drug testing cases do in their own way in the USA. For one must not forget that the German case was litigated in the early fifties. It is thus arguably right to suggest that the legal decision must be seen against the political realities that prevailed at that time. The final conclusion of the German court, that limiting the speech rights of the dismissed employee is admissible if it serves to protect some other competing legal value (*Rechtsgut*), can thus be sees as a sham. A sham that clothes in legalistic language a decision of political expediency that the climate of the times made almost unavoidable. That such a (harsh) interpretation is not entirely fanciful can be seen from the fact that the court found no constitutional text to peg such an approach but, instead, chose to trump constitutional protected speech rights by relying on previous court practice and academic writings.[104]

4.4 Some tentative conclusions

Three, I believe, are in order.

First, the treasures of German law have to be mined at great personal effort. The effort lies in discovering the basic idea behind complex theorising. This makes the German legal model, despite its undoubted intellectual virtues, a difficult one to follow. To put it differently, it makes it a model worth studying for the sake of tapping its undoubted intellectual originality but not ideal for the purposes of literal transplantation. As I put it elsewhere, German law must first be "deconstructed" and then "reconstructed" before English lawyers can use it.[105]

Secondly, American law is far too varied, too complex and, on the whole, too rooted in private market philosophies to lend itself to facile comparisons.

---

[104] BArbGE 1, 185, 194–5 (1954). A second constitutional challenge in that case was based on the idea that the dismissal violated Art. 3 (3) of the Constitution, which prohibits discrimination on grounds of political opinion. Though the Court held that this constitutional provision as well had a horizontal effect it, again, held that it had not been violated in this instance. Subsequent case law has, however, shown greater sensitivity to the employee's political views, especially if the facts of the case suggested that the employer had, by dismissing the employee, over-reacted to the latter's stance. Thus, see: BArbGE 47, 363 (1984).

[105] Markesinis and Dannemann, "The Legacy of History on German Contract Law", 1–28, in *Essays for Roy Goode* (Cranston ed., OUP, 1997).

Searching for factual equivalents of the *Drittwirkung* phenomenon may be, if not impossible, certainly too perilous an exercise to be undertaken with any conviction of reliability. Yet, workable models for comparing legal systems in a meaningful way are needed so the effort to devise them should, at least, be made; and in my submission the attempt made above can serve as a working model.

Finally, and at a most technical level, the German case law may suggest an interesting phenomenon. For given the fact that at the end of the day the "dissenting" American employee was protected whereas his German counterpart was not, I am left with the impression that the German courts often seem to be establishing a distinction between horizontal application and the substance of the obligation. This means that while on the one hand they seem to be drawing individuals into the sphere of obligations created by the relevant provisions of their Constitution, on the other they are also diluting the substance of the obligation for a variety of reasons which are often not obvious from the judgments. This is not the place to consider whether this is the result of being influenced by wider and not always, strictly speaking, legal considerations. But it is appropriate to make the point, even in a passing manner, since I think we may, once again, be finding echoes of this phenomenon in recent English and American decisions.

5. FUTURE DEBTS AND WAYS OF PAYING THEM OFF

I would now like to bring these brief observations to a close by means of seven propositions.

First, I believe there is a tendency, deeply rooted in human nature, to look around and borrow, where possible, good and tested ideas. The doctrine of binding precedent is, after all, in part based on this belief. Increased travel, common education programmes and the pursuit of a growing number of common economic aims will, in my view, broaden this natural habit so as to include foreign experiences and ideas. To be sure, the coming together and borrowing will decreasingly be the product of an inspired decision of a few widely educated judges and jurists and become a by-product of contemporary cosmopolitanism and enhanced, trans-border interaction. Though I am no particular fan of mass movements, I welcome the interaction that is brought about by shrinking our world. One can see this changing trend even within the relatively short space of time that I have been in the teaching profession. For, when I started my academic life in Cambridge in the late 1960's, our only guide (in English) to foreign law was the already dated (but) excellent manual of German law written by the late Professor Cohn. Matters were not really much better for French law even though in the post-War years the intellectual contacts with that country were very strong. For here, too, we basically had our book in English—the attractive but increasingly out-dated little book of the late Professors Amos and Walton. Even the bible of contemporary comparatists—Zweigert and Kötz's *An Introduction to Comparative Law*—had not yet seen the light of day in the original let alone in English. I need hardly give illustrations of how much the scene has changed; and changed not only in the classroom but even in the courtroom where the use of foreign material, though not an every day occurrence hardly raises an eyebrow any longer. This is no mean achievement for those of us who have fought for this change.

Secondly, our task in disseminating legal ideas will be facilitated if we abandon the habit of a particular breed of comparatist who saw the subject largely (if not exclusively) as one which pursues a *mission civilisatrice*. This approach nearly killed off the cultivation of a subject that had been taken to such heights, mainly in the late twenties and thirties, by the *Kaiser Whilhelm Institut* of Berlin. For many of us it thus contributed to an almost unforgivable decline of the subject in the seventies—certainly in France, Italy, and our country— though, of course, honourable exceptions can be mentioned.[106] Instead, we must put the method to the service of practitioners and judges and persuade them that it can improve the quality of their work, especially where local law does not possess a clear and convincing solution to a particular problem. A learned judge recently admitted that this could work. He thus said: "If the advocate can show that in other legal systems which we respect the problem facing the court is solved by the use of a concept which, while novel here in the relevant context, is a practicable one to adopt, then he may find that the court welcomes the stimulus which this can provide."[107]

Thirdly, though I see many areas of private law—mainly connected with the topics of court structures, procedure, and restitution—still offering many topics worthy of comparative discussion, I think the time is ripe for English comparatists to shift their attention to public law. By this I mean not only French Administrative law which, for years, has been a wonderful source of inspiration (and controversy) but also German and Italian public law. Re-reading Maitland convinced me that such a switch of emphasis is right. For, in one of his little

---

[106] In France, for instance, the names of Denis Tallon and André Tunc spring to mind. In Italy we have the ubiquitous Rodolfo Sacco who literally changed the Italian landscape by introducing comparative law as an undergraduate course in most Italian Universities. In my own country the towering figure of Tony Honoré must be mentioned alongside the very sui generis contribution made by Tony Weir, mainly through his elegant translations of numerous foreign texts. In my view, only Germany escaped this decline as it can boast an impressive array of comparatists such as Zweigert, Werner Lorenz, Stoll, Drobnig, Kötz, Schlechtriem, Grossfeld, Lutter, Schwarze, Zimmermann, Coester-Waltjen, von Bar, Muller-Graff, Ebke and others.

[107] Lord Justice Schiemann reviewing in 114 (1998) *LQR*, 515, at p. 523, my two volume work *The German Law of Obligations* (co-authored with Professor Werner Lorenz and Dr. Gerhard Danemann) (Oxford, 1998). The learned judge, emphasizing the utility of the comparative method, continued: "Future editors of English [sic] text books on contract, restitution or tort owe it to their readers to take the time to absorb these books and, at the very least, to incorporate the appropriate references in their footnotes . . ." Lord Goff expressed similar views in his Child lecture, reprinted in 1987 *Denning Law Review* 79 at 94. Thus he wrote: "If, as I hope and expect, [the English jurist] extends his vision to the study of those subjects as treated in other systems of law, his statement of English law can, and should be, set . . . in a comparative context. In this way, practitioners in common law countries, and especially judges in those countries, will be exposed to new ideas which will not only enrich their understanding of their own law, but may influence them to develop it in ways which previously might not have been thought possible."

remembered essays[108] I noted that he perceived (and praised) the 19th century as the era of codification of private law. This started me thinking what would he have said if he were writing at the close of our century? I feel reasonably confident that the growth of administrative law would have attracted the attention of the great historian. And that must be right because the most notable feature of our century has been this switch from rules regulating horizontal relationships (citizen with citizen) to rules dictating how the vertical relationships (state and citizen) should be ordained. My guess is that in the years to come we will be forced to look at a new variant of this problem—new to us but not our German friends—and that is why I have started stressing the need to include German public law within our purview.[109] This inquiry, incidentally, leads us to another aspect of public law: human rights. But this is not where our comparative inquiries should stop. I think another area in which political events will force us into comparative study will be variations of federalism or, to put it less provocatively, constitutional problems resulting from conflicts that are bound to arise between the central government, the states and their variously independent regions. In both these areas of public law I think our German and Italian colleagues have much information and, I would add, ideas, to impart.[110] We should be ready to look at this with interest rather than take the easy way out and say, if federalism becomes an issue, the American or Australian models can provide us with all we need and more. The urge to opt for that easier option will, of course, be strengthened by the fact that studying American, Canadian or Australian law requires no particular linguistic effort. But, once again, I am sure that the onward rush of political developments in Europe will make the move towards studying Continental European public law more widely felt.

Fourthly, I think we must recall, especially in the context of what I have said in the previous section of this paper, that what we are primarily interested in is the broader ideas rather than the concepts, the organising categories, or the systems of analyses. The evolution of our administrative law supports my thesis and predilection. For pause and think how our administrative law came about. For, having started in the shadow of the Dicey legacy, it was mercilessly (and unfavourably) compared to the French *droit administatif* for most of the fifties and early sixties. Then, came the work of some influential scholars, such as Sir William Wade, and some great judges, such as Lords Reid, Denning, Diplock

[108] "A Survey of the Century", a lecture delivered in 1901 and republished in *The Collected Papers of Frederick William Maitland* Fisher (ed.), vol. III (1911), 432 ff. See, also in the same volume at pp. 474 ff., "The Making of the German Civil Code".

[109] For instance in my Wilberforce Lecture entitled, "Privacy, Freedom of Speech and the Horizontal application of the Human Rights Legislation" (1999) *LQR*, 47 ff.

[110] I am encouraged to see that leading American comparatists share this view. Thus, see: Kommers, "Kann das deutsche Verfassungrechtsdenken Vorbild für die Vereinigten Staaten sein?" *Der Staat*. 37 Zeitschrift für Staatslehre, öffentliches Recht und Verfassungsgeschichte 1998, 335 ff. Another topic, which I recently discussed with Professors J. B. Auby, D. Coester-Waltgen and Dr. S. Deakin is the *Tortious Liability of Statutory Bodies* (Oxford, Hart Publishing, 1999)—an area of English tort law which is increasingly affected by the case-law of the Strasbourg Court of Human Rights.

and Wilberforce. And our law, finally, more than redeemed its original deficiencies by coming up with its own, native, solution: a *droit administratif à la anglaise*, as the Master of Rolls—himself a leading scholar of the subject—put it so felicitously. This blend of local features with foreign and indigenous ideas seems to me to hold the key to the way forward as far as the new study of comparative public law is concerned. But it will require more than a passing acquaintance with European legal thought. In this area of the law I think we can say that this "new awareness" already exists to an impressive degree. For never before in our history can I find so many judges writing about matters of administrative law and human rights and demonstrating in their writings such a predilection for wider, jurisprudential and comparative material. Listing the names of some of those who have written such pieces—Lord Scarman,[111] Lord Woolf,[112] Lord Bingham,[113] Lord Browne-Wilkinson,[114] Lord Hoffman,[115] Mr Justice Laws,[116] Mr Justice Sedley,[117] Madame Justice Arden,[118] and, indeed, the current Lord Chancellor, Lord Irvine of Lairg[119]—amply makes my point. This material will require a continued willingness to comb it for ideas when faced with problems that are new to us.

Fifthly, we must redouble our efforts on the language front. The aforementioned achievements of our judges are not, in themselves, enough to bring the cultural re-orientation that I wish and recommend. For a time, language differences and difficulties will still cause insurmountable difficulties. Some of our indigenous authors have, in fact, expressed their scepticism about our ability to overcome this hurdle.[120] Again, however, I remain optimistic. And I ask my readers to ponder three developments, all linked with what has been happening

---

[111] Most noteworthy, of course, is his Hamlyn Lecture, *English Law: the New Dimension* (1974)—the *fons et origo* of much of the contemporary debate on the need to acquire a human rights legislation.

[112] *Protecting the Public: A New Challenge* (1990). See, also, "Droit Public—English Style", the text of the F. A. Mann lecture [1955] *Public law*, 51 ff.

[113] Gordon and Wilmot-Smith (eds.), *Human Rights in the United Kingdom* (OUP, 1996): "The European Convention on Human Rights: Time to Incorporate", The Denning Lecture, 1 ff.; "Should there be a Law to Protect Rights of Personal Privacy?" [1996] *European Human Rights Law Review*, 450 ff.

[114] "The Infiltration of a Bill of Rights" [1992] *Public Law*, 397 ff.

[115] "A Sense of Proportion in Community Law in English Courts" in Jacobs, F. and Andenas, M., "English Public Law and the Community of Europe" (Oxford, 1998).

[116] "The Ghost in the Machine: Principle in Public Law" [1989] *Public Law*; "Is the High Court the Guardian of Fundamental Constitutional Rights?" [1993] *Public Law*, 59 ff.; "Law and Democracy" [1995] *Public Law*, 72 ff.; "The Constitution: Morals and Rights" [1996] *Public Law*, 622; "The Limitations of Human Rights" [1998] *Public Law*, 254 ff.

[117] "The Sound of Silence: Constitutional Law Without a Constitution" (1994) 110 *LQR*, 270 ff. "Human Rights: A Twenty First Century Agenda" [1995] *Public Law*, 386 ff.

[118] "The Future of the Law of Privacy" (not yet published).

[119] "Judges and Decision-Makers: The Theory and Practice of Wednesbury Review" [1996] *Public Law*, 9 ff.; "Response to Sir John Laws" [1996] *Public Law*, 636 ff.; "The Development of Human Rights in Britain" [1998] *Public Law*, 221 ff.

[120] Weir, "Die Sprachen des europäischen Rechts: Eine skeptische Betrachtung" (1995) 3 *Zeitschrift für Europäisches Privatrecht*, 368 ff., convincingly refuted by Professor Zimmermann in his "Savigny's Legacy" etc., 112 *LQR*, 595–6.

in Europe since the Second World War. In my view, all point in the direction that I wish us to take.

Thus, first, we already have, by my own reckoning, at least half a dozen senior judges who are proficient in German (more, if we add other languages) and who are giving increasing signs that they are prepared to use this linguistic expertise in their work. Secondly, over the past ten or fifteen years, through a handful of published works, English speaking jurists have acquired translations of over five hundred leading cases in contract and tort alone. Extracts, often lengthy, from almost as many decisions of the German Constitutional Court are also now available provided one knows how to look for them! Thus, in volume terms there is more German material available in English than the average English student would ever read using his English casebooks on contract, tort or constitutional law. The language problem is not thus insurmountable; and with the passage of time it will be proved to be an excuse but not a reason for not studying foreign law. Thirdly, and most importantly, we have a growing itiner- ant student population which will go on increasing in numbers and which, in twenty years time or less, will be on stream as senior practitioners, civil servants, and judges. Their European experiences, enriched by study leaves and training programmes in various European countries, are bound, in my view, to be reflected in the law they pass, administer, or adjudicate on, as past experience with similarly educated young lawyers clearly shows.

Sixthly, I wish to stress the need for greater intellectual honesty when it comes to transplants of ideas. This is, in one sense, such an obvious proposition that I would not have felt the need to make it at all. Yet recently, the readers of the Law Quarterly Review will have read a learned piece by a Scottish colleague in which he documented the extent of borrowing from Scottish law that took place in shaping some of the leading cases of contemporary English law.[121] Yet some of the readers of this learned article may have been impressed more by the fact that this borrowing from the civil law had to be concealed than that it happened at all. There may have been good reasons why such "loans" had to be sup- pressed. But the temptation to do so in the future would, in my view, be a dan- gerous concession to a kind of legal chauvinism which is neither attractive nor likely to prove viable during the next millennium.

So I come, finally, to my sixth and last proposition which, because it tres- passes on Professor von Bar's paper I shall keep brief.

I said this before and I repeat it now: comparative law is not a one way street. The question that occupies me most is where can we make our greatest contri- bution. In my opinion, our contribution to the emerging new Europe will spring from our main strengths which I find not in dogmatic analysis of the law but in our procedure, advocacy, pragmatism, and preference for a properly under- stood notion of incrementalism. To these I would add our teaching of the law,

---

[121] R. Evan-Jones, "Roman Law in Scotland and England and the development of One Law for Britain", 115 (1999) *LQR*, 604.

not least because it involves all of these attributes which over the years I have come to admire. These we are well-advised to combine with the intellectual strengths of our neighbours and partners; and history suggests that such a combination of foreign and indigenous ideas can be made to work. For as Professor Simpson put it so felicitously, "in the history of Western European legal tradition of private law successful creative work consists in a combination between intelligent plagiarism and systematisation of what is lifted from others".[122] If it worked for private law—and the 1980's and 1990's have shown how fruitful the comparative methodology has been in the area of contract and tort—I see no reason why it should not work for public law. And I have already stressed that it is here that I think lies much of the future of comparative law.

So, I conclude this paper with two statements from two eminent judges whom I greatly admire and, I hope, I can even refer to as friends: Lords Goff and Bingham. In his Child lecture[123] the first predicted that ". . . we are bound to see an enrichment of our legal culture on an unparalleled scale though the increasing study of comparative law . . .". In his Mann lecture the second looked forward to the day when "England joined, or more accurately rejoined [sic] the mainstream of European legal tradition . . .".[124] Sufficient time has elapsed since these statements were made to describe them both as prophecies. And, despite this, neither of their authors has met with the fate usually reserved for prophets. That must be a good sign.

---

[122] *Op. cit.*, at p. 254.
[123] "Judge, Jurist and Legislature" [1987] *Denning Law Review*, 79 at p. 93.
[124] *Op. cit.* at p. 528.

4

A *New Jus Commune Europaeum and the Importance of the Common Law*

CHRISTIAN V. BAR

A NEW JUS COMMUNE EUROPAEUM

The linguist Simeon Potter once remarked that an Englishman feels much more comfortable receiving a "hearty welcome" rather than a "cordial reception."[1] I fear that the same is true of "common law" and "jus commune": although both terms literally mean the same, the Latin term[2] feels far more foreign and formal on this side of the Channel than the English. But anyone invited to speak in England on the importance of the Common law for a developing jus commune europaeum has more than only psychological barriers to overcome. He must first try to give his broad and vague subject some shape: even the term Common law is definable only in terms of opposites and that of the new jus commune europaeum covers not only a legal reality but also a programme.

The term "jus commune" gives rise to a shimmering array of associations. In the context of early continental European tradition it refers to a Roman-type law developed primarily by university academics. Jus commune, in the sense of civil law is thus almost the exact opposite of the Common law. Nonetheless, both Common law and jus commune relate to those areas of law which, having been developed by generation after generation, are viewed as being people's common heritage. *Friedrich-Carl* v. *Savigny* described this law as being "the good and the true, created by the silent strength of a people rather than a barbaric act of legislation."[3] To him, the *Code Napoléon* was such an act.[4] Now however, after almost two hundred years, that *Code Civil* contains precisely that which a French lawyer would consider to be his country's *droit commun*.

---

[1] Simeon Potter, *Our Language* (London 1976) 25. *Cf*. Bill Bryson, *Mother Tongue. The English Language* (London, 1991), 51.

[2] Unlike the word "common", the word "law" is of Scandinavian rather than Latin origin: "The Lat[in] . . . *lex* is not now generally believed to be cognate" (*The Oxford English Dictionary*, vol. viii, 2nd edn. Oxford, 1989, *sub verbo* "law").

[3] Friedrich-Carl v. Savigny, *Vom Berufe unserer Zeit für Gesetzgebung und Rechtswissenschaft* (Heidelberg, 1840), 11.

[4] *Loc. cit.*, p. 54–81.

When we speak of a new jus commune europaeum in the year two thousand, most of us probably imagine that it must be possible to break down the nationalities of and divisions between the European private law systems and create a feeling for their internal relationships and interaction. The term jus commune europaeum comprises ideas of similarity, relationship, and material and procedural equality—common elements which transcend national borders without denying the existence of differences. It should not be forgotten however that a common law can only lay claim to being jus when it is binding. It is in the nature of law that it is binding; the creative arts are the subject of other faculties.

Where and how to seek the importance of the common law for the new common European law? I believe there are three areas worthy of consideration: firstly, modern comparative law with its effects on member state national law, secondly, the law imposed from above by European Union treaties and legislation and thirdly and most importantly, the question as to how far a statutory system of pan-European concepts of the central areas of private law can be created, neither causing sharp breaks with tradition nor provoking rebellious reaction.

COMPARATIVE LAW

Some time ago, as I spoke in Oxford of Tony Weir's masterly translation[5] of Franz Wieacker's *Privatrechtsgeschichte der Neuzeit*,[6] Lord Goff commented rather dryly that Wiecker had paid as much attention to the common law as an English lawyer normally pays Channel Islands law. Indeed, the English common law lay for centuries outside the scope of continental legal science. Whereas the libraries of the old English research establishments possess nearly all the classics of early jus commune—what St. John's College, Oxford has to offer would greatly honour any German institute of legal history—the corresponding collections in Germany and Italy comprise barely any original old English case report collections. In the view of even my grandparents, England was to Europe what Louisiana was and is to the United States of America. Scotland, the Faculty of Advocates of which, in the second half of the nineteenth century, required that its students have some knowledge of German,[7] almost belonged to Europe but was geographically so distant that its law was not really bothered with. Scotland also looked to Germany but Germany failed to look to the United Kingdom.

The change came after the Second World War, and then with an unsurpassable intensity. A new subject occupied the place previously occupied in the nationalist Europe of the nineteenth century by the study of a single, academic

---

[5] Franz Wieacker, *A History of Private Law in Europe* (Oxford, 1995), translation by Tony Weir.
[6] Franz Wieacker, *Privatrechtsgeschichte der Neuzeit* (2nd edn., Göttingen, 1967).
[7] See further Alan Rodger, "Scottish Advocates in the Nineteenth Century: The German Connection" 110 (1994) *LQR* 563.

discipline: comparative law.[8] This comparison of laws remained bound in name and outlook to the territorial realities of multiple legal systems but since the nineteen fifties at least, it has attempted to develop knowledge and understanding of the methods of others. In common with the jus commune, it had its intellectual roots in academia. Whilst only a method of legal science, the study, unlike the early comparative work undertaken in Germany and other European states, was always concerned with at least one common law system. The first reason for this lies in the fact that its judgment culture provides the ideal starting point for a "functional legal comparison." With its concentration on the conflicting interests and the policy considerations pertinent to the conflict's solution, and its avoidance of systematic structures and nightmarish "terminological jurisprudence", it was seen at the time as being the non plus ultra, the highest attainable objective. Legal comparison, it is still taught today, should be undertaken essentially on the basis of court judgments,[9] so how could such comparison be carried out ignoring the common law? With only little overstatement, it can be said that the common law set the methodological example followed by post-war comparative law. The second reason for this development was political and a consequence of the Second World War. A never-ending stream of young lawyers, in particular from Germany made a pilgrimage to America and England, and subsequently Scotland, Ireland and even the one-time British colonies of Asia and Africa which had retained the common law. In England and the United States, many of those young lawyers were initially assisted by German Jewish refugees, who had belonged to the legal elite of my country.[10]

Today, only two generations of lawyers later, the extent of comparative legal education and research all over Europe is barely believable, and comparative research almost always means to submerge oneself in, and allow oneself to be entrapped by, English legal culture. English became the *lingua franca* of modern times. For that reason also, not only did comparative studies include the common law but attributed to it special value. Indeed at times this can be worrying, for England is one of the smaller countries in the greater Europe. But we must look even further and no longer be concerned with France, England or Germany: our concern must be to make available the entire treasury of European knowledge of law and justice.[11]

Despite the influence of the common law on comparative legal study, and hence its importance for modern legal education, it is remarkably difficult to

---

[8] Whilst the study of comparative law has a considerably longer history, it blossomed only after the Second World War. See further Zweigert/Kötz, *Einführung in die Rechtsvergleichung* (3rd edn., Tübingen, 1996), p. 47.

[9] Markesinis, "L'enseignement du droit comparé sous l'éclairage de la jurisprudence", (1985) *Revue de la Recherche Juridique (RRJ)* 866.

[10] See further Jabs, *Die Emigration deutscher Juristen nach Großbritannien* (Osnabrück, 1999), including biographies of Ernst Joseph Cohn, Rudolf Graupner, Otto Kahn-Freund, Kurt Lipstein, F.A. Mann und Clive M. Schmitthoff.

[11] v. Bar, *A Common European Law of Torts* (Rome, 1996; Centro di studi e ricerche di diritto comparato e straniero. Saggi, conference e seminari vol. 19) 8.

demonstrate its concrete effects on the alteration or modernisation of any particular Scandinavian or continental system of private law. Much is shadowy and probably impossible to prove by research. Certainly, legal language is becoming ever more saturated with English terms: contract lawyers all over Europe speak of "leasing", "factoring" and "franchising", corporate lawyers of "corporate governance" and tort lawyers of "wrongful birth" and "wrongful life". It is also true that the new Netherlands *Burgerlijk Wetboek* has here and there adopted English thinking,[12] that the Scandinavian liability laws cannot deny some common law influences[13] and that there are even cases in which German courts have adopted English law and English courts German law to support their own positions.[14] But all of these are merely individual events the importance of which should not be overestimated so long as their examples are not followed. Insofar as comparative legal study has opened reception channels, these are directed far more often at the USA than at England,[15] and are in any event restricted to narrow areas of the law of obligations. It must also be appreciated that the development of law through comparison, is subject, especially in Germany, to the filter of academic literature,[16] with the result that foreign examples act only very indirectly on German judgments. In view of the German courts' tradition of basing their judgments on intensive study of academic materials, the existence of a whole series of reception channels can be strongly argued but nevertheless rarely strictly proven. A fundamental climate change is nonetheless undeniable. German non-contractual liability law today contains whole areas of solely judge-made law, having no genuine basis in our codification.[17] German judges, like others, have become more confident, not least because comparative legal study and foreign experience have given them courage. They have not however adopted the controlling mechanism of binding precedents, which has hardly promoted legal certainty.

---

[12] Mistakes do appear however to have been made in the comprehension of the English method. See e.g. tortious liability for representatives under Art. 6:172 BW. *Cf.* v. Bar, *The Common European Law of Torts*, vol. i (Oxford, 1998), 217 and 356.

[13] See further Sundberg, Civil Law, "Common Law and the Scandinavians", *Scand.Stud.L.* 13 (1969), 179.

[14] See further v. Bar *loc. cit.*, (fn. 12), p. 414.

[15] Großfeld, "Vom Beitrag der Rechtsvergleichung zum deutschen Recht", *Archiv für die civilistische Praxis (AcP)* 184 (1984), 289.

[16] The sometime president of the German Federal Supreme Court Professor Odersky once correctly observed that "Not only is the national judge entitled to consider the opinion of other legal systems and courts; within the boundaries of his national law and whilst weighing up all aspects relevant for the interpretation and development of law, he may also emphasize the fact that the solution in question could help to harmonize European law. In conclusion, he could then use this argument to turn towards foreign legal systems for the solution of the problem. Such reasoning ought to be used increasingly as part of the European process of unification" (*Zeitschrift für Europäisches Privatrecht* [ZEuP] 1994 p. 1, 2). The German courts have so far ignored these comments.

[17] Two examples are liability for infringements of the general law of personality and for information. See v. Bar, "Liability for Information and Opinions causing Pure Economic Loss to Third Parties: A Comparison of English and German Case Law", in Markesinis (ed.), *The Gradual Convergence* (Oxford, 1994) p. 98.

UNIFIED AND HARMONISED LAW

The English common law is not only definable solely as an opposite of civil, equitable, or statutory law but also of local law. Common law is that law which, whether statutory or otherwise, is binding on all persons in a jurisdiction. Thus viewed, a new jus commune europaeum is easily recognisable, rooted in international treaties and the European Union's constitution and legislation.[18] In this context, the fact that international treaties and directives are binding only upon states rather than their inhabitants can safely be ignored. What cannot, however, be ignored is the fact that the EU was established between states for which a written constitution and a distinction between private and public law were only natural. All those states had given and continue to give the separation of powers constitutional status; nowhere would it be conceivable to grant the judicial committee of a legislative organ judicial power. Nowhere is the judgment of a court to be viewed as a source of law outside constitutional disputes.[19] There was and is nowhere only one High Court and one Court of Appeal. The judges of the founding member states, with the exception of those of the constitutional courts, were and are to a man career judges, accustomed to working under a codification. All those states applied a broadly similar legislative system, a world apart from the surgically precise approach of English legislation. European Union law is of necessity written law.[20] It was begun in the belief that it needed to create a jus commune rather than merely intervene as a corrective in an already extant common law. In English terms, European Union private law is statutory rather than common.

Given that background, it is understandable that there is more scepticism in England than elsewhere of the Brussels Union law. But one should not be over hasty in believing that it is pure civil law independent of any common law influence. European Union law is a unique type of law which has repeatedly demonstrated its openness to all influences as well as an ability to compromise. Its interpretational methods may indeed be more strongly associated with continental than English tradition[21] but even this latter is changing; and in the area

[18] See Lipari (ed.), *Diritto Privato Europeo* (Milan, 1997) for summary and analysis of the principle sources.

[19] It is interesting to study how English courts initially dealt with European Communities law. Judgments of the ECJ were cited without reference either to the terms of the Treaty of Rome and subsidiary legislation or whether ECJ decisions were even of any authority in British courts. See Hans-Claudius Ficker, "Die Rechtsentwicklung innerhalb der Europäischen Gemeinschaften und ihre Auswirkungen auf die EFTA-Staaten", *Zeitschrift für Rechtsvergleichung* (ZfRV) 1973 161, 168.

[20] Usher, "The Influence of the Civil Law, via Modern Legal Systems, on European Community Law", in David L. Carey Miller and Reinhard Zimmermann (eds.), *The Civilian Tradition and Scots Law* (Berlin, 1997), 321, 325.

[21] European Union law has since its inception employed the teleological interpretative method under which legislation is interpreted according to the intentions of the legislature. An analogical interpretative method has also at times been adopted. *Cf. Union Française de Céréales* v. *H.Z.A. Hamburg-Jonas*, Case 6/78, ECJ [1978] E.C.R. 1675 and Usher *loc. cit.* (previous fn.) 326

of unimplemented Union law[22] is moving ever further towards continental customs.[23] The European legislative technique in respect of Directives is indeed remarkably close to the English. In comparison with Scandinavian and continental regulatory standards, Directives are remarkably detailed.

Whilst banal, it is perhaps not entirely superfluous to mention the fact that for as long as the United Kingdom and Ireland were not members of the European Communities, the common law could have no influence over the content of European private law or the treaties between the member states relevant to it. I am thinking here of the 1968 Brussels Convention on international jurisdiction and the enforcement of foreign awards. The position is rather different in respect of the 1980 Rome Convention on the law applicable to contracts but it can at least be said with certainty firstly that it was a result of British pressure that the convention was restricted to contracts[24] and secondly, that its central technique, the connection with the place of habitual residence of the person responsible for the performance characteristic of the contract has its roots not in the EU but rather in Switzerland.[25]

This detail might appear almost anecdotal but it brings us to fundamental observation. This is that whilst the common law may in content have had relatively little influence over recent European private law, that is not something which separates English private law from that of the other European systems to any significant degree. It is not legal systems but rather economic and social interests which compete in Brussels. Of course there have on occasion been Directives effecting within a narrow scope existant English law more than most other systems[26] but those other systems could probably say the same of other occasions. Apart from that, it is difficult to attribute specific text formulae in the multilingual directives to particular national sources. Thus the German language text of Art. 6 (1) (b) of the Product Liability Directive[27] disguises the importance of the English reasonableness test in respect of the concept of defectiveness.[28] Far clearer is the influence of English legal thinking on the formula-

---

thereon. See further Everling, "Rechtsvereinheitlichung durch Richterrecht in der Europäischen Gemeinschaft", *Rabels Zeitschrift für ausländisches und internationales Privatrecht (RabelsZ)* 50 (1986) 193, 209 on the interpretative methods employed by the judges.

[22] See Zweigert/Kötz *loc. cit.* (fn. 8) 260 on the interpretative methods employed by English courts in respect of EU legislation.

[23] *Pepper* v. *Hart* [1993] A.C. 593.

[24] Dicey/Morris/Collins, *The Conflict of Laws*, vol. ii (12th edn., London, 1993), 1191. A "Rome II" convention also covering conflicts between non-contractual liabilities is currently in preparation.

[25] See further v. Bar, *Internationales Privatrecht*, vol. ii (Munich, 1991), 358.

[26] See e.g. the road traffic liability insurance Directives. *Cf.* v. Bar *loc. cit.* (fn. 12), 400.

[27] Council Directive 85/374/EEC of 25 July 1985 on the Approximation of the Laws, Regulations and Administrative Provisions of the Member States Concerning Liability for Defective Products, O.J. L 210, 7/9/1985, 29.

[28] The German text refers to the use of the product "which may equitably be expected" ("mit dem billigerweise gerechnet werden kann"), rather than to "what might reasonably be expected to be done with . . . the product". The French construction "l'usage qui peut en être *raisonnablement* attendu" was previously unknown there.

tion of Art. 2 of the Product Safety Directive.[29] In other cases, English law other than the true common law has played a weighty role. Thus was the statutory Unfair Contract Terms Act 1977 together with the German AGBG (Law on General Terms of Trade) one of the main sources of inspiration for the Directive on Unfair Terms in Consumer Contracts.[30] Equally, whilst one may view the liberalisation of insurance law as a United Kingdom victory, it cannot be viewed as being a common law victory. The position is of course different where the structures and approaches of the United Nations Vienna Convention on the International Sale of Goods have had an indirect effect on Union private law, as the influence of English law on the Vienna Convention was undeniably strong[31] and the Convention in turn had considerable influence on the many details of the draft Directive on the Sale of Consumer Goods and related Guarantees.[32] I am thinking here of the system of remedies available to the consumer in case of the defectiveness of the goods delivered under Art. 3 (4) of the proposal. Lastly, there have even been occasions on which the EU wished to base its legislation on English experience and rules, only to encounter English fear that European legislation will inhibit English control of its own laws, as in the case of the Directive on Takeovers, still awaiting promulgation.[33]

In addition, three other particularities of European directive law should not be ignored.

Firstly, it is important that EU directives have to date affected only very specific areas of contract and liability law. The foundations of the European legal systems have been left effectively untouched. This can be seen in the contexts of both tort and contract law. For eg. the Product Liability Directive avoids working with the concept of *Eigentumsverletzung* ("property damage"), which is central to German tort law and instead relies on the damaging or destruction of goods. That, it seems, more or less corresponds with the English negligence concept of damage to property. In truth however, it cannot have been the objective to adopt the common law approach for European product liability law but rather to avoid altogether the problematic boundary between damage to property and pure economic loss. Similar aims obtained when the self-damaging of

---

[29] Council Directive 92/95/EEC of 29 June 1992 on General Products Safety, O.J. L 228/24, 11/8/1992.

[30] Council Directive 93/13/EEC of 5 April 1993 on Unfair Terms in Consumer Contracts, O.J. L 095, 21/4/1993, 29.

[31] The unified concept of breach and non-fulfilment of contracts is based largely on the influence of the common law. Vendors' compensation liability is also considerably closer to the English than the German or Austrian law. See further Schlechtriem, *Internationales UN-Kaufrecht* (Tübingen, 1996), 111 and Karollus, *UN-Kaufrecht* (Vienna, 1991), 205 ff. The compromise in Art. 28 CISG in respect of the right of enforcement is also remarkably close to the English law.

[32] Amended Proposal for a European Parliament and Council Directive on the Sale of Consumer Goods and associated Guarantees of 19/1/1999, COM/99/0016 final—COD 96/0161.

[33] Amended Proposal for a Thirteenth European Parliament and Council Directive on Company Law Concerning Takeover Bids of 11 November 1997, O.J. C 378 of 13/12/1997, 10. See further on later version Mülbert, "Die Zielgesellschaft im Vorschlag 1997 einer Takeover-Richtlinie—zwei folgenreiche Eingriffe ins deutsche Aktienrecht", *Internationales Steuerrecht (IStR)* 1999 83.

a product was kept outside the ambit of the directive under Art. 9 (b). In contract law on the other hand, European directives have left untouched the English doctrine of consideration. The directives very rarely create rules as to the formation of contracts. Instead they presuppose such formation[34] and restrict themselves to limiting its consequences for the consumer. Additionally, they are themselves restricted to contracts for value: contracts lacking consideration are beyond their scope. Rules governing rescission and unjust enrichment are generally also left to national law.[35] Fundamental questions of property law have in any event been left untouched, with the result that the concept of trust has neither influenced nor been affected by European Union law.

Secondly, it should be recognised that the Directives have generally been concerned with relatively new areas of law, in which the common law has yet to develop either fixed standards or particularities. Examples are the Directive on the Protection of Consumers in Respect of Distance Contracts[36] and the proposed Directive on Electronic Commerce.[37] It further appears that several Directives deal with social conflicts which as a matter of fact are of less concern in England than elsewhere in Europe. Thus is time sharing of greatest economic importance in the Mediterranean holiday regions of France, Spain and Italy and cases involving the contract law of the Isle of Man (!) have been particularly prevalent in Germany.[38] A further example is that of door step sales, which are apparently relatively rare in England. That at least would be an explanation why the Consumer Protection Regulations 1987, which implemented the corresponding Directive[39] in the United Kingdom, have so rarely been applied.[40]

The third point that should not be overlooked is that EU directives have normally been concerned with consumer protection law, an area in which the value of claims is only moderate. Accordingly, the majority of trials thus affected are

---

[34] E.g. Art. 5 (1) Directive 94/47/EC of the European Parliament and the Council of 26 October 1994 on the Protection of Purchasers in respect of certain Aspects of Contracts relating to the Purchase of the Right to use Immovable Properties on a Timeshare Basis, O.J. L 280, 29/10/1994, 83 ("The Member States shall make provisions in their legislation to ensure that . . . in addition to the possibilities available to the purchaser under national laws on the nullity of contracts, the purchaser shall have the right . . .").

[35] See e.g. Art. 5 (3) (1) Timesharing Directive (previous fn.) and Art. 7 Council Directive 85/577/EEC of 20 December 1985 to Protect the Consumer in Respect of Contracts Negotiated Away from Business Premises, O.J. L 372, 31/12/1985, 31 ("If the consumer exercises his right of renunciation, the legal effects of such renunciation shall be governed by national laws, . . ."). There are however examples to the opposite effect, such as Art. 6 (2) (1) Directive 97/7/EC of the European Parliament and of the Council of 20 May 1997 on the Protection of Consumers in Respect of Distance Contracts, O.J. L 144, 4/6/1997, 19.

[36] Previous fn.

[37] Proposal for a Directive of the European Parliament and of the Council Concerning the Distance Marketing of Consumer Financial Services and Amending Council Directive 90/619/EEE and Directives 97/7/EC and 98/27/EC, O.J. C 385, 11/12/1998 10; Proposal for a European Parliament and Council Directive on Certain Legal Aspects of Electronic Commerce in the Internal Market, O.J. C 030, 5/2/1999, 4.

[38] Fundamentally BGH 19 March 1997, BGHZ 135 124.

[39] See fn. 35 above.

[40] Basedow, "Einführung: Zur Umsetzung der Richtlinie über den Widerruf von Haustürgeschäften", *ZEuP* 1997 1075.

heard before the County rather the High Court or even the Court of Appeal and not being reported, hardly contribute to the development of the common law. It therefore appears to be no coincidence that English consumer protection law is generally statutory rather than common law. An example already mentioned is the Unfair Contract Terms Act 1977. It should also be remembered that in this area, the directives seek only to achieve a minimum of harmonisation: the member states are free to enact legislation granting consumers greater protection than that provided under the Directives.[41]

In conclusion it may be said that the Brussels legislation has left the core material of the European national private law systems untouched. The Brussels jus commune europaeum, no matter how praiseworthy, is still far from becoming substantive European common law. Some people may be relieved to hear that, believing that the hour has not yet struck for large scale political measures in the area of private law. Nonetheless, it is impossible to overlook the efforts made by European legal academics for some considerable time in laying the foundations for the next steps towards integration.

EUROPEAN PRIVATE LAW: THE ROAD TO COMMON BASIC RULES OF THE LAWS OF OBLIGATIONS AND CREDIT SECURITIES

A new legal discipline has been since the beginning of the nineteen nineties at the latest: European private law.[42] The comparative study of law has thereby lost some of its occasionally eclectic elements. It now clearly serves the objective of European harmonisation and no longer merely attempts to deal with individual problematic areas[43] but rather to present and analyse whole areas of law on a basis common to as many European states as possible. The earliest results have already arrived or will shortly, concerned mostly with general tort, contract and (unjust) enrichment law.[44] New journals on European private law have appeared,[45] and Professor van Gerven is compiling an entire case book series on

---

[41] See e.g. Art. 8 Directive 85/577/EEC (fn. 35 above), Art. 11 Directive 94/47/EC (fn. 34 above), Art. 14 Directive 97/7/EC (fn. 35 above) and Art. 15 Council Directive 87/102/EEC of 22 December 1986 for the Approximation of the Laws, Regulations and Administrative Provisions of the Member States Concerning Consumer Credit, O.J. L 042, 12/02/1987 48.

[42] This development was initiated by Kötz, "Gemeineuropäisches Zivilrecht", *Festschrift für Konrad Zweigert zum 70. Geburtstag* (Tübingen, 1981), p. 481. Gebauer, *Grundfragen der Europäisierung des Privatrechts* (Heidelberg, 1998) provides a historical review.

[43] There is a whole series of impressive "common European" studies, including Sinde Monteiro, *Responsabilidade por Conselhos, Recomendações ou Informações* (Coimbra, 1989) and Hesselink, *De Redelijkheid en Billijkheid in het Europese Privaatrecht* (Deventer, 1999).

[44] Already in print are Kötz, *Europäisches Vertragsrecht* (vol. i, Tübingen, 1996 with English translation *European Contract Law*, Oxford 1997, by Tony Weir) and v. Bar, *Gemeineuropäisches Deliktsrecht* (vol. i, Munich, 1996 with English translation [fn. 12 above] Oxford, 1998; vol. ii, Munich, 1999). Schlechtriem expects to publish a two volume work on European unjust enrichment law in Summer 2000.

[45] *Zeitschrift für Europäisches Privatrecht* (Munich 1.1993); *European Review of Private Law* (Deventer 1, 1994); *Europa e Diritto Privato* (Milan 1, 1994); *Maastricht Journal of European and Comparative Law* (Antwerp 1, 1994).

the subject in Belgium.[46] Extensive representations of foreign legal systems are becoming more available,[47] those considering case law being particularly successful.[48] Whilst the earnest world of first instance courts, notaries and national justice ministers may not be overly affected by what is happening here, it will at least contribute to the future legal elite's perception from the outset of private law within a European context. Lawyers will no longer allow themselves to be suffocated by the intellectual straits of a single national system. The EU's Erasmus programme and others already ensure that there is hardly a lecture theatre in Europe in which only students of that nation have sat. As a result, comparative teaching became necessary, which in turn led to extraordinary attention's being paid to the common law.

The importance of the common law lies not merely in the fact that its judgments are amongst the most oft-cited in European legal literature. Rather it proves repeatedly to be an extremely effective tool in identifying strengths and weaknesses in European theories. Anyone who does not wish to limit themselves to the analysis of particular social conflicts, as in medical negligence liability and consumer protection, but rather feels he must present a whole area of law such as contract, tort or (unjust) enrichment law in its European context, must extend the scope of his work much further than was originally believed necessary or even possible. He must also turn to the great structural questions of legal systems, of the intersection between different areas, and of the performance of particular central concepts. What are the central concepts of a tort? What does intention mean? What is fault, what is damage? Which is the better concept to work with, the breach of rights or the breach of a duty? Would torts such as nuisance be better accommodated within a law of things, torts such as conversion better within a law of (unjust) enrichment? What is really behind the old idea of damage *per se*? Is a link now recognisable between this and the Italian concept of biological damage? Where do other legal systems provide for punitive damages? How should strict liability for breach of statutory duties be viewed? What should one think of the possibility of the extension of limitation periods by judicial decision? Without the common law, a great number of questions would never be posed in continental Europe. Loaded with theoretical luggage as we are, we continental Europeans would stay with and eventually be petrified by our nineteenth century ideas. But the same is clearly also true in reverse. Without wishing to be impolite to my English hosts, may I suggest that the English defamation law can hardly be viewed as a European ideal, and that

---

[46] See van Gerven (ed.)/Lever/Larouche/von Bar/Viney, *Torts: Scope of Protection* (Oxford, 1998). This is merely one of several planned volumes on the subject of tort. Other areas are to follow.

[47] A classic of the genre is Ferid/Sonnenberger, *Französisches Zivilrecht* (2nd edn., Heidelberg, 1986).

[48] Basil Markesinis, Werner Lorenz and Gerhard Dannemann, *The German Law of Obligations. Vol. 1: The Law of Contracts and Restitution. A Comparative Introduction* (Oxford, 1997) and Markesinis, *Vol. 2: The Law of Torts: A Comparative Introduction* (3rd edn., Oxford, 1997) are as yet unparalleled.

the doctrine of consideration is unlikely to be a model for European emulation, given its exclusion of third parties from contracts.

I believe that the true significance of the common law for the gradually developing new *jus commune europaeum* does not lie in specific rules. In terms of practical results, European private laws remarkably rarely differ from one another and where they do, there are normally good reasons within the system for the difference. It is not the solutions to particular problems which are recognisably national nowadays but rather their positions within the legal systems and the thought structures which dictate our approach. The national differences lie in the grounds on which we base our decisions. It is on this point that the question as to the importance of the common law in a new jus commune europaeum thus must concentrate: of which areas of substantive law will we continentals need to alter the systematic positions to correspond with the common law, simply because the common law structure is the better?

No one has as yet conclusive views on this question: answers will appear only gradually through pan-European discussion. We already have the benefit of some experience, both in the context of the UN Vienna Convention on Sales Law and within the Commission on European Contract Law. If the "Principles"[49] set out by the commission are considered in their entirety, it may albeit with some simplification be said that the rules on "interpretation" in chapter 5 PECL have a universal character, that chapter 4 on "validity" are influenced primarily by civil law and that chapters 8 on "non-performance and remedies in general" and 9 on "particular remedies for non-performance" are essentially based on common law ideas. If I had the opportunity, I would also be able to cite a whole series of Articles of the PECL in which the Commission has attempted to distil the ideal out of the current legal systems and condense that into rules. Common law influences are recognisable everywhere, although often interwoven with continental ideas. The definition of "reasonableness" under Art. 1:302 PECL is a simple example, containing as it does the concept of "good faith". The law governing formation of contracts is also replete with such examples. Thus whilst the doctrine of consideration has not been adopted,[50] the Anglo-German view that "*causa* has no role in the formation and validity of contracts"[51] has. The rules under Art. 2:202 PECL on the revocation of offers demonstrate a true compromise. The basic rule, as under the common law but not in Germany, is that an offer is not binding and may be revoked at any time

---

[49] The conclusions of the first Commission were published in Lando/Beale, *The Principles of European Contract Law. Part I: Performance, Non-performance and Remedies* (1995). Drobnig/Zimmermann, "Die Grundregeln des Europäischen Vertragsrechts", ZEuP 1995 864 provide a German translation. The "Principles" have been published in French in de Lamberterie/Rouhette/Tallon, *Les principes du droit européen du contrat* (1997). The conclusions of the second Commission, including some new thoughts on the work of the first, have been published with a reprint of the first edition late in 1999. The third Commission expects to complete its work in 2000. The citations employed here refer to the 1999 edition.

[50] Art. 2:101 PECL: "(1) A contract is concluded if: (a) the parties intend to be legally bound, and (b) they reach a sufficient agreement, *without any further requirement*" (italics added).

[51] Note 3 (b) Art. 2:101 PECL.

until acceptance. Nonetheless, we felt it would be unacceptable if an offer which the offeror himself had described as binding could be thus revoked. This followed from our refusal to adopt the doctrine of consideration. Indeed no other rule would comply with the ideal of good faith which runs through all the principles.

I presume that a similar method of working and open-mindedness will be the mark of the newly founded *Study Group on a European Civil Code*. Do not be worried by the words "civil code". We have merely adopted the terminology of the European Parliament, which has often called upon legal academics to begin the preliminary work on such an undertaking.[52] But what is a "code"? In the foreseeable future at least we do not mean a continental-type comprehensive civil law. Rather, we intend merely to analyse the principle areas of the law of obligations, that is the laws of contract, tort and unjust enrichment, to an extent that will allow us to propose a model European law comprising the essential concepts of justice common to the national European systems. The code will also cover credit securities. Whilst we hope that the national systems will be persuaded of the value of this private basic law and will be able to agree upon it, it is recognised that they will retain unique national details for a long time and perhaps even for ever. Europe must find its own route to legal harmonisation and unification. Commercial and consumer-related law will not be able to continue in its current multiplicity, although other areas may remain in disharmony, thus contributing to the Europe of the regions. I believe both tendencies to be important: the development of a core of common legal concepts and the continued existence of regional and national peculiarities. Where however we can and must move towards each other, we should reach out from our inherited systems and grasp this historical chance to jettison ballast. Such process should not commence centrally from Brussels. Rather we should ourselves attempt to assess without prejudice the advantages and disadvantages of our private law systems, which have for so long been developed in national isolation. It is the usefulness of each law and system which counts, not its territorial origin. We should not forget that none of us is obliged to serve a French, German or English justice, but rather justice *simpliciter*. I accordingly have no fear for the future of German or French private law, no do I see any reason to be concerned for the future of the common law.[53] It will enrich the legal thinking of the whole of Europe. Equally, I hope also that we continentals may have something to offer the common law.

---

[52] The first such Resolution was passed on 26 May 1989 (Text in *RabelsZ* 56 [1992] 320 and *ZEuP* 1993 613). It was repeated and reinforced on 6 May 1994 (*ZEuP* 1995 p. 669). In Autumn 1998 the Parliament commissioned from the Study Group on a European Code a report on discrimination on the basis of nationality and the chances of the realisation of a European Civil Code. The report is as yet unpublished.

[53] Lord Goff of Chieveley's 1997 Wilberforce Lecture, entitled "The Future of the Common Law" at 46 [1997] 745 dealt primarily with the retention of the identity of the common law in the context of European unification. *Cf.* now Beatson, *Has the Common Law a Future?* (Cambridge, 1996).

5

Interpretation: Legal Texts and their Landscape

JOHAN STEYN

The case-by-case development of the common law has been the source of its enduring strength. Judges have concentrated on the fair resolution of the case at hand, anchoring their decisions in custom and tradition, and at the same time exposing their reasoning processes in detail thereby facilitating the development of the law. This methodology is distinctively English in origin and is to be contrasted with the civilian tradition, influenced by systematic codes and cultural traditions favouring doctrine over pragmatism. Thus the continental systems recognise an overarching duty of good faith in the performance of contracts. The common law achieves similar results by a resort to implied terms, rectification and estoppel. In civilian systems there is generally a wider incidence of liability in tort or delict for intentional wrongdoing than in the English system of particular torts. Similarly on the continent a general principle of unjust enrichment has predominated while in England the common law has covered the same ground by the recognition of particular restitutionary remedies. The growth of the English system has been controlled by precedent. It has ensured relatively consistent results and by and large the attainment of practical justice. Precedent depends on the evaluation of the analogical force of earlier decisions. This is a form of legal interpretation. The process of interpreting a discursive judgment is, however, qualitatively very different from the interpretation of a legal text agreed by the parties to a contract or a legal text enacted by a legislature. This article is concerned with the interpretation of such legal texts.

The importance of the subject is not always fully appreciated. The curricula offered by our universities, the articles appearing in our legal journals, and the legal treatises published in this country overwhelmingly create the impression that the common law is the dominant source of law. And that is how as academic lawyers, practitioners, and judges we generally tend to think about law. The reality is very different. In the High Court, the Court of Appeal, and the House of Lords the great preponderance of civil issues involve points of interpretation of statutes, regulations, bye-laws, various types of "soft" laws, and so forth. If one then also takes into account adjudications by lower courts and tribunals the conclusion is irresistible that statute law is the dominant source of law in our time. And the output of enacted law increases year by year, notably as a result of the social welfare system and the integration of our civil law into European legal culture. Interpretation of legal texts is therefore of paramount importance to a modern lawyer. But our skills in explaining and applying the common law are not matched by comparable skills in the interpretation of legal texts. As English lawyers we are not as at ease in the field of statutory interpretation as our continental colleagues for whom logically coherent codes and broadly drafted statutes are acknowledged to be the predominant source of law. English lawyers instinctively approach a statute from the perspective of the common law while civilian lawyers search for the guiding principles in the design and structure of the legal text. It is true that we have a number of excellent books on the drafting and interpretation of statutes. Perhaps we still need a major jurisprudential work focused on interpretation in the English legal system as well as a comprehensive technical treatise on the lines of the brief account of Miers and Page.[1] Moreover, as Professor Zimmermann has cogently argued, we need a better alliance between the legislature, courts and universities in improving the quality of our legislation.[2]

This article does not aim to fill any gap. It does not put forward a theory of interpretation. For my part this elusive subject will always evade encapsulation in a theory. But as the result of the work of legal philosophers, academic lawyers, and judges it is possible to take stock of some insights which throw light on the subject of interpretation. And negatively it is possible to state what ought not play a part in the interpretative process. In stating the position we have reached I shall discuss three types of legal text, namely commercial contracts, statute law and constitutional instruments. But it will be obvious that much of what I say is relevant to legal texts generally.

TWO PRELIMINARY GENERALISATIONS

In law broad generalisations rightly excite scepticism and require strict proof. Nevertheless I shall venture to state two general propositions which (if correct) may go to the heart of the problem of interpretation of legal texts. First, the interpretation of a legal text must aim to assign to the text, be it a contract or enacted law, a meaning derived from its nature and contents. It cannot aim to discover what the parties to a contract or the collective body of individuals constituting the legislature subjectively intended. Such a subjective enquiry cannot be expected to yield realistic results. Moreover, the idea of such an enquiry is logically incoherent: it is excluded by the very concept of interpretation which involves the ascertainment of the objective meaning of a text.

---

[1] *Legislation*, 2nd edn. (London, 1990).
[2] "Statuta Sunt Stricte Interpretanda? Statutes and the Common Law: A Continental Perspective" (1997), *C.L.J.* 315 at 326.

In the case of contracts the subjective desires of the parties will be divergent. Yet they choose a text to govern their relationship and to be the ground upon which disputes are to be resolved. When a dispute as to the interpretation of the contract arises the matter in contention will usually be a risk unforeseen by the parties. How the matter should be resolved depends on the allocation of risks in the contract, the application of default rules, or rarely, the incidence of rules of defeasibility. All these impinge on interpretation. But, leaving aside rectification and estoppel by convention, the subjective views of the parties are irrelevant. The emphasis must be on what the parties, circumstanced as they were, must reasonably be taken by their chosen contractual text to have said to one another.

For somewhat different reasons the text of an enacted law must always be the touchstone. At stake is not the interpretation of the legislative history of a statute but of the text itself. This principle is anchored in the democratic ideal. The rule of law in a democracy requires that the rights and duties of citizens should be publicly promulgated in enacted law. And it is the meaning of an enacted text which is controlling. The individual views of the members of the legislature, even if there is a large measure of agreement, do not have legal significance. It is the fact that in accordance with constitutional rules a particular text has been enacted which is decisive. The critical thing is what the text of the law provides.

The second proposition is closely allied to the first. The mandated point of departure must be the text itself. It does not mean that contextual materials in aid of interpretation of a text must be ruled out or down-graded. After all, a statement is only intelligible if one knows under what conditions it was made. But extrinsic materials are subordinate to the text itself. The primacy of the text is the framework of reference for the judge considering a point of interpretation. But all legal texts must be construed against the contextual setting in which they come into existence. Taking full account of such aids to construction the judge must concentrate on the different meaning which the text is capable of letting in. What falls beyond that range of possible meanings will not be a result attainable by interpretation. Principles of institutional integrity which bind all judges set those limits for judges.

The two propositions advanced do not justify a narrow textual theory of interpretation. It is certainly not a plea for a search for the "original" intent of the framers of the document. It is my main thesis that the intent of the framers of a text is irrelevant to interpretation. Moreover, it is well settled in English law, in the context of statutory interpretation, that *prima facie* the instrument is to be considered "an always speaking statute." The text "has a legal existence independently of the historical contingencies of its promulgation, and accordingly should be interpreted in the light of its place within the system of legal norms currently in force."[3]

---

[3] Cross, *Statutory Interpretation*, 3rd edn. (London, 1990), 52.

COMMERCIAL CONTRACTS

The interpretation of a contract is an enquiry into the meaning of particular language in a contextual setting, with the aid occasionally of rules of interpretation, which are founded essentially on common sense criteria. It is therefore not surprising that English law does not differentiate between the interpretation of a rudimentary cobbled together contract and a sophisticated standard form contract; the interpretation of a consumer contract and a commercial contract; or the interpretation of a domestic and transnational contract. That is not, however, to say that in working out what is the best interpretation of a contract a court may not take into account, for example, a consumer as opposed to a commercial context, or the need for uniformity in international transactions.

The purpose of the interpretation of a contract is not to discover how the parties understood the language of the text which they adopted. The aim is to determine the meaning of the contract against the relevant contextual scene. In other words, the question is what the contract must reasonably be taken to mean, its language being considered against the contextual world against which it was concluded. It is sometimes argued by counsel, and even asserted by judges, that an ambiguity is a precondition to admitting evidence of the setting of the contract. That is wrong. Language can never be understood divorced from its context. That is why a dictionary can never solve a problem of interpretation. Some factual information is always necessary in order to interpret a contract. Occasionally, the contract may contain the necessary factual material in preambles or otherwise. More often extrinsic evidence is necessary to explain the circumstances in which the parties concluded a contract. The full import of the classic judgment of Lord Wilberforce in *Reardon Smith Line* v. *Yngvar Hansen-Tangen (trading as Hansen-Tangen)*[4] is not always appreciated. Lord Wilberforce said: "no contracts are made in a vacuum: there is always a setting in which they have to be placed."[5] About surrounding circumstances Lord Wilberforce said: "In a commercial contract it is certainly right that the court should know the commercial purpose of the contract and this in turn presupposes knowledge of the genesis of the transaction, the background, the context, the market in which the parties are operating."[6] And Lord Wilberforce made clear that the court is *always* entitled to be informed of the setting of a contract.[7] The type of evidence of surrounding circumstances which may be allowed to influence a question of interpretation is often controversial. Two recent decisions in the House of Lords explored the extent to which the context may impress a meaning on contractual language. In *Mannai Limited* v. *Eagle Star Assurance Company Limited* the issue was whether a contractual notice by a

---

[4] [1976] WLR 989.
[5] At 995H.
[6] At 995H–996A.
[7] At 997B.

tenant to determine a lease, which wrongly named the day upon which the tenant would do so as 12th January rather than 13th January, was valid.[8] The majority held that the notice was nevertheless valid. Essentially, they regarded it as wholly implausible that the tenant only wanted to terminate if he could do so on 12th rather than 13th January. Given this position the majority concluded that a reasonable recipient would have understood that the option was being exercised. The minority held that the notices failed to conform to the requirements of the options reserved in the lease. Having been a member of the majority in *Mannai* I would acknowledge that the decision is regarded by some as controversial.

The case of *Investors Compensation Scheme Limited* v. *West Bromwich Building Society*[9] is even more important. The Court of Appeal held that "Any claim (whether sounding in rescission for undue influence or otherwise)" could not be interpreted to mean "Any claim sounding in rescission (whether for undue influence or otherwise)". By a majority of 4 to 1 the House of Lords upheld the conclusion of the judge that something had probably gone wrong in the drafting and reversed the ruling of the Court of Appeal. Lord Hoffmann, speaking for the majority rejected the contention that judges cannot, short of rectification, decide on an issue of interpretation that parties had made mistakes of meaning or syntax. Lord Hoffmann summarised the five principles as follows:[10]

(1) Interpretation is the ascertainment of the meaning which the document would convey to a reasonable person having all the background knowledge which would reasonably have been available to the parties in the situation in which they were at the time of the contract.

(2) The background was famously referred to by Lord Wilberforce as the "matrix of fact," but this phrase is, if anything, an understated description of what the background may include. Subject to the requirement that it should have been reasonably available to the parties and to the exception to be mentioned next, it includes absolutely anything which would have affected the way in which the language of the document would have been understood by a reasonable man.

(3) The law excludes from the admissible background the previous negotiations of the parties and their declarations of subjective intent. They are admissible only in an action for rectification. The law makes this distinction for reasons of practical policy and, in this respect only, legal interpretation differs from the way we would interpret utterances in ordinary life. The boundaries of this exception are in some respects unclear. But this is not the occasion on which to explore them.

(4) The meaning which a document (or any other utterance) would convey to a reasonable man is not the same thing as the meaning of its words. The meaning of words is a matter of dictionaries and grammars; the meaning of the document is what the parties using those words against the relevant background would reasonably have been understood to mean. The background may not merely enable

---

[8] [1997] AC 749.
[9] [1998] 1 WLR 896.
[10] At 912H–913E.

the reasonable man to choose between the possible meanings of words which are ambiguous but even (as occasionally happens in ordinary life) to conclude that the parties must, for whatever reason, have used the wrong words or syntax. See *Mannai Investments Co. Ltd.* v. *Eagle Star Life Assurance Co. Ltd* [1997] *A.C.* 749.

(5) The "rule" that words should be given their "natural and ordinary meaning" reflects the common sense proposition that we do not easily accept that people have made linguistic mistakes, particularly in formal documents. On the other hand, if one would nevertheless conclude from the background that something must have gone wrong with the language, the law does not require judges to attribute to the parties an intention which they plainly could not have had.

Except for the second proposition Lord Hoffmann's summary of the legal position seems to me uncontroversial. The second proposition has caused concern in two Court of Appeal decisions. In *National Bank of Sharjah* v. *Delborg and Others* in unreported judgments the Court of Appeal mildly protested about this part of Lord Hoffmann's judgment.[11] In *Scottish Power PLC* v. *Britoil (Exploration) Ltd. and others* Lord Justice Staughton (with the agreement on this point of Otton L.J. and Robert Walker L.J.) questioned whether Lord Hoffmann's second proposition is part of the *ratio decidendi* of the *I.C.S.* case and plainly regarded it as too widely expressed.[12] Lord Hoffmann's statement that "it includes absolutely anything" is startling but it is immediately qualified by the requirement that it *"would* have affected the way in which the language *would* have been understood by a reasonable man." Relevance of the extrinsic evidence to the objective setting of the contract is the expressed criterion. The concern caused by Lord Hoffmann's observation is not in my view justified by the terms of his judgment. The actual decision in the case may, however, be said to lie close to the outer limit of what can be achieved by interpretation.

The implication of terms is also part of the process of interpretation of written contracts. Three types of implied terms must be distinguished. First, there are usages of trade and commerce which are so regularly observed as to justify an expectation they will be observed in respect of relevant transactions. This is part of interpretation because the question is whether the usage can be accommodated in the framework of the written contract read as a whole. Secondly, there are terms implied by law. This occurs when the terms are annexed to particular forms of contract, such as contracts for building work, sale, hire, and so forth, by operation of law. Such terms operate as default rules. It is again part of interpretation because the question arises whether the terms of the particular written contract permit such supplementation.

The third category is terms described as implied in fact. This terminology is capable of creating confusion. Two tests have been developed to ascertain whether such an implication is justified, namely the officious bystander test which poses the question whether the proposed implication is so obvious that it

---

[11] CA Transcript, 9th July 1997.
[12] CA Transcript, 18th November 1997; reported in *The Times*, 2nd December 1997.

can be said that it goes without saying (*Shirlaw* v. *Southern Foundries (1926) Ltd.*)[13] and the business efficacy test which poses the question whether the implication is necessary to make the contract workable (*The Moorcock*).[14] These are simply practical tests developed by judges to ascertain whether the proposed implication is strictly necessary if the reasonable expectations of the parties are not to be defeated. In *Tolstoy* v. *Aldington* (with the agreement of Simon Brown L.J.) I explained this point in some detail.[15] In essence such an implication is constructional in nature: proceeding from the effect of the express terms of the contract, in its relevant setting, the question is whether the proposed implication is strictly necessary. The implication is certainly not based on an inference of the actual intention of the parties. It is a term which in the light of the terms of the contract and its objective setting the law imputes to the parties. The background material, which may be admitted in aid of the determination whether a term ought to be implied, is the same as the evidence admissible in aid of the construction of an express term.

STATUTE LAW

In 1882 Pollock described the approach of judges to statutes as follows: "Parliament generally changes law for the worse, and that the business of the judges is to keep the mischief of its interference within the narrowest bounds."[16] This was an accurate description of the judicial mindset in Victorian times. The outcome of this approach was restrictive interpretation by literalist methods. It remained the approach of judges until some time after the Second World War. But it is no longer an accurate description. By and large, English judges are now used to applying purposive methods of construction of statutes. A major cause of this shift has been to the teleological approach of European Community jurisprudence, as well as the influence of the European Court of Human Rights.

It is an appropriate time to take stock where we have arrived. Judges frequently assert that the purpose of interpretation is to determine the will of Parliament. It is, however, a fairy tale to think that the subjective views of members of Parliament, sitting in two separate chambers, can be determined. That is not what statutory interpretation is about. Reference to the intention of Parliament is simply convenient shorthand for the appropriate meaning of the statutory text. Statutes are enacted in accordance with the principles of our unwritten constitution, and only the text so enacted is law and susceptible to interpretation. The text, and not its history, is the starting point. In emphasising this truism I am not making a plea for literal methods of construction. On

---

[13] [1939] K.B. 206, at 227.
[14] [1989] 14 P.D. 64, at 68.
[15] CA, Transcript, 15th December 1993. This judgment is only reported briefly in *The Times*, 16th December 1993.
[16] Pollock, *Essays on Jurisprudence and Ethics* (1882), 85.

the contrary, a recognition that interpretation is concerned with the meaning of publicly promulgated texts is the foundation upon which purposive construction rests.

In cases where the correct interpretation of a statute is uncertain the contextual scene of the legislation will be important. Such material includes, of course, the genesis of the statute, its major purposes, the structure of the statute, the legislative technique employed, and so forth. But it is important to bear in mind that the text must be viewed in the light of the world to which it relates: it speaks with reference to the circumstances in which it came to be passed. Far more important than rules of interpretation, or presumptions, is for the court to be fully informed of the contextual background of the statute.

It will be rare for a statute to have one obvious meaning which can be determined without taking into account the context of the legislation. One might say that a statutory provision that an important notice must be lodged within 30 days requires no resort to contextual material. But even this proposition is not necessarily correct. The context may throw light on the relative plausibility of interpretations holding that days include every day of the week or only week days. While the text of the statute is of pre-eminent importance, it cannot be understood in a vacuum: legislative language can only be understood against the backcloth of the world to which it relates. Sometimes judgments do not fully take into account the different levels of reasoning at which the context is relevant. As in the case of commercial contracts, and other legal texts, the context is relevant to what possible different meanings the language of the text may let in. But when the judge comes to select among the possible interpretations the best one the context is again relevant. It is therefore a fundamental misconception to say that the background to the statute may only be admitted in the event of an ambiguity.

Professor Reinhard Zimmermann, a distinguished observer of the English legal scene, has pointed out that the idea that common law and statutes constitute two separate components of the law lingers on in England.[17] And the result is still a somewhat negative attitude to legislation. He has pointed out that by contrast in Germany it is accepted that the courts have to develop statute law in accordance with the Basic Law of 1949. He observed that "It is hard to understand why the courts in England should not be able, in a similar manner, imaginatively to develop and elaborate the statutory law so as to co-ordinate it with the common law." There is substance in this observation. In England we have some way to go to a full hearted acceptance of the fact that: common law and statute coalesce in one legal system; statute law draws heavily on the concepts and techniques of the common law and may be developed accordingly; and, the common law may in turn be developed on the basis of the analogical force of the statute law. Possibly the constitutionalisation of our public law, devolution legislation and the Human Rights Act 1998 may speed on an even better understanding of and approach to statute law.

[17] *Op. cit.*

A discussion of statutory interpretation must, of course, take into account the landmark decision of the House of Lords in *Pepper* v. *Hart*.[18] There are principled arguments for and against allowing a statute to be interpreted in accordance with an explanation ventured in debate by a minister promoting the bill. On the one hand, there is the consideration that the executive, which plays a decisive role in the passing of legislation, ought not to be able to get away with saying in a Parliamentary debate that the proposed legislation will mean one thing in order to secure the passage of legislation and then to argue through counsel in court that the legislation bears the opposite meaning, thereby prejudicing particular individuals. This is the core reason of the majority in *Pepper* v. *Hart*. This argument is formidable. On the other hand, there is a contrary contention, which can be advanced on behalf of society generally. It is the argument that the law should be accessible to anyone who reads the statute against its objective contextual scene. It may be said to be inconsistent with the principles of a parliamentary democracy which legislates by enacting texts in the forms of bills, to allow evidence of the views of promoters of a bill to contradict the text. This too is a cogent argument.

In a Bentham lecture delivered in 1996 I welcomed the decision in *Pepper* v. *Hart*.[19] Now I am far less confident that the balance of principled arguments favoured the *Pepper* v. *Hart* decision. It is a difficult point on which there is force in the arguments deployed on both sides. I would therefore not wish to re-examine the merits of those arguments of principle. Instead I question whether in the light of experience since 1992 the ruling in *Pepper* v. *Hart* has been shown to be a desirable one in the interests of our legal system as a whole. Lord Renton, Q.C., in a lecture delivered in 1995 commented on *Pepper* v. *Hart*. Speaking with enormous experience of the Parliamentary process and statute law he trenchantly observed:[20]

> "None of the Law Lords who decided that had ever had to pilot a Bill. If they had, they would have known that in doing so one often had to change one's mind on particular clauses, or even on a principle, in order to get the Bill passed. So Hansard inevitably contains contradictions or ambiguous statements by those responsible. How much better it would be to make the drafting clear, so as to avoid consulting Hansard! *Pepper* v. *Hart* causes the word of the courts and of barristers to be longer and more expensive, and will one day be superseded."

In 1997 Lord Hoffmann stated extra-judicially, on the basis of his experience as an appellate judge, that the time and money spent in researching Parliamentary history of an enactment seldom produces anything worthwhile. He added that "trying to find guidance in a minister's attempt to make sense of his or her departmental brief at short notice while standing at the despatch box is usually a hopeless quest."[21]

---

[18] [1993] AC 593 (H.L.).
[19] Steyn, "Does Legal Formalism Hold Sway in England?" (1996) *CLP* 43, at 50.
[20] The Inaugural Lecture of the Statute Law Society (1995).
[21] Hoffman, "The Intolerable Wrestle with Words and Meanings" (1997), 114 *SALJ* 656.

While *Pepper* v. *Hart* arguments have often been advanced in cases in which I have sat in the Court of Appeal and the House of Lords they have never produced anything significant. That is also the experience of many other appellate judges. But I accept that the *Pepper* v. *Hart* principle can occasionally produce something useful, as it did in that very case. But it does so rarely and at exorbitant cost. One has to bear in mind not only the cases where the searches have produced materials which counsel felt able to place before the court but the countless cases where even counsel's enthusiasm for exploring Hansard produced nothing whatever of value. In the light of the experience of our courts since 1992 I am now inclined to agree with Lord Renton Q.C. and Lord Hoffmann that the *Pepper* v. *Hart* decision has by the judgment of experience probably been shown to be an undesirable luxury in our legal system. The pragmatic case against the decision in *Pepper* v. *Hart* is strong.

CONSTITUTIONAL ADJUDICATION

One may legitimately enquire whether there is any reason why the approach to the interpretation of a constitutional instrument should differ from the interpretation of an ordinary statute. In a democracy there is at least one sufficient answer to this question. Ultimately, the people are the source of power. The people resolve to embody the ground rules of a representative democracy in a written constitution in order to place beyond doubt the only way in which they are prepared to be governed. Such written constitutions typically contain a diversity of provisions. A major part would be the allocation of power between the legislature, executive, judiciary, and other agencies. Another major feature would be the protection of fundamental rights of individuals, often called the Bill of Rights provisions of the constitution. It would be unrealistic to say that there is a single theory of interpretation capable of explaining the correct approach to interpretation in divergent contexts and in relation to constitutional rights of different kinds. What one can with confidence say is that provisions are incorporated in a constitution in the expectation that they will be afforded a higher normative force than other rules. This generalisation does not solve many concrete cases but it is the indispensable point of departure for constitutional adjudication.

Some would say this is all true but not relevant to law in the United Kingdom in 2000. The argument is that we do not have a written constitution and therefore the subject of constitutional interpretation does not arise. It is true that the development by the courts of constitutional rights, such as freedom of speech, the right of access to the courts, the right to a fair trial, and so forth, does not involve interpretation of a text. Until the promulgation of the Scotland Act 1998 and the Human Rights Act 1998 the English courts, other than the Privy Council in Caribbean and other foreign appeals, were not called on to decide issues of constitutional interpretation. Now there is an entirely new landscape. It is a controversial point whether the two new statutes have a constitutional dimension. It may be said that the Scotland Act 1998 is revocable at the will of the Westminster Parliament and that it is therefore not a constitutional measure. This is a tenable view. If it prevails, it may have an impact on the meaning to be given to the "reserved matters" which are outside the competence of the Scottish Parliament.[22] A broader view is possible. A court may rule that the intention was that there should be a durable settlement in favour of Scotland which may justify the conclusion that the relevant provisions of the Scotland Act 1998 should be regarded as constitutional in character or, in any event, that those provisions should be interpreted on the same principles as a constitutional measure. On this supposition a broader and more flexible approach to what constitutes reserved matters, not tied to the circumstances at the time of devolution, may be justified. This view may be reinforced by the fact that it is also outside the legal competence of the Scottish Parliament to legislate incompatibly with convention rights under the Human Rights Act 1998.[23] The argument may be that the Scotland Act is more than an ordinary "always speaking statute." This is a question of supreme importance upon which it would not be right for me as a serving Law Lord to express a concluded view at this stage.

It may also be said that the Human Rights Act 1998 is revocable at the will of Parliament and that this Act is therefore not a constitutional measure. It must, however, be borne in mind that it was passed against the background of the clear jurisprudence of the European Court holding that the European Convention is to be interpreted as a living text in the light of contemporary conditions. Moreover, the Privy Council has held that provisions modelled on the European Convention contained in Caribbean constitutions must be given "a generous interpretation avoiding what has been called 'the austerity of tabulated legalism', suitable to give individuals the full measure of the fundamental rights referred to."[24] Given this context it seems clear that the Human Rights Act 1998, and convention rights, must be interpreted in the same way as Bill of Rights provisions in a constitution.

CONCLUSION

The interpretation of legal texts raises baffling problems. It is best to recognise that there is no integrated theory of interpretation which can assist in the decision of difficult cases. The answer is to be found in the detail. But there are some modest insights to be recorded. Foremost among these is the core idea that a legal text has a public character, and that it must be read in the light of publicly

---

[22] See Sections 28 and 29. Section 29(2)(a) provides that reserved matters as listed in Schedule 5 are beyond the legislative competence of the Scottish Parliament. Schedule 5 is almost impenetrable in its complexity.

[23] See section 29(2)(d).

[24] *Ministry of Home Affairs* v. *Fischer* [1980] AC 319 at 328.

available evidence. Dictionaries, a grammar book, and precepts of syntax, will not by themselves yield the contextual meaning of words and sentences. It is true that in a dictionary words are given a limited range of conventional meanings. But in a legal text a word forms part of a sentence and sentences are unlimited in their variety of the arrangement of words. Moreover, the sentence is embedded in a text which by virtue of its major purposes and the general effect of its provisions may add colour to words and sentences. A subtle interplay between word, sentence and text is involved. A problem of interpretation therefore requires an intense focus on particular language in its contextual setting. The first impression of the average reader is a useful starting point but cannot be a conclusive guide. The judge may have to wrestle analytically with the problem, and he or she may have to weigh consequentialist arguments in search of the best interpretation of the legal text.

6

Managing the European Union: For Better or for Worse?

W. VAN GERVEN[1]

When accepting Professor Markesinis' invitation to take part in this prestigious conference as a member of the panel discussing commercial law in the Emerging Europe I knew that it would not be easy to define the term commercial law. This is not because the concept is insufficiently clear—it relates, I would think, to business transactions between traders—but because I feel, as I have always felt, that commercial law is to be viewed as part of economic law. This means that it includes not only rules dealing with transactions between traders but also rules laying down the ways and passing the instruments through which governmental agencies can affect economic life. Thus, both these aspects of the law must be included in the inquiry.

Defining commercial law as (part of) economic law may be regarded as heretical in the eyes of a continental lawyer because it ignores the division between private and public law. I assume this not to be the case for lawyers who come from the common law legal family. Be that as it may, a fringe benefit of ignoring this division is that it facilitates compliance with Professor Markesinis' request to make my paper as "European" in its orientation as possible. For European Community law, on which I wish to concentrate is, and remains, essentially economic law. Initially, European law was concerned with the free establishment and free movement—within the European internal market—of persons, goods, services and capital, regardless of nationality or origin. Nowadays, however, it has now come to look upon even at ethical questions— such as abortion or *in vitro* fertilisation—from a viewpoint of free movement of services.[2]

Between being invited to participate in the present event and writing this paper, I was designated by the European Parliament as one of five members of

---

[1] At the time of writing the author is a member of the Committee of Independent Experts instituted by the European Parliament to examine cases of fraud, mismanagement and nepotism within the European Commission. The views expressed herein are strictly personal.

[2] See ECJ, case 159/90, *Society for the Protection of Unborn Children Ireland Ltd* v. *Stephen Grogan* [1991] ECR I–4685 and the Opinion of the Advocate-General at I–4703 (abortion); *Reg. V. H.F.E. Authority, ex parte Blood* (1996) 3 W.L.R. 1176. Fam. D.; (1996) 2 W.L.R. 806, L.A. (in vitro).

the Independent Committee of Experts (hereafter the "Committee"). Its purpose was to examine the way in which the Santer Commission (hereinafter "the former Commission") of the European Union dealt with fraud, mismanagement and nepotism. The Committee was asked to submit its first report on 15 March 1999,[3] which resulted, as will be recalled, in the collective resignation of the European Commission. The Committee's second report is to deal with an analysis of the financial and employment contracts which the Commission concludes, the procedures to deal with fraud, mismanagement and nepotism, as well as the administrative culture in the Commission.[4] This must be submitted by the beginning of September 1999 so that the newly elected European Parliament and the new Commission under President Romano Prodi can take account of its recommendations. The issues dealt in the first Report (and, possibly, in the second Report which at the time of writing has not yet been published)[5] are, I believe, of great importance for the constitutional framework of economic law in the emerging Europe. Taking advantage of the wide discretion left to the speakers to define their own subject, I would like to address in this paper some of these constitutional aspects.

The issues I have in mind concern the relationship between the responsibility of the European Commission, as a body, and of its individual members (the Commissioners) in laying down economic policy (mainly), and the responsibility of the heads of departments (the Director Generals) and their services, in implementing such policy. It will be obvious from the choice of my subject that it will have some bearing as well on the subject of the following seminar group on "Protecting the Citizen" but that, I hope, should not present any particular problems.

THE EUROPEAN COMMISSION'S LEGISLATIVE AND ADMINISTRATIVE STRONGHOLD

The policy and ensuing law-making activity has become more and more complex over the years.[6] That is the consequence mainly of the growth of the role of the European Parliament and the need resulting from this to organise the co-operation, and mediation, between the three participating institutions: the Commission, the Council and the Parliament. That is also the consequence of the ever-growing input of national technocrats and national interest groups

---

[3] First Report on *Allegations regarding Fraud, Mismanagement and Nepotism in the European Commission*, 1999.

[4] Thus the decision of the European Parliament at its session of 23–24 March 1999 outlining the agreements reached at the Conference of Presidents of 22 March 1999.

[5] After this paper was completed, the seventh (and last) chapter of the second Report has been published. It concerns the questions discussed in this essay. The text of chapter 7 can be found on Internet: http://www.europarl.eu.int.

[6] Craig and De Burca, *European Union Law* (2nd edn., Oxford, 1998), at 143 ff; also Kapteyn and VerLoren van Themaat, *Introduction to the Law of the European Communities* (3rd edn., edited and revised by L.W. Gormley (1998)) at 389 ff.

through "the EC's complex committee structure known generally as Comitology".[7] Within the limited sphere of competence attributed to the Community (and, as a consequence, the necessity to find a legal basis in the Treaties to justify any Community action[8]), and subject to the application of the subsidiarity principle,[9] the Commission remains an important actor. That is primarily so because of its right of legislative initiative in practically all cases, and under all legislative procedures, laid down in the Treaties. A second reason for this is the large amount of delegated legislative powers assigned to it.[10] Of course, as stated by Craig and de Burca,[11] legislative proposals from the Commission "do not emerge out of thin air". Instead, they are the result of interaction not only between the three institutions but also, before the Commission submits its proposal to the Council and/or the Parliament, between the services of the Commission and various kinds of interest groups at the national and Community level. A similar interaction takes place regarding the exercise of delegated legislative power by the Commission, which has been subjected by the Council to institutional constraints, in the form of committees through which the interests of the Member States can be represented.[12] As to decision-making within the Commission, itself, "the relevant Commissioner will assume overall responsibility for a proposal which comes within his or her area. It will have been fashioned by the relevant Directorate-General, and by the appropriate Directorates and Divisions which are part of that bureaucracy . . . Once the Commissioner is satisfied with the draft it will then be submitted to the College of Commissioners (since) legislative proposals, once formulated, require the endorsement of the whole Commission".[13]

The foregoing refer to the role of the Commission in the policy- and law-making process, i.e. in its role as part of the Community legislature. No less important but, it would seem, less explored is the Commission's executive role, that is its role in implementing approved policy by means of normative acts or documents and by means of individual decisions or programmes.[14] A distinction must be made here between two areas of activity. First, administrative management tasks, which the Commission carries out itself—e.g. in the fields of the customs union, competition policy and the application of safeguard clauses

---

[7] Craig and De Burca, at 156.
[8] See further W. van Gerven, "Community and national legislators, regulators, judges, academics and practitioners: living together apart?" in *Law Making, Law Finding, and Law Shaping* Markesinis (ed.) (Oxford, 1997), at 13 ff.
[9] Craig and De Burca, at 125.
[10] *Ibid*, 138.
[11] *Ibid*, 150–151.
[12] *Ibid*, 138.
[13] *Ibid*, 151.
[14] That is even more regrettable because the Commission's task progressively shifts "from drafting new legislation and developing new policy initiatives (towards) tackling the less glamorous, but increasingly important, task of managing existing programmes: thus F. Herman, MEP, "Report on improvements in the functioning of the Institutions without modification of the treaties" of 26 March 1999 before the EP's Committee on Institutional Affairs at B 34.

(direct management). Secondly, administrative supervisory tasks through which the Commission ensures the observance by the Member States of management obligations imposed upon them by primary or secondary Community law rules, e.g. in the field of agricultural policy (shared management). In the first report of the Committee, a third form of implementation (or rather a sub-category of direct management) came to the fore in the cases analysed by the Committee. This third form consists in the "outsourcing" to the private sector of direct management tasks, which the Commission services themselves are not capable of carrying out because of shortages of human resources.[15] It leads to a proliferation of private entities, which are often commissioned to fulfil public functions and to manage important operational resources. Such "outsourcing" is not always the object of sufficiently rigid rules on financial and managerial status and behaviour on the part of those private entities. Nor is it subject to sufficiently watertight techniques of surveillance on the part of the Commission services. The Committee's analysis of individual files has shown that this practice is apt to lead to fraud and mismanagement on the part of those private entities, sometimes in concert with one or more civil servants.[16] This unsatisfactory state of affairs stems, more often than not, from a decision of the Commission, not infrequently at the request of the Council, Parliament, or one or another Member State, to take on tasks for which only insufficient resources are made available.[17] Taking on tasks without securing sufficient resources is an open invitation for services or third parties to ignore sound management practices, and to interpret rules in too flexible a manner, thus contributing to the emergence of a culture of unruliness and irresponsibility.

THE EUROPEAN PARLIAMENT'S BUDGETARY WEAPON

The reluctance of the European Commission to open up its corridors of power to scrutiny has, of course, been criticised on many an occasion. The desire of the European Parliament to increase its grip over such activities, stimulated by the occurrence of fraud, mismanagement, and favouritism on the part of some civil servants and of third contracting parties, also came to light in the course of parliamentary discussions. It culminated in the refusal by the majority of Parliament to give a discharge to the Commission in respect of the implementation of the 1996 budget, as provided for in Article 276 (ex-206) EC.[18] Parliament was particularly unhappy with the way in which it had been denied access by the

[15] See also Birkinshaw and Parkin, "Standards in British Public Life: Responsibility, accountability and ethics", *Acta Universitatis wratislaviensis*, no. 2047, 1997, 235 ff. at 238.

[16] First Report, at 4.2.3 ff. and 9.4.5 ff.

[17] See, however, art. 270 (ex-201a) EC.

[18] For a discussion of the provisions of Article 272 (ex-203) EC on the drafting and approval of the budget, and their inter-institutional dimension, see Craig and de Burca, at 99 ff. The provisions of Article 276 EC on the discharge in respect of the implementation of the budget have been strengthened by the TEU: see Kapteyn a.o., cited in 5, at 386 ff.

Commission to information which it regarded necessary for the examination of the accounts and to which, in its view, it was entitled according to Article 276 (ex-206, par. 2), EC.[19]

As a result of the (former) Commission's perceived lack of transparency and openness, Parliament went as far as considering a motion of censure. Had this been carried by a two-thirds majority of the votes cast it would have compelled the Commission to "resign as a body", as is required by article 201 (ex-144) EC. However, reluctant to go to such extremes, the majority in Parliament voted, on 14 January 1999, a compromise resolution, which led to the appointment of the Committee of Independent Experts already alluded to above. At the same time Parliament obtained from the Commission a concession. Thus, among other things, the Commission agreed to submit three codes of conduct, the first laying down rules of conduct for members of the Commission, the second governing relations between Commissioners and Commission departments, and the third setting out a code of ethics for officials. Of these three codes, the first two are of particular importance here. They were drafted by the Commission before its collective resignation, following the publication of the Committee's first Report, and have been published on the Internet.[20] They will be dealt with hereafter.

The above is a clear-cut example of how "the budgetary process cannot . . . be separated from more general issues of institutional power within the Community. History is replete with such examples of legislative bodies at national level, which have used their power over the purse as a lever to improve their position in the overall constitutional hierarchy. The European Parliament is no different in this respect".[21]

THE RESPONSIBILITY OF COMMISSION AND COMMISSIONERS FOR NOT BEHAVING IN ACCORDANCE WITH STANDARDS IN PUBLIC LIFE

The most crucial issue with which the Committee had to deal with in its first Report was whether the Commission as a body could be held responsible for mismanagement (eventually fraud, or nepotism) committed by individual Commissioners. The Committee first referred to the terms of reference governing its mandate, according to which "the first report could seek to establish to what extent the Commission, as a body, or Commissioners individually, bear specific responsibility for the recent examples of fraud, mismanagement or

---

[19] See the Working Document of 3 December 1998 prepared by Ms. Theato for the EP's Commission of Budget Control, at no. 1 ff., where the standpoint of the EP is set out. Parliament later on also refused to give discharge for the 1997 budget, as proposed in a document of 26 March 1999 prepared by Mr. Brinkhorst for the same EP Commission.

[20] http://europa.eur.int/comm/codes of conduct/index_en.htm. The third code on officials is still under preparation, while the incoming Commission has already amended and supplemented the first two codes with proposals of its own (to be adopted formally when it assumes office).

[21] Craig and De Burca, at 102.

nepotism".[22] The Committee then held that the responsibility to be investigated by it was to be distinguished from the "political" responsibility dealt with in Article 144, now Article 201 EC, as well as from the "disciplinary" responsibility dealt with in Article 160, now Article 216 EC. The former is to be determined by Parliament and leads, according to the present wording of Article 144, to the resignation of the Commission as a body. The latter is to be determined by the Court of Justice, on application by the Council or the Commission, and leads to the compulsory retirement of the Commissioner who "no longer fulfils the conditions required for the performance of his duties" or who "has been guilty of serious misconduct". In the Committee's view, its ability to determine the responsibility of the Commission as a body, or of Commissioners individually, regarding recent cases of fraud, mismanagement or nepotism, had nothing to do with the ability of Parliament (or the Court) to decide, on the findings of the Committee, political (or disciplinary) responsibility.[23] The Committee was of the opinion that the task assigned to it was about "ethical responsibility, that is responsibility for not behaving in accordance with proper standards in public life".[24]

The latter point needs further clarification. It allows me moreover, considering the objective of this Conference, to illustrate the impact, which the common law has exerted on this particular instance. Looking for standards which the Committee wished to apply, it held that Commissioners were to comply "with the highest standards of conduct in European public administration" and "the higher the Office, the more demanding those standards are in requiring the holders to conduct themselves properly in appearance and behaviour".[25] Taking into account the "Seven principles of public life", as set out in the first report of the U.K. "Committee on Standards in Public Life",[26] and referring to Article 157—now Article 213 EC—relating to the requirements that members of the Commission must fulfil, the Committee identified the common core of "minimum standards". These were: acting in the general interest, in complete independence, with integrity and discretion, and with a sense of accountability, openness, and leadership.[27] More precisely, with regard to "mismanagement" the Committee regarded it to be proof of poor or failed management if the prac-

---

[22] First Report, point 1.1.4.

[23] Point 1.6.2, last sentence.

[24] *Ibid.*, second sentence.

[25] Point 1.5.1 and point 1.5.2 respectively.

[26] The Committee chaired at the time by Lord Nolan, now by Lord Neill of Bladen, was established in October 1994. Its terms of reference are: "To examine current concerns about standards of conduct of all holders of public office, including arrangements relating to financial and commercial activities, and make recommendations as to any changes in present arrangements which might be required to ensure the highest standards of propriety in public life". See further the first report presented by the Prime Minister to Parliament in May 1995, at 15 ff.

[27] Point 1.5.4. In the meantime similar, and even more specific, standards for public service have been elaborated at the supranational level, that is in the framework of the OECD, and adopted by its Council on 23 April 1998 under the title "Principles for Managing Ethics in the Public Service": http://www.oecd.org/pume/gvrnance/ethics/pubs/rec98.

tices and procedures applied by the Commission did not allow it, and its members, to deal properly with fraud, mismanagement and nepotism committed by officials working in the Commission, or by third parties working on behalf of, or under contract with, the Commission.[28]

In the light of these considerations the Committee concluded that it amounts to mismanagement for a member of the Commission, or for the Commission as a whole, not to react to the malfunctioning of a program (for which another Commissioner is directly responsible) at time when such malfunctioning is common knowledge within the Commission and its services. As a consequence all Commissioners were to be held collectively responsible for it. The Committee held more specifically, regarding one programme—the Leonardo da Vinci programme—"that the allegations raised . . . at an early stage of operation, and even before . . ., were so serious and illustrative of a dysfunctional organisational climate and structure that they should have been seen by those who were in charge. They are a demonstration of the weaknesses of the information channels and control mechanisms within the Commission, up to the highest level".[29] What made things worse is that the information about the malfunctioning of the private contractor in charge of the implementation of the programme, was not made available to Parliament when the latter had to take a decision on the successor programme (which was assigned to the same contractor).[30]

It is to be hoped for that the standards in public life set out in the Committee's first Report will, in the years to come, be further developed and applied not only to high officials of the Commission but also of the European Parliament and other European Institutions. To set up an independent committee on Standards in Public Life at the European level, modelled after its UK counterpart, might serve a double purpose. First, it would encourage the finding and shaping of proper standards through general recommendations but, secondly, also it could help determine them on a case to case basis, that is at the moment when advice was sought by high officials on the acceptability of one or another practice. Such incremental approach seems preferable to a purely regulatory approach whereby the Commission draws up a code of conduct for its own (and only for its own) members, and then leaves its application in concrete cases to its president. That approach should not prevent individual Community institutions or bodies to adopt special codes of conduct that are consistent with such independent committee's recommendations, with a view of adapting them to the characteristics of each institution.

It is also to be hoped for that the concept of collective responsibility will be fleshed out in a positive manner, encouraging Commissioners to intervene on all

---

[28] Point 1.6.1. The Committee referred in this respect to Article 195 (ex 138e) EC Treaty, establishing the Office of Ombudsman where the term "maladministration" is used and to the definition attached to this term in the Ombudsman's reports.

[29] First Report, at point 5.8.1.

[30] *Ibid.*, at point 5.6.1 ff.

matters in cabinet decisions (since they can all be held to account).[31] In the draft code of conduct for Commissioners prepared by the former Commission, the concept is defined in a purely negative way, in that "Commissioners shall not make any comment which would call into question a decision taken by the Commission".[32] Without further qualification, this might be read as an illustration of a "self-protective" mentality on the part of the Commission.

It follows from the Committee's findings that standards in public life relate not only to blameworthy personal behaviour of high officials for failing to act in complete independence and with integrity and discretion. They also relate to blameworthy functional and managerial behaviour, namely for not acting in the exercise of their function with a sense of accountability and openness[33] i.e. for not acting in accordance with principles of sound management, or for not exerting leadership. Since the entry into effect of the Amsterdam Treaty on 1 May 1999, it is stated in Article 219 (ex 163) EC that "The Commission shall work under the political guidance of its President". This provides a special responsibility for the President of the Commission to promote collective leadership on the part of the Commission as a whole.

COMMISSIONERS, THEIR DEPARTMENTS AND PRIVATE OFFICES, AND THE PRINCIPLE OF OPENNESS

In its first Report the Committee stressed the principles of openness, transparency and accountability for being "at the heart of democracy and . . . the very instruments allowing it to function properly".[34] It continued: "Openness and transparency imply that the decision-making process, at all levels, is as accessible and accountable as possible to the general public. It means that the reasons for decisions taken, or not taken, are known and that those taking decisions assume responsibility for them and are ready to accept the personal consequences when such decisions are subsequently shown to have been wrong".[35] The Committee found that the relationship between Commissioners and Directors-General did not always meet this standard. It stated that "the separation between political responsibility of Commissioners (for policy decisions) and the administrative responsibility of the director-general and the services (for the implementation of policy) should not be stretched too far".[36]

---

[31] The corollary of collective responsibility is that Commissioners who disagree with the course of policy adopted by the Commission as a whole, or who do no longer enjoy the confidence of their colleagues resign, and/or can be forced to resign.

[32] In that draft code, rules are fixed on outside activities, financial interests and assets, activities of spouses, missions, receptions, gifts. There are also a few rules on the composition of the private Offices of the Commissioners, and on collective responsibility (see further in the text).

[33] Article 1 (ex A) TEU provides that "decisions are (to be) taken as openly as possible and as closely as possible to the citizen".

[34] Point 9.3.3.

[35] Ibid.

[36] Point 9.3.4.

The draft code on Commissioners and Departments prepared by the (former) Commission may seem to part from different principles. After stating the obvious, *i.e.* that the "relations between Commissioners (their Offices) and departments shall be based first and foremost on loyalty and trust", the code emphasises that "Commissioners shall assume full political responsibility. Directors-General shall be answerable to their Commissioner for the sound implementation of the policy guidelines laid down by the Commission and the Commissioner". It would seem that the distinction between laying down "policy guidelines" and "their implementation" cannot be made as clearly as it is suggested. Moreover, emphasising the Commissioner's full political responsibility is misleading if it does not stress at the same time that Commissioners and the Directors-General bear joint responsibility for the implementation of policy and that the latter (as the draft code recognises) are to be associated closely to the laying down of policy guidelines by their Commissioner. The Committee's first Report underlines, correctly I believe, "that Commissioners must continuously seek to be informed about the acts and omissions of the directorates-general for which they bear responsibility and the Directors-General must keep their Commissioners informed of all major decisions they take or become aware of. This requirement of mutual information implies that Commissioners must be held to know what is going on in their services, at least at the level of the Director General, and should bear responsibility for it".[37]

Separating policy and implementation, as envisaged in the (former) Commission's proposed draft, may be correct insofar as it relates to one of the essential tasks of the Commission, i.e. its participation—together with the Council *and* the Parliament—in policy and law-making activities. It ignores, however, that the Commission is also, and in the first place, at the head of the Community's executive function. Feeling primarily responsible for the legislative part of their function may correspond with how Commissioners see themselves, but that only reflects half of their duties. They are also responsible for the implementation of approved policies and legislation, a task for which they are to bear joint responsibility with the heads of their departments.

Another matter of concern is the way in which the draft code views the tasks of the Commissioner's Private Office (or Cabinet). Not so much because it stresses, correctly it would seem, that the Commissioner's Cabinet shall help to ensure that the principle of collective responsibility operates correctly by keeping the Commissioner informed about matters outside his or her own area of competence. But, because it emphasises subsequently that it is for the Private Office to inform the departments about the Commission's proceedings and about decisions taken by the Commissioner and that the Office will "keep the Director-General fully informed about its contacts with the outside on matters falling within the portfolio". Also, because the draft code states that the private Office "shall take part in the major stages of policy formulation by consulting

---

[37] *Ibid.*

the departments on the priorities set. It shall ensure that priorities and pro-
gramming are complied with". A matter of concern in these statements is the
distance, which they seem to express between the Commissioner and his/her
department, including the Director-General, as well as the interference of the
Office with tasks, which are obviously those of a Director-General. Knowing
that the Private Office of a Commissioner is composed of persons he has chosen
personally on the basis of trust and loyalty,[38] it is not to be excluded that it will
function as a screen between the Commissioner and the Director-General.

Coming from a country where the private Office of cabinet ministers has seen
an exorbitant expansion, I happen to know that Private Offices may well be
counter-productive in that they give rise to a dual administration and result in
de-motivating the civil servants working in the Administration. To avoid this,
the tasks entrusted to Private Offices must consist only in assisting the
Commissioner in reading documents and preparing notes for the weekly
Commission meetings and, chiefly, keeping him or her informed on what is
going on in other departments, and on the outside. Taking part in the actual formulation of policy is not part of their task. In other words Private Offices should
be regarded merely as the personal emanation ("eyes, ears and mouth") of the
Commissioner concerned and should not be allowed to express their own opinions.

In the draft code further principles and rules are spelled out on the working
relations between the departments and their Commissioner and his or her Office
in respect of policy implementation and management of human resources. One
of the rules to be respected is that no cross contacts should be made between the
Office of one Commissioner, or the department for which he or she is responsible, and a department, or the Office, of another Commissioner. However, on
matters of horizontal importance, joint meetings of Directors-General and chefs
de cabinet *may* be held. All this may illustrate the hierarchically organised and
bureaucratically regulated structure of discussions carried on between officials
within the Commission. It is doubtful whether such compartmentalisation promotes constructive collegiality and collective responsibility.

RELATIONS BETWEEN COMMISSIONERS AND PARLIAMENT TO BE CHARACTERISED BY ACCOUNTABILITY AND RESPONSIBILITY

As indicated above, the underlying reason for the Commission's decision to
resign as a body, following the first Report of the Committee, was Parliament's
refusal to discharge the Commission for the implementation of the 1996 budget.
The motive for refusing that discharge was, in substance, Parliament's conviction that the Commission did not comply with its obligation, as laid down in
Article 276 (ex 206), para. 2, EC "to submit any necessary information to the

---

[38] If the members of the Private Office were to be entrusted with more "substantive" tasks, they
should at the least be selected on the basis of purely objective criteria of merit.

European Parliament at the latter's request". On the basis of this text Parliament claimed that it was not for the Commission, but for Parliament itself, to decide which documents it needed. At the end of the day, it could not agree with the Commission's practice, agreed earlier on between the two institutions with respect to one specific file, that the Commission would transmit the whole file but delete names and, as it later appeared, for reasons of confidentiality, allow many blank spaces which made the documents difficult to read and to understand. Although Parliament admitted that measures must be taken to preserve individual rights as well as the secrecy of judicial procedures, it wanted to lay down itself the rules under which documents were to be transmitted confidentially, but fully.[39]

As mentioned earlier, the issue of the Commission's obligation to account to Parliament came also to the fore, and in a wider context, during the Committee's investigation of the Leonardo da Vinci file. For it was then discovered that Parliament, at the time that it had to speak out on the successor programme, was not fully informed by the Commission of the irregularities having occurred in the management of the first programme.

The broad issue underlying these incidents concerns the constitutional relationship between the Commission, as head of the Executive, and Parliament, as part of the Community Legislator. Even although the European Parliament does not have (yet) the same legislative prerogatives as a national Parliament in any one of the Member States,[40] the issue of accountability arises substantially in the same terms. Here, again, much can be learned from the British situation where "the relationship between government and Parliament is a matter of profound constitutional concern".[41] Recent developments, as chronicled in the Scott report,[42] show that the questions which are at the centre of the constitutional debate concern the distinction between constitutional (or political) accountability of Ministers on the one hand, and their personal responsibility on the other. Sub-questions relate to the scope of the Ministers' obligation to inform Parliament, the sanctions for not complying with that obligation, and the

---

[39] See the EP's Working Document of 3 December 1998, quoted above, at n. 18. See also in the meantime the report of 8 March 1999, prepared by Mr. Giovanni for the EP's Committee on Institutional Affairs containing proposals of special confidentiality arrangements.

[40] But see the judgment of the ECHR of 18 February 1999, *Matthews* v. *UK*, concerning the interpretation of Article 3 of Protocol no. 1 of the European Convention Human Rights where the Strasbourg Court held that the European (Union's) Parliament "represents the principal form of democratic, political accountability in the Community system" and ". . . whatever its limitations . . . (deriving legitimation from the direct elections by universal suffrage) best reflects concerns as to 'effective political democracy'" (para 52 of the judgment).

[41] Tomkins, "Ministers and Parliament" in *The Constitution after Scott* (Clarendon Press, Oxford, 1998), at 25. On the role of the European Parliament in general and its place within the European Union's institutional set-up, see Delwit, De Waele and Magnette (eds.), *A quoi sert le Parlement européen?* in collection "Etudes européennes" (ULB), 1999, 231.

[42] *Report of the Inquiry into the Export of Defence equipment and Dual Use Goods to Iraq and related Prosecutions* by Sir Richard Scott, ordered by the House of Commons to be printed 15th February 1996.

distinction between policy and operational matters as a controversial guideline for delineating the ministerial responsibility to Parliament and the management responsibility of civil servants.[43] Thus far, the outcome of this constitutional debate is reflected, apparently with all party consent, in resolutions passed in both the House of Lords and the House of Commons, on principles which should govern the conduct of Ministers of the Crown in relation to Parliament.[44] The result thereof is that ministerial responsibility is no longer merely an unwritten constitutional convention. Nor is it any longer a matter to be decided by government but a matter for Parliament to rule upon.[45]

Taking advantage of the constitutional debate in the UK but also in other Member States,[46] and in the light of what has already been said, the following comments may be in order.

Accountability is the keyword to describe the relationship between Commission and Parliament. It consists of two complementary aspects to be characterised as the "obligation to give an account" and the "liability to be held to account".[47] The former obliges "the executive . . . to provide full information about and explain its actions in Parliament so that [it is] subject to proper democratic scrutiny".[48] It means that "ministers should give accurate and truthful information to Parliament, correcting any inadvertent error at the earliest opportunity. Ministers who knowingly mislead Parliament will be expected to offer their resignation to the Prime Minister" (thus the aforementioned resolution passed in the UK in both Houses of Parliament).[49] The latter specification is important as it underlines that the sanction for giving inaccurate information to Parliament is not always, or necessarily, resignation.

The second aspect of accountability, i.e. "liability to be held to account", refers in my understanding to the Minister's (or, in the present context, the Commissioner's) responsibility to Parliament, i.e. what has already been called the "political" responsibility to Parliament. That responsibility concerns the political consequence drawn by Parliament from wrongful (personal, functional, managerial) conduct on the part of the Minister or Commissioner him or herself, or on the part of civil servants for whom he/she bears (vicarious) responsibility. In other words, it would seem, that a distinction has to be made between personal, or functional or managerial responsibility of the Minister/Commissioner him or herself, and responsibility for behaviour of his/her civil servants. The first form of responsibility comprises responsibility for reprehen-

---

[43] For a full account on these, and other issues, see Tomkins, cited in n. 40.

[44] As quoted in Tomkins, *supra* n. 40, at 61–62.

[45] Tomkins, at 62.

[46] To cite only one example amongst many others, see the elaborated Dutch report "Steekhoudend ministerschap" of the Scheltema commission on the meaning and application of ministerial responsibility presented to the second chamber of the Dutch Parliament on 1 June 1993.

[47] Thus the *Public Service Committee* of the UK House of Commons in *Ministerial Accountability and Responsibility*, H.C. (1995–96), 313, quoted by Tomkins, *supra* n. 40, at 58.

[48] Tomkins, *ibid.*, at 58.

[49] *Ibid.*, at 62.

sible or blameworthy acts or omissions of the Commissioner (and his/her Private Office) in the exercise of his/her functions for failing to act with integrity and/or in accordance with principles of sound management in instructing, or omitting to instruct his/her civil servants, or in organising his/her departments to provide in the proper framework through which policies are delivered and resources are allocated. The second form of responsibility refers to responsibility regarding reprehensible or blameworthy acts or omissions of civil servants acting within the Minister's or Commissioner's sphere of competence, and for which he/she bears constitutional or political responsibility, even when he or she (or his/her Private Office) is not personally to be blamed for it. Whilst the latter form of responsibility should only exceptionally be censured at all (e.g. because of the impact on public opinion), the former must normally be censured in due course, but not necessarily by way of voluntary or imposed resignation. In other words lesser sanctions, such as a resolution for corrective action, or a resolution of disapproval or discontent, may in such instance be more commensurate with the action or omission concerned.

As discussed above, the (personal) responsibility, and the political consequence drawn from it by Parliament, may be a joined responsibility for which several Ministers, or Commissioners, or even the whole government, or Commission, may be held to account. In the case of the Commission, the situation under the present provisions of Article 201 (ex 144) EC is such that, when Parliament (by a two thirds majority of the votes cast representing a majority of its members) votes in favour of a motion of censure, "the Members of the Commission shall resign as a body. They shall continue to deal with the current business until they are replaced . . .". Obviously, collective dismissal, as incorporated in that Article, is not a very useful sanction in a case, like the one at issue in the Committee's first Report, where only one individual Commissioner is seriously blamed for mismanagement and favouritism. It would thus be helpful if a more proportionate political sanction (individual resignation or dismissal) were to be introduced in the Treaties at the occasion of the next Inter-Governmental Conference. But apart from that, it would have been constitutionally more correct if the Commission, following the publication of the Committee's report, had not imposed the sanction of collective resignation upon itself but had left it to Parliament to draw the political consequences of it, as prescribed in Article 201 EC.

Be that as it may, already under the present Treaty provisions nothing prevents Parliament to express its displeasure towards an individual Commissioner. Moreover, according to Declaration 32 attached to the Amsterdam Treaty amending the EC Treaty: "the President of the Commission must enjoy broad discretion in the allocation of tasks within the college, as well as in any reshuffling of those tasks during a Commission's term of office". That, along with a declaration of intent on the part of Commissioners when they accept office to resign voluntarily, at the request of the President of the Commission, were parliament to vote a resolution of discontent in the course of their term, goes a long way in sanctioning an individual Commissioner's political responsibility.[50]

CONCLUSION: NATIONAL CONSTITUTIONS TO BE TAKEN SERIOUSLY

As I had the occasion to stress on other occasions,[51] there is an urgent need for Community law, and Community Institutions creating it, to take stock, in a systematic way, of general principles and legal rules, which are part of the legal systems of the EU Member States. That is particularly true for the shaping of constitutional rules and traditions in areas of the law, so sensitive and significant for the public image of the European Union as the ones discussed herein. The role of the common law, and of Britain with its great constitutional traditions is, therefore, of crucial importance. It is to be hoped for (and not unlikely) that in its second Report the Committee will be able to make a further contribution to the shaping of such common constitutional rules.[52]

---

[50] In this respect, see the recommendations in chapter 7 of the Committee's second report at 14.19–7.14.22.

[51] See my contribution on extra-contractual liability of Member States and Community Institutions "Taking Article 215 (2) EC seriously" in J. Beatson and T. Tridimas, eds., *New Directions in European Public Law*, (Hart Publishing, Oxford, 1998) at 35 ff.

[52] In the meantime, it is clear that the second report will make such further contribution. See n. 5, above.

7

Common Principles of Corporate Governance in Europe?

KLAUS J. HOPT

INTRODUCTION: THE CONVERGENCE OF THE COMMON LAW AND THE CIVIL LAW IN THE FIELD OF CORPORATE AND CAPITAL MARKET LAW

The convergence of the common law and the civil law is an old dream—or nightmare—an outlook that depends less on which side of the Channel or the ocean the idea is held, and more on how international the outlook of the academic or practitioner is. Academics who have studied abroad or are even comparativists[1] look at this differently than those who are firmly and exclusively embedded in their own national law and its legal subtleties. The same is true for the practitioners both in the legal profession and the enterprises, though a growing number of them are exposed professionally to European law and to international legal issues.[2] Sometimes one has the impression of witnessing a battle in which the adversaries are labeled as "a-historic" and "unpatriotic" or else "backward-minded" or "outright provincial". This is by no means just a

---

[1] *Cf.* Markesinis, The Comparatist (or a Plea for a Broader Legal Education), *Yearbook of European Law* 15 (1995) 261. A great many of the German commercial and business law professors have studied in the USA. Whole fields of law, such as corporate law, antitrust, securities regulation, banking, and telecommunications, show the influences of this. It would be interesting to look into this fertilization in a more systematic way. See also the critical piece by Stiefel/Maxeiner, "Why Are U.S. Lawyers Not Learning from Comparative Law?" in Vogt (ed.), *The International Practice of Law, Liber Amicorum for Thomas Bär and Robert Karrer* (Basel, The Hague et al., 1997), 213.

[2] An indicator is the merger movement in the legal profession which goes across national borders and beyond mere strategic alliances to outright international mergers, most recently between large British and German law firms. This will not only change the professional scene, but will have a deep impact also on procedural and substantive law. This impact is already felt in areas like mergers and acquisitions and financial transactions, which are the domain of international practice and standards. It suffices to look at the German words of the trade, which are English—for example, share deal, asset deal, due diligence, Chinese walls, compliance, letter of intent, asset-backed securities, insider dealing, etc. *Cf.* also André, Cultural Hegemony: The Exportation of Anglo-Saxon Corporate Governance Ideologies to Germany, *Tulane L.Rev.* 73 (1998) 69. As to Switzerland, see the remarkable influence of American law as described by Böckli, "Osmosis of Anglo-Saxon Concepts in Swiss Business Law", in Vogt, *loc. cit.*, 9; same, Droit des marchés de capitaux—La vis se resserre, *SZW* 1995, 219 at 222: invasion des idées anglo-saxonnes. See also Wiegand, "The Reception of American Law in Europe", 39 *A.J.Comp.L.* 229 (1991) and same, "Americanization of Law: Reception or Convergence?" in Friedman/Scheiber (eds.), *Legal Culture and the Legal Profession* (Boulder, Oxford, 1996), 137.

difference of opinion; though it is seldom admitted, there are turfs to defend for which professional investment, knowledge, and language skill (or lack of it) count.

While a commercial or corporate lawyer may find this amusing, he or she is more interested in facts, and these facts differ considerably depending on the legal field one looks at. This is obvious for fields like family or inheritance law, which remain national domains untouched by European harmonization. But also in the law of goods, tangible—and even more so intangible—concepts of common law and civil law are very different. As an example, consider credit securities and compare the British floating charge and the German "Sicherungs-übereignung".[3] Still, international legal practice finds its way. In other fields, famous inimical brethren are, for example, Trust und Treuhand, the title of a well-known book by my colleague, Kötz, at the Max Planck Institute.[4] Yet as irreconcilable as both concepts seem to appear, there are parallel problems and developments.[5] In the field of corporate and capital law, things move quicker due to market forces and economic actors who are facing competition on a transnational level, but also because of political factors which further harmonization. This is also true for corporate governance, where there are strong trends towards the coming together of Anglo-Saxon and Continental law. These trends are not so much due to the European Union and its harmonization efforts, although some of the convergence can be attributed to this (infra III). What proves to be more important, thoroughgoing, and probably irreversible is market-driven approximation (infra I). As important as market forces are, though, there are still other forces such as tradition, history, and culture which have shaped and still determine the law. Modern theory calls this path-dependency[6] (infra II).

What is corporate governance? Although the concept is not yet very old, it is being discussed worldwide and with great controversy, and has already led to the production of a vast body of legal and interdisciplinary literature. Corporate governance relates to the internal organization and power structure of the firm; the functioning of the board of directors in the one-tier and the two-tier system; the ownership structure of the firm; and the interrelationships among management board, shareholders, and other stakeholders, in particular the company's

---

[3] Cf. von Wilmowsky, *Europäisches Kreditsicherungsrecht* (Ribuster, Tübingen, 1996); Röver, *Vergleichende Prinzipien dinglicher Sicherheiten* (München, 1999); Dalhuisen, "Security in Movable and Intangible Property, Finance Sales, Future Interests and Trust", in Hartkamp et al., *Towards a European Civil Code* (Nijmegen, 1994), 361; Drobnig, "Mobiliarsicherheiten—Vielfalt oder Einheit? Ein Vergleichender Generalbericht", in Kreuzer (ed.), *Mobiliarsicherheiten—Vielfalt oder Einheit?* (Baden-Baden, 1999), 9.

[4] Kötz, *Trust und Treuhand. Eine rechtsvergleichende Darstellung des anglo-amerikanischen trust und funktionsverwandter Institute des deutschen Rechts* (Göttingen, 1963). Cf. Helmholz/Zimmermann (eds.), *Itinera Fiduciae, Trust and Treuhand in Historical Perspective* (Berlin, 1998).

[5] Grundmann, "The Evolution of Trust and Treuhand in the 20th Century", in Helmholz/Zimmerman, *loc. cit.*, p. 469 at 492 *et seq.*

[6] Cf. Roe, "Chaos and Evolution in Law and Economics", *Harv.L.Rev.* 109 (1996) 641. See also Teubner, "Rechtsirritationen: Der Transfer von Rechtsnormen in rechtssoziologischer Sicht", in *Festschrift für Blankenburg* (Baden-Baden, 1998), 233.

workforce and its creditors.[7] Internal corporate governance, or insider control system, is commonly distinguished from external or outsider control system. The former concerns the forces working inside the corporation. The latter are external actors and the market forces, in particular the market on corporate control (takeovers), capital and labour markets, and, in Germany, the banks. Somewhere between inside and outside are disclosure and auditing, which hold this position because they take place inside the corporation but are effective on and addressed to the market. This article shows that, while corporate governance is a different mix of legal and other norms and institutions in various countries, common principles of corporate governance in Europe do appear.

While it would be challenging to develop this in a strictly comparative way,[8] this article focuses on German and European Union law and the influences of British law and corporate governance on them, rather than on the influences of the former on British law, which may be better perceived from the inside. In a way, therefore, this article should be considered as a kind of comparatist advance payment in the hope that a similar inquiry will soon be made in the reverse direction.

I. MARKET-DRIVEN APPROXIMATION OF CORPORATE GOVERNANCE
IN ANGLO-SAXON AND CONTINENTAL COUNTRIES, PARTICULARLY GERMANY

Internal Corporate Governance: One-Tier and Two-Tier Boards

The core of internal corporate governance is the board. Traditional wisdom is that there are two fundamentally different board systems, the one-tier and the two-tier board. The Anglo-Saxon and many other—in particular Southern European—countries have a one-tier board; Germany and some other Continental European countries (German-speaking as well as Northern European countries) have a two-tier board through which the tasks of management and supervision are split up by mandatory law and entrusted to two separate organs, the management board (Vorstand) and the supervisory board (Aufsichtsrat). The latter is elected by the shareholders and elects and dismisses the former.[9]

Much of the literature seems to be devoted to showing the advantage of one system over the other. Not so surprisingly, each evaluator's own system is usually found to be the one that is better, more logical, and certainly not to be

---

[7] Hopt/Prigge in Hopt/Kanda/Roe/Wymeersch/Prigge (eds.), *Comparative Corporate Governance—The State of the Art and Emerging Research* (Oxford, 1998), p. v; see also the selected bibliography, *idem* at 1201–1210.

[8] See, for example, Wymeersch, *A Status Report on Corporate Governance Rules and Practices in Some Continental European States, idem* at 1045.

[9] See Art. 76 *et seq.*, 95 *et seq.* of the German Stock Corporation Act 1965. *Cf.* Hopt, "The German Two-Tier Board (Aufsichtsrat), A German View on Corporate Governance", in Hopt/Wymeersch (eds.), *Comparative Corporate Governance, Essays and Materials* (Berlin/New York, 1997), 3.

given up. This shows also in practice. In Britain, the Hampel Report poll found that there is "overwhelming support in the UK for the unitary board, and virtually none for the two tier board".[10] On the other hand, the one-tier board model is "rejected by the majority of German business leaders as well as German academics".[11]

Upon closer inspection, the seemingly fundamental difference appears less marked. First, the two-tier model is mandated by German law only for stock corporations. Other companies, including the limited liability company (GmbH), are free to have a one-tier or a two-tier board, and—apart from labour codetermination, which is also mandatory in the GmbH and is considered to be tolerable for enterprises only under the two-tier system—nearly all GmbHs have just a management board under the direction of the general assembly of the associates. Reality counts: there are around 5,500 stock corporations versus more than 650,000 limited liability companies.

What is even more important is that in both German and Anglo-Saxon practice, the homogeneity of the board is split up. In the latter there is a clear movement towards independent outside directors who are part of the one-tier board but have special functions. In critical cases, management and control are divided.[12] Furthermore, the Cadbury Report has already recommended against having the same person as CEO and as chairman of the board.[13]

In addition, there is a certain approximation of the practical functioning of the one-tier and the two-tier board. In both countries there have been recent board reforms, though enacted in each country's different style. British board reform[14] has come about by the code movement, which finally led to the supercode of the stock exchange and is thereby binding on listed companies. German board reform has taken the form of a law.[15] Candidates for reform were, inter alia, more division between management and supervision, more transparency and reporting, installation or improvement of the company's system of internal control, more and better committee work, more outside advice, and more concentration on the job (limits to the number of board seats held by the same person in other companies). A reform that was not possible in Germany was the deregulation of the mandatory size of the board, which in large codetermined enterprises is 20 (in the coal and steel industry 21). This was due to the influence of the trade unions and the Federal Ministry of Labour, which held up the reform for more than half a year and finally had their way, although the Federal

[10] Hampel Report (Committee on Corporate Governance, Final Report, London, January 1998), Summary no. 10.

[11] Theisen, "Empirical Evidence and Economic Comments on Board Structure in Germany", in Hopt/Kanda/Roe/Wymeersch/Prigge, *loc.cit.*, 259 at 260.

[12] Windbichler, "Zur Trennung von Geschäftsführung und Kontrolle bei amerikanischen Großgesellschaften", ZGR 1985, 50.

[13] Cadbury Report, London 1992, 4.9 and the Code of Best Practice No. 1.2.

[14] *Cf.* Cheffins, *Company Law: Theory, Structure, and Operation* (Oxford, 1997), 602 *et seq.*

[15] So-called Law on Control and Transparency in the Corporate Sector (KonTraG) of 27.4.1998, BGBl I 786. A short summary of the reforms can be found in OECD Financial Markets Trends 71, November 1998, 21 *et seq.*

Ministry of Justice, which had prepared the draft law, and legal experts, comparativists, and business representatives all agreed that this would have been an important improvement to a better working body of supervision. Here and in other financial matters the Swiss are much more flexible and quicker to learn.[16]

The standards of conduct for the directors are also broadly similar. In particular, in German law like in American and English law the duty of care is determined by an evolving business judgement rule. As to the duty of loyalty, which was traditionally less developed in German corporate law, the courts and legal authors have become aware of the problem and are quickly elevating the requirements to international standards. Enforcement presents an acute difference not between English and German law, but between American and European law. While there is a clear tendency in German law towards more liability cases of directors both under stricter procedural law (minority rights to sue) and enforcement practice,[17] the number of cases and the amounts of claims and settlements are inordinately higher in the USA. In Germany and probably also in the United Kingdom it is common opinion that this is legally and socially undesirable and to be avoided.[18]

Problems and different outlooks on how to solve them remain. In particular, it is an open question how far the independence requirement for non-executive directors should go, or else how to find the right line between independence and expertise of the outside board members. In the German supervisory board, there is of course mandatory independence of management for all—not just for some—of the supervisory board members. This goes beyond the British requirements. On the other hand, the Cadbury Code of Best Practice already recommended that a majority of the non-executive directors should not only be independent of management but also "free from any business or other relationship which could materially interfere with the exercise of their independent judgement, apart from their fees and shareholding".[19] This is of course not the case for the typical German supervisory board member (of the shareholder side) who is appointed to the board precisely because of the banking, business, or

---

[16] *Cf.* Böckli, "Corporate Governance: The 'Cadbury Report' and the Swiss Board Concept of 1991", *SZW* [1996] 149 at 158: "The traditional large and unwieldy Swiss Board of Directors is being phased out".

[17] A recent study has counted 90 D & O insurance cases (corporation v. management) from 1886–1995, and 166 insurance cases (third party v. management); 1976–1985, 113 cases; 1986–1995, 206 cases; see Ihlas, *Organhaftung und Haftpflichtversicherung* (Berlin, 1997), 317 *et seq.* The most recent and comprehensive commentary on directors' liability can be found in Hopt/Wiedemann (eds.), *Großkommentar Aktiengesetz*, 4th edn., § 93 (Hopt) (Berlin, New York, 1999).

[18] *Cf.* the study on procedural law reform (associations' action and class action) by the Max-Planck-Institute for Foreign Private and Private International Law in Hamburg, which was commissioned by the Federal Ministry of Justice. The study is published in a more detailed book form: Basedow/Hopt/Kötz/Baetge (eds.), *Die Bündelung gleichgerichteter Interessen im Prozeß—Verbandsklage und Gruppenklage* (Tübingen, 1999); Miller, "Political Structure and Corporate Governance: Some Points of Contrast Between the United States and England", *Columbia Business Law Review* 1998, 51.

[19] Code of Best Practice No. 2.2.

other relationship he or his employer has with the corporation.[20] This leads to a further more fundamental distinction. In Germany, a widespread practice has developed not only of personal links between enterprises and their boards, but also of share crossholdings. Despite a number of restrictions, such as voting in case of reciprocal shareholdings, German law has not yet come to grips with this networking. Reform proposals are on the table, but they remain controversial. They reach from outright prohibitions,[21] in particular for banks, to smoother arrangements which would make use of legislative and judge-made rules on conflicts of interest. Some consider this to be the sensitive center of the German internal corporate governance problem. It is revealing that the American institutional investor CalPERS in its "Principles for Good Governance in Germany" considers this to be an important draw-back.[22]

External Corporate Governance: The Market for Corporate Control

An even more impressive example of the coming together of British and Continental European law is takeover regulation. This is not at all self-evident. As already mentioned above in the context of board reform, there are very different traditions of self-regulation in Great Britain and in other countries, particularly Germany. In Britain, takeover regulation is mainly self-regulatory by the Panel with its City Code on Takeovers and Mergers. After initial difficulties with this kind of self-regulation in the fifties and sixties, the City Code of 1968 and the obligatory bid requirement of 1972 with revisions of 1974 and 1976 proved to be a tool which the Panel was able to administer in a highly successful way. At least this is the impression abroad.[23]

In contrast, German experiences with this kind of self-regulation proved to be disappointing. The German Insider Trading Guidelines of 1970, which were administered by Insider Trading Inquiry Commissions at the various German stock exchanges, were severely criticized from the very beginning as being toothless and secretive and in the end aimed more at preventing legislation than honestly solving the problem. Under the impression of clear competitive disadvantages for the German stock exchanges and under the pressure of the European Insider Trading Directive of 1989, the Guidelines were replaced by a

---

[20] For data, see Korn/Ferry International, Board Meeting In Session, European Board of Directors' Study, London 1996; Prigge, "A Survey of German Corporate Governance", in Hopt/Kanda/Roe/Wymeersch/Prigge, *loc. cit.*, p. 943 at 955 *et seq.*

[21] F. ex. Italy has prohibited cross-shareholdings over 2 per cent in 1974, but has just introduced a provision that if a takeover bid is made this limit is not applicable any more. In France cross-holdings seem to have faded away.

[22] CalPERS, Intenational Corporate Governance, Germany Market Principles, II 7 B: Cross-Shareholding, 1999. CalPERS also advocates "a substantial number of independent directors", *idem.* II 6 A: Independent Directors.

[23] There are several well-researched theses in Germany on the British model, for example, Lüttmann, *Kontrollwechsel in Kapitalgesellschaften* (Baden-Baden, 1992); Krause, *Das obligatorische Übernahmeangebot* (Baden-Baden, 1995).

law.[24] The German Takeover Code of 1995, as revised in 1997 and administered by the Takeover Commission in Frankfurt, is more successful, but not successful enough. In February 1999, the Stock Exchange Experts Commission at the Federal Ministry of Finance, which was the father of this self-regulation, concluded that the Takeover Code had proven its worth in its practical application, but that the goal of its all-encompassing recognition by German industry had not been achieved.[25] Therefore, a takeover law is now generally deemed to be unavoidable, quite apart from the fate of the 13th European Directive. It remains to be seen whether, as in the case of insider dealing regulation, this takeover law will replace self-regulation completely or will leave self-regulation working in the shadow of the law, which in my opinion would have the advantages of flexibility and practical experience.[26]

In the substance of takeover regulation, the British model proved very attractive indeed. It is safe to say that it has developed into the standard all over the Continent. Modern takeover regulations, for example, in Spain, Portugal, Italy, Switzerland, Austria, Denmark, Sweden, Norway and Finland. are very much influenced by the British example.[27] So is the draft 13th European Directive on takeovers. While this is true for many principles of takeover regulation, such as information and disclosure, takeover procedure, conduct during the offer, partial offers, and competing offers, two more controversial points shall be stressed, namely the neutrality of the board and the mandatory bid. Both are dealt with in American law very differently from the British example and the Continental European laws which follow the latter.[28]

The neutrality principle says in the words of Rule 21 of the British Code that "(D)uring the course of an offer, or even before the date of the offer if the board of the offeree company has reason to believe that a bona fide offer might be imminent, the board must not, except in pursuance of a contract entered into earlier, without the approval of the shareholders in general meeting" engage in frustrating action such as issuing shares, selling, disposing or acquiring assets of a material amount or "enter(ing) into contracts otherwise than in the ordinary course of business". This neutrality principle has been taken up by nearly all

---

[24] This development is described by Hopt, "Auf dem Weg zum deutschen Insidergesetz—Die Vorüberlegungen vom Herbst 1992", *Festschrift für Beusch* (Berlin, 1993), 393.

[25] Börsensachverständigenkommission beim Bundesministerium der Finanzen, Standpunkte zur künftigen Regelung von Unternehmensübernahmen, Bonn, February 1999. More generally on the German experiences with self-regulation, see Hopt, "Self-Regulation in Banking and Finance—Practice and Theory in Germany", in *La Déontologie bancaire et financière/The Ethical Standards in Banking & Finance* (Brussels, 1998), 53.

[26] Hopt, "Europäisches und deutsches Übernahmerecht", *ZHR* 161 (1997) 368 at 407 *et seq.*

[27] For comparative law, see Hopt/Wymeersch (eds.), *European Takeovers—Law and Practice* (London, 1992); Kozyris (ed.), *Corporate Takeovers Through the Public Markets* (The Hague, 1996); Wymeersch et al., The Proposal for a 13th Company Law Directive on Takeovers: A Multi-jurisdiction Survey, *European Financial Services Law* 3 (1996) 301, 4 (1997) 2.

[28] As to American takeover law, see Gilson, *The Law and Finance of Corporate Acquisitions* (New York, 1986) with supplement; Auerbach (ed.), *Corporate Takeovers: Causes and Consequences* (Chicago, 1988); Romano, "A Guide to Takeovers: Theory, Evidence and Regulation", in Hopt/Wymeersch, *loc.cit.*, 3; Lüttmann, loc. cit., 83 *et seq.*

Continental European countries which have enacted laws or codes on takeovers. In Germany this took some time. In 1993 the issue was still the subject of controversial debate during a meeting of the leading German general counsels and law professors. The majority still thought that it was up to the management board to take all measures necessary in case of a hostile takeover in order to keep harm away from the company. The concepts of full competence for management (section 76 of the German Stock Corporation Act)[29] and of shareholder sovereignty stood in opposition to one another. Finally, however, the view of the management board as trustee for the shareholders and of section 76 as but an emanation of general civil law rules on the mandate with its principle of sovereignty of the mandator carried the day. In 1995 the new German Takeover Code expressly adopted the neutrality principle, and it is virtually a certainty that the future German Takeover Law will do the same.[30] This is not to say that in Europe the problem of defenses against hostile takeovers has been solved; Gucci would not have been successful in fighting off the recent hostile bid if it had not chosen to incorporate in the Netherlands. There will be more work to do for the European Union.[31]

The mandatory bid is a feat of British self-regulatory takeover law. The essence of the mandatory bid is a right for all shareholders to sell their shares to the bidder for full consideration. They are thereby able to leave the corporation before the possible dangers resulting from the control of the bidder are felt, and they need not rely on group law provisions which may or may not protect them later on when the bidder has taken and exercised control in his own interest or in the interest of the group of companies which he is running. I shall come back to this issue later on when we deal with group law. Here it suffices to say that the mandatory bid requirement has swept all over Continental European takeover laws and codes. Despite the fact that Germany has a far-reaching group law, the German Takeover Code of 1995 has at its core a mandatory bid requirement, and such a rule will certainly also be part of the coming German Takeover Law. Even Sweden, where the mandatory bid was rejected by the Swedish Company Law Committee in 1995 with remarkable economic and country-specific arguments,[32] adopted the mandatory bid rule in 1999.[33] The reason for this, however, seems to have been not so much care for the minority shareholders at large, but rather the more subtle thought of the leading industrialist family in Sweden which, in a world of globalization and threats of hos-

---

[29] Section 76 subsection 1 of the Aktiengesetz 1965 reads: "The managing board is charged with the personal responsibility of directing the company."

[30] *Cf.* Hopt, Aktionärskreis und Vorstandsneutralität, ZGR 1993, 534 with further references; Article 19 of the German Takeover Code reads: "Following publication of a public tender offer . . . the executive or managing body of the target company, including the executive or managing bodies of the related companies of the target company, may not take any measures that run counter to the interest of the holders of securities in taking advantage of the tender offer."

[31] See infra III 2 at the end.

[32] Skog, *Does Sweden Need a Mandatory Bid Rule? A Critical Analysis* (Stockholm, 1995).

[33] The 1999 Swedish Takeover Recommendations: NBK Recommendations concerning public offers for the acquisitions and transfers of shares etc, Stockholm 1999.

tile takeovers by foreigners, might feel better off with a mandatory bid rule: such a rule makes bids more difficult because the bidder has to come up with more capital, but if he does, even large minority shareholders can walk away under better conditions. This may also have been the reason why some major Swedish stock corporations, like for example Nokia, have inserted a mandatory bid rule in their articles of incorporation even before the 1999 recommendations.

Apparently there is again a great difference between European law, including British law, and American law. Apart from a number of states which have adopted so-called control share acquisition statutes,[34] American corporate law (which is state law) allows the board of directors to fight off hostile takeovers. Similarly there is no general requirement of a mandatory bid to all shareholders of the target. At first glance this is surprising because American corporate and securities law has long been very far-reaching with much influence on other countries. The very movement of shareholder value originated in the USA and swept from there over Europe. Yet things are more complicated. It is true that the American board has a crucial role in taking stands in case of a hostile takeover bid. But it is vital to see that the board can act only as a fiduciary of the shareholders. These strong fiduciary duties are upheld by the American courts[35] under a procedural law which, as mentioned before, is extremely plaintiff-friendly. If one takes into account this pivotal role of American procedural law and courts, then it is clear that American takeover rules would have a very different effect in European states. What appears to be a great difference in law may be much less different in fact.

Similar problems exist with the mandatory bid, which is not common in the USA. But if one looks at the takeover practice it is said that as many as 95 per cent of all bids are for all shares and today most US bidders agree on a non-premium bid. As to remaining differences it must not be forgotten that in a country with many more public corporations (i.e., corporations without controlling or even major stockholders) and with very developed securities markets, the shareholders are much less likely to be locked into a stock corporation in which the bidder takes over control. In Continental Europe, in contrast, where stock ownership is much more concentrated and securities markets are more narrow and less deep, the minority shareholders are better protected by a mandatory exit right opened up by a mandatory bid. The corresponding effect, of course, as stated before, is that the hurdle a bidder must surmount is higher and the chances for the old, possibly inefficient, management to remain in office are better. But there is a natural tradeoff between two principal/agent problems: the one between the shareholders and the board—this is the emphasis of American law and American economic and legal theory—and between the minority shareholders and the bidder, i.e., the possible future majority shareholder.

---

[34] For details, see Lüttmann, *loc.cit.*, 90 *et seq.*
[35] *Cf.* Sullivan/Conlon, Crisis and Transition in Corporate Governance Paradigms: The Role of the Chancery Court of Delaware, *Law & Society Rev.* 31 (1997) 713; Miller, *loc cit.*, at p. 54 *et seq.*

Corporate Governance between Inside and Outside: Disclosure, Auditing, and Intermediation

Disclosure is a regulatory instrument which is nowadays used nearly everywhere in commercial and corporate law and, in particular, in corporate governance. Of course there is a host of detailed disclosure regulation that differs from one country to another. It suffices to say that even the 4th European Directive, which has striven to harmonize the law of accounting and balance sheets of the corporation, contains no less than 40 options for the Member States. This is quite apart from all the hidden regulatory and interpretative differences, and from all those points which openly have not been harmonized at all.[36] In particular, the true and fair view principle, which is the overriding principle of British balance sheet law, though embodied as a general principle into the 4th Directive, has been "uncoupled" in the transformation laws of some Member States such as Germany.[37]

Furthermore, there are deep-rooted patterns of behaviour that are not easy to change. Many German corporations still have the practice of trying to stick to the same dividends each year in the short-sighted belief that this is needed to maintain continuity and keep confidence. This, of course, is incompatible with the shareholder value concept. Hidden reserves continue to play a prominent role in the balance sheets of German banks and insurance companies, and it is a fact for all enterprises that as far as the 4th Directive allows, German balance sheet law is creditor-friendly, not shareholder-friendly. This is the greatest difference as compared with American law and the US GAAP.

Yet what is really remarkable is not so much these traditional differences, but the extent to which globalization, and more specifically the attractions of the US American capital markets and the access to them via the New York Stock exchange, have brought about changes. The large German enterprises aiming in this direction had first tried jointly to obtain exemptions from the US GAAP when seeking listing at the NYSE. But these efforts failed spectacularly when Daimler-Benz unilaterally left this coalition and, in order to be the first German enterprise to be listed at the NYSE, gave in completely to American demands.[38]

---

[36] *Cf.* Ernst & Whinney, *The Fourth Directive, Its Effect on the Annual Accounts of Companies in the European Economic Community* (London, 1979); Albach/Klein (eds.), *Harmonisierung der Rechnungslegung in Europa* (Wiesbaden, 1988).

[37] *Cf.* Schön, "Entwicklung und Perspektiven des Handelsbilanzrechts", *ZHR* 161 (1997) 133 at 152 *et seq.* See also the critique by van Hulle (charged with corporate law and accounting at DG XV of the European Commission), Das Europäische Bilanzrecht—Entwicklungen und Herausforderungen, *Schriftenreihe des Zentrum für Europäisches Wirtschaftsrecht der Universität Bonn*, No. 34, Bonn [1994], 5 *et seq.*; same, "True and Fair View", im Sinne der 4. Richtlinie, Festschrift für Budde (München, 1995), 313 at 318.

[38] See the report by Bruns (Daimler-Benz), "Der Gang an die New York Stock Exchange: Das Beispiel der Daimler-Benz AG", *Wirtschaftsprüferkammer-Mitteilungen* (*WPK-Mitt*), *Sonderheft* Juni 1997, 31.

Other major German corporations had no other choice but to follow this path, albeit with a scowl at Daimler-Benz. The consequence was the need to prepare two different balance sheets, one complying with German (and harmonized European) accounting law, one with American GAAP. This was time-consuming, expensive, and potentially misleading for German investors. Accordingly, industry leaders exercised pressure on German legislators to achieve freedom of choice between the traditional German standards and "internationally recognized balance sheet principles", at least when preparing group accounts. This was aimed in particular at the option of using International Accounting Standards (IAS). German legislators gave in in 1998 in order to facilitate capital raising by German enterprises, but they limited this option until 2004 in the hope that by then there would be a breakthrough in the international harmonization of balance sheet law.[39] Meanwhile, the European Union is working hard not to be left behind. While it has been made clear that departures from the 7th Directive will not be acceptable,[40] the Commission announced a new strategy concerning international accounting harmonization[41] and has begun the process of reforming European accounting law.[42] In the meantime, the accounting profession and its national and international bodies, together with accounting economists and lawyers, are in the middle of comparing US GAAP, IAS, and national accounting standards in view of reaching harmonization from the bottom up and a German Accounting Standards Committee has begun its work similarly to the International Accounting Standards Committee.[43]

It has been said that accounting and balance sheets are only as good as their certification. While this may be an exaggeration, it is certainly true that in the market, and particularly in the international market, certification by auditors is a must. The 4th and 8th European Directives have already achieved some harmonization as to auditing and auditors. But the legal requirements for auditors in the European Union are still very different. This is true also as to the independence of the auditor, a point on which the 8th Directive has not brought much clarity and progress. In its 1996 Green Book on "The Role, the Position and the Liability of the Statutory Auditor within the European Union", the

---

[39] Kapitalaufnahmeerleichterungsgesetz—KapAEG of 20.4.1998, *Federal Gazette* 1998 I 707. Section 292 a subsection 2 No 2 b makes clear that the balance sheet must not depart from the 7th European Directive.

[40] No. 61 of the Mitteilung der Kommission zu Auslegungsfragen im Hinblick auf bestimmte Artikel der Vierten und der Siebenten Richtlinie des Rates auf dem Gebiet der Rechnungslegung, O.J.E.C. 20.1.1998 C 16/5.

[41] Mitteilung der Kommission, Harmonisierung auf dem Gebiet der Rechnungslegung: Eine neue Strategie im Hinblick auf die internationale Harmonisierung, 14.11.1995, KOM(95) 508 endg. See the comments by von Hulle, "International Harmonisation of Accounting Principles: A European Perspective", *Wirtschaftsprüferkammer-Mitteilungen* (*WPK-Mitt*), *Sonderheft* Juni 1997, 44.

[42] See, for example, European Commission, DG XV, Proposal for amending Directive 78/660/EEC on annual accounts as regards the use of the fair value method, Brussels 19.6.1998.

[43] *Cf.* Schön, *loc. cit.*, 154 *et seq.*; Born, *Rechnungslegung international* (Stuttgart, 1997); Ballwieser (ed.), *US-amerikanische Rechnungslegung* (3rd edn., Stuttgart, 1998), each with further references; Ebke, "Der Deutsche Standardisierungsrat und das Deutsche Rechnungslegungs Standards Committee . . .", *ZIP* 1999, 1193.

Commission came up with new ideas.[44] It is significant to see that in this paper, the Commission relied, inter alia, on the Cadbury Report and on other reports and codes concerning corporate governance.

In the meantime, some Member States have taken the lead and have started to integrate the auditors into their corporate governance system much more intensively. It is clear that these reforms were driven by the desire to keep up with international competition. In Germany, for example, the aforementioned board reform of 1997 extended the role of the statutory auditor considerably by making him a corporate governance partner of the supervisory board.[45] While he still is elected by the general assembly of shareholders, it is no longer the management board but the supervisory board which concludes the contract with the auditor and to whom he reports, and the auditor is required to attend the meetings of the supervisory board or of its financial audit committees held to approve the annual accounts.[46] The tasks of the auditors encompass now, inter alia:[47]

—auditing the report of the management board on the risk of future business development which is to be contained in the management report (Lagebericht), and
—organizing the audit in such a way that errors and violations against law, company statute, and by-laws which may have material effects on the true and fair view of the assets, finance, and profit situation of the corporation will be discovered.

This goes together with a clearer formulation of the auditing report and more nuanced formulas for the certification of the financial statements, with stiffer requirements of independence (namely incompatibility if the auditor has received more than 30 percent of his income in the last 5 years from a specific company) and with a (modest) modernization of professional liability.

Among the reform proposals which German legislators did not dare to touch are the merits of a rotation requirement for auditing firms (not just of individual members of the firm)[48] and of liability of the auditor towards third parties.[49]

---

[44] European Commission, Green Book, 2.10.1996, O.J.E.C. 28.10.1996 C 321/01; Hommelhoff, "Europäisches Bilanzrecht im Aufbruch", *RabelsZ* 62 (1998) 381.

[45] *Cf.* Hommelhoff, *Die neue Position des Abschlußprüfers im Kraftfeld der aktienrechtlichen Organisationsverfassung* (Teil I, II) (BB, 1998), 2567, 2625; Mattheus, Die gewandelte Rolle des Wirtschaftsprüfers als Partner des Aufsichtsrats nach dem KonTraG, *ZGR* 1999, 682.

[46] Section 111 subsection 2 of the Stock Corporation Act; section 321 subsection 5 of the Commercial Code; section 171 subsection 1 of the Stock Corporation Act.

[47] See sections 289, 317, 321, 322, 319 subsection 2 No 8 and 323 of the Commercial Code.

[48] See section 319 subsection 3 No. 6 of the Commercial Code: rotation of the individual auditor after having audited 6 annual reports during the last 10 years. *Cf.* a similar proposal made by the Cadbury Report, 5.12: no compulsory rotation of audit firms, but periodic change of audit partners in the case of listed companies.

[49] Pro, for example, Ekkenga, *Die Fahrlässigkeitshaftung des Jahresabschlußprüfers für Insolvenzschäden*, Dritter, WM Sonderbeilage 3/1996; contra, for example, Ebke/Struckmeier, "The Civil Liability of Corporate Auditors: An International Perspective", in *Capital Markets Forum, International Bar Association* (London, 1994). As to the similar controversy in Great Britain *cf.* Cadbury Report, 5.31 *et seq.* and Appendix 6 on *Caparo Industries plc* v. *Dickman and Others* (1990) 1 All ER 568.

Both are extremely controversial from both economic and legal standpoints. It remains to be seen whether the trust placed in the auditing profession by the legislator will prove to be well-founded. The misperformance of leading auditing firms in the scandalous case of the Bayerische Hypotheken- und Wechselbank in 1998 and the thunderous failure of the building enterprise Holzmann (in which the Deutsche Bank held a major participation) in November 1999 may dampen hopes—or induce the profession to do some rethinking

Let me finish this part on market-driven approximation of corporate governance in Anglo-Saxon and Continental countries with a few words on intermediation. Intermediation is usually seen as the function of going between two partners in the market who otherwise would have difficulties in coming together. Yet intermediation also has another function, namely improving information, helping with advice, and even protecting the one side from the other by the professional or legal standards of the intermediator. While there is a clear trend in financial transactions to cut back in bank intermediation business (disintermediation and securitization), there seems to be the inverse trend as to the second function. This is also true in corporate governance. One example which has just been mentioned are the auditors who are entrusted by law with the task of helping the board in its supervisory tasks. Another example is the financial intermediaries, such as banks, which are getting more and more burdened with duties to inform, to warn, and to give advice[50]—a development which may also be seen in the light of a contribution to improve corporate governance from the transaction or market side.

I shall mention here another example, namely the rules on independent advice to be taken during a takeover bid. Rule 3 of the British City Code requires the board of the offeree company to obtain competent independent advice on any offer and the substance of such advice must be made known to the shareholders. Similarly, the board of an offeror must obtain competent independent advice on any offer when the offer being made is a reverse takeover or when the directors are faced with a conflict of interest; again the substance of such advice must be made known to its shareholders. The first draft of the 13th Directive contained a similar requirement—but only for the board of the target—namely obtaining a report by an independent expert in cases in which the offered consideration comprises non-listed securities. This was dropped in later drafts during the process of slimming down the 13th Directive in order to reach a compromise limited to the essentials of takeover regulation. Yet even without a European law provision, it seems fair to say that such a duty to obtain competent independent advice may already result from general legal principles on the duty of care and the duty of loyalty of the board members. The Cadbury Code of Best Practice holds in No. 1.5 that there should be an agreed procedure for

---

[50] *Cf.* the critical comment by Breen Haire, "The Fiduciary Responsibilities of Investment Bankers in Change-of-Control Transactions: In re Daisy Systems Corp.", 74 *N.Y.U.L.Rev.*, 277 (1999).

directors in the furtherance of their duties to take independent professional advice if necessary, at the company's expense. This may very well be the direction in which the corporate law of Germany and some other Member States will develop even beyond mere takeover situations.

Many differences, some fundamental, still remain between the corporate governance of Anglo-Saxon and Continental European countries. Without going into much detail, I should like to take three examples. Each of these examples not only presents many legal problems, but it is embedded in the particular country's tradition, history, and culture, thus making it more difficult to describe and explain. For this reason, in Part II the outlook shall be narrowed down to path-dependent differences in corporate governance between Great Britain and Germany.

Labour Codetermination vs. Shareholder Value?

The most obvious difference in internal corporate governance between Great Britain and Germany is labour codetermination on German corporate boards. Is this opposed to the British (and American) idea of shareholder value? The answer should start with a glimpse at the old, detailed German discussion of the aims of the stock corporation and the duties of the management board towards shareholders as well as other stakeholders. This discussion has been carried on in Germany as well as in Great Britain.[51] The traditional German view, which is clearly the majority view, holds that the aims of the corporation include the interest of the shareholders (for example, voting rights, dividend rules, minority rights, shareholder suits, etc.), the interest of the creditors (for example, minimum capital and relating rules), and, as a separate category of the latter, the interest of the employees of the corporation. Unlike under the Stock Corporation Act of 1937,[52] the public interest, i.e., interest of the people

---

[51] Cf. Lord Wedderburn of Charlton, "The Legal Development of Corporate Responsibility, For Whom Will Corporate Managers Be Trustees?" in Hopt/Teubner (eds.), *Corporate Governance and Directors' Liabilities* (Berlin/New York, 1985), 3; Deakin/Hughes (eds.), *Enterprise and Community: New Directions in Corporate Governance* (Cambridge, 1997).

[52] Section 70 subsection 1 of the Stock Corporation Act of 1937 said: "The management board is charged with the personal responsibility of directing the corporation in such a way as required by the welfare of the enterprise and its workforce and the common benefit of the people and the Reich." Despite this wording, which was the language of the Third Reich, the content of the provision was not Nazi, but corresponded to a much longer tradition. See Riechers, *Das Unternehmen 'an sich'* (Tübingen, 1966), 166 *et seq.*, 191; see for example the explanations of the 1930 Draft for a reform of the Stock Corporation Act: "shareholders have to acknowledge that the modern stock corporation is not only for the individual pursuit of profit but it also has to serve to varying degrees the general interests of the people", quoted by Riechers, p. 102. As to the Stock Corporation Act of 1997 *cf.* Mann, "The New German Company Law and Its Background", 19 *J. of Comparative Legislation and International Law* 220 (1937). See also Spindler, Recht und Konzern, *Interdependenzen der*

and the state, is no longer part of the aims of the corporation. Yet this discussion need not be restated here in detail, for despite its theoretical pomp, its practical relevance is small. Not only is it restricted to stock corporations (while the limited liability company is clearly steered by the partners themselves who can give detailed instructions to their manager), but the medium-term interest of the shareholders together with the business judgment rule cover nearly all activities of the board in favour of the employees, and even many public activities of the corporate good citizen, such as donations, the creation of a foundation, and environmental measures. It is true that this stakeholder interest provision holds a clear danger that, under the cover of stakeholder interest, the management board could pursue its own interest, for example, in the course of a hostile takeover. Yet this is a well-known problem that we know also from the stakeholder statutes of a number of US American states. Of course, as in many other states, the concept of shareholder value has also been more recently discussed in Germany.[53] But this discussion has also been carried on at a rather theoretical level, and it has not changed the above-mentioned view on the aims of the corporation and the rights and duties of the board under the current law.

On the contrary, eminent practical differences between British and German law as to stakeholder interest appear under boardroom codetermination. The content and the consequences of this form of labour codetermination have been described elsewhere.[54] Therefore, a few words suffice. First of all, this boardroom

---

Rechts- und Unternehmensentwicklung in Deutschland und den USA zwischen 1870 und 1933 (Tübingen, 1993).

[53] For example, Mülbert, Shareholder Value aus rechtlicher Sicht, *ZGR* 1997, 129; Busse von Colbe, Was ist und was bedeutet Shareholder Value aus betriebswirtschaftlicher Sicht, *ZGR* 1997, 271; R.H. Schmidt/Spindler, *Shareholder-Value zwischen Ökonomie und Recht, Freundesgabe für Kübler* (Heidelberg, 1997), 515; F.W. Wagner, "Shareholder Value: Eine neue Runde im Konflikt zwischen Kapitalmarkt und Unternehmensinteresse", *BFuP* 49 (1997) 473; Brühner/Tuschel, "Zur Kritik am Shareholder Value—eine ökonomische Analyse", *BFuP* 49 (1997) 499; Hachmeister, "Shareholder Value", *Die Betriebswirtschaft* 57 (1997) 823; Kübler, "Shareholder Value: Eine Herausforderung für das Deutsche Recht?" in *Festschrift für Zöllner* (Cologne, 1998), p. 321; Drukarczyk, *Shareholder Value*, Conference held at the European Business School, Schloß Reichartshausen, 13.4.1999.

[54] *Cf.*, for example, Hopt, "Labour Representation on Corporate Boards: Impacts and Problems for Corporate Governance and Economic Integration in Europe", 14 *International Review of Law and Economics* 203 (1994); same, "Arbeitnehmervertretung im Aufsichtsrat—Auswirkungen der Mitbstimmung auf corporate governance und wirtschaftliche Integration in Europa", *Festschrift für Everling* (Baden-Baden, 1995), 235; Raiser, *Bewährung des Mitbestimmungsgesetzes nach zwanzig Jahren? Freundesgabe für Kübler* (Heidelberg, 1997), 477; Roe, "German Codetermination and German Securities Markets", *Columbia Business Law Review* 1 (1998) 167; Bainbridge, "Privately Ordered Participatory Management: An Organizational Failures Analysis", 23 *Del.J.Corp.L.* 979 (1998); Bertelsmann-Stiftung/Hans-Böckler-Stiftung (eds.), *Mitbestimmung und neue Unternehmenskulturen—Bilanz und Perspektiven* (Bericht der Kommission Mitbestimmung, Gütersloh, 1998); Gerum, *Mitbestimmung und Corporate Governance* (Gütersloh, 1998); Kübler, "Aufsichtsratsmitbestimmung im Gegenwind der Globalisierung", in Kübler/Scherer/ Treeck (eds.), *The International Lawyer, Freundesgabe für Döser* (Baden-Baden, 1999), 237; Oetker, "Mitbestimmungsgesetze", in Hopt/Wiedemann (eds.), *Großkommentar zum Aktiengesetz* (Berlin/New York, 1999); Endres (former member of the board of Deutsche Bank), "Organisation der Unternehmensleitung aus der Sicht der Praxis", *ZHR* 163 (1999) 441 at 454 *et seq.*

co-determination, which comprises all kind of decisions of the supervisory board, must be clearly distinguished from the codetermination of the works council at the plant level under the Works Council Statute of 1988, which extends only to conditions of labour. Second, there are three different systems of boardroom codetermination with the following characteristics: (1) full-parity codetermination: only coal and steel, only stock corporations, and limited liability companies, more than 1,000 employees, boards up to 21 members; (2) quasi-parity codetermination under the Codetermination Law of 1976: stock corporations, limited liability companies, and some other company forms, more than 2,000 employees, boards up to 20 members; and (3) the general one-third labour codetermination: stock corporations, limited liability companies, and other company forms, more than 500 employees, board up to 21 members. To all these forms there exist various exemptions, inter alia, for partnerships and for media-, church-, union-, and politics-related companies.

German business seems to have adjusted quite well to labour codetermination. Of course, as always, there are advantages and disadvantages. Counted among the advantages are better integration and motivation of the workforce and their leaders and better and quicker execution of decisions that have been approved by the codetermined supervisory board. In particular, it is said that in difficult times, having labour representatives as members of the board helps to make unpopular but unavoidable decisions, including layoffs and rescue operations. It is reported from some Eastern German enterprises that labour codetermination helped considerably in coping with the enormous difficulties of adaptation. Disadvantages are, inter alia, a marked slow-down of the decision-making process, a generally observed fractionalization of the board into the shareholder and the labour side, undeniable problems for board secrecy, and, as a result, hesitation by the management board in informing the normal members of the supervisory board about sensitive issues at an early stage. The conclusion of the merger between the management board of Daimler-Benz and the Chrysler board is a good example: the supervisory board of Daimler-Benz, whose consent was needed as a matter of law, was informed only when the deal was fully negotiated. Yet Daimler-Chrysler is also an example of a transnational merger in which the German labour codetermination system was fully maintained and (at least verbally) has been praised by Schremp as an asset for the merged corporation. On the other side, there is the example of the Hoechst/Rhône-Poulenc merger in which it was decided to have the holding in Strasbourg/France, resulting in not having labour codetermination at the holding level. The merger report contains a brief provision according to which the management board of Hoechst will endeavor to get the consent of the management board of Aventis for creating a committee that contains representatives of both the management board of Aventis and Hoechst as well as representatives of labour. This committee shall inquire into whether codetermination of labour in the board of Aventis on a voluntary basis will be feasible.

On the whole it is fair to say that outside of Germany and the Netherlands, transnational enterprises shy away from (voluntary) boardroom codetermination. This is why Dutch law, when introducing its far-reaching labour codetermination system in 1973, made sure to grant certain exemptions to Dutch transnational enterprises.[55] German experience also shows that normal employee representatives and union members on the board do show a rather different outlook and behaviour in the codetermined supervisory boards. Nevertheless, labour codetermination works quite well in Germany because in principle the trade unions are upholding the system. Indeed, labour codetermination was introduced after World War I and extended after World War II when it was vital for capital and labour to work together in reconstructing the destroyed country. This is a very good example of path dependency, and may be fundamentally different in a number of other countries that have trade unions which still live and act in the old Communist tradition. In any case, labour codetermination has for many decades now been the major stumbling block for European company law and has held up the Statute of a European Stock Corporation and the 5th, 11th, and 14th Directives. As recently as 1999, Spain vetoed the enactment of a long- and well-prepared European compromise on the European Stock Corporation, allegedly because of the minimum labour codetermination rules in the draft which it still considered to be too harmful to the Spanish business and labour environment.

Universal Banks vs. Capital Markets?

Another far-reaching difference between Great Britain and Germany is the different role played by universal banks and capital markets. It is well known that in Germany the capital markets developed much slower than in Great Britain. This has important consequences for corporate governance since the disciplining forces of the capital market and, as mentioned above, particularly those of the market of corporate control, are less effective than in Great Britain. Part of the financing functions that elsewhere are exercised by the capital markets are exercised in Germany by the universal banks. The universal banking system in Germany is characterized by letting banks combine both the credit business and the investment business. There is no legally mandated separation between both kinds of banks and banking business such as that which exists most obviously in the USA under the Glass-Steagall system, a system that has been under attack in the United States for decades but has prevailed until autumn 1999 when the long-expected reform was finally embarked upon. In Germany there has been much ado about the "power of the German universal banks". This fear is an old

---

[55] See Hopt, Grundprobleme der Mitbestimmung in Europa, *ZfA* 1982, 207 at 233 *et seq.*; Dorresteijn, "Corporate Governance Issues in the Netherlands, The Legal Structure for Large Companies", in Wymeersch (ed.), *Further Perspectives in Financial Integration in Europe* (Berlin/New York, 1994), 209.

one and from time to time has led to public attempts to curb bank power in one way or another. In the international corporate governance discussion, the influence of the banks is also considered to be characteristic of German corporate governance. German universal banks, it is said, stabilize management to the detriment of the shareholders and are one of the reasons why the German capital markets have developed more slowly than in other countries, in particular the USA and Great Britain.[56]

There is some truth in this, though also some exaggeration. This has been discussed in more detail elsewhere.[57] It suffices here to say that German universal banks do indeed enjoy four important sources of influence on the corporations which, in conjunction, give them more leverage than banks and financial institutions in Great Britain and many other countries. Apart from the credit business links that allow the credit-giving bank deep insights into the credit-taking corporation, there is an old and intensive pattern of German universal banks holding major participations in key industrial enterprises. In 1994, the 10 largest private banks held a total of 135 participations with over 5 percent of the shares of the respective corporations. 30 of these participations were in listed companies. Furthermore, the German universal banks hold many directorships in large German corporations. According to a poll of the German Association of Private Banks of 1993, 89 of the largest 100 enterprises had a supervisory board. The total amount of seats in these boards were 1,561. Representatives of the private banks held 99, and representatives of other credit institutions (including savings banks) and of insurance companies held another 53. Labour held 760 seats under boardroom codetermination. The shareholder side alone is composed of 152 representatives of financial and insurance companies, 427 representatives of industry and other business enterprises, and 155 other directors such as lawyers, public notaries, representatives of shareholder associations, and so forth. Finally, the so-called depository voting right must be mentioned. It is common practice of shareholders in Germany to let the bank which holds their shares in custody vote these shares in the general assembly. Under corporate law this can be done only under rather severe restrictions. For example, the banks must ask the client for a specific mandate to represent him and for instructions on how to

---

[56] As to this, *cf.* most recently Charny, "The German Corporate Governance System", *Columbia Business Law Review* 1 (1998) 145 with further references.

[57] *Cf.*, for example, Mülbert, "Bank Equity Holdings in Non-Financial Firms and Corporate Governance: The Case of the German Universal Banks", in Hopt/Kanda/Roe/Wymeersch/Prigge, *loc. cit.*, 445; Hopt, "Corporate Governance und deutsche Universalbanken", in Feddersen/Hommelhoff/Schneider (eds.), *Corporate Governance* (Cologne, 1996), 243; Westermann, Vollmachtsstimmrecht und Streubesitzaktionäre in der Hauptversammlung deutscher Aktiengesellschaften", in Feddersen/Hommelhoff/Schneider, *loc. cit.*, 264; Kohler, "Zur Neuregelung des Vollmachtsstimmrechts insbesondere bei Eigenbesitz von Banken", in Kübler/Scherer/Treeck, *loc. cit.*, p. 225; Hertig, "Western Europe's Corporate Governance Dilemma", in Baum/Hopt/Horn, eds, *Developments in Economic Law—Festschrift in Honour of Professor Buxbaum* (in print). A rather different, bank-bashing view is presented by Wenger/Kaserer, "German Banks and Corporate Governance: A Critical View", in Hopt/Kanda/Roe/Wymeersch/Prigge, *loc. cit.*, 499. The most recent policy study is by Hoffmann, *Systeme der Stimmrechtsvertretung in der Publikumsgesellschaft* (Baden-Baden, 1999).

vote. The bank must state clearly how it will vote if it does not get such instructions. And the law makes clear that the bank must act only in the interest of the client, otherwise it makes itself liable for damages. Still, the fact is that the banks usually receive these mandates without specific instructions, and they usually vote for the proposals made by the management. These four factors combined do indeed give the banks influence and may dampen corporate governance of the shareholders more than in countries in which the forces of the capital markets play a more important role.

To state the fact that German universal banks have such an influence is one matter. To evaluate the impact of this influence both on the single enterprises and on corporate governance in Germany as a whole is of course much more difficult. It is astonishing how quick some of the (German and foreign) observers are in presenting theories and making judgment on possible reforms. At a minimum, more clarity about the economic facts is needed. The studies of Edwards and Fisher[58] and the most recent and comprehensive report by Prigge[59] may be recommended as excellent sources. So is the study of Mülbert as to whether reforms limiting the influences of credit institutions on stock corporations are to be recommended to legislators.[60]

In the Board Reform Act of 1998, legislators put the emphasis on the board and the auditors and—apart from more transparency and a few incompatibility rules—refrained from fundamental reforms concerning the universal banks and their influence on the stock corporations. This was, of course, controversial and against the proposals of the then opposition which now is in power. Yet the proposals made in the reform discussion are in part very problematic, such as, for example, excluding banks from proxy voting and instead hoping that auditors and other commercial trustees take their place; or limiting shareholdings of banks to 5 percent of the shares of any corporation; or cutting back by law the number of seats the banks hold in supervisory boards while leaving the seats held by labour untouched, etc. It remains to be seen whether the new government coalition will come back to the plans it made while it was still the opposition, though this is doubtful because many other clearly much more important structural reforms are overdue in Germany.

This does not mean that the universal banks as they are now in Germany will remain untouched. But this is not the task of the legislators, for they should refrain from interference with the market, particularly if they are not sure about the consequences of their interference on the system as a whole. After all, the universal banking system is not forcing the banks to be universal banks, but rather letting them if they feel that this is more successful in the market than

---

[58] Edwards/Fisher, *Banks, Finance and Investment in Germany* (Cambridge, 1994).

[59] Prigge, "A Survey of German Corporate Governance", in Hopt/Kanda/Roe/Wymeersch/Prigge, *loc. cit.*, 943.

[60] Mülbert, "Empfehlen sich gesetzliche Regelungen zur Einschränkung des Einflusses der Kreditinstitute auf Aktiengesellschaften? Gutachten E für den 61". *Deutschen Juristentag* (Karlsruhe, 1996).

offering specialist banking services. In this perspective, the universal banking system is the banking system which is most free, deregulated, and market conformed. Yet international and global competition do exercise market pressures on the German universal banks. Investment banks, in particular from the USA, have entered the market and proven that their banking business is much more profitable than the traditional credit business. The Deutsche Bank and other major players have already tried to react by reorganization and national and international mergers. Whether this will be successful is another difficult question. The situation is also changing in other respects. The German capital markets and the stock exchanges are growing quickly and undergoing fundamental, internationally driven changes which by themselves are eroding traditional credit banking business. The process of securitization is in full swing and blurs the traditional distinction between bank-based and market-based countries viz. systems. Also in Germany the market for bond issues by enterprises is growing fast and the traditional housebank relationships are quickly eroding and have been called a mere myth.[61] And one last remark: it has been said that German universal banks are opposed to hostile takeovers and will impede their rise in Germany. In my opinion this is wrong. The pressures of the market and of an international clientele combined with high profit margins will also convince the German universal banks in the near future that this type of business is attractive. The (unsuccessful) bid of Krupp for Thyssen and the role of the German banks in this affair has already marked the change of the trend.

Groups of Companies Law vs. Exit, Fiduciary Principles, and Veil-Piercing?

The third example of deep-rooted, path dependence-driven differences between Great Britain and Germany is the law of groups of companies. This particularity of German corporate law has already been presented to an English-speaking audience several times[62] and has been the object of early and quite unsuccessful harmonization endeavors of the European Commission in its predraft of a 9th Directive. It should be enough to mention three characteristic elements of the German law of groups of companies as distinguished from British law. For many other differences, reference is made to the host of books and articles about the subject.[63] The first is that the control concept is substantive instead of formal. This means that under German group law, provisions apply if there exists a de facto control by the parent. It is not necessary for the parent to hold more

---

[61] Gerke, bank and stock exchange economist, in an interview with the Frankfurter *Allgemeine Zeitung*, July 13, 1999, No 159, 27.

[62] See, for example, Wiedemann, "The German Experience with the Law of Affiliated Enterprises", in Hopt (ed.), *Groups of Companies in European Laws* (Berlin/New York, 1982), 21; Hopt, "Legal Elements and Policy Decisions in Regulating Groups of Companies", in Schmitthoff/Wooldridge (eds.), *Groups of Companies* (London, 1991), 81.

[63] *Cf.* the well-documented book by Emmerich/Sonnenschein, *Konzernrecht* (6th edn., Munich, 1997).

than 50 percent of the shares or voting rights in the subsidiary. This, of course, goes very far and extends the reach of group law considerably. Second, there is a fundamental distinction between so-called contractual and merely factual groups of companies. In contractual groups, the creditors of the subsidiary are protected by the legal obligation of the parent towards the subsidiary to make good the losses at the end of the year. Outside shareholders of the subsidiary have a right to periodic compensation payments and must be offered the opportunity of selling their shares to the parent as against equitable indemnity. As a quid pro quo for entering into such an enterprise contract, the parent is permitted by law to instruct the subsidiary to act not in its own interest, but in the interest of the group as a whole. Third, there are several provisions which try to protect minority shareholders and creditors also in a de facto group. In particular, the controlling enterprise may not use its influence to induce the subsidiary to enter into transactions disadvantageous to it or to take or refrain from taking measures to its disadvantage unless compensation is granted for such disadvantage, usually within the same fiscal year. If compensation is not granted, the controlling enterprise and its board are liable to the subsidiary unless they have acted in a diligent and prudent way.

On the other side, German law of groups does not trust instruments which British law uses, inter alia, to cope with group situations, such as, for example, exit rights, fiduciary principles, and piercing of the corporate veil both before and after insolvency. As to exit rights, it has been stated above that there is no general early exit right by the requirement of a mandatory bid procedure. Rather, there are some special cases in which special exit rights are granted to the minority shareholders in the group, for example, when a contractual group is formed (sections 305 and 306 of the Stock Corporations Act) or in case of statutory mergers (sections 29 and 34 of the Fundamental Changes Act, Umwandlungsgesetz). Fiduciary principles are less needed in German group law because of the above-mentioned statutory provisions, but are developed by the courts for groups of limited liability companies. Finally, the doctrine of piercing the corporate veil is known in civil law, but it is seldom used for groups of companies out of fear of disavowing the overriding principle of separate entity.

The distrust of the just-mentioned general civil law instruments in group situations and instead the formation of a specific law of corporate groups in Germany is a particular path German law has taken as a result of the fundamental stock corporation law reform in 1965. It was the result of a very controversial legislative debate in which academia had a fair deal of influence. The fact that the German Cartel Act had just been enacted some years before and that the state of the law under the old stock corporation act of 1937 was very unsatisfactory added to this. In particular, the courts were not able to develop principles of group law capable of dealing with the major group problems. Be this as it may, what counts today is that since 1965 there is a huge amount of legal doctrine and many cases applying principles developed from this. This jurisprudence and case law, in addition to the detailed group law provisions in the Act of 1965, have a strong momentum of their own. Therefore, a change within German group law cannot be expected.

I do not think that this will change by harmonization measures of the European Union. Certainly there will be no change through exporting German group law concepts to the other Member States of the European Union by way of harmonization. The 9th Directive must be considered dead. There is more chance of importing certain concepts concerning groups from other countries and to try to reach a certain harmonization in this way. The Forum Europaeum Group Law has just tried to make proposals for such a European Law of Groups. These proposals will be presented to the English audience both orally[64] and in writing in the near future.[65] The first reaction to them when they were presented on an international conference sponsored by the German Ministry of Justice at Bonn in April 1999 was positive and apt to create hopes for some further progress on this way.

III. LEGAL HARMONIZATION OF CORPORATE GOVERNANCE IN
THE EUROPEAN UNION?

The Present State

Corporate governance appeared only fairly recently on the agenda of possible harmonization of the European Commission. In the most recent German book on "European Corporate Law" of 1999,[66] not even a hint at corporate governance can be found, and this is not to be criticised, but rather an accurate reflection of the state of European company law harmonization. It was only at the "Conference on Company Law and the Single Market", held in Brussels on December 3, 1998, under the auspices of the European Commission, that Paul Davies was asked to present his views about "Issues in Corporate Governance".[67] This relatively late start is not too surprising. The European Commission has experienced political and other difficulties with company law harmonization for some time. Major projects such as the Statute of the

---

[64] Hopt, "Towards a Corporate Group Law for Europe", Annual Lecture of the Centre of European Law at King's College London, October 11, 1999.

[65] Forum Europeanum Konzernrecht (Forum Europaeum Corporate Group Law), Corporate Group Law for Europe (in print for 2000); Hopt, "Europäisches Konzernrecht—Zu den Vorschlägen und Thesen des Forum Europaeum Konzernrecht-", in *Festschrift in Honour of Professor Buxbaum*, *loc. cit.* (in print).

[66] Habersack, *Europäisches Gesellschaftsrecht* (Munich, 1999). A more general inquiry is the one by Franzen, *Privatrechtsangleichung durch die Europäische Gemeinschaft* (Berlin, 1999).

[67] Davies, "Issues in Corporate Goverance", paper prepared for the Brussels conference on December 3, 1998. Here the written version, which is more detailed, is used. A shorter oral version is printed in European Commission, Acts of the Conference on Company Law and the Single Market, Office of Official Publications of the European Communities, Luxemburg 1998. See also Berglöf, "Reforming Corporate Governance: Redirecting the European Agenda", (1997) 24 *Economic Policy* 93.

European Stock Corporation and the draft directives of the 5th, 11th, 13th and 14th Directives were held up, some of them for decades, because the Member States (in particular Germany, which was not prepared to make compromises on labour codetermination) could not agree on a common regulatory core. Member States predicted crisis or even the end of European company law harmonization. This was exactly what some political players—but also many academics, most of them economists—wanted, for federalist reasons or for reasons of economic theory. Politically and legally, the subsidiarity principle embedded in the European Community Treaty (formerly Art. 3 b, now in the consolidated version under the Amsterdam Treaty Art. 5) served as the bastion. For academics it was the concept of competition of legislators which counted. In this unfavourable climate, the European Commission had to look for new beginnings and ideas, and corporate governance became one of the possibilities for exploration.

In his paper to the Commission, Davies explains why corporate governance, i.e., in particular the accountability of those in control of companies to the shareholders (and possibly certain stakeholders), has recently received so much attention in many Member States. He mentions, inter alia, the blurring of the public and private sectors, the growth of old age/pension funds and other institutional investors, but most important globalization and competition. The latter are bound to lead to the question of comparative corporate governance, which has already become a separate field of international research.[68]

To be sure, there already exists a certain body of European law touching corporate governance, part of which is already in force and part of which has been proposed by the European Commission and is still in the draft stage. As to internal corporate governance, much of the company law harmonization must be mentioned, even though key parts as far as corporate governance is concerned are not yet in force, such as the 5th Directive on company structure. This deals, inter alia, with the board and shareholder rights in the general assembly and the decision on and the auditing of the annual accounts; the Statute of the European Stock Corporation and its corresponding provisions on the shareholders and the board; and the 11th and 14th Directives, etc. As to external corporate governance—i.e., harmonization of the corporate control and securities markets— the record looks better, even though the key piece on takeover regulation, namely the 13th Directive, has still not yet been finally enacted, and even if it will be has been watered down considerably.[69] Stock exchange harmonization in particular has come a long way. A short mention must be made also of the area in which the Commission was particularly successful, namely bank supervision. Insofar as well-led, risk-conscious banks contribute to corporate governance, the harmonization of bank supervision, including consolidated bank supervision,

---

[68] See Hopt/Kanda/Roe/Wymeersch/Prigge (eds.), *Comparative Corporate Governance—The State of the Art and Emerging Research* (Oxford, 1998) with many further references.

[69] *Cf.* Brüssel will Schutz von Minderheitenaktionären ausweiten, *Frankfurter Allgemeine Zeitung*, June 21, 1999, No. 140, 19.

must not be forgotten, even though its focus is, of course, elsewhere, namely on risk. It is true, however, that the credit for this regulation belongs not only to the European Commission, but to a high (and maybe even higher) degree to the Bank of International Settlements and its Basel Committee.

Further Plans of the European Commission as to Corporate Governance

This is not the place to describe the further plans of the European Commission concerning the just-mentioned well-known proposals for a European company law. I have done this and evaluated the prospects of it elsewhere.[70] What is interesting is whether the Commission will pursue its ideas of specifically harmonizing some corporate governance measures. The Commission had already mentioned corporate governance as one of its concerns in its Action Framework of October 1998, which was the basis for the above-mentioned Brussels Conference of December 1998. In the meantime, the Commission also included corporate governance as a topic in its finalized Action Program of May 11, 1999.[71] Under the heading of "General Conditions for an Efficient EU Financial Market", the Commission mentions: (1) structure of the corporation, and (2) tax provisions. The Commission says there that differences in the structure of corporations may lead to unnecessary uncertainties for the investors and might create impediments for the development of the EU financial market. The example given is the practical rules for the exercise of voting rights by the shareholders in the different Member States. Another concern of the Commission is that current national codes on corporate structure and governance might create legal or administrative impediments for the development of uniform EU financial markets. The Commission therefore intends to commission an inquiry into the content of such codes and their possible impeding effects on the internal market.

It is hardly deniable that this action program remains rather vague as to corporate governance, and that the two projects on the agenda of the Commission relating to it are piecemeal. But this is hardly surprising. The fact is that corporate governance is a very difficult task which does not promise to give quick and palpable results of the kind the Commission needs in the political process.

If one looks critically at the prospects of legal harmonization of corporate governance in the European Union, one must start with the premise that all legislative activism in this field is wrong. The legal principle of subsidiarity as

---

[70] Hopt, Europäisches Gesellschaftsrecht—Krise und neue Anläufe, *ZIP* 1998, 96; Hopt, "Company Law in the European Union: Harmonisation and/or Subsidiarity?" *Int. & Comp. Corp. L. J.* 1 (1999) 41; Magnier, *Rapprochement des droits dans l'Union européenne et viabilité d'un droit commun des sociétés* (Paris, 1999).

[71] Kommission der Europäischen Gemeinschaften, Umsetzung des Finanzmarktrahmens: Aktionsplan, Mitteilung vom 11.5.199, KOM(1999) 232 endg., reprinted in *ZBB* 1999, 254; Mogg, "Looking Ahead to the Next Century: EU Priorities for Financial Services", *Revue Européene de droit bancaire et fiancier/European Banking and Financial Law Journal (Euredia)* 1999, 9.

embedded in the European Community Treaty, as well as the economic concept of competition—also among legislators—put the burden of proof on those who plead for European harmonization. Therefore, it must not only be shown that a particular legislative interference with unregulated corporate governance is legitimate—for example, because of market failure, or external effects, or the necessary implementation of the political decision of bringing about the internal market. Very often the answer and the right way will not be regulation, but rather non-regulation, or even deregulation. But it is further necessary to prove that this kind of legislation, in order to be successful, needs to be undertaken by the European Commission at the European level and not just at the level of the Member States.

This in turn would require scientific, comparative, and in certain cases interdisciplinary preparation of major legislative projects by the European Commission or the European Parliament just as it is done in many Member States, for example, in the preparation of the German insolvency law reform or more recently of the German stock exchange law reform.[72]

If these principles are observed and the legislative work is well prepared, what would be possible candidates for corporate governance reforms, and how should this legislative task be divided between the Member States and the European legislators? There is of course no short answer to either of these questions. For answering the latter, it is necessary in principle to search for those parts of corporate governance which need to be unified in an internal market. These are typically those provisions which will help to cut down impediments to open markets and lead to more competition, and by this to better corporate governance. It is evident that both the 11th and 14th Directives point in this direction. But are there more concrete examples for candidates for a body of European corporate governance law?

Davies mentions with all due restraint:

—principal-agent and minority protection;
—voice and exit, with more weight on the first in some countries, and in others more on the second;
—accountability (and dismissal) of directors;
—buy-out and possibly squeeze-out rights; and
—disclosure.

All these can be happily debated, but they would need to be scrutinized in more depth to determine whether different national legal rules relating to them will be impediments for the internal market.

---

[72] See the study on stock exchange reform by the Max Planck Institute for Foreign Private and Private International Law in Hamburg, which was commissioned by the Federal Ministry of Finance. The study is published in a more detailed book form: Hopt/Rudolph/Baum (eds.), *Börsenreform—Eine ökonomische, rechtsvergleichende und rechtspolitische Untersuchung* (Stuttgart, 1997). See on this study Hellwig, Möglichkeiten einer Börsenreform zur Stärkung des deutschen Kapitalmarkts, *ZGR* (1999) (in print).

In this respect, there is no decisive difference whether the impediments result from the law or from private codes, be they stock-exchange-made or other codes on corporate governance. For example, if a national stock exchange admits a foreign corporation to be listed only if it has a one-tier board, this would be an impediment to the internal market. Thus far the European Commission is right in commissioning an inquiry as to whether the codes movement in the different Member States may contain rules which function as such impediments. This is not to say that the stock exchanges should not take the lead in furthering corporate governance. The Combined Code of the London Stock Exchange— "Principles of Good Governance and Code of Best Practice" as of June 25, 1998, an appendix to the listing rules[73]—is an example to be imitated by German and other national stock exchanges.[74] Depending on the circumstances and on different national traditions, such self-regulatory efforts may have better chances for success in practice than legislation.

A further suggestion could be to mandate free choice for corporations between a one- and two-tier system, as already exists in France. It is true that only a small percentage of French corporations opts for the two-tier board, namely around 3,000 out of 158,000 companies. But among these there are some very successful and international enterprises.[75]

Disclosure also plays a key role in the international context and for investors and shareholders who want to invest in foreign corporations and securities. Therefore, the core of disclosure regulation is rightly European. This does not preclude individual Member States as well as single enterprises from going further in disclosure and thereby trying to outcompete their competitors. On the other hand, the use of disclosure requirements as a means to systematically keep out foreign competitors, be it by mandating too high disclosure standards or, worse, too specific disclosure formats, must be avoided. An unresolved question in this context is whether it is warranted to restrict harmonization of disclosure to listed companies. This seems to be practical and less demanding, but checks should be made as to whether it may have distortive effects on competition.

As to external corporate governance, possible candidates for European harmonization efforts could be, inter alia, keeping the securities markets open to foreign enterprises and their securities; setting core rules for the development of an open market for corporate control; cutting down defensive measures if they are used systematically to keep out foreigners; and looking into structural and institutional conditions which function as a defense against takeovers.[76]

---

[73] *Cf.* Pettet, "The Combined Code: A Firm Place For Self-Regulation in Corporate Governance" (1998) *J.I.B.L.*, 394.

[74] *Cf.* CalPERS, Intenational Corporate Governance, Germany Market Principles, 1999. See also the OECD Principles of Corporate Governance, Paris, April 1999.

[75] According to a recent American study directed by Kraakman in Harvard 20 per cent of the large companies have opted for the two-tier board.

[76] *Cf.* Maeijer/Geens (eds.), *Defensive Measures against Hostile Takeovers in the Common Market* (Dordrecht, 1990); see also the contributions by Hopt, Davies, Schaafsma, Simont and Maier-Reimer in Hopt/Wymeersch (eds.), *European Takeovers, loc. cit.*, ch. 6–8.

Corporate governance of institutional investors, in particular of banks and insurance companies, is another possible item for the agenda. Good corporate governance of the banks themselves is not only in the interest of the bank's shareholders, but indirectly contributes also to more competition and to the better functioning of the financial and economic system. Common principles of corporate governance in Europe for banking and insurance business may be even quicker to come about than elsewhere because market forces are particularly strong and joint efforts of the regulators could help. It may even be that developments in these fields will stimulate corporate governance more generally, as is the case for internal risk management systems which, since 1998, are mandatory for all German corporations, not only banks.

Summary and Conclusion: Sovereignty and Globalization at the Beginning of the New Millennium

This leads back to the opening question: are there common principles of corporate governance in Europe? My answer is yes and no, but more yes. As shown in the first part of the article, there has already been and will be more convergence of the Anglo-Saxon and Continental European countries in the field of corporate and capital market law, and specifically in corporate governance.

Most of this convergence will be market-driven. The forces of globalization and international competition are enormous, and have led or are leading to harmonization of legal and economic practice even under very different legal systems and rules. The examples of the practical approximation of the one-tier and two-tier board system, the development of the market for corporate control in countries in which hostile takeovers were virtually unknown, and the increased importance of disclosure, auditing, and intermediation in the different countries illustrate this development.

On the other hand, there remain path-dependent differences in corporate governance that are deeply embedded in the country's tradition, history, and culture, and will therefore not change or change only very slowly and in an unpredictable way. The examples given for German corporate governance are labour codetermination, the universal banking system, and the existence of a special law of groups of companies. They stand for particular political arrangements, historically grown economic systems, and particular legal doctrines that are upheld by an influential academia and active courts. Any changes to these are bound to affect vested rights and interests. But even here market forces can be expected to be stronger, at least in the long run.

Legal harmonization of corporate governance could be a way by which common principles of corporate governance could be furthered in Europe. Indeed, there is already an important body of European company and capital markets law which affects corporate governance. Yet the action program of the European Commission as to corporate governance more specifically remains rather vague. This is not surprising given the complexity of internal and external corporate governance, i.e., corporate governance between the board and the markets. But there is more: even if a particular interference of the legislature with unregulated corporate governance turns out to be legitimate—for example, because of market failure or external effects or the necessary implementation of a political decision to bring about the internal market—it is by no means sure that this kind of legislation must be done by the European Commission at the European level. The legal principle of subsidiarity and the economic concept of competition, also among the legislators, put the burden of proof on those who plead for European harmonization.

The conclusion goes beyond corporate governance and corporate and capital market law. The traditional idea that each sovereign state is free to choose which law should reign in the land is no longer true in a world of international competition and of globalization.[77] As far as we can see, at the beginning of the new millennium market forces will have their way across borders and legal systems. It remains a task for transnational political and legal cooperation to see that the necessary rule of law is not lost.

---

[77] *Cf.* The chairman of the board of DaimlerChrysler Schrempp in a speech at the Übersee-Club Hamburg on May 7, 1999 (Reden zum 50. Übersee-Tag, Hamburg, 68 at 74): "Nationale Regierungen und ihre Organe können nur noch begrenzt beeinflussen und steuern. . . . (Es) werden im globalen Dorf schonungslos die Fehler staatlicher Reglementierungen offengelegt. Industrienationen können nicht von den Vorteilen der Weltwirtschaft profitieren und gleichzeitig auf die notwendigen inneren Reformen verzichten."

8

The Additional Responsibilities of the Judiciary in the New Millennium

LORD WOOLF

INTRODUCTION

As this new millennium begins, the constitutional landscape of the United Kingdom is being transformed. Devolution is a reality in the case of Scotland, Wales and Northern Ireland. It is still possible to hope that this will also be true soon in the case of Northern Ireland. The Human Rights Act 1998 will come in to force in October 2000. The emphasis in public law will then move from enforcing the duties of public bodies to upholding individual rights. The future of the Appellate Committee of the House of Lords is under debate. The Privy Council will be the final court of appeal for devolution issues. This will for the first time give the Privy Council some of the powers of a constitutional court in relation to the United Kingdom.

In addition, the Civil Procedure Rules which came into force in April 1999 move the English common law civil justice system closer to that of the civil law jurisdictions. Now the English judge has the final responsibility for managing civil litigation.[1] The reforms place less emphasis than before on the trial; instead issues are disposed of sequentially. Oral advocacy and evidence are to be controlled. Discovery is restricted. The single expert witness is becoming a much more common figure on the litigation scene. The control of costs has become a major responsibility of all judges. The assessment of costs is no longer almost a monopoly of the Cost Judge, or as he used to be known, the Taxing Master.

There is a further important change involved in the civil justice reforms. It is the cultural change involved in making decisions as to how to manage cases "justly". The judiciary are now entitled to take into account the effect of their decisions on the resources of the courts and on other cases which are proceeding before the courts. It will certainly come as a surprise to many non-lawyers and, I suspect, lawyers as well, that before April 1999 in reaching a decision, the

---

[1] For the purpose of the Access to Justice report the procedure of the civil jurisdictions particularly France were examined and the validity of the traditional English approach tested by comparing it with its civil justice counterpart. Detailed information was obtained as to the system of fixed costs used in Germany. The German approach to costs (see Access to Justice, An Interim Report, Annex V p.263) was the model for fixed costs on the *fast track*, a reform only partially implemented.

courts could not have regard to the effect of their decision on other than those to which it related. A high water mark of this approach was the fact that, even where there was inordinate delay in pursuing litigation, the courts were not entitled to strike out any proceedings unless the *defendant* could show that the "delay had caused him prejudice or was contumacious".[2] The fact that the administration of justice was prejudiced was not sufficient. The former approach reflected the view of the courts that in so far as they were able to do so, they *should* seek to achieve a result in a particular case which was as "just" as possible. For this purpose a decision was "just" if it was one which came as close as possible to producing the right result. The fact that the costs involved in achieving the result were excessive or the delay in doing so inordinate were of less significance than achieving the "just" result.

The blinkered approach to which I have referred was not confined to civil proceedings. The same criticism can be made of the inquiry system in this country which still can involve disproportionate expense and delay. To an extent it applies to sentencing in criminal proceedings. When imposing a sentence of imprisonment the judge takes into account many factors. He takes into account the needs of society for retribution, the need to deter and the need to reform. What is not taken into account is the capacity of our prisons to absorb satisfactorily the defendant who is being sentenced; the cost of keeping the offender in prison and the effect of the number of prisoners in custody on the ability of the prison service to perform its mandate. This is a mandate which requires the prison service not only to keep a prisoner in custody but also to help them to lead law abiding and useful lives both while in prison and after release. The prison service is not fulfilling its role unless, when a prisoner is released at the end of his sentence, he is less and not more likely to commit further offences. The corrosive effects of imprisonment are immeasurably greater if prisons are overcrowded and therefore incapable of providing a constructive regime.[3]

As we enter the new millennium it is at last accepted, without qualification, that the judges are lawmakers; that they have a constitutional role to keep the common law under review and to develop and refurbish the principles to be derived from our case law; that there are crevices which have to be filled and decay which has to be removed if our law is to remain capable of effectively meeting the needs of contemporary society; that there is law making to be done which the legislator will not undertake. In addition there is general recognition that it is part of the role of appellate courts to provide policy guidance in the form of guideline judgments. This role has been well developed in relation to sentencing in criminal cases. It promotes consistency which is important. The guidelines on the whole are used to place the sentences for particular crimes into the correct position in relation to the tariff for sentencing as a whole. What the English courts have not done is to consider the validity of that tariff. The ques-

---

[2] *Birkett* v. *James* [1978] AC 297.
[3] See the Report of an Inquiry into Prison Disturbances 1990, February 1991, Cm.1456. HMSO.

tion has not been asked as to whether the objectives of sentencing could not be equally well achieved by, for example, reducing sentences in general by 20%.[4] The position is much the same in relation to damages for non pecuniary loss in the case of personal injuries. However in a recent report the Law Commission, having recommended that the level of this class of damages should be substantially increased, added that at least initially there should not be legislation. "Instead we hope that the Court of Appeal and the House of Lords will use their existing powers to lay down guidelines, in a case or series of cases, which would raise damages in line with the increases recommended".[5]

The final responsibility of the judiciary to which I should refer is not new. It is one which has evolved and will continue to evolve in the next millennium. It is the responsibility of the judiciary to promote the rule of law, and increasingly human rights, not only in this country, but also overseas. Overseas, this has been the role of the Privy Council for over a century. At one time it performed this role for a large proportion of the total population of the world because, at its zenith, the Privy Council was the final court of appeal for what would now be a third of the countries of the world. Unfortunately, the Privy Council never developed, as I believe it could have done, into being the final court of appeal of the Commonwealth. So today, while it is still a significant appellate court, it is no more than a shadow of what it once was or could have been.

This, however, does not mean that the responsibilities of our judiciary to jurisdictions overseas has been reduced to the same extent. In many parts of the common law world the judicial system of this country is still held in great respect as the historical home of their legal system. They still look to this country for leadership. The fact that we have a more modest role on the world stage may make it easier for some new independent countries to turn to this country for guidance as to common law values. They do not have the fear of domination by this country as they have of the States. In addition our closer relationship with Europe means that we are in an ideal situation to act as a bridge between the civil law and common law systems. The result is that both in the former colonies and in new democracies of eastern Europe our judiciary has a role to play in providing judicial support and assistance. We also have a role within the European Union to assist in developing understanding of the common law system and encouraging the process of harmonisation between the two legal systems which is beginning to take place. Both in this country and abroad the fact that the European Convention on Human Rights is to be part of our domestic law will enhance this role. The new responsibilities which the judiciary will have as they enter the new millennium are therefore formidable. The question which arises is how well placed are the judiciary to meet them?

---

[4] This is what happened in the Federal Republic of Germany in the late 80s. *Op. cit.* 259 para. 10.148.

[5] Law Com. no. 257 (1999) para. 3.165 p.85.

RESOURCES

The message received loud and clear at the end of the twentieth century is that the resources available for all forms of public services are limited. The courts, and therefore the law, are in competition, in particular with health and education authorities for their proper share of those resources. This means that the law is not in a strong position. Lawyers may need no persuading about how important an efficient and effective court system is to society, but the majority of politicians are not going to be easily persuaded that votes are to be won by increasing the resources available to the courts. This will remain the position even though it can be shown that the responsibilities being placed upon the courts are continually expanding. The extent to which the courts' resources will be increased to meet those responsibilities is still unclear, though there is an assurance by the Government that the judiciary will receive the IT equipment that it requires.

WHAT HAS ALREADY BEEN DONE

The Court Service is already well organised and directed and is in a better position to provide the judiciary with the support that it will require to meet the challenges posed by the judiciary's increased responsibilities. On the whole the courts are meeting the targets which are being set for them.[6] In addition, throughout the country, cases are being heard by judges of the appropriate seniority. To ensure this happens, criminal, civil and family work is now being managed by an administrative hierarchy of judges with administrative responsibilities.

The judiciary is better trained today than it has ever been. The Judicial Studies Board provides essential training. Its training for the introduction for the civil procedural reforms, and the family law reforms, was agreed to be excellent. The demands on the judiciary meant however that even if the Judicial Studies Board had been in a position to provide more intense training, the judges could not have been spared for the time which increased training would have required. While it is obvious that greater training will reduce the number of appeals and ensure the more expeditious handling of litigation, the current needs for judicial deployment cannot be ignored for the long term gains which the training would provide. While a pragmatic approach to training is required, balancing current needs against future benefits, the judiciary has a responsibility to insist that they receive at least the minimum training necessary for the competent performance of their role. Fortunately this has been recognised in relation to the bringing in to force of the Human Rights Act. Part of the explanation for the

---

[6] For example, in the financial year 1998–1999, 95.2% of administrative work in the civil courts was dealt with within target time, and the quality of service provided to court users exceeded the target of 82% by 1.4%. *The Court Service Annual Report 1998–1999.*

delay to October 2000 in the Act's implementation is to enable that training to have already taken place.

The civil procedure reforms also mark a move in the right direction. An important plank of the reforms is a development of pre-action protocols, which set out the best practice for resolving disputes without the need to have recourse to litigation. The support which the judiciary is required to give to the protocols and the pre-litigation offers to settle, which are intended to encourage settlement, should result in unnecessary litigation being avoided. However, where litigation is unavoidable, it should be dealt with more efficiently and expeditiously. This not only benefits the parties to the dispute but also the public in general. It allows the courts to focus on providing a better service. The civil procedure reforms should therefore assist. However, the extent to which the objectives of the reforms are being met will have to be carefully monitored. The system will need continuous fine tuning and the courts will need to demonstrate that they are moving with the times in order to meet the changing requirements of the public

WHAT ELSE NEEDS TO BE DONE?

1 Greater support for the senior judiciary

If the courts are to develop the law in the way they should the appellate courts must have greater assistance than they have at present. The tradition has been to rely on counsel to do the research that is necessary to make sure that the court is aware of the relevant authorities. Such reliance is possible if the court is only to be informed of binding relevant authorities decided by the courts of this country. It is not possible if the court is to be provided with all the relevant comparative and academic material to be considered as it should be, if a thorough approach to constructive law making is to be adopted. The advocate's primary role is to advance his client's case and it is unreasonable to expect the advocate to become involved with all the wider issues with which the court should be concerned. Furthermore it can be unreasonable to expect the client to pay for counsel's time in exploring arguments which are of no interest to the client.[7] Of course the judge can carry out research himself out of court, but this is an expensive indulgence which may give the judge satisfaction, but is, in the case of the initial spade work, an uneconomic use of the judge's time.

In the Court of Appeal we have, by the standards of most developed countries, a modest scheme for the deployment of judicial assistants, which is proving to be a success It greatly assists the court and equally benefits the assistants. They enable the Court of Appeal to manage its work in a way which is still not possible in the House of Lords. A case by case approach to the development of

---

[7] The House of Lords were told this was the position so far as the local authority was concerned in *Westdeutsche Landesbank* v. *Islington Borough Council* [1996] AC 669. The issue of whether compound or simple interest should be awarded took three days to argue!

the law can be too haphazard. The type of issues which will arise under the Human Rights Act will mean that appellate courts will need to have to adjust to many more individuals and organisations wishing to intervene or place before the court *Brandis* style briefs and that material will have to be marshalled. The Act itself requires the court to have regard to the *Strasbourg* jurisprudence. But if our senior courts are to perform their additional responsibilities properly they will have to spread their net wider and consider decisions in numerous other jurisdictions as well. There may be different instruments giving effect to human rights but their application is universal and whenever possible what is required is a harmonised approach to their application..

It is not without significance that on the second hearing in the Lords in the *Pinochet case* important arguments were advanced which were not considered at the first hearing. All the relevant material needs to be available to ensure that law making by the courts is of the highest possible quality.

Related to the judiciary's responsibility to develop the law, there is the need to clarify the law. Clear guidance can avoid similar disputes in the future. The judiciary also has a responsibility to simplify the law so as to make it more readily understood. As I will explain later, there could be greater use of the courts' declaratory jurisdiction for this purpose. It is difficult for judges to perform this task if they have nobody to assist them to collect the available material. The Court of Appeal has found that it can be of the greatest assistance if it contacts the courts of other jurisdictions to find out how they deal with a particular problem. This was done in the case of controversy as to whether judicial assistants' memoranda for members of the courts should be disclosed. The response from other jurisdictions was unanimous that they should not be disclosed. This influenced our decision to adopt the same practice.

2 Promoting public understanding of the role of the courts

The judiciary and the courts should adopt a broad approach to their role in society. It is essential that the public understands the importance of the work of the courts. Admirable initiatives are already taking place in a number of courts to improve this understanding. However a comprehensive approach is required. Together with the court service, the judiciary should actively be involved in a comprehensive programme for promoting an understanding among the public of the court's role in society and the importance of the rule of law and human rights. Visits to courts by the public and visits by the judiciary to suitable centers need to be organised regularly, during which the role of the courts and the judiciary can be explained.

This is particularly important in relation to the young. We want the public to feel a sense of ownership of the courts and our legal system. The present and future health of the rule of law depends on this perception being as widely shared as possible. It is also relevant to broadening access to justice, which is another contemporary responsibility of the court service and the judiciary. The courts and the judiciary are in an ideal position to promote the message. Access to justice does not necessarily mean access to the courts. There are disputes which are more satisfactorily resolved in the courts but a great many disputes are more satisfactorily resolved by other methods. It is now part of the courts role to ensure that potential litigants are made aware of the alternative methods of resolving their disputes.

MORE EFFECTIVE DECISION MAKING

I treat the subject of effective decision making as a separate topic because it is one to which I believe too little attention has been attached in the past, and one on which a great deal of attention needs to be focused in the future. It has three dimensions. The first is the research which should be undertaken as to what have been the consequences of decisions of the courts and the remedies which have been provided. The second is the material which should be placed before the courts so that they can anticipate more accurately what is likely to happen as a result of their decisions, and the third is the need for precision remedies which are at the same time more flexible in their application. For the future, remedies need to mirror the qualities of key hole surgery—providing with the minimum necessary intervention the precise effect which is necessary. In considering these three aspects, I will focus primarily on public law because this is the area where decisions of the courts have their widest impact.

A great deal has been written about how the scope of judicial review has been expanded. There has been vigorous debate as to what is the true basis of the courts' jurisdiction. The extent to which it is derived from the previously private law principle of ultra vires is still controversial. However, very little information is available as to how constructive the process has been. It is largely a matter of unsupported belief that judicial review has improved administrative practice. One of the areas where intervention of the courts can be relatively easily charted is in relation to prison discipline and the grant of parole. The standards which are objectively required are now clearly established. But whether as a result of the intervention of the courts the decision making is in fact fairer and whether individual prisoners have greater confidence in the parole system has not been, so far as I am aware, the subject of any structured research.

The most frequently granted remedy on an application for judicial review is almost certainly an order of certiorari. The result is that the offending decision has to be taken afresh. Again, as far as I am aware, there is hardly any authoritative research as to what happens thereafter. Are the decisions in fact taken again with a different outcome? Does the remedy improve the position of the applicants?[8]

---

[8] Maurice Sunkin, Lee Bridges and George Meszaros are currently compiling the results of a cohorts study they have done which follows the progress of applicants after they have taken review proceedings.

The remedies available in judicial review are discretionary. If the courts are going to use those remedies in the most effective manner, they need to benefit from the experience which should have already been accumulated as a result of past decisions. This is particularly true in the case of delay where the court is required to take into account whether the effect of the delay would be detrimental to good administration.[9]

EXPLANATION AND EXAMPLES

Some judicial review decisions, by their nature, will affect only one person, or perhaps a few people. An example is the decision by a local authority to resile from a promise made to a person that council housing would be provided in a particular place or that care would be provided to a particular level or standard. By contrast, another decision may have very broad effects on vast numbers of people not party to the litigation. A typical example is a case determining the proper interpretation of a statutory provision governing entitlement to a state-funded benefit. Sometimes the one decision under review will have both types of effect at the same time.[10]

Where a decision with broad effect is determined by a court to be unlawful, or made subject to an unlawful procedure, then the question that next arises is what is the status of those affected, apart from the applicant to the court, by the courts decision? What happened to the previous decisions made on a similar basis? If all past decisions must be re-examined and perhaps re-decided, then the administrative body concerned may be put to enormous expense.

Such a situation arose in the case of *R* v. *Secretary of State for Social Services, ex parte Child Poverty Action Group*;[11] (a case perhaps better known for its decision on standing). In that case the DHSS suffered a serious breakdown in their administrative arrangements with the effect that a vast number of people had not been paid their full benefit entitlement. The average amount due was thought to be about £25. However the Department's own estimate put the number of people to whom payments were due to be around 16,000 people. This would mean total refunds coming to around £440,000; not a crippling sum in the scheme of things. However the problem was in identifying the people who were owed money. The Department initially took the view that it would pay any valid claims, but that it would not itself go to the trouble of working out who was entitled to payment. The reason for this was that to do so would involve re-opening 15 million papers and deploying 420 full-time staff for a year. The cost

---

[9] S.31(6) Supreme Court Act 1981.

[10] An example is *R* v. *North East Devon Health Authority, ex parte Coughlan*, Court of Appeal [1999] (yet to be reported), concerning both the breaking of a promise which was only relevant to three people, and the interpretation, inter alia, of the government's duty under s.1(1) of the National Health Service Act 1977 to "continue the promotion . . . of a comprehensive health service".

[11] *The Times*, 15 August 1984.

of this endeavour would come to £4.8m to the taxpayer; ten times the amount refunded. The Department understandably argued that they would rather spend this money on their current welfare recipients. The issue for the courts was the black and white one as to whether there was a duty to carry out this mammoth and uneconomic task. At first instance I thought there was such a duty but the Court of Appeal decided there was no duty. If there had been broader powers available to the court, a more pragmatic and sensible answer could have been given. The court could have said what was the reasonable course to take in the circumstances.

LIMITED RE-DETERMINATION

Express and implied provision to revisit decisions

The extent to which administrative bodies must revisit their past decisions is also rarely called into question. Some statutes specifically provide for the revision of decisions. Examples include s.29(3) of the Taxes Management Act 1970 and s.104 of the Social Security Act 1975. However where there is no such provision, in what circumstances and to what extent can the courts require administrative bodies to revisit decisions?

An interesting case on this issue is the Court of Appeal decision in *Cheung* v. *Hertfordshire County Council*.[12] In 1978 the *Hertfordshire County Council* refused Mr Cheung, then a student, an education grant on the basis of a particular interpretation of the relevant legislation. In 1982 the House of Lords heard combined appeals in cases brought by a number of different applicants, but not Mr Cheung, challenging decisions made by different local authorities, but not by the *Hertfordshire County Council*.[13] The point before the House of Lords was precisely the same as the one that had been determined adversely against Mr Cheung three years earlier by his local authority. Their Lordships held that the interpretation of the statute favoured by the local authorities was incorrect. This meant that local authorities had been unlawfully refusing grants for many years, perhaps as far back as 1962.

The local authorities were then faced with the problem of broad effect outlined above. The government arrived at a compromise solution. The Secretary of State for Education issued a circular, part of which is quoted below, advising local authorities to only reconsider grants going back to the 1979/80 academic years on the basis that this was the year in issue in the House of Lords case, but not to reconsider earlier year's applications.

Mr Cheung's original grant application had related to the 1978/79 academic year. In accordance with the government policy the *Hertfordshire County Council* refused to reconsider his grant on the basis that it fell outside the

---

[12] *The Times*, 4 April 1986. See the excellent note of the case in (1987) PL 21.
[13] The case was *R* v. *Barnet LBC; ex p. Shah* [1982] 2 AC 309.

Secretary of State's criteria. Mr Cheung and another applicant sought leave to review the original 1978 decision made against them, on the basis recognised by the House of Lords as unlawful, as well as extensions of time in which to apply. They also challenged the Secretary of State's and local authority's policy of limiting the reconsideration of grants to certain cases only.

The Court of Appeal refused leave to challenge this decision because the application was well out of time, and because a change in the law was not a sufficient excuse for the delay.[14] However in the same decision the Court of Appeal did grant leave to challenge the 1983 decision. On the substantive appeal the Court of Appeal upheld the Secretary of State's general policy approach, but held that the local authority was under a duty to consider exercising its discretion to reconsider the application.[15] The Court held that there was nothing unlawful about the local authority giving limited effect to the House of Lords decision. However the Court did hold that the precise cut-off date chosen by the Secretary of State was incorrect, as one of the students in the House of Lords appeal had applied for a grant in the 1978/79 academic year. Therefore the reconsideration of past grant decisions should be extended to that year as well. Mr Cheung succeeded, but only on that rather technical basis.

I will return to this ruling later in the course of discussing the theoretical problems associated with limiting relief. For now it is sufficient to note that public bodies may have limited power to determine the means by which they will give effect to judicial review rulings that have impugned their past decisions. It is also worth noting that the exercise of this power will itself be the subject of supervision and control by the courts.

In the *Cheung* case Parliament itself attempted to limit the significant potential effect of the House of Lords decision by approving regulations designed to effectively override the House of Lords case.[16] However, in a separate case these regulations were held to be effective only in respect of applications for grants lodged after the regulations had come into force.[17]

PROSPECTIVE DECLARATIONS

An approach to the problem of broad effect could be the greater use of prospective declarations.[18] The first point to note is that the term "prospective declarations" may be slightly misleading. The important point is not that such remedies, when granted, have prospective effect, as the vast majority of decla-

---

[14] Court of Appeal, 20 March 1985; reported in *The Times*, 2 April 1985.

[15] Court of Appeal, 26 March 1986; reported in *The Times*, 4 April 1986.

[16] See the Education (Mandatory Awards) (Amendment) (No. 2) Regulations 1983 SI No. 477.

[17] See *R* v. *Haringey LBC; ex p. Lee*, *The Times*, 31 July 1984.

[18] Another approach which I have canvassed previously is the use of anticipatory rulings. This is where administrative bodies go to the courts prior to the making of an administrative decision to clarify the legality of a proposed course of action. For my discussion of this see pp.47–50 of my Hamlyn lectures, *Protection of The Public—a New Challenge* (London, 1989).

rations are assumed to have this in any case. The relevant point is that a "prospective declaration" may be prospective *only*. A more accurate term is therefore "non-retrospective declarations". But this description is too clumsy to adopt.

The concept has a number of variations. The two main primary ones are: first, that the declaration is to have no retrospective operation whatsoever. In such a case the judicial review judgment only provides guidance for future decisions and does not invalidate the decision in issue or other decisions taken on the same basis. The Law Commission refers to this as "a hybrid case where a remedy is refused due to the detriment to good administration but where the court grants declaratory relief as a guide for the future".[19] Alternatively the declaration could invalidate the decision under review but leave intact other decisions already made on the same impugned basis. The two different forms of prospective declaration have different implications for the place of this remedy in public law, as will be illustrated shortly.

Relevance

The relevance of prospective declarations to the present issue should be immediately apparent: if courts granted such declarations on a more frequent basis, then the disruptive effect of judicial review decisions on completed administrative action would be reduced. As one writer has put it:

> "Such declarations allow the court to tread a middle-path which enables them to deliver guidance on the law to ensure it is properly applied in future, whilst recognising limitations on the use of judicial review to quash decisions with the automatic consequences that flow from the rather blunt instrument of retrospective nullity."[20]

In many cases prospective declarations will clearly be inappropriate. For example, if an applicant makes out a case for impugning a disciplinary ruling against him on public law grounds, then a prospective declaration of the first type mentioned above would deny to the litigant what may have been his only reason for going to court, in a situation where there may be no danger of the decision having broader implications for administrative resource allocation.

The remedy in practice—legislation

The European Court of Justice has always had the power, provided by article 174(2) of the Treaty of Rome, to limit the effects of retrospective invalidation of

---

[19] The Law Commission, *Administrative Law: Judicial Review and Statutory Appeals*, Consultation Paper No. 126, London, HMSO, p.78.

[20] C. Lewis, *Judicial Remedies in Public Law*, 1992, Sweet & Maxwell at p.198. The second edition of this excellent work was, at the time of writing, due for publication at the end of 1999.

regulations.[21] There are numerous United Kingdom statutes which provide for the retrospective operation of some or all of their provisions, or empower the making of decisions or regulations with such effect,[22] or seek to retrospectively validate actions.[23] However express statutory limitation[24] or exclusion[25] of retrospective effect is less common. The only statutory provisions of which I am aware[26] which expressly empower courts to grant prospective declarations are the recent devolution acts: s.102(2) of the Scotland Act 1998; s.110(2) Government of Wales Act 1998; and s.81(2) Northern Ireland Act 1998. These are all identical and provide that if a court or tribunal finds that a devolved body did not have the power to make a decision, regulation or act (as the case may be) then:

"The court or tribunal may make an order—
(a) removing or limiting any retrospective effect of the decision, or
(b) suspending the effect of the decision for any period and on any conditions to allow the defect to be corrected."

Clive Lewis, in his excellent analysis of prospective declarations, deals with a number of cases in which prospective declarations were considered or discussed.[27] He also mentions other cases in his book.[28] The cases most frequently cited are the two cases on the susceptibility to judicial review of the Panel on Take-Overs and Mergers: *R* v. *Panel on Take-Overs and Mergers, ex parte Datafin Plc*[29] and *R* v. *Panel on Take-Overs and Mergers, ex parte Guinness Plc*.[30] I would caution against placing too much emphasis on these cases as the central authorities for the use of prospective declarations. The context of take-overs battles presents very particular problems for both regulators and courts. The subject matter imposes very different demands on courts in fashioning their

---

[21] See *Re 1986 Budget: EC Council* v. *European Parliament (Case 34/86)* [1986] 3 CMLR 94.

[22] For examples of such empowering provisions, see Northern Ireland Act 1998, ss.25(2), 26(5), 80(2)(a), 85(1)(a); Police Act 1996, ss.50(5), 51(3); Finance Act 1996 Schedules 6, 15, 32; Child Support Act 1991, s.51; Finance Act 1990, s.50.

[23] E.g. Schedule 5 of the Pensions Act 1995, amending s.37(2) of the Pension Schemes Act 1993; Town and Country Planning (Costs of Inquiries etc.) Act 1995, s.2.

[24] For two examples of the placing of restrictions on retrospective effect, see s.7(3) of the Remuneration of Teachers Act 1965 (since repealed) ("nothing in this subsection shall be construed as authorising the remuneration of any teacher to be reduced retrospectively") and Schedule 2, Order 6(2) of the Finance Act 1957 ("no such order shall have retrospective effect for the purpose of increasing the duty chargeable on any goods"); s.15(1)(a) of the Abolition of Domestic Rates etc. (Scotland) Act 1987, limiting the power of a registration officer to make orders having retrospective effect to within two years.

[25] For example see Article 17 of the Rome Convention on contractual obligations, incorporated by the Contracts (Applicable Law) Act 1990; s.163 of the Pension Schemes Act 1993; s.69(6) of the Social Security Act 1973.

[26] I am grateful to Clive Lewis for pointing these provisions out to me.

[27] See Lewis (1988) at pp.79–95.

[28] Lewis, *Judicial Remedies in Public Law*, above n. 20 at pp.196–199; other cases of note include *R* v. *Dairy Produce Quota Tribunal, ex parte Caswell* [1989] 1 WLR 1089; *R* v. *Secretary of State, ex parte Association of Metropolitan Authorities* [1986] 1 WLR 1.

[29] [1987] 1 QB 815.

[30] [1990] 1 QB 147.

procedure and remedies than does, say, the judicial review of subordinate social security legislation. An important issue in the *Take-Overs* cases was not just the desire not to upset decisions already made, but to ensure that any contemporaneous review had a minimal impact on the extremely tight timescale operating in that case. The majority of judicial review cases do not present the same problems of extreme urgency and contemporaneous effect, or at least not to anything like the same degree. Most cases can wait at least for a few days.

However this does not mean that the use of prospective declarations should be restricted to such extreme situations. The position should be the opposite: just because the main cases cited in association with this remedy present a situation of extreme urgency, it should not be assumed that the remedy is restricted to such extreme cases.

One case which may not be a landmark in the area, but I nonetheless have some attachment to, is *R* v. *Attorney-General; ex parte ICI Plc.*[31] ICI sought a declaration that the Revenue's assessment of its competitors was an underassessment. They were partly successful before myself at first instance. There was separate argument as to the appropriate remedy. I granted a declaration with only prospective effect and held that as a matter of principle and discretion it would be wrong to grant a retrospective declaration. The Court of Appeal took a different view, largely on the basis that such a result would deprive ICI of the fruits of the litigation.[32] I will return to this reasoning below.[33]

Retrospective and prospective relief and the Human Rights Act

The incorporation of the European Convention on Human Rights into domestic law by the coming into force of the Human Rights Act 1998 will pose new challenges not just to our substantive law but also to our procedural law, including the law of remedies. Professor Gearty has posed a number of questions raised by the Act. He says:[34]

> "Let us suppose by way of example that the terms of an old statute under which a number of persons are currently in prison has been radically reinterpreted under section 3(1) (of the Human Rights Act 1998) in a way that makes clear that such incarceration would not now be permitted. Should these prisoners be released? Are their convictions not now manifestly unsafe? Do they have a right to damages for false imprisonment? If so, from what date: the date of the launch of their legal action? The coming into force of the Act? Some earlier date? Could property owners who have been penalised by the terms of the War Damage Act 1965 launch actions for compensation based on new, human rights-invigorated, versions of the Act's terms? Would

[31] (1989) 60 Tax Cases 1. My first instance decision on the issue presently under consideration is at pp.31–34.
[32] *Ibid.* at p.65 per Lord Oliver; also see Lloyd LJ at p.78 and Nourse LJ at p.90.
[33] See p 21.
[34] C.A. Gearty, "The Impact of the Human Rights Act 1998" in A. Loux (ed.), *Human Rights and Scots Law* (Hart, Oxford, forthcoming, 2000).

such a reading of the Act be a possibility? If Parliament's recent legislation on the right to silence were found to require radical reinterpretation so as to comply with certain of the incorporated ECHR rights, would those whose convictions had been secured in large part by robust application of the pre-human rights law be entitled to their immediate freedom, or to a retrial, or to nothing at all? Of course problems of retrospectivity occasionally arise in the current framework of law, but the coming into force of the Human Rights Act will greatly increase their frequency and their importance."

These difficult questions will ultimately have to be addressed by the courts, and they will seek to draw assistance from more tightly framed remedies such as prospective declarations. Of course in doing so courts will have to ensure that any denial of retrospective relief is consistent with article 6 of the Convention. It is likely that some balancing of interests will need to be carried out, with an assessment of whether the proposed denial of retrospective relief is a proportionate response to the administrative problem raised.

It should also be noted in this regard that the Human Rights Act places heavy reliance on the principle of non-retrospectivity. Declarations of incompatibility under section 4(2) are to have prospective effect only.[35] They may not directly benefit the litigant who may have raised the issue in the first place. This is not just a minor side-effect of the Act; it is a vitally important provision in terms of the structure and philosophy behind the incorporation of the Convention. The prospective nature of declarations of incompatibility is the key to reconciling the incorporation of the Convention with the doctrine of parliamentary sovereignty.

However it has already been noted that one of the provisions of the Act has some element of retrospective effect. Section 22(4) of the Act provides that s.7(1)(b) of the same Act:

"applies to proceedings brought by or at the instigation of a public authority whenever the act in question took place; but otherwise that subsection does not apply to an act taking place before the coming into force of that section".

These provisions were considered recently by a Divisional Court consisting of Lord Bingham CJ, Laws LJ and Sullivan J in the case of *R* v. *DPP, ex parte Kebilene*.[36] Lord Bingham CJ agreed with the observation that s.22(4) "introduces an element of retrospectivity on which victims of acts made unlawful by the Convention may rely when section 7(1)(b) is brought into force".[37] The devolution legislation also enables the law officers to refer devolution issues to the Judicial Committee of the Privy Council for, in effect, advisory opinions, thus bringing the Judicial Committee's role closer to that of its historic cousin, the Conseil d'Etat.

---

[35] Note also Schedule 2, Order 1(4) of the Act, which provides in relation to remedial orders that "No person is to be guilty of an offence solely as a result of the retrospective effect of a remedial order".

[36] [1999] 3 WLR 175, DC.

[37] *Ibid.* at 185.

An aid to expansion of judicial review

The use of more precisely directed remedies will enable the courts to extend the protection offered by judicial review. This was a factor in the *Datafin* decision. The Court of Appeal would not have subjected the Panel to review as Sir John Donaldson MR made clear if to do so would have destroyed the efficacy of the Panel's important and delicate work. It was also a factor in my decision to grant standing in the *ICI* case. As I made clear in that case, I would have been less willing to grant ICI standing to challenge the Revenue's assessments of its competitors' tax bills if I were being asked to strike down a particular valuation, as opposed to pronouncing upon a particular approach to valuation.[38] However in that case wiser minds took exception to this sentiment, stating that they found it "difficult to understand".[39] None the less, the subsequent decade has seen a progressive expansion of the circumstances in which the courts will grant declaratory relief. To this has to be added the power of the courts to grant interim declarations and the provisions of the devolution legislation which I have already cited.

The problem with the development of the declaratory remedies is that they can result in successful litigants being deprived of any remedy which for them has any value. The decision may establish a principle, but most litigants are after more material rewards.

The present position can also result in the court granting a remedy to a particular litigant or litigants but denying relief to other people in a similar position who did not bring judicial review proceedings. This may produce results which are arbitrary, or at least perceived as such.

However, the disparity in relief granted between those who seek redress for their complaint and those that do not is just a natural consequence of the time limits found in almost all areas of non-criminal law. Justice is not arbitrary because it is available to those that seek it in time but is not available to those that do not. It is accepted that time limits operate irrespective of the validity of the claim.

There remain a number of problems with such an approach. Sir John Donaldson MR made the point in one of the decisions in the *Cheung* litigation[40] that if a public law test case is before a court, it would not be right to require all people similarly positioned to begin proceedings in order to protect their positions. In addition, we may be faced with the problem as touched upon previously that in the case of prospective declarations the merit of the claim has already been established, whereas in a time barred case the litigant is being prevented from testing a claim of undetermined merit. It may be one thing to say

---

[38] (1989) 60 Tax Cases at p.33.

[39] See *ibid*. at p.78F per Lloyd LJ and p.90D per Nourse LJ; also see Lord Oliver's more lengthy analysis of the issue at pp.65–66.

[40] The Court of Appeal decision handed down on 26 March 1986.

that in the furtherance of good administration a party is barred from challenging a decision on the ground of delay. But it may be quite another thing to say that although a court has just held that a public authority acted unlawfully in its treatment of a citizen and has seen fit to grant one citizen a remedy against this injustice, the demands of good administration require that other citizens in the same position be denied a remedy. Such a result risks bringing the administration of justice into disrepute.

The Court of Appeal has at least once stated its view on this issue. In the *Cheung* case the Court of Appeal saw nothing arbitrary about a government policy which gave some form of prospective effect to judicial review rulings. It was held that distinguishing between applicants who had been unlawfully denied education grants on the basis of whether or not they applied for a grant in the same year as the litigants in the original judicial review case establishing the invalidity was not a lawful basis for determining entitlement to relief. The principle of good administration required that all those that applied in the same year as the public law litigant should be treated alike. It is worth setting out the relevant part of the Secretary of State's circular considered in that case, as it is of interest to the present issue. The Secretary of State advised local authorities that

> "the guiding principles should be the requirements of good administration and the desirability of reviewing cases where the courts would be likely to grant leave for an application for judicial review without forcing the student first to have recourse to the courts . . . the courts would probably regard delay while the test cases were pending as wholly justified. While students who were refused an award less than three months before leave to appeal was first given in the test cases would have a stronger case than those whose award was refused earlier . . . it would be consonant with good public administration to treat all students who started their courses in the autumn of 1979 similarly."

Such a rule gives guidance and sets limits on the manner in which the general principle of good administration is to be applied to the issue of prospective declarations. However it may still be questioned whether the government's approach to the problem in so far as it was restrictive was a proper and lawful one. In the Divisional Court the policy was held by McNeill J to be unreasonable as it was reached purely for reasons of administrative convenience and in an attempt to limit the financial consequences of declared unlawfulness.[41] The Court of Appeal held that the policy was lawful, on the basis that the statutory duty to consider and determine awards does not also imply a duty to pay awards.[42] The law on this subject is clearly in need of further development. So far there has been no attempt to introduce group or representative actions into judicial review.

---

[41] Queen's Bench Division (Crown Office List) 5 July 1985, reported in *The Times*, 15 July 1985.
[42] See the report in *The Times*, 4 April 1986.

DAMAGES FOR PERSONAL INJURIES

Our law in relation to damages is still fault based. It is necessary to show a breach of a duty of care. In what circumstances a duty of care exists is a constant subject of litigation and academic discussion. The courts have to define the parameters. The approach of the courts varies from time to time. It swings back and forth like a pendulum. At one stage the approach is expansive. At other stages it is restrictive. The explanation for the oscillation is the courts' perception of which approach best reflects the public interest. The approach is however largely instinctive rather than scientific. The court has to speculate as to what will be the consequences of the approach which it has adopted. Sometimes the result of a change of direction of the courts will be to prejudice one insurance company rather than another. But even where this is the position there will be economic consequences as to which the courts, on the information available, can do no more than speculate.

In its report *Damages for Personal Injury: Non-Pecuniary Loss*, to which I have already referred, the Law Commission has recommended that there should not be immediate legislation but instead it should be left to the courts to implement the increase in damages which the Commission considers desirable. This is not as novel a recommendation as it may first appear. The level of damages for non-pecuniary loss have always primarily been a matter for the courts. However an increase on the scale proposed by the Law Commission would have far reaching economic consequences. It would have substantial consequences for insurers. It would have substantial consequences for the insured who will have to pay increased premiums. Further more, if the matter is dealt with by the courts, which I agree is the preferable course, then the decisions will have a retrospective effect in relation to those cases which have not already been resolved. The insurers will have to meet liabilities which are greater than they could reasonably expect, liabilities for which they have made no provision.

In respect of future pecuniary loss, the approach to calculating the amount which is payable was drastically reconsidered by the House of Lords in the recent case of *Wells* v *Wells*.[43] Since that decision the court is required not to calculate future loss on the basis that the capital sum which is awarded will be invested in a mixed portfolio of equities and fixed interest stock but on the basis that the capital sum which is payable to a claimant in respect of future pecuniary loss will be invested in index linked government stock. The logic set out in the speeches in the House of Lords for coming to this approach is based on well established principles. The House of Lords was influenced by a carefully reasoned report of the Law Commission, *Structured Settlements and Interim and Provisional Damages*.[44] It is now up to a claimant to decide whether he should take the risk of investing in equities in the hope of beating the return on the

[43] [1998] 3 All ER 481.
[44] Report 224 of 1994.

inflation protected stock. As it is, the position of insurers was changed overnight from one where they had to meet future losses by the payment of a capital sum producing, for example, a discounted return of 3% instead of a discounted return of 4% to 5%. The new calculation may be more accurate than the old. But what cannot be disputed is that both calculations are speculative. What the court did not do was to order that in future, damages should be awarded on an instalment or structural basis which would meet the actual fluctuating needs of the claimant.

SENTENCING POLICY

The courts have not had the advantage of the reports by the Law Commission on sentencing policy. The courts have taken no steps to consider the policies which should inform sentencing discussions, taking into account the economic impact of the policies adopted.[45] No long term consideration has been given by the courts to the relative benefit to the public of spending more money on education and less on prisons.

The courts cannot be blamed for this. They have not been given the material which would be needed for such an exercise

The judiciary do, however, complain if Parliament seeks to reduce their discretion as to sentencing. They are right to do so in my judgement. However, if they are to retain their discretion, they must also accept the responsibility of ensuring they obtain the material they need to answer the major questions which arise in determining an enlightened policy on sentencing.

CONCLUSION

I do believe we have a judiciary of the quality we need as we enter the next millennium. We also have a court service which is better structured to meet the challenges which lie ahead.

However, the judiciary need greater support if they are to achieve the improvements in the legal system which their additional responsibilities make necessary. A greater emphasis on judicial training is essential. The judiciary need to be able to adopt a global approach. Decisions have to be made, having taken into account what is happening in the other major legal systems.

There is also a need for more research. Research is needed as to how the judiciary is performing, as to the consequences of our discussions, and as to the

---

[45] The prison population rose between 1992–1998 from 40,606–66,516 (64%). In the case of women prisoners it rose from 1,353–3,189 (136%). During the same period and in the case of young prisoners it rose from 6,783–11,636 (72%). The sharpest rise has been in local prisons where it is most difficult to provide a constructive regime. The rise in the prison population is not due to the increase in the number of offences appearing before the court but harsher sentencing. See the paper of the Penal Affairs Consortium, *The Prison System*, August 1999.

relative merits of alternative policies. It must also be accepted that the task of the courts is to make the maximum contribution to society by promoting good citizenship and respect for the rule of law. In addition, by example and encouragement, we can and should support our colleagues in other jurisdictions who do not have the benefit of our traditions, to achieve the same objectives.

If we are provided with the backup we need, I am confident we can make the contribution which is required. The judiciary is capable of meeting the challenges of the next millennium.

9

The Protection of Human Rights in Germany

JUTTA LIMBACH

THE GUARDIAN OF BASIC RIGHTS

When the men and women who framed the Basic Law set about drafting a constitution in 1948, they were animated by the desire to draw lessons from the 1933–45 reign of terror. The promise "Never again!" presided over the work in the Parliamentary Council. But the failure of the Weimar Republic, the constitution of which had offered no adequate defences against the foes of democracy,[1] also guided the search for principles and institutions able to guarantee coexistence befitting human dignity in a free, democratic polity. It was with that intent that the fundamental rights, the principle of separation of powers and the rule of law were made part of the Basic Law. Experience of the preceding dictatorship did not just induce the framers of the constitution to cast the human rights and freedoms as actionable subjective rights. They went further, to provide for a Federal Court as guardian of the constitution. This court was not merely to check whether statutes were in harmony with the Basic Law. It was to have the task of "vouchsafing to every inhabitant of Germany the needful protection against encroachments on their constitutionally assured fundamental rights".[2]

Anyone who feels that their fundamental rights have been infringed by the public authorities may lodge a constitutional complaint. It may be directed against a measure of an administrative body, against the verdict of a court or against a law. A constitutional complaint requires acceptance for adjudication. It must be accepted if it is of fundamental constitutional importance, if the claimed infringement of fundamental rights is of special severity or if the complainant would suffer particularly severe detriment from failure to decide the issue. The Federal Constitutional Court itself has to decide as to the prerequisites for acceptance before deciding the constitutional complaint.

A constitutional complaint is as a rule admissible only after the complainant

---

[1] Cf. *Benda/Klein*, Lehrbuch des Verfassungsprozeßrechts, Heidelberg 1991, p. 1.

[2] In the words of Representative *Süsterhenn*. See the *Stenographic Report of the Parliamentary Council*, Bonn 1949, p. 25. The Parliamentary Council ultimately rejected inclusion of the constitutional complaint in the Basic Law. It was brought in first by the Federal Constitutional Court Act, and later anchored constitutionally in the Basic Law.

has resorted unsuccessfully to the otherwise competent courts. In the German system all constitutional organs have to respect the supremacy of the constitution. It is statute in the first Article of the Basic Law that the following basic rights shall bind the legislature, the executive and the judiciary as directly enforceable law. But only the Federal Constitutional Court decides on the interpretation and application of the constitution with final binding force. The Federal Constitutional Court is not a general court of review which examines the decisions of the ordinary courts for any error of fact or law. Its exclusive responsibility is to decide questions of constitutional law and to interpret the Basic Law. The Court enjoys the last word on the meaning of the Basic Law, and its word is law. But as long as no fundamental right has been infringed, the Federal Constitutional Court is bound by the decisions of the other courts.

THE JUDGE'S CREATIVE RELATIONSHIP TO THE LAW

The Federal Constitutional Court performs a predominantly checking function, delimiting and restraining power. Its job is to tie policy to law, and subordinate it to law. For the Basic Law has "resolved the age-old tension between power and law in favour of the law".[3] The Court's task is the limited one of interpreting the Constitution in Court proceedings; the expediency considerations of politics are not its concern.[4] The Federal Constitutional Court is "designed as an organ of law, not of politics"; even if its decision may, inevitably, have political repercussions.[5] Nonetheless it is a crucial question whether constitutional adjudication can at all be separated with logical distinctness from lawmaking.

For the extent of the Federal Constitutional Court's decision-making power, the method of constitutional interpretation is of fundamental importance. The question of the right method continues to be controversial in jurisprudence. First, the specific nature of the text has to be taken into account. The Articles of the Basic Law are marked by a low degree of certainty. The Basic Law, considered from a structural viewpoint, is a framework system. With very few exceptions, it formulates no directly applicable individual provisions. Its articles are norms with great openness, with margins of interpretation that are hard to delimit.[6] The Basic Law essentially contains—apart from the law on the organisation of the State—principles that must first be spelled out before they can be

---

[3] Helmut Simon, *Verfassungsgerichtsbarkeit*, in: *Benda/Maihofer/Vogel* (eds.), *Handbuch des Verfassungsrechts*, 2nd ed. 1994, pp. 1137, 1661.

[4] So the Federal Constitutional Court refrains from considering wheter the legislature has chosen, the wisest, justest and most expedient solution. Cf. BVerfGE 36, 174 ,189; 38, 312, 322.

[5] As rightly put by Thomas Clemens in his article: *Das Bundesverfassungsgericht im Rechts- und Verfassungsstaat: Sein Verhältnis zur Politik und zum einfachen Recht; Entwicklungslinien seiner Rechtsprechung*, in: Michael Piazolo (ed.), *Das Bundesverfassungsgericht—ein Gericht im Schnittpunkt von Recht und Politik*, Mainz—München 1995, pp. 13, 16 f.; and Dieter C. Umbach, *the German Democracy and the Federal Constitutional Court as Promoter and Guardian of the Rule of Law*, in: *Democracy and the Rule of Law in Germany*—in Jordan, 1992, p. 25 f.

applied.[7] Furthermore, they open up semantic room for manoeuvre, allowing not just one correct decision. Judicial decision is not only finding, but always also law-making. "In every act of judicial application of law . . . cognitive and volitional elements form an indissoluble combination".[8] The judge creates law in the process of finding a decision. Adjudication accordingly always has a political dimension too. This is certainly true of constitutional jurisdiction.

Given the openness of the constitution, the question arises what normative viewpoints judges orient themselves by. There is no binding constitutional theory. What is meant is a theory that supplies information about binding viewpoints in interpretation, as well as about the substantive scope of the constitution and its norms. Certainly, calls for the development of such a constitutional theory are repeatedly heard. But differing constitutional views continue to compete with each other. This emerges especially with the attempt to define the scope of fundamental rights. Some understand fundamental rights as essentially defensive rights against governmental interference. Others see the bill of fundamental rights as more, as an objective value system radiating out into all areas of law. The view of the constitution as an objective value system demands political activism from the Constitutional Court. Consideration of the boundary-setting function of the constitution (in the relation between citizen and State), by contrast, favours a more reticent role for the Court. The Federal Constitutional Court's case law examined below may illuminate the Court's understanding of fundamental rights. The selected case law on the principle of constitutionality, on equal rights for men and women and on the law of freedom of opinion is inteded to illustrate how the Federal Constitutional Court marks out the boundaries of the rights and freedoms that the bill of fundamental rights in the Basic Law guaranteed.

JUDICIAL FUNDAMENTAL RIGHTS

Through the judgements on fair hearing[9] and due process[10] the Court shaped the outlines of the principle of the rule of law and broke with many authoritarian traditions.[11] This is true not least of the elimination of the legal concept of the "special relationship of subordination". In reference to the monitoring of a prison inmate's letters by the penal institution, the Court decided in 1972 that

[6] K. Hesse, *Grundzüge des Verfassungsrechts der Bundesrepublik Deutschland* (Heidelberg 1995) p. 20, and W. Zeidler, in: *Verfassungsgerichtsbarkeit, Gesetzgebung und politische Führung, Ein Cappenberger Gespräch* (Köln 1980), p 46.

[7] On the foregoing cf. E.-W. Böckenförde, *Die Methoden der Verfassungsinterpretation*, in: *idem, Staat, Verfassung und Demokratie* (Frankfurt a.M. 1992) pp. 53 ff., 58.

[8] Dieter Grimm, *Politik und Recht*, in: *Eckart Klein* (ed.), *Grundrechte, soziale Ordnung und Verfassungsgerichtsbarkeit, Festschrift für Ernst Benda zum 70. Geburtstag*, Heidelberg 1995, pp. 91, p. 100.

[9] BVerfGE 47, 182, 187 f.

[10] BVerfGE 38, 105, 111.

[11] Klaus Schlaich, *Das Bundesverfassungsgericht*, 4th ed. 1997, marginalnr. 195, p. 133.

inmates' fundamental rights could "be restricted only by or on the basis of a law". It would contradict the comprehensive bindings of State power by fundamental rights if these could be restricted arbitrarily or by discretion in the course of execution of sentence.[12]

In this connection one further landmark decision of the Federal Constitutional Court deserves mention. In 1977, the Court had to decide on the constitutionality of life imprisonment as the punishment generally inflicted on murderers.[13]

A policeman, then aged 31, was accused of having killed a drug addict in order to cover up his own drug dealing activities. The Verden district court, before which the defendant was to be tried, deemed him to be guilty of murder, but regarded the sentence of life as incompatible with the Basic Law. The court referred to several psychological studies on the impact of life imprisonment on the human personality, stating, that after a period of ten to twenty years the convicted person suffered a decline of good instincts, being replaced by resignation and dullness, resulting in an inability to cope with life and ultimately in stultification. Having served about twenty years of imprisonment, the convicted person would be both mentally and physically wrecked.

The Constitutional Court's First Senate stated that the life sentence in general is—under certain conditions—compatible with the Basic Law. Having surveyed different psychological case studies offering a broad variety of results, the Court concluded that life imprisonment might—at least in certain cases and after a certain period of time—have deforming effects on the human personality.[14]

Taking this eventuality into account, the Court stressed the impact of human dignity—as guaranteed in Art. 1 (1) of the Basic Law— on criminal proceedings and punishment. The free human person and his dignity being the highest values of the constitutional order, the state is obliged to respect and defend those. State authorities therefore have to regard every individual as having equal worth. The constitutional guarantee of human dignity consequently forbids turning an offender into a mere object of crime prevention; it demands, on the contrary, that any convicted person is to be treated in a meaningful way finally aimed at resocialization. Furthermore, it would be intolerable for the state to deprive a person of his freedom without at least providing him with "a ray of hope" of someday regaining it.[15]

Human dignity and the principle of the rule of law demand set rules for the granting of pardon, which sufficiently guarantee this hope. A right of pardon granted in each separate case at the government's discretion does not comply with these rules. Instead, it is up to the law to set the conditions under which the remainder of the sentence is suspended on probation.[16]

---

[12] BVerfGE 33, 1, 11.
[13] BVerfGE 45, 187.
[14] BVerfGE 45, 187, 237.
[15] BVerfGE 45, 187, 227–229.
[16] BVerfGE 45, 187, 243.

Soon after this decision, German parliament amended the Criminal Code by stating the conditions under which courts have to place a convicted person—having served at least fifteen years of his life sentence—on probation.[17]

EQUALITY OF MEN AND WOMEN

In its first decades the Federal Constitutional Court interpreted the constitutional clause "men and women shall have equal rights" (Art. 3 para. 2 GG) as an inhibition to discriminate. The Court ruled: "This constitutional command prohibits in principal and once and for all the legal distinction on the ground of sex."[18] Consequently, the aim is formal equalisation, i.e. the creation of a legal order, which does not refer to the sex of a person anymore. In accordance with this jurisdiction the statutory law—particularly the family law—of the Federal Republic of Germany is worded widely in an egalitarian manner.

In view of the fact that egalitarian law by itself does not ensure the equalisation of man and woman in social reality, the discussion evoked a more dynamic interpretation of the equalisation command of the constitution. The attention no longer turns to rules which differentiate between man and woman. The focus lies on positive (or affirmative) action for women. The central question is, whether these—e.g. the quotas—are in accordance with the Constitution. Indeed, the Constitutional Court has already ruled in earlier decisions that the function of Art. 3 para. 2 GG is also to accomplish the equalisation of the sexes in the future.[19] But it was only in the decision concerning pensions in 1981, that the Court added a compensatory element to its previous understanding of Art. 3 para. 2 GG as a prohibition to discriminate: it argued that the legislator is authorised to adopt unequal treatment, if he—motivated by the idea of the social state— orders standardised compensation of disadvantages, which themselves stem from biological differences. This is not, the Court ruled, a discrimination "on the ground of sex", but a measure, which aims at the compensation of suffered inequalities.[20]

The main turn-around in the court's interpretation of Art. 3 para. 2 GG was the decision concerning the prohibition of work at night for women in 1981.[21] The case concerned the question, whether the statutory rule which prohibited women to work at night was in accordance with the equalisation command and the ban of discrimination in the Constitution. In its ruling the court stated: "the clause 'men and women shall have equal rights' does not only intend to abolish all legal rules which attach advantages or disadvantages to the gender of a person, but also intends to enforce the equalisation of the sexes in future". It aims

---

[17] § 57 a StGB, inserted by law of Dec. 8th, 1981.
[18] BVerfGE 37, 217, 244.
[19] BVerfGE 57, 335, 345 f.
[20] BVerfGE 74, 163, 180.
[21] BVerfGE 87, 1, 42.

to equalise the reality of social life. Consequently women need to have the same opportunities in employment relations as men. Traditional understanding and stereotypes concerning the role of women, which lay a stronger burden or other disadvantages on them, may not be fortified by public actions. Factual inequalities, which are typically suffered by women, may in view of the equalisation command of Art. 3 para. 2 GG be removed by way of positive action. Thus the equalisation command is given a dynamic, reality correcting task.

On the tracks of this jurisdiction the Basic Law was supplemented with a new sentence 2 in Art. 3 para. 2 GG. Its wording reads: "The state shall promote the actual implementation of equal rights for women and men and take steps to eliminate disadvantages that now exist." This wording is an absolute compromise in formula. The Social Democrats would have preferred a wording which expressly allows positive action for women in order to counterbalance historical disadvantages. With such a compensation clause the ban of discrimination in Art. 3 para. 2 GG could have been partially lifted, which would have invalidated the argument of reverse discrimination. But the ever present ghost of a strict quota suffocated the readiness of the conservative parties to negotiate from the very beginning. However, with the formula of compromise in Art. 3 para. 2 sent. 2 GG at least an anchor is fixed in the constitution, which obliges the state to alter reality in the sense of the equalisation command.

A FREEDOM OF SPEECH CASE

An early decision of the Federal Constitutional Court, the Lüth decision[22] articulated the standards and methods for protecting fundamental rights. It set the course for the radiative effect of fundamental rights in all other areas of law.

The facts of the Lüth case can be quickly related:[23]
Veit Harlan was a popular film director under the Nazi regime and the producer of the notoriously anti-semitic film Jud Süss. In 1950 he directed a new movie entitled "Immortal lover". Erich Lüth, Hamburg's director of information and an active member of a group seeking to heal the wounds between Christians and Jews, was outraged by Harlan's re-emergence as a film director. Speaking before an audience of motion picture producers and distributors, he urged his listeners to boycott the movie "Immortal lover". In his view, the boycott was necessary because of Harlan's Nazi past: he was one of the important exponents of anti-semitism. And Lüth was concerned that Harlan's re-emergence would terribly renew distrust against Germany. The film's producer and distributor secured an order from the Superior Court of Hamburg forbidding Lüth to call for a boycott. The Court regarded Lüth's action as an incitement to violate the law of

---

[22] BVerfGE 7, 198.

[23] The presentation of the facts and the grounds of judgment below draws on the translation by Donald P. Kommers, *The Constitutional Jurisprudence of the Federal Republic of Germany*, 2nd ed., 1997, p. 361 ff.

torts. Lüth successfully filed a constitutional complaint asserting a violation of his basic right to free speech[24] by the Superior Court of Hamburg.

In deciding this case, the Federal Constitutional Court laid down for the first time the doctrine of an objective order of values and clarified the relationship between fundamental rights and private law. We are used to understanding human rights as negative entitlements which enable the individual to defend himself against government intrusions into his sphere of freedom. In its ground-breaking Lüth judgment, the Federal Constitutional Court understood basic rights in our constitution not only as subjective rights, but also as objective principles. As an objective order of values the basic rights penetrate the whole legal and social order.

The Court said in the Lüth decision:

> The primary purpose of the basic rights is to safeguard the liberties of the individual against interferences by public authority. They are defensive rights of the individual against the state . . . It is equally true, however, that the Basic Law is not a value-neutral document. Its section on basic rights establishes an objective order of values, and this order strongly reinforces the effective power of basic rights. This value system, which centres upon dignity of the human personality developing freely within the social community, must be looked upon as a fundamental constitutional decision affecting all spheres of law (public and private). It serves as a yardstick for measuring and assessing all actions in the areas of legislation, public administration, and adjudication. Thus it is clear that basic rights also influence the development of private Law. Every provision of private law must be compatible with this system of values, and every such provision must be interpreted in its spirit. [25]

The decision focused attention on the so-called radiative effect of fundamental rights. The Court thus developed a variety of affirmative or protective duties, which oblige the State, especially the legislature, to protect human rights against threats from private individuals or groups. In the course of more than forty-five years of jurisprudence, the Court has drawn several conclusions from the premise that human rights are also objective principles.

This decision leads to an "omnipresence of the fundamental rights in the process of interpreting and applying ordinary statute law".[26] This has proved enormously rich in consequences, especially for civil law. For thinking in private law has changed fundamentally since the beginning of the 20th century. Certainly, private autonomy continues to be the guiding principle of the civil law. But alongside this principle, the principle of the Social State is termed one of the main pillars of the civil law. Under the influence of the fundamental rights and the Social-State clauses, a social law of obligations has been developed, by an interaction between case law and legislation. What this means is a kind of

---

[24] The freedom of speech is laid down in Art. 5. It reads: "Every person shall have the right freely to express and disseminate his opinions in speech, writing, and pictures and to inform himself without hindrance from generelly accessible sources."

[25] BVerfGE 7, 198, 204 f.; *Kommers*, op. cit. fn. 23, p. 363.

[26] Thus Ossenbühl, *Verfassungsgerichtsbarkeit und Fachgerichtsbarkeit*, in: *Festschrift für H.P. Ipsen*, 1977, pp. 129–138.

law that takes the power gap or power imbalance between contractual partners into account and protects the economically inferior, the socially weak. Examples of this are socially-just tenancy law and consumer protection law.

The Court's most recent decision concerns the law of suretyship. The case concerned a young woman who had rendered herself hopelessly over-indebted through a surety bond. She had stood surety for a high bank credit to her father, although she had only a small income (DM1,150 per month). The Federal Constitutional Court decided that the civil courts ought to monitor the content of such contracts and where necessary declare them void, provided always that there be a structural inferiority of the guarantor and that the sure-tyship be an unusually heavy burden on him or her.[27]

The Federal Constitutional Court's case law on the radiative effect of the fundamental rights has not only been applauded. Especially recently, it has been heavily criticised. This is connected on the one hand with the crisis of the Social State and the desire to set bounds on a case law seen as paternalistic. On the other hand, the case law on the radiative effect of the fundamental rights favours a great breadth and intensity of supervision by the Federal Constitutional Court, which may endanger the separation of powers.

PRESS FREEDOM AND THE RIGHT OF PRIVACY

One problem which has concerned German justice until very recently is the tension between press freedom and the right to privacy. Both principles are recognised in the Basic Law. It lays down freedom of the press in Article 5, which reads: "Freedom of the press and freedom of reporting by means of broadcasts and films shall be guaranteed. There shall be no censorship." As against this, Article 1 declares the dignity of the person inviolable, while Article 2 protects the free development of the personality. The interaction of the two last-mentioned Articles implies that every person enjoys an autonomous sphere of private life. Only that person can decide whether and how far others are to be allowed access to that space. Both fundamental rights are of equal value. That is how the German constitution itself describes the basic conflict between press freedom and protection of the individual sphere.

The Federal Constitutional Court was called upon in the seventies to set criteria for weighing up the public's interest in information against protection of the intimate sphere of the individual. A convicted accomplice to murder lodged a constitutional complaint because his deed was to be presented as a television documentary. The court's conclusion was as follows: "Solving the conflict has to start from the point that it is the Constitution's desire that both constitutional values should be essential components of the Basic Law's free democratic basic order, so that neither of them may claim any primacy in principle." It argued

---

[27]   BVerfGE 89, 214.

that on the one hand the Constitution's image of the person and the structure of the national community required acknowledgement of the autonomy of the individual personality. On the other hand, they also called for the securing of a free climate of life, something possible only through freedom of communication. The decision continues: "Both constitutional values must accordingly in the event of conflict be brought to a balance as far as possible; if that cannot be achieved, it must determine which interest will defer to the other in the light of the type of the case and its special circumstances. It must be decided which interest must succumb. In doing so, the court must consider both constitutional values in their relation to human dignity as the centre of the Constitutions's value system". Applying these principles and considering that the complainant was about to be released, the Court found that at this time the documentary ought not to be broadcast. The complainant's right to an unencumbered new start outweighed the television viewer's interest in information.[28]

In German constitutional law theory we term this weighing-up procedure the restoration of "practical concordance":[29] According to it, conflicting constitutional principles are as far as possible to be brought into balance, and delimited in such a way as to take as far-reaching effect for all concerned as possible. That is more or less elegantly formulated. But this formula of practical concordance only describes the problem, without laying down any criterion for solving it. (We lawyers are after all the masters of that). The decisional practice of both the German courts and the German Press Council illustrates the difficulty of weighing up conflicting principles and interests against each other in the specific case.

SUMMARY

The protection of fundamental rights in the Federal Republic of Germany has a history of success. That may be said even by a President of the Federal Constitutional Court without distasteful self-praise, for the credit lies primarily with the previous generations of judges. The Federal Constitutional Court set up in 1951 has in the 48 years of its existence become an important core element in the German constitutional system. Its case law, especially on fundamental rights, has not only caused the Basic Law to take on concrete form and develop roots in our political system.[30] More, it has created an awareness in the people that they are not exposed defencelessly to measures of the State.[31] And not least, the rulings have sharpened both public actors 'and the ordinary citizens' sense that the catalogue of fundamental rights constitutes directly applicable law.

---

[28] So the Federal Constitutional Court in the famed *Lebach Case* (1973) BVerfGE 35, 202, 225 f.
[29] Cf. K. Hesse, op. cit. fn. 6, 142.
[30] K. Hesse, *Verfassungsrechtsprechung im geschichtlichen Wandel*, in: JZ 1955, 265, 266.
[31] Benda/Klein, *Lehrbuch des Verfassungsprozeßrechts*, 1991, marginalnr. 313.

It certainly cannot be denied that the Federal Constitutional Court has taken the Basic Law beyond mere application and developed it further. Consider only the example of the right to informational self-determination. Occasionally its political activism has been criticised. Since the force of law inheres in its rulings that overthrow norms, the competition with the legislature cannot fail to be seen. This is ultimately a consequence of the primacy of the constitution. All the same, the Court must be wary of juridifying politics too much, or narrowing the legislature's or the executive's creative power excessively.[32] Its working ethos here, continually to be pondered, must accordingly be scrupulously to demarcate its own sphere of tasks, and not poach on the preserves of the other powers.

---

[32] *Hans Vorländer* sees a problematic tendency here towards juridification of politics by the Federal Constitutional Court, in *idem, Die Verfassung—Idee und Geschichte*, 1999, p. 94. Examples continually cited here are the second abortion case (BVerfGE 88, 203, 210-213) and the wealth-tax decision (BVerfGE 93, 121).

10

The Response of the French Constitutional Court to the Growing Importance of International Law

NOËLLE LENOIR

INTRODUCTION

The national courts and the globalisation of the law

The globalisation of the law[1] is generating an upheaval in the practice of the courts and, especially, in the way national courts conceive and perform their task. Rules of international law of whatever origin—bilateral or multilateral treaties, instruments adopted by international organisations, Community secondary legislation and so on—play an ever growing role in the decisions of national courts, implicitly or explicitly. The legal world is now an open world. Legal systems communicate between countries, between continents even. And in Europe, the decisions of two international courts—the European Court of Human Rights and the European Court of Justice—seriously influence national case law. In France, for example, even though the judgments given by the two courts are not directly enforceable and have no value as binding authorities to be followed by the French courts, the courts tend to follow them all the same. The Court of Cassation, for instance, recently departed from earlier decisions on transsexualism in order to adopt a decision of the Strasbourg Court. In four leading cases decided in 1990,[2] the Court of Cassation held that "transsexualism, even if medically recognised, cannot be analysed as a genuine change of sex", which meant that those concerned could never have their entries in the registers of births and deaths altered. The European Court of Human Rights then

---

[1] Mireille Delmas-Marty, *La mondialisation du droit, chances et risques*, Revue Dalloz-Sirey, 1999, 5ème cahier, chronique, p. 43. See also "Democracy and the Global Order" (Polity Press, London, 1995).

[2] Cass. Ière civ.; 21.5.90; JCP 1990.II.21588, with report by Counciller Massip and submissions by Madame Flipo, Advocate-General; and JCP.1990, I, 3475, M. Gobert, "*Le transsexualisme ou la difficulté d'exister*".

gave judgment against France—in *B.* v. *France* on 25 March 1992[3]—for refusing to modify the status and forename of a transsexual who had become a female, whereupon the Court of Cassation immediately reversed its earlier decision, accepting the applicant's request for changes to entries in the register of births (*Marc X* v. *Procureur général*, judgment given on 11 December 1992). The Council of State also tends to adapt its case-law. An example can be found in a disciplinary case: in *Subrini* (judgment given on 11 July 1984), it had refused to follow decisions of the European Court in Strasbourg holding that Article 6 of the European Human Rights Convention imposed a duty to ensure that hearings of disciplinary courts were open to the public. But it departed from its own decision in *Maubleu* on 14 February 1996 and followed the Strasbourg Court's policy.[4] The Council of State, on the other hand, stood by its position, deciding that there was no obligation for the submissions of the Government Commissioners before administrative courts to be presented in the course of an adversarial procedure.[5]

Even if national courts do not always follow decisions given in Strasbourg and Luxembourg, they refer to them more and more often, sometimes going so far as to incorporate the decisions of foreign courts in their *ratio decidendi*. A shining example can be seen in the German Constitutional Court in Karlsruhe. In a decision given on 13 December 1977 on the immunity to be enjoyed by foreign governments in court proceedings, the Court considered the legislation and case-law of 108 foreign countries and several decisions of the International Court of Justice.[6] The French Court of Cassation, even before its famous judgment in *Administration des Douanes* v. *Société des Cafés Jacques Vabre* on 24 May 1975, where it upheld for the first time the primacy of a treaty over domestic legislation, even if that legislation was enacted subsequently, reviewed the law concerning the relationship between international and domestic law in the then five other Member States of the European Community.[7] Even the Supreme Court of the United States, breaking new ground in the country's judicial history, now has no qualms about referring to decisions of foreign and international courts and the European Human Rights Convention.[8]

---

[3] By judgment No 63, the Strasbourg Court ordered France to pay the applicant, converted to feminine gender by surgical operation, 100 000 francs damages and 35 000 francs costs, holding that the applicant was daily in a situation that was incompatible with respect for her private life within the meaning of article 8 of the European Human Rights Convention.

[4] See judgment with submissions by Government Commissioner Marc Sanson, in RFDA, Nov Dec. 1996, p. 1186.

[5] See judgment of 29 July 1998 *Mme Esclatine* in AJDA, 20 January 1999, p. 69.

[6] See *The integration of international and European Community law into the national legal order*, ed. Michel Eisemann, (Kluwer Law International, The Hague, 1996), p. 102.

[7] See submissions of Adolphe Touffait, General Prosecutor at the Court of Cassation, in Revue Dalloz, 1975, 27e cahier.

[8] In a dissenting opinion when judgment was given in *William D. Elledge* v. *Florida* on 13 October 1998 (extradition of an American citizen previously condemned to death), Judge Breyer refers to a judgment and to article 3 of the European Human Rights Convention prohibiting cruel, inhuman and degrading treatment applied to the situation of people waiting on Death Row in the United States. He did so in the following terms: " Finally, a reasoned answer to the "delay" question

These court practices express new forms of solidarity. There is an emerging international dialogue between courts which goes far beyond the bounds of the official cooperation expressed through judicial assistance in criminal and civil matters. This is an ongoing, often informal dialogue. It is established in the course of the direct contacts that arise on the occasion of colloquia, conferences, symposia, visits and exchanges as well as via information and communication technologies. The decisions of the major courts are now accessible in real time thanks to the internet. A databank such as that compiled by the Venice Commission[9] is an exemplary source of information from all the supreme or constitutional courts of the States belonging to the Council of Europe. In democratic countries, the courts are using language that is converging more and more all the time. Looking beyond the cultural gaps dividing the common law from the civil law or influencing the specific modes of judicial organisation in different countries or even in specific regions (Scotland or Alsace, for example), bridges are being built between different legal systems. Just as public international law has conventionally been regarded as being based on "the general principles of law recognised by civilised nations", so, in recent times, it has been found logical to regard the "constitutional traditions common to the Member States" of the European Union as one of the sources of the principles of Community law.[10] Clearly, then, the principles of domestic law will serve as the basis for the principles of international law just as international law will "impregnate" domestic law.

There is a two-way movement. This interdependence of national legal systems is one of the salient features of the globalisation promoted in both legal and economic terms.

Does this mean that the courts are in effect putting an end to the sovereignty of the State that has been affirmed in Europe since the Middle Ages? Certainly not. But there is little room for doubt that the concept of sovereignty is in a state of flux. The concept of sovereignty, linked to the concept of the State, exercising its absolute centralised power over a clearly-defined territory—as is explained in the writings of Bodin, one of the first theorists of the modern

could help to ease the practical anomaly created when foreign courts refuse to extradite capital defendants to America for fear of undue delay in execution. See *Soering* v. *United Kingdom*, 11 Eur.H.R.Rep.439 (1989) (holding that the extradition of a capital defendant to America would be a violation of Article 3 of the European Convention on Human Rights, primarily because of the risk of delay before execution. "

[9] The Venice Commission is an advisory body consisting of independent experts whose task is to promote knowledge of the legal systems of the member countries of the Council of Europe with a view to harmonising them and reinforcing the democratic institutions of the relevant countries. It was set up by the Council of Europe in 1990. Its very rich legal database can be accessed at www.coe.fr/venice.

[10] This expression, taken over from the case-law of the Court of Justice of the European Communities, is used in article F(2) of the Maastricht Treaty, now article 6 of the Amsterdam Treaty, which provides "The Union shall respect fundamental rights, as guaranteed by the European Convention for the Protection of Human Rights and Fundamental Freedoms, signed in Rome on 4 November 1950, and as they result from the constitutional traditions common to the Member States, as general principles of Community law".

republic[11]—was the original source in law of national independence. Two centuries later it was reviewed on a contractual basis by the likes of Locke[12] and Rousseau; sovereignty, the fundamental attribute of statehood, has also been seen as the underlying principle of the relationship of trust that is supposed to unite the government and the governed. Sovereignty thus became democratic, as exemplified in Rousseau's statement that "sovereignty . . . is no more than the exercise of the general Will" that is incarnate in the Nation. Source of legitimate power, "every act of sovereignty" may thus be conceived as "absolute, independent of what went before it; the sovereign does not act because he has willed it but because he now wills it".[13] This is still the dominant conception in the French constitutional system, where sovereignty is the lifeblood of democracy and national sovereignty is treated as being the sovereignty of the people combining in a political community. This is the inspiration for Article 3 of the Declaration of Human and Civic Rights of 1789, which declares that "the principle of sovereignty resides in the Nation". Article 3 of the Constitution of 1958 likewise states that "National sovereignty shall belong to the people, who shall exercise it through their representatives and by means of referendum."

Sovereignty and democracy thus have shared roots, and it is hardly surprising that, after the Second World War, States built up the international community on the basis of the equal sovereignty of each of them. Article 2(1) of the United Nations Charter provides that "the Organisation is based on the principle of the sovereign equality of all its members".

Is it not surprising that, at the same time and in what might seem a paradoxical way, these States agreed to transfer certain of their sovereign powers to international organisations like the UN and its specialised agencies or, in the case of European States, to organisations such as the Council of Europe and the European Communities? Is it not surprising that they even agreed to submit their disputes to the jurisdiction of international courts, so much so indeed that they allow their citizens to bring their actions direct in the two European courts—in Strasbourg and in Luxembourg?

True, accepting limitations on one's own sovereignty is a defining sovereign act. But the fact remains that the effect of establishing European regional entities with ever-expanding areas of activity is to constrain national legal systems within a growing volume of common norms.

In this kind of context, national courts are faced by a wholly new kind of challenge. They must continue to play their fundamental role of preserving the values expressed by domestic law as the "expression of the general will" while endeavouring to reconcile this domestic legal order and an international legal order that is constantly evolving.

[11] J. Bodin, *Les Six Livres de la Republic*, (Paris, Fayard, 1986) (First edition, 1576).
  J.L. Holzgrefe, "The Origins of Modern International Relations Theory", *Review of International Studies*, 15/1/89, p. 11.
[12] See J. Dunn. *Locke*, (Oxford University Press, 1984).
[13] In *Fragments politiques*, III, 11, Œuvres complètes, (Paris, Gallimard, La Pléïade), Tome IV, p. 485.

The purpose of this paper is to describe how the French constitutional courts approach international law, particularly European human rights law, when exercising the jurisdiction conferred on them by the Constitution of 1958.

The status of public international law in the French legal system

France is a country where written law predominates; it has a Constitution containing detailed provisions governing the relationship between public international law and domestic law. Their effect is that the French system is of the unitary rather than the dualist kind.[14]

It will be remembered that for the main proponents of the unitary approach, the best-known of whom are the Austrian constitutional theorist Hans Kelsen and the French international law theorist Georges Scelle, international law and domestic law constitute a single legal order in which international law dominates. For the proponents of the dualist approach, the international and domestic legal orders are radically separate entities, and no litigant in a national court can plead a rule of international law that has not been incorporated by statute in the domestic legal order. The Member States of the European Union are either unitary (Belgium, Spain and France, in particular[15]) or dualist (Ireland, Italy,[16] the United Kingdom and Germany[17]).

In France, a unitary country, the position is clear. Treaties can in principle be pleaded against individuals, provided only that they have been duly ratified and published in the *Journal Officiel de la Republic Française*. There is no need, as there is in the "dualist" countries, for them to have "naturalised", as it were, either by a statute making them enforceable or by some other instrument

---

[14] Rebecca M.M. Wallace, *International Law*, (Sweet and Maxwell, London, 1997), p. 36.

[15] In Belgium, the attachment to the unitary system flows from the cases rather than a specific provision of the Constitution. In Spain, article 96.1 of the Constitution of 27 December 1978 provides that "International treaties properly concluded and officially published in Spain shall be part of the domestic legal order . . . ".

[16] The Italian Constitution of 27 December 1947 contains no provisions on the insertion of treaties in the domestic legal order beyond a provision that "The Italian legal order shall comply with generally recognised rules of international law", which draws the mind to article 25 of the German Basic Law of 23 May 1949, which provides: "The general rules of public international law shall be an integral component of federal law . . .". In Italy, if a treaty provision is to be applicable in the domestic legal order, there must a statute either making the treaty enforceable and reproducing its provisions in an annex or transposing the treaty 's provisions into domestic legislation.

In Ireland, the situation is clearer still under article 29.6 of the Constitution of 1 July 1937, whereby "no international agreement shall form part of the law of the State except as determined by Parliament". Likewise in the United Kingdom, the common law rule is that treaty provisions are applicable only of they have been expressly incorporated in the domestic legal order by an Act of Parliament: *Brind* v. *Secretary of State for the Home Department* [1991] 1 All ER 720, HL).

[17] B. Verf G74, 358 [370] of 26 March 1987. The Federal Constitutional Court at Karlsruhe held that the statute inserting the European Human Rights Convention into the domestic legal order had given the Convention the status of a statute. But some lawyers argue that in fact the legislature had renounced the possibility of enacting statutes conflicting with it, which in practice thus gave it supra-legislative, or in some eyes, constitutional status.

transposing them in whole or in part into domestic law. Article 55 of the French Constitution of 1958, partly based on the previous Constitution of 1946, provides that "treaties or agreements duly ratified or approved shall, upon publication, prevail over Acts of Parliament, subject, in regard to each agreement or treaty, to its application by the other party". The French legal system is thus in theory a welcoming host to international law. Reality, however, is not quite so black-and-white. Experience has shown that the distinction between the unitary and the dualist countries is by no means as sharp as the theories might suggest. The fact is that there is a wide variety of techniques for inserting rules of international law into national legal systems "so that we see unitary systems with dualist features and dualist systems with unitary features".[18]

Let us take the example of France. Even though the negotiation and conclusion of treaties is within the powers of the executive branch, Parliament is entitled to express its views on certain international commitments, which it can accordingly delay or even block altogether. Article 53 of the Constitution requires statutory authorisation for the ratification and approval of the most important treaties and agreements—peace and trade treaties, treaties or agreements relating to international organisations and those that commit the finances of the State, that modify provisions that are matters for statute, those relating to the status of persons, and those that involve the cession, exchange or addition of territory.

For the French courts, as for the courts in other countries, it will not suffice for a treaty to have entered into force for it to be automatically capable of being pleaded against an individual. This will be the case only if the court holds its provisions to be sufficiently precise to operate without national implementing measures, in the form of primary or subordinate legislation. For the Court of Cassation, the provisions of the New York Convention on the Rights of the Child 1990 "cannot be pleaded in the courts as they solely create obligations incumbent on States which are not directly applicable in domestic law".[19] The Council of State, however, has held that a distinction must be made between provisions of the Convention which are directly applicable and those which are not.[20]

The effectiveness of international law in terms of domestic law thus often depends on the common attitude of the executive, legislative and judicial branches. Community secondary legislation is, however, the exception. In all Member States of the European Union there is machinery for the direct incorporation of the instruments enacted pursuant to the European treaties (Community directives and regulations) into domestic law, irrespective of whether the State is unitary or dualist. Moreover, the intervention of the

---

[18] Jean Dhommeaux, *"Monismes et Dualismes en droit international des droits de l'homme"*, in Annuaire Français de International law (AFDI), XLI, 1995, p. 447.

[19] Judgment of 10 March 1993, *Lejeune*, RGDIP, 1993, p. 1051.

[20] Judgment of 29 July 1994, *Préfet de la Seine-Maritime v/ Abdelmoula*, RGDIP, 1995, p. 502.

European Court of Justice promotes unification of the application and interpretation of these instruments. This does not exclude differences of interpretation as between the European Court of Justice and the national courts, but at least the divergences gradually narrow down in such a way as to strengthen the impact of this body of legislation. The French Council of State, for instance, now acknowledges that Community directives that have not been transposed by the deadline can none the less have legal effects. It has held that national authorities could not in such a case "maintain provisions of subordinate legislation that are incompatible with the declared objectives of the relevant directives",[21] thus accepting the philosophy of the Luxembourg Court.

The French Constitution does not merely define the conditions for the applicability of an international instrument in the domestic legal order. It also states the position occupied by international law in the hierarchy of norms, at least as regards the relationship between treaty and statute. The 1946 Constitution was the first to make detailed provisions on this subject. It did so in a fashion that was distinctly favourable to the reception of international instruments into domestic law. Admittedly, after the war, great hopes were placed in the United Nations set up by the San Francisco Charter, to which the Preamble to the Constitution of 1946[22] implicitly refers when it allows the "limitations of sovereignty needed for the organisation and defence of peace". Going beyond this position of principle, the authors of the 1946 Constitution displayed an undeniable openness towards international law, declaring unequivocally that treaties prevailed over domestic statutes, whether they predated (article 26[23]) or postdated (article 28[24]) them. The point at the time was to avoid certain mistakes of the past by preventing Parliament from enacting statutes designed solely to enable France to evade the obligations it had entered into. Between the two wars, statutes had been enacted to exclude nationals of certain foreign countries from the benefit of treaties relating to commercial and industrial property (rents, in particular).[25]

---

[21] Judgment of 3 February 1989, *Compagnie Alitalia*, RFDA, 1989, 391, with submissions by the Government Commissioner, Mr Chahid Nouraï.

[22] The Preamble to the Constitution of 1946, alongside the Constitution of 1958 and the Declaration of Human and Civic Rights of 1789, is part of the "bloc de constitutionnalité" which serves as the reference for Constitutional Council's constitutional review function.

[23] By this article, "diplomatic treaties that have been properly ratified and published shall have the force of statute even if they are contrary to French statutes, and their application shall require no further legislative provisions than those whereby they were ratified".

[24] By this article, "since diplomatic treaties that have been properly ratified and published enjoy greater authority than domestic statutes, their provisions may be repealed, amended or suspended only by virtue of a proper denunciation, notified by diplomatic channels". "Where one of the treaties referred to in article 27 (treaties whose ratification requires the prior authorisation of Parliament) is concerned, denunciation may be authorised by the National Assembly, except as regards trade treaties".

[25] Lawrence Preuss, *"Droit international et Droit interne dans la Constitution de 1946"* in Revue international d'histoire politique et constitutional, 1951, p. 199.

The authors of the 1958 Constitution maintained the principle that treaties prevail; this is expressed in Article 55. But the 1958 Constitution is substantially less internationally-minded than its predecessor. Both the letter and the spirit are more "sovereignty-oriented" ("*souverainiste*"), to use the currently fashionable epithet in France to describe those who oppose globalisation and the transfer of state powers that it entails. Two innovations illustrate the point. The first is the procedure introduced by Article 54, which confers on the new French constitutional court (the Constitutional Council was first set up by the Constitution of the Fifth Republic) jurisdiction to verify on application by a public authority whether a treaty contains clauses that would be contrary to the Constitution; if so, the treaty cannot be ratified without prior revision of the Constitution. The second innovation is to be found in Article 55 which, while stating the principle that treaties prevail over statutes, imposes an unprecedented condition for their implementation, namely the "application of the treaty by the other party". This "reciprocity" clause aroused considerable academic hostility on the ground that it would theoretically be sufficient for French authorities to rely on it in relation to this or that country for France to feel free of its own commitment. The reluctance of the authors of the 1958 Constitution to accept international law flows from the parliamentary debates of the early 1950s on the Treaty establishing the European Defence Community (EDC). Ratification of that treaty was ultimately rejected by the National Assembly on 30 August 1954. One of those opposed to the Treaty, Michel Debré, who was a Senator, subsequently became one of the principal authors of the Constitution as Minister of Justice under General De Gaulle, Prime Minister in 1958. In 1952 he had stated before the Council of the Republic (as the Senate was known in the Fourth Republic) that the EDC treaty was "thoroughly unconstitutional" by reason of the sovereignty that it would require France to abandon.[26]

This historical backdrop will help to clarify the system of the 1958 Constitution, under which the primacy of public international law is now no more than relative and conditional.

In such a context, it was difficult to foresee the likely attitude of the French constitutional courts to the relationship between international law and domestic law. But their attitude quickly became clear. In the 1970s, the Constitutional Council used actions based both on article 61 of the Constitution (constitutional review of statutes) and on article 54 (jurisdiction of the Council to review treaties for compatibility with the Constitution prior to ratification) to develop its case-law, its jurisprudence—and commentators were quick to observe, its prudence. As a response to the inexorable rise of international and especially European law, this prudence can perhaps be seen as expressing the concerns of a court whose chief parameter for review is the Constitution and which is wary of shifting the balance of its components once it proceeds on the basis of inter-

---

[26] These views are cited and commented on in Nguyen Quoc Dinh, "*La Constitution de 1958 et le droit international*", RDP, 1959, p. 516.

national law. These scruples are not confined to the French judiciary. And the position of the French judiciary is presumably not fixed for all time, since constitutional is basically a "living law", as the Italian constitutional judge Gustavo Zagrebelsky has so brilliantly demonstrated.[27] Constitutional courts give their rulings in the light both of the economic, social and cultural context and of the legal environment. It is all the more difficult for them to ignore the phenomenon of the internationalisation of the law as the phenomenon is particularly strong in the area of the protection of fundamental rights where the constitutional courts are by definition especially active.

THE CONSTITUTIONAL COUNCIL, WHEN REVIEWING STATUTES FOR CONSTITUTIONALITY, HESITATES TO REVIEW STATUTES DIRECTLY FOR CONFORMITY WITH TREATIES

The first point to be made is that the constitutional review of statutes in France is a preventive review, that is to say it is undertaken before the statute comes into force. The second paragraph of article 61 of the Constitution reads: ". . . Acts of Parliament may be referred to the Constitutional Council, before their promulgation, by the President of the Republic, The Prime Minister, the President of the National Assembly, the President of the Senate or sixty deputies or sixty senators". Other constitutional courts in Europe exercise a comparable form of review. The French experience, however, is unique in that the preventive review of a statute is the only kind that that the Constitutional Council can exercise in principle.[28] The right to bring an action to attack a statute in France is thus limited in terms of both time and place. On the other hand, the procedure in the Constitutional Council is highly efficient. Cases are decided very quickly as the Council has only one month (or eight days in urgent cases declared by the Government[29]) to come to its decision: it cannot, therefore, evade the

---

[27] See "*La doctrine du droit vivant*" AIJC, 1986, p. 55. See also the forthcoming thesis by JJ Pardini, "*Le juge constitutionnel et le fait, en Italie et en France*", which emphasises the influence of social reality on constitutional case-law, a reality which neatly explains every development in it. The author also shows that this influence is exerted both in the case of post-promulgation review of statutes that are already in operation, as in the Italian model, and in the more abstract pre-promulgation review in the French model.

[28] This statement cannot, however, be made in black and white terms. Although a statute can be referred to the Constitutional Council only before promulgation, the Council claims jurisdiction to review a statute that is already promulgated if the statute referred to it "amend, amplify or affect the scope of the" existing statute. In decision DC. 99-410 of 15 March 1999 (institutional act changing the status of New Caledonia, an overseas territory enjoying extensive autonomy), the Constitutional Council saw fit to rule exceptionally on a provision of a statute enacted in 1985 whereby in the event of personal bankruptcy the bankrupt was automatically disqualified from public elective office. The Constitutional Council held that an automatic disqualification was contrary to the principle that penalties must be both necessary and proportionate as laid down by the Declaration of Human and Civic Rights of 1789. The other administrative and ordinary courts will now have to draw the conclusions that flow from this declaration of unconstitutionality. See JP.Camby, "*Une loi promulguée frappée d'inconstitutionnalité?*" in RDP, No 33, 1999.

[29] The Government has never yet made such a declaration.

difficulties raised by a case by simply not setting it down on its cause-list.[30] What is more, a legislative provision held to be unconstitutional disappears from the domestic legal scene as if it had never been enacted. A statute censured by the Constitutional Council is published in the *Journal Officiel* without the provisions found to be contrary to the Constitution. The Constitutional Council can even hold an entire statute to be contrary to the Constitution and annul it *ex toto*.[31]

The short time available to the Constitutional Council is one of the important factors behind the Council's refusal to review statutes for conformity with rules of international law. In its IVG (voluntary termination of pregnancy, or abortion for short) decision of 15 January 1975, the Constitutional Council held that, despite the principle of the primacy of treaties established by article 55 of the Constitution, it had no jurisdiction to review statutes for conformity with France's international commitments. This was no trivial case: the Act referred was to decriminalise abortion, previously severely punishable under legislation dating from 1920. Abortion was now authorised in medical establishments under certain conditions. The bill had been presented by the Government of President Giscard d'Estaing, but its enactment was possible only thanks to the support of the left-wing opposition in the National Assembly. Several leading political figures in the governing majority were firmly against it. The President of the Senate, who signed the reference to Constitutional Council, pleaded violation of the right to life secured by article 2 of the European Human Rights Convention.[32] How was the right to life to be reconciled with the woman's freedom to "manage" her own body to the point of being able to abort? Many constitutional courts in Europe have had to tackle this dilemma.[33] A comparative study of their decisions shows that they have gone about it in all sorts of different ways. Some have held that the right to life did not concern the embryo and was enjoyed by the child only after its birth (Austria and Spain, for instance), whereas others have held that the embryo enjoyed a right to life under both the European Human Rights Convention and the national Constitution (German Constitutional Court, decision of 25 February 1975[34]).

The French Constitutional Council refrained from examining the value and scope of the right to life secured by the European Convention. It declined to consider the argument, purely and simply declaring it inadmissible as exceeding its jurisdiction. The decision holds that it is not for the Constitutional Council,

---

[30] For example, the Spanish Constitutional Court, on a reference in 1988 by members of parliament concerning a bioethics statute which raised the question of the constitutionality of human embryo research, had still not come to a decision in 1999.

[31] This was what happened to the Falloux Act on investment aid to private educational establishments by local authorities: DC n° 93-329, 13 January 1994, recueil p. 9.

[32] This article requires the right to life to be protected by law.

[33] See the 1986 volume of the International Yearbook of Constitutional Justice (AIJC), the central theme of which was "Voluntary termination of pregnancy in comparative constitutional case-law", particularly the summary report by Professor Franck Moderne, p. 218.

[34] Report by Professor Georges Ress, in AIJC (*op. cit.*), p. 89.

hearing an application pursuant to article 61 of the Constitution, to "review a statute for conformity with a treaty or an international agreement".[35]

This decision is not necessarily *sui generis* but it cannot be seen in isolation from its context. The Act in question, which was eventually passed after lengthy and very difficult debates led on the Government side by Simone Veil, Minister for Social Affairs at the time,[36] had achieved a form of equilibrium between those who were against any form of legalisation of abortion (the Catholic Church, in particular) and supporters of a more advanced degree of liberalisation. Produced in response to the demands of feminist movements that had placed the decriminalisation of abortion at the centre of their concern, the Act was also a response to the expectations of the general public. The effect of the ban on abortion was to encourage clandestine operations, exposing women to serious risks, sometimes fatal, and this was the situation which the reform sought to remedy, among other things. The Constitutional Council, therefore, was at pains to avoid entering the political arena and relaunching a debate that was only just closed. The unusually brief grounds given for its decision are evidence of this. It was, after all, in this decision that the Constitutional Council, for the first time, held by way of *obiter dictum* that it did "not enjoy the same power of discretion or the same decision-making power as Parliament". Since then the Constitutional Council has used this expression whenever it felt moved to exercise only limited review of a statute, leaving the other public authorities with their extensive discretionary powers.

In any event the 1975 decision came as a bombshell. It had not been expected that the Council would deny its own jurisdiction. Indeed, not long before, it had posited an extensive concept of its jurisdiction, when it decided of its own motion that the parameters for its review could extend beyond the Constitution of 1958 and include the Preamble to the Constitution of 1946[37] and the Declaration of Human and Civic Rights of 1789.[38] How, then, are we to explain the fact that it refused to apply the principle of the primacy of treaties when article 55 of the Constitution seemed to indicate it should? With a very few exceptions, commentators—some of whom subsequently actually became members of Constitutional Council, for instance Professor François Luchaire and Professor Jacques Robert—deplored a decision which seemed to them to

---

[35] See commentary on decision 74-54 DC of 15 January 1975 in Louis Favoreu et Loïc Philip, *Les grandes décisions du Conseil Constitutionnel* Dalloz, 9th edition, 1997, p. 305, which gives references to all other commentaries on that decision that have appeared in the legal journals.

[36] She became a member of the Constitutional Council in 1998.

[37] DC 71-44, 16 July 1971, on freedom of association, which the court ranked among the fundamental principles recognised by the laws of the Republic mentioned in the Preamble to the Constitution of 1946: recueil p. 25.

[38] DC 73-51, 27 December 1973, on tax assessments by the authorities; the Constitutional Council held that the "principle of equality before the law set out in the Declaration of Human and Civic Rights of 1789" had constitutional status: recueil p. 25.

deprive the article of its real effect by allowing statutes that were contrary to treaties to enter the domestic legal order.[39]

The justification for the abortion decision is difficult to identify as the Council's proceedings are strictly secret.[40] Sittings are held *in camera* and no person other than a member of the Constitutional Council is admitted, not even the advocates.[41] The procedure is exclusively a written procedure. The secrecy of discussions and voting is absolute, and dissenting opinions are not allowed. Explanations by academic writers of the decisions given by the Constitutional Council are inevitably, therefore, based on supposition. That said, however, an interesting explanation for the decision of 15 January 1975 has been offered by Professor Jean Rivéro, one of France's most eminent legal theorists. In an article entitled: "Judges declining to govern", Professor Rivéro describes what he sees as a "new institution, breaking with a long tradition of absolute parliamentary sovereignty and entering a legal environment that was not keen to welcome it, so that it had to remain modest if it was to gain acceptance and takes its ultimate place in the general political and judicial set-up".[42] This is a plausible interpretation. But it does not suffice. It must not be forgotten that at the same time the Constitutional Council was taking a bolder line, creating the concept of the "bloc de constitutionnalité" and in the process putting itself forward as a veritable Constitutional Court, contrary to the intentions of the authors of the Constitution, who did not wish to give it this kind of power. Consequently, other practical and legal considerations have to be factored into the equation.

The first—practical—consideration lies in the specific difficulties facing the constitutional judge in France. France, of course, like other countries in Europe, is bound by a considerable number of international commitments involving provisions that are commonly difficult to interpret, and the Council is given but a month to come to its decision. This time-limit is tight enough already, but the problem is aggravated in the case of Community law by the need for a reference

[39] Mr François Luchaire pointed out that in an earlier decision of 19 June 1970 (DC 70-39), the Constitutional Council had brought "the entire body of international law . . . into the-legislative category", by treating decisions of the Council of the Communities under the Community treaties in the same way as the treaties. He saw it as consequently paradoxical that the Constitutional Council failed to draw the obvious conclusion as regards the constitutional review of statutes. See "*Le Conseil Constitutionnel et la protection des libertés*" in Mélanges Waline, Tome II, p. 561. Mr Jacques Robert, writing in Le Monde on 18 January 1975, regretted that the Council was not exercising its full jurisdiction.

[40] The institutional act of 7 November 1958 on the Constitutional Council specifies the oath that each member is to take before the President of the Republic upon appointment: all must swear "that they will properly and faithfully discharge their functions, perform them fully impartially in respect for the Constitution, preserve confidentiality as to proceedings and voting, make no public statement and enter into no consultancy with respect to matters within the Council's jurisdiction". This paper is by no means affected, as it offers no more than a dynamic historical account of the Constitutional Council's decisions in an area where controversy is the most common.

[41] The position is different when the Constitutional Council sits to hear electoral cases. Following amendments made to its Standing Orders in 1995, the Council has made provision for the parties and their legal advisers to be heard, albeit *in camera*.

[42] See his article in the March 1975 issue of l'Actualité Juridique du Droit Administratif (AJDA), p. 134.

for a preliminary ruling to the Court of Justice of the European Communities, which often takes a very long time before giving its ruling.[43] Evidence in support of the hypothesis that these purely practical considerations influence the Constitutional Council's decision can be found in the change in its attitude in electoral cases.[44] Here the time-limits do not apply, and the Council has no hesitations about referring to international law as a supra-legislative source. When sitting as an electoral court, it has no objections to entertaining a plea requiring it to review electoral legislation for conformity with treaties.[45]

Even so, the decision of 15 January 1975 does not recite any such practical considerations. It merely sets out substantive grounds in support of its inability to review the statute for conformity with instruments of international law. These grounds manifest a highly traditional approach to international law seen in purely contractual terms, the application of which depends on the goodwill of States—the comity of nations—alone. The decision states that the principle of the primacy of treaties asserted by article 55 of the Constitution is "both relative and contingent", whereas its decisions are absolute and definitive.[46] The point about the superiority of treaties over statutes being relative is that it applies "only within the field of application of the treaty". And the reason why it is contingent is that is "subject to a condition of reciprocity the realisation of which can vary with the conduct of the State or States that signed the treaty and the time when the question whether the condition is met falls to be answered". This vision of international law refers to the legal positivism of the early 20th Century, when the mandatory force of international law was seen as depending on the will of the sovereign State. This approach was that taken by Italian writers such as Anzilotti and Cavaglieri, and more recently by a certain strand of academic thinking in France. The international courts show little inclination to take it, except perhaps in the decision given in 1927 by the Permanent Court of International Justice (PCIJ) in the well-known *Lotus* case.[47]

Since this doctrine emerged, much water has flowed under the bridge. Nowadays the effectiveness of international instruments more and more commonly depends on their own machinery. This is particularly true of European

---

[43] Two courts that can be regarded as constitutional courts have decided to make such references—the Belgian Court of Arbitration and the Land Court of one of the German Länder.

[44] The Constitutional Council has had jurisdiction to consider whether elections to the National Assembly and the Senate have been properly conducted since this jurisdiction was withdrawn from the two Houses by the Constitution of 1958. The Constitutional Council has the same jurisdiction in relation to referendums and Presidential elections.

[45] It did this twice in 1988 (decision of 21 October on the legislative elections in the département of Val d'Oise and decision of 8 November on the legislative elections in the département of Seine Saint-Denis) and again in 1998 by decision of 29 January on the legislative elections in the département of Rhône.

[46] The absolute effect of decisions of the Constitutional Council flows from article 62 of the Constitution of 1958, which provides: ". . . decisions of the Constitutional Council . . . shall be binding on public authorities and on all administrative authorities and all courts".

[47] In this judgment, given on 7 September 1927 (series A, No 10) the PCIJ stated that international law governs relations between independent States. The rules of law that bind States accordingly depend on their will.

instruments, the ones that are most likely in practice to be pleaded by litigants in the countries where they operate. Community rules are enforced by a courts system consisting of national judges and the two Community courts (Court of First Instance and Court of Justice of the European Communities). The European Human Rights Convention is likewise enforced both by the national courts and by the Court in Strasbourg. Admittedly, at the time of the abortion decision in 1975 France had not yet recognised the possibility of direct action in that Court. But it was generally accepted that the European Human Rights Convention was in the category of treaties that directly engender rights and obligations for individuals, irrespective of the will of the States that sign them.[48] The Constitutional Council was not unaware of this. The grounds given for the decision of 15 January 1975 must accordingly be seen as being conceived in general terms. Since the Constitutional Council made no distinction as between types of treaties, it must have been arguing strictly in terms of general principles. After this decision of the Constitutional Council declining the jurisdiction, the way was open for other courts to take its place. The Constitutional Council's decision looked in every respect like an invitation to the ordinary courts to enforce the primacy of treaties over statutes as it was unwilling to do so.

That, at any rate, was the message perceived by the Court of Cassation. In the case already mentioned above, *Administration des Douanes* v. *Société Jacques Vabre* (judgment given on 24 May 1975[49]), that Court held that article 95 of the Treaty of Rome, prohibiting barriers to competition, prevailed over statutory provisions regulating the taxation of imported coffee even though they had been enacted after the treaty. The submissions of Mr Prosecutor-General Adolphe Touffait, after this case, make abundantly clear that the Court of Cassation felt that it had jurisdiction to disapply provisions that were contrary to the treaty precisely because of the decision of the Constitutional Council excluding all actions at that level. Since then the ordinary courts have consistently followed the decision and upheld the primacy of international law over statutes, even where they were enacted later.

The Council of State did not immediately conclude that it had jurisdiction to exercise this review for conformity with treaty-law. For a long time it applied the theory of the "statutory veil", whereby treaties enjoy superior authority only

---

[48] The Human Rights Commission of the Council of Europe had stated, for example, in the *Fall* case on 11 January 1961, that by concluding the European Human Rights Convention, the contracting States had not sought to confer reciprocal rights and obligations for the purpose of pursuing their respective national interests but of attaining the objectives and ideals of the Council of Europe as set out in the Statute and of establishing a communal public order. . . the obligations entered into by the contracting States to the Convention were basically objective in that they aimed to protect the fundamental rights of individuals against encroachments by contracting States rather than to create subjective reciprocal rights between the two. Professor Léo Hamon cites this judgment in his commentary on the Constitutional Council decision of 15 January 1975 in Dalloz-Sirey, 1975, jurisprudence, p. 529.

[49] See text of judgment with submissions by the General Prosecutor at the Court of Cassation, Adolphe Touffait, in revue Dalloz-Sirey, 1975, jurisprudence, p. 497.

over statutes that predate them. On the other hand the courts would have to enforce statutes post-dating the treaty as through a veil before the treaty, and its primacy could no longer be sustained. The case-law here, which the Council of State followed for more than thirty years, proceeded from the idea that if it were to disapply a statute that was contrary to a treaty, it would have to review the legislation, that role being reserved for the Constitutional Council. A famous textbook on litigation in the administrative courts puts it this way:

> "the administrative courts, by arrogating to themselves the constitutional review of statutes of which the Constitution deliberately deprives them but rather meanly allows the Constitutional Council to exercise, upset the whole balance of public authority [with the effect that] the administrative courts are hardly well-placed to claim to ensure that other administrative authorities remain within the bounds of their own powers".[50]

This restrained attitude shown by the Council of State is easy to understand. The Council of State was set up by Napoleon I in the image of the King's Council and only a century later did it present itself as an administrative court that was independent of the Executive while maintaining its function as an advisory body to the Government. Consequently, being close to the State, it has traditionally been concerned, as a superior administrative court, to avoid encumbering the public authorities in the exercise of their functions. As a judicial review body, it has held since 1936 that it has no power of constitutional review of statutes.[51] It is there to censure administrative malpractice but not the policies of the Government of the day, and has scrupulously refrained from interfering in the international relations of the State.

The evolution and changing views of international law finally laid to rest the theory of the "statutory veil" and it was abandoned in 1989. In the *Nicolo* decision[52] on the elections to the European Parliament, the Council of State held that the Treaty of Rome must prevail over a French statute of 1977 on the organisation of these elections. It is clear from the submissions of the Government Commissioner that the Council of State based its decision primarily on the jurisdiction, implicitly conferred on the other courts by the Constitutional Council's abortion decision, to enforce the primacy of treaties themselves. Review for conformity with treaty-law is thus now a matter for the ordinary and administrative courts. They exercise the function all the more readily as they see the primacy of treaties as a public policy ground that they can raise of their own motion, in other words even if the parties to the case do not raise it.[53] Moreover,

---

[50] Raymond Odent, *"Contentieux administratif"*, lectures given at the Institut d'Etudes politiques de Paris (Institut d'Etudes politiques de Paris, Paris, 1981) p. 182.

[51] *Arrighi*, judgment given on 6 November 1936, recueil p. 966.

[52] Plenary judgment of the Council of State given on 20 October 1989, Recueil p. 190, with submissions by the government Commissioner, M. Frydman. The Government Commissioner at the Council of State is a member of the court who acts as prosecutor with full independence from the Executive.

[53] *Doyon*, judgment given by the Council of State on 23 February 1990, recueil p. 773.

just a few months after *Nicolo*, the Council of State went on to hold that it could itself interpret a treaty, whereas previously it was required to seek the opinion of the Minister for Foreign Affairs.[54]

These developments in the case-law have radically transformed the legal landscape in France. In next to no time, the courts at all levels, not just the two supreme courts—the Court of Cassation and the Council of State—have acquired the power to apply international law. They have endeavoured to interpret statutes in such a way as to find them compatible with international law. But where they were unable to do so, they have purely and simply disapplied them.

The foregoing considerations might tend to support the idea that the French constitutional court has stood aside in an environment where the influence of international law in domestic law has been boosted to an extraordinary extent. But that would be wrong. The Constitutional Council is naturally familiar with the changes that are going on, particularly in Europe. Its awareness of this phenomenon is all the stronger as it is obliged to observe that parliamentarians who refer statutes to it almost invariably plead violations of European law. In theory, the Constitutional Council strictly follows the rule in its decision of 1975 and refrains from reviewing statutes in terms of their conformity with whatever international instrument is pleaded before it. It reiterated its position, using the very terms used in the abortion decision, when rejecting as inoperable an argument based on violation of Community competition law in the case of a statute allowing public-sector social security bodies to operate in the area of supplementary welfare protection, traditionally reserved for private-sector insurers.[55] But in other, more recent, cases, the Constitutional Council opened up the possibility of a departure from its case-law. New refinements appearing in the grounds for its decisions reveal its hesitations: for example, it used the theory of the "acte clair" to reject a plea that a Community directive on pharmaceutical products was violated;[56] it also took account of the Community principle of the free movement of goods in the European Union, holding that the Act referred did not violate it.[57] These semantic exercises are evidence of a growing willingness to accept international law. This willingness is further attested by decisions of the Constitutional Council in cases concerning constitutional review of treaties pursuant to article 54 of the Constitution.

---

[54] *GISTI*, judgment given by the Council of State on 29 June 1990, recueil p. 171, with submissions by the government Commissioner, R. Abraham. The ordinary courts, since 1839, had agreed to interpret treaties, provided only private interests were involved. This restraint placed by the ordinary courts on their own jurisdiction to interpret treaties may disappear as the European Human Rights Court has held that the national courts should exercise their full jurisdiction and interpret treaties themselves with reference to the executive branch (*Beaumartin v France*, 24 November 1994, series A, No 296.B).

[55] DC 99-416 of 23 July 1999 on the Universal Sickness Insurance Act, with commentary by Jean-Eric Schoettl, AJDA, 20 September 1999, p. 700.

[56] In decision DC 97-393 of 18 December 1997 on the Social Security (Finance) Act for 1998, it held that "the directive does not provide clearly" that it was contrary to the statute, recueil, p. 320.

[57] DC 98-402 of 25 June 1998 (Economic and Financial Measures Act), recueil, p. 269.

IN ITS CONSTITUTIONAL REVIEW OF TREATIES, THE CONSTITUTIONAL COUNCIL SEEKS TO
PRESERVE A BALANCE BETWEEN THE PRINCIPLE OF NATIONAL SOVEREIGNTY AND THE
PRINCIPLE THAT FRANCE MUST OCCUPY ITS PROPER PLACE IN THE INTERNATIONAL
COMMUNITY

The Constitutional Council is necessarily in touch with the major developments in international law since, by article 54 of the Constitution, it is directly involved in the treaty ratification process. Under that article, the question of whether a treaty that France is planning to ratify contains clauses that are contrary to the Constitution may be referred to the Constitutional Council by the President of the Republic, the Prime Minister, the President of one or other assembly or by sixty deputies or sixty Senators. If in response the Constitutional Council "has declared that an international commitment contains a clause contrary to the Constitution, authorisation to ratify or approve the international commitment in question may be given only after amendment of the Constitution".

This procedure for prior constitutional review of treaties is an unprecedented innovation in French constitutional history. In some ways it can be seen as illustrating the cautious approach taken by the authors of the 1958 Constitution to international law, in particular to the transfers of sovereignty flowing from the European integration process. Let us just remember the debates that preceded the elaboration of the Constitution; they illustrate how the main aim of those who inspired the Fifth Republic was to give the Executive the means of preventing France from ratifying treaties that encroached on its sovereignty. They were not thinking only of the treaty on the European Defence Community. They were probably also thinking of how to enable the Executive to control the process of European integration. This is the context in which the Constitutional Council—originally founded, it will be recalled, to prevent Parliament from hampering the Government—was empowered by article 54 of the Constitution to review treaties for constitutionality before they could be ratified. Many commentators on the new Constitution regretted at the time that France was displaying what they regarded as a retrograde attitude that augured ill for the future. But one of them had already realised the value of the new procedure in that it could "eliminate endless controversies between the executive and legislative branches as to the compatibility or incompatibility of a draft treaty or agreement with the Constitution".[58] History has borne out his view. The decisions given by the Constitutional Council in cases under article 54 of the Constitution have had a pacifying effect. They have helped to dilute the often bitter controversies between 'sovereignists' and 'internationalists'.[59]

---

[58] M. Nguyen Quoc Dinh, in his article cited above on *"La Constitution de 1958 et le droit international law"*, RDP, 1959, p. 516.

[59] So far the Constitutional Council has been asked to rule on the constitutionality of a treaty prior to ratification eight times. The relevant decisions are DC 70-39 of 19 June 1970 on the Treaty of Luxembourg; DC 76-71 of 30 December 1976 on the election of the European Parliament by universal suffrage; DC 85-188 of 22 May 1985 on the Additional Protocol to the European Human

Evidence for this can be seen in the way in which the constitutional amendments were enacted following the decisions on the unconstitutionality of certain treaties. When the European treaties (Maastricht and Amsterdam), like the Statute of Rome establishing an International Criminal Court, came in for sharp criticism from certain strands of political thinking, the amendments to the Constitution required by the relevant decisions of the Constitutional Council eventually secured large majorities in Parliament.[60] Admittedly, in another case a decision of the Constitutional Council fed controversy. This was the decision of 15 June 1999 holding that the European Charter for Regional or Minority Languages "undermines the constitutional principles of the indivisibility of the Republic", notably by recognising the "inalienable right" of speakers of these languages in geographically specific regions (such as the Basque Country or Corsica).

Can we take stock of the decisions given by the Constitutional Council in cases under Article 54 of the Constitution? Perhaps, but only on a provisional basis, as there have not yet been many decisions. The Constitutional Council has received only eight referrals, most of them from the executive, i.e. the President of the Republic or the Prime Minister. There are, however, likely to be more and more of them as France enters into more and more international's commitments.

If one salient feature is to be identified in the current state of the case-law, it has to be that the French Constitutional Council is clearly at pains to safeguard national sovereignty while at the same time doing its utmost to uphold France's responsibilities as an actor on the international scene. The Council's decisions clearly bear witness to its endless balancing act as between the principles of national sovereignty and France's proper place in the international community.

The Council applies three main criteria to decide whether a provision of a treaty is contrary to the Constitution.

First, a treaty clause may be directly contrary to a provision of the Constitution. This was the case, for example, of the Maastricht Treaty's provisions on the right of (non-French) Community nationals to vote and stand as candidates at municipal elections, which violated the letter of article 3 of the Constitution. It was also the case of provisions of the Statute of the International Criminal Court whereby Heads of State did not enjoy immunity from criminal liability, contrary to article 68 of the 1958 Constitution conferring

---

Rights Convention on the abolition of the death penalty; DC 92-308 of 9 April 1992 on the Maastricht Treaty; DC 92-312 of 2 September 1992 on the Maastricht Treaty; DC 97-394 of 31 December 1997 on the Amsterdam Treaty; DC 98-408 of 22 January 1999 on the Statute of Rome establishing an International Criminal Court; DC 99-412 of 15 June 1999 on the European Charter (Council of Europe) on regional and minority languages.

[60] Under article 89 of the Constitution, revision of the Constitution proceeds in two stages. First, the draft or proposal must be approved by a majority in each of the two houses in identical terms. Then, the text is put to the people at referendum or to the two houses in joint session, where it must be passed by a majority of three fifths of the votes cast.

such immunity for acts done by the President of the Republic, "except in the case of high treason".

Second, any clause jeopardising constitutionally guaranteed rights and freedoms would also be contrary to the Constitution. This criterion, which is comparable to the one used by the German Constitutional Court in its analysis of the European treaties,[61] was brought clearly to the fore for the first time in the Constitutional Council in the 1999 decision on the International Criminal Court. But so far the Constitutional Council has not had a single occasion to declare a treaty unconstitutional on this ground. If it did so, the public might reasonably be expected to abandon any plans to ratify the treaty. Georges Scelle, a great French internationalist, went so far as to argue that a treaty that violated fundamental rights would even be "internationally unconstitutional" as it would violate "the firmly established principles of international law".[62]

The third and final criterion concerns the preservation of national sovereignty. There have been many positive cases of application. By definition, national sovereignty is limited by the international commitments entered into by France, and the Constitutional Council has held that the Constitution does not prohibit all limitations of sovereignty. The only ones that are actually unconstitutional are those which imperil the "essential conditions for the exercise of national sovereignty". It is not possible to produce a list of examples of cases of unconstitutionality as the decisions are basically pragmatic, but it is possible to cite a few typical cases. First, the Constitutional Council has regard to the manner in which powers transferred to an international organisation are exercised. Thus in 1997 the Constitutional Council held that Community measures on visas, asylum and the free movement of persons that were to be taken by qualified majority and not unanimously were unconstitutional for that very reason. Then, consideration is given to the nature of the power that is transferred; it was only to be expected in 1992 that the establishment of the single currency by the Treaty of Maastricht would be regarded as not provided for by the Constitution. The Constitutional Council sets great store by preserving the will of Parliament in areas where the national legal culture finds its most eloquent expression. In the 1999 decision on the International Criminal Court, it held that the Constitution was violated by the possibility that the Court could cause the French authorities to hand over to it a person who had been given an amnesty

---

[61] Decisions of the German Constitutional Court at Karlsruhe on the level of protection of fundamental rights secured by the Community legal order echo this approach by the Constitutional Council. See decisions of 29 May 1974 '*Solange I*', B. Verf. GE 37, 271, and 22 October 1986, '*Solange II*', B. Verf GE, 73, 339.

[62] In '*Sur la prétendue inconstitutionnalité interne des treaties*' RDP 1952, p. 1012, at a time when the European Defence Community (CED) Treaty was being hotly debated in France, Professor G. Scelle opposed the very concept of the unconstitutionality of treaties in the domestic legal order, an argument advanced by the opponents of the EDC Treaty. Even so, he considered the possibility that a treaty might violate constitutionally secured rights and freedoms. But as there was no court with jurisdiction to hear such cases at the time, he merely pointed out that in such a case it would be up to the public authorities to refuse to ratify the treaty.

in due form by the French Parliament.[63] Amnesty does not exist in all legal systems, not in the British system for instance, but it is firmly rooted in the French tradition. A State's conception of its sovereignty is clearly bound up with the identity it has forged for itself in the course of its history, and that is what this decision is all about. The Constitutional Council, anxious to avoid all possibility of ouster of the national judicial authorities, held in the same decision that the investigation powers of the Prosecutor at the International Court, even if they were confined to 'public places', were contrary to the principle of sovereignty in that they allowed him to operate alone in the territory of a State.

Otherwise the Constitutional Council has approved most of the transfers of power made by the treaties referred to it. What is more, its decisions have adopted a formula comparable to article 24(1) of the German Constitution,[64] holding that in general France had the opportunity "of participating in the creation or development of a permanent international organisation, enjoying legal personality and decision-making powers".[65] It has likewise held that the Constitution empowered France to participate in the establishment of an international court, the International Criminal Court as it happens, to "protect the fundamental rights of the human person . . . with jurisdiction to try the perpetrators of crimes that are so serious as to affect the international Community".[66]

The decisions of the Constitutional Council thus set out to establish an equilibrium. They endeavour to balance out the restrictions on sovereignty that a State which is part of the international legal order is bound to accept and the transfers of powers which, by going somewhat against the concept of sovereignty and therefore of national identity, depend on the express will of the authors of the Constitution. The Constitutional Council did not invent this approach all by itself. France's participation in an international legal order is expressly provided for in the Preamble to the Constitution of 1946 (which the Constitutional Council—as we have seen—included in the 'body of constitutional instruments', giving it the same status as the Constitution itself), two paragraphs of which are clearly designed to ensure "more constant communication" between international law and domestic law.[67] The fifteenth paragraph, already mentioned, states that "subject to reciprocity, France accepts the restrictions on sovereignty needed for the organisation and defence of peace", an implied reference to the powers conferred on the UN Security Council and to the

---

[63] An example might be the French Generals condemned at the time of the Algerian War and amnestied by a statute of 1982.

[64] Which provides, "The Federation may by statute transfer rights of sovereignty to international institutions".

[65] See decision of 9 April 1992 on the Maastricht Treaty as regards the European Union.

[66] See decision of 15 June 1999 on the International Criminal Court. This formulation in some ways goes further than article 24(3)of the German Basic Law, which merely provides that "To permit the settlement of disputes between States, the Federation shall accede to conventions establishing an international court of arbitration having general, universal and mandatory jurisdiction".

[67] See Jacques Donnedieu de Vabres, "*La Constitution de 1946 et le droit international*", in Recueil Dalloz hebdomadaire (1948), Chronique II, p. 6.

principles of mutual collective security.[68] The fourteenth paragraph states solemnly that "France, faithful to its traditions, respects the rules of public international law . . .".[69] This has been a particularly useful clause: it has helped to set the line of demarcation between the restrictions on sovereignty authorised by the Constitution and the transfers of powers that require amendments of the text of the Constitution. The reasoning behind it can be summed up as follows: although the spirit of the Fifth Republic requires the constitutional courts to protect national sovereignty, they are also required to consider how far the fourteenth and fifteenth paragraphs of the Preamble of 1946 allowed exceptions to be made. The Constitutional Council interprets the fourteenth paragraph in a very broad sense as implying that France must respect all international rules, written or not. In its 1999 decision on the International Criminal Court, it refers expressly to the concept of the "general principles of public international law", which covers all the forms of sources of international law: treaties, custom and general principles of law.[70]

The decision of 9 April 1992 on the Maastricht Treaty was the first to elevate to the status of parameter for constitutional review the customary rule that goes by the Latin tag of "*Pacta sunt servanda*", whereby States parties to a treaty must comply with it in good faith. The rule is, admittedly, codified in article 26 of the Vienna Convention on the law of treaties 1969;[71] and it has constantly been recalled by the international courts for a long time now.[72] But this codification did not deprive it of its custom status, especially as for France—which has not yet ratified the Vienna Convention—it is not a treaty rule.[73] The Constitutional Council's 1999 decision on the International Criminal Court also treats other customary principles as being of constitutional status, in particular the punishability of international crimes that are regarded as exempt from all limitation rules.

[68]   Exactly the same idea is expressed in article 24(2) of the German Basic Law of 1949.

[69]   Here again there is a striking convergence with the German Constitution, article 25 of which provides that "The general rules of public international law shall form part of federal law . . .".

[70]   This concept refers to the one in article 38 of the Statute of the International Court of Justice in The Hague, which refers to the general principles of law recognised by civilised nations". See Bin Cheng, *General Principles of Law as Applied by International Courts and Tribunals*, (Stevens, London, 1953).

[71]   The "*Pacta sunt servanda*" rule is also found in the Treaty establishing the European Community (article 10 following the Amsterdam Treaty) in an explicit form: "Member States shall take all appropriate measures, general or particular, to ensure fulfilment of the obligations arising out of this Treaty or resulting from action taken by the institutions of the Community. They shall facilitate the fulfilment of the Community's tasks. They shall abstain from any measure which could jeopardise the attainment of the objectives of this Treaty."

[72]   In 1910, in an award given in the *North Atlantic Fisheries* case, concerning the application of a treaty governing British fishing rights in Canadian waters, granted to American nationals, the Permanent Court of Arbitration, relying on the "principle of international law that treaty obligations must be discharged in the utmost good faith" held that the treaty engendered an obligation whereby the right of Great Britain to exercise its sovereignty by making fisheries regulations was confined to regulations made in good faith and without violating the treaty. (United Nations Compendium of arbitral awards XI, p. 188).

[73]   Its main go-round is its opposition to the mandatory status of the jus cogens.

The fact that the Constitutional Council has regard to international custom illustrates the transformation of national legal cultures by international law. These changes have come about in stages. The Court of Cassation has for years accepted that certain customary principles (such as State immunity and humanitarian rights) are mandatory but the Council of State followed only in 1997,[74] though without drawing the conclusion that they could enjoy primacy over statutes. The Constitutional Council, beginning in 1999, now intends to assess treaties in terms of unwritten international law as the expression of an international ethic: an ethic which, for instance, requires States to meet in good faith the commitments they have entered into and to abide by the principles of humanitarian law and human rights.

The fact that the French courts, imbued with the law as inspired by Napoleon, refer to custom in this way is all the more remarkable as the courts in the Common Law countries are no more substantially open to general international law. As two writers have pointed out,

> "explicit references to customary international law in the Common Law countries (United Kingdom, Ireland), even though they are used to unwritten sources of law, are rare; the courts usually prefer to base their findings on more familiar concepts such as 'comity' or 'public policy'.

In fact, they add,

> "the preference for a reference to custom ultimately depends on the judges' background and knowledge . . . and it is noteworthy here that the only countries where there is an abundance of case-law relating to customary international law are Germany and Greece, where the identification of the customary rule is facilitated by the preliminary ruling procedure whereby the court can refer a case to a superior court (Constitutional Court in Germany, Special Upper Court in Greece) for a ruling on the position as to the customary law".[75]

IN GENERAL TERMS, THE FRENCH CONSTITUTIONAL CASE-LAW IS HEAVILY INFLUENCED BY INTERNATIONAL LAW

The impression given by the abortion decision of 1975 that the Constitutional Council refuses to ensure that statutes observe treaties is to some extent misleading. Actually the point at which it held that it must do so is not without its impact on the Council's subsequent decisions. For one thing, the Council has been at pains to clarify the point; for another, through the technique of interpretative distinctions, it regularly reminds the public authorities of their duty to ensure that the law has its proper effect.

---

[74] See *Aquarone*, 18 June 1997, recueil p. 206.
[75] Christian Dominicé et François Voeffray, 'L'Application du Droit International Général dans l'ordre juridique interne', in *The Integration of International and European Community Law into the National Legal Order*, ed. Pierre Michel Eisemann, (*supra*), p. 58.

In a 1977 decision on provisions of a Finance Act relating to Community levies on imported milk products,[76] the Constitutional Council saw fit to point out that the contested statute was "merely the consequence of international commitments entered into by France within the scope of article 55 of the Constitution". The point of this formula is that the Council was recalling the fact that the Treaty of Rome had been incorporated into the domestic legal order and that the legislature was bound to observe it. The Council followed a similar logic some years later when reviewing the Treaties of Maastricht and Amsterdam for constitutionality. It felt the need to specify that the earlier European treaties remained in force unchanged but also that the new treaties had to be seen in the light of earlier international commitments. Without actually conferring constitutional status on the '*acquis communautaire*' constituted by these older treaties, the Council nevertheless attached decisive importance to them in the interpretation of the amending treaties. The '*acquis communautaire*' is an internationally accepted neologism to refer to the set of rules and practices that applicant countries must accept as a condition of their accession to the European Union. It is touching to see the French constitutional courts imposing the same requirement on themselves when considering legal progress in European integration.

Another interesting decision is the one given on 3 September 1986 on a statute to combat terrorism and regulate the right of asylum for refugees in France. It states that the treaty—in this case the Geneva Convention on the status of refugees of 1951—must be respected "even if there is no statutory provision to that effect . . . and the various authorities of the State must ensure that the provisions of international conventions are applied in their respective areas of responsibility". Similarly, in a decision of 1991 concerning a statute that restricted advertising for alcohol,[77] the Council stated that the regulatory authorities responsible for implementing the statute should comply with Community rules applicable to alcoholic beverages.

Like other European courts, and in the same spirit, the Council endeavours to avoid all conflicts between international law and domestic law by interpreting them in such a way as to make them compatible. This technique of '*interprétation conforme*' is a powerful means of adapting bodies of domestic law to the constraints of international law. A good example is the 1993 decision on the Code of Nationality,[78] in which the Council interpreted the Act referred to it as impliedly conforming with a bilateral convention between France and Algeria. The provision, contested by the members of parliament making the reference required French nationals having dual nationality to perform national service in France, without leaving them the option of performing it in the other country of which they also had nationality. The Council held that this provision would not jeopardise the exception provided for by the French-Algerian Convention

---

[76] DC 77-89 of 30 December 1977 on the "co-responsibility levy", recueil, p. 46.
[77] DC 90-283 of 8 January 1991 on various measures to combat alcoholism, recueil, p. 11.
[78] DC 93-321 of 20 July 1993 on the Nationality Code, recueil p. 196.

whereby young people with dual nationality could do their military service in one or other country at their own option.

When reviewing the constitutionality of treaties, the Constitutional Council has further reinforced the effect of article 55 by removing the ambiguity as to the implementation of the principle of primacy of treaties that had persisted since 1958. It will be remembered that article 55 of the Constitution operates subject to 'reciprocity'—the requirement that the treaty also be applied by the other party. This unprecedented provision, inspired by the law applicable to contracts between private individuals, was criticised at the outset as being out of line with international law since it left the Government free to decide whether and when France could consider itself unbound by its commitments. In particular, when applied to the European Community, the clause struck many commentators on the 1958 Constitution as especially perilous.

The Constitutional Council got round the difficulty in two stages. First, it held that the reciprocity clause was inapplicable to Community treaties, which had their own judicial review machinery. In its decision of 1998 on the institutional act transposing the Community instruments giving all Union citizens the right to vote and stand as candidates at municipal elections, it held that "should a Member State fail to conform to the obligations arising from the first paragraph of article 8b, France could refer a case to the Court of Justice on the basis of article 170 of the Treaty establishing the European Community".[79] In the 1999 decision on the International Criminal Court, it took the radical step of holding that the reciprocity clause was inapplicable to humanitarian and human rights treaties. This is already clear from article 60(5) of the Vienna Convention on the law of treaties 1969. The same point has been made for many years by the international courts, as these treaties directly generate rights and obligations for individuals irrespective of the conduct of the State to which they are attached. In terms of the Constitutional Council, this decision set a precedent. It is no easy matter for a constitutional court to deprive the Constitution of its legal effects. Moreover, the decision could be taken much further. Although the Constitutional Council has not overruled its 1975 abortion decision, the fact is that it has shaken the theoretical foundations for it. It is no longer possible for it to hold that all treaties are by their nature precarious and that the primacy of treaties is always no more than contingent.

The Constitutional Council's case-law on the relationship between international law is thus evolving. The Council has gradually clarified the scope and legal force of article 55 of the Constitution. In terms of substance, it is more and more inclined to follow the reasoning techniques of international courts such as the one in Strasbourg, in particular as regards fundamental rights. The decisions of the Strasbourg Court have had a spectacular impact on the decisions of the Constitutional Council, even though this may sometimes be imperceptible. This

---

[79] DC 98-400 of 20 May 1998 on the right of Community nationals to vote and stand as candidates at municipal elections, recueil p. 253.

lack of visibility is partly attributable to the secrecy surrounding the Council's decisions and to the fact that there are no dissenting opinions (already mentioned). Many French writers are now rather in favour of dissenting opinions,[80] but the fact is that a practice which comes naturally to the judges in the United Kingdom or the United States is radically contrary to the French legal culture. It must be admitted that, in the absence of a procedure as transparent as that of certain other countries, it is not always easy to ascertain where the French constitutional courts are seeking their inspiration or what their decisions really mean. For one thing, the Constitutional Council has no prosecutors or equivalents[81] (as there are in other French courts, though dissenting opinions are not allowed there either) with the function of publicly setting out the points of law in issue and proposing solutions. For another, the grounds given for decisions of the Council are often laconic. This concision is partly due to the rather abstract nature of constitutional litigation France, but only partly. The drafting techniques used in decisions of the Constitutional Council, based on the practice of the Council of State, are evidence of its concern to avoid binding itself as to the future. This is quite comprehensible. After all, the Council is required to give a ruling on instruments whose longer-term implications are not all immediately apparent; and since every decision given by the Council is seen as establishing points of principle and is immediately and absolutely enforceable, the Council tends to be economical with the arguments.

It is only now after the event that it is possible to understand how open to the decisions of the European Human Rights Court the Council has actually been. The phenomenon may be perceptible only now, but in fact it has been evolving for more than ten years.

The originality of the French situation lies in the fact that the Constitutional Council does not indicate where it has been inspired by international law in general and the decisions of the international courts in particular. Incidentally, there is no provision in the French Constitution similar to article 10(2) of the Spanish Constitution, which requires the courts to have regard to international human rights instruments as a source for the interpretation of constitutional provisions relating to freedom.[82] Even so, experience has shown that this is exactly what the Constitutional Council does. More and more often, it defines and interprets the rights and freedoms secured by the Constitution by reference—implicitly—to the European Human Rights Convention and the case-law of the Strasbourg Court. This approach, which promotes dialogue with the European courts, is most helpful when the Constitutional Council has to supply lacunae in the provisions of the Constitution governing fundamental rights. The

---

[80] See forthcoming issue of *Cahiers du Conseil Constitutionnel* (April 2000).

[81] The presentation of the public interest in a case is made by the prosecutor in the ordinary courts and by the Government Commissioners in the administrative courts.

[82] Under this, "the rules relating to fundamental rights and freedom recognised by the Constitution shall be interpreted in conformity with the Universal Declaration of Human Rights and with international treaties and agreements covering the same subjects which have been ratified by Spain".

Constitution of 1958 does not contain a catalogue of fundamental rights as most written Constitutions do. From the 1970s onwards, the Council accordingly incorporated in the set of constitutional rules it applies (the *"bloc de constitutionnalité"*) the Declaration of Human and Civic Rights of 1789 and the Preamble to the Constitution of 1946 (economic and social rights), the two instruments together constituting a sort of "Bill of Rights". But they are not always perfectly explicit. Nor are they up to date with the aspirations of the people of today. Consequently, without laying claim to a creative role, which would run counter to the official principle that the courts merely express the law as it is, the Constitutional Council has "discovered" in the *bloc de constitutionnalite* such principles as are not expressly stated there but which seem to flow from it. This particular form of deductive reasoning is not the sole preserve of the French constitutional court but it is all the more exceptional in France as the Constitutional Council was not set up to arbitrate on rights and fundamental freedoms. Certainly, the Constitutional Council always makes sure it can rely on a written constitutional provision to deduce a new constitutional principle, which it definitely does not claim to be inventing from scratch.[83] But at the same time it cannot operate in total isolation from the socio-political and legal environment of a Europe which is seeking to fructify a common heritage of fundamental rights defined at the time of the Liberation.[84] And it is by drawing on this heritage that it enriches the debate that in turn generates new constitutional principles.

The Constitutional Council's 'borrowings' from concepts drawn from European human rights law are so numerous that they cannot all be cited here. Let a few examples suffice to illustrate the convergences[85] that now exist between the French constitutional system and the European system for the protection of fundamental rights, in particular the case-law of the Strasbourg Court. The case-law of the Luxembourg Court has not so far been so influential. The Constitutional Council is highly reluctant to have regard to the principles of Community law, as it feels them to be somewhat alien to the principles of French constitutional law. For example, it has held that there is no constitu-

---

[83] Sometimes the Constitutional Council can be quite creative. For instance, it took a sentence in the first paragraph of the Constitution of 1946 to propound the constitutional principle of the dignity of the human person in its decision on the bioethics statutes. The sentence reads: "On the morrow of the victory won by free peoples over regimes which sought to enslave and degrade humankind, the French people once again proclaim that all human beings, without distinction as to race, religion or creed, possess inalienable and sacred rights. . . " (DC 94-343/344 of 27 July 1994, recueil, p. 100).

[84] Patrick Gaïa, "Les interactions entre les jurisprudences de la Cour européenne des droits de l'homme et du Conseil Constitutionnel", in *Revue française de Droit Constitutionnel* (RFDC), 28, 1996 ; and JF. Flauss, "Des incidences de la Convention européenne des droits de l'homme sur le contrôle de la constitutionality des lois en France", in *Les Petites Affiches* (LPA), 1988, No 148, p. 3. These articles, in the current state of the case-law of the Constitutional Council, which does not apply the Convention directly, refer to the "effets indirects" doctrine.

[85] The same idea can be found in Basil Markesinis, *The Gradual Convergence*, (Clarendon Press, Oxford, 1994).

tional norm guaranteeing a principle of "legitimate expectations".[86] And yet a few months after so holding it went on to acknowledge the legal status of a principle resembling it very closely and upheld by the European Human Rights Court—the principle of certainty as to the law.[87] This attitude can perhaps be explained by the specific 'tone' of Community law, the principles of which seem ultimately designed to uphold economic liberalism, which is by no means the proper concern of a court like the Constitutional Council.[88]

In its report to the Ninth Conference of European Constitutional Courts in Paris in 1993, the Constitutional Council highlighted only the influence of the Strasbourg Court, though it specified that "similarities in interpretation and review techniques are the result of convergence factors that have emerged over the years rather than through any direct influence of European case-law". The point here was to avoid giving the impression that the Strasbourg Court might enjoy some kind of primacy. But the fact remains that the case-law of that Court is being followed more and more perceptibly by the Constitutional Council. This is clear at three levels.

First, the types of fundamental rights secured by the Constitution. The new rights that the Constitutional Council deduces from the general provisions of the Constitution often correspond to those deduced by the European Human Rights Court. The right to respect for one's private life is an example. Neither the Constitution of 1958, nor the Preamble to the Constitution of 1946, nor, *a fortiori*, the Declaration of 1789, mentions a principle along these lines. The Council deduced it from the principle of liberty set out in the Constitution. Yet the right to privacy[89] is also secured by article 8 of the European Human Rights Convention, and there has been a long line of cases on the subject in Strasbourg. The same applies to freedom of marriage. This was held to be a component of individual freedom in 1993,[90] but it is expressly provided for by article 12 of the European Convention. And there is no doubt that the Constitutional Council

[86] DC 97-395 of 30 December 1997 on the Finance Act for 1998, recueil, p. 333. The principle of legitimate expectations has been upheld by the Court of Justice of the European Communities as a general principle of Community law since a decision of 5 June 1973 in Case 81/72 *Commission* v. *Council* (recueil p. 575).

[87] In *Sunday Times* v. *United Kingdom* (26 April 1979, Case No 30), the Strasbourg Court linked the principle of certainty as to the law to the question of the accessibility and foreseeability of the law, holding that as there is more to the law than a text or a rule, a principle of certainty as to the law must necessarily be included. This philosophy of the law flows from the concept of democracy that the European Human Rights Convention sets out to promote. The Constitutional Council applies the principle without actually mentioning it by name and by linking it rather to the stability of the law. In its decision on the Social Security (Finance) Act for 1999 (DC No 98-404 of 18 December 1998, recueil, p. 315), the Constitutional Council found against retroactive tax provisions obliging firms to pay an additional tax on their turnover for the past four years, as this deprived the firms of their certainty as to the law.

[88] It was only in 1969 (Case 11/70 *Stauder*, recueil, p. 1125) that the Luxembourg Court acknowledged its own jurisdiction to protect fundamental rights. That jurisdiction was formally conferred by the Amsterdam Treaty (articles 6(2) and L).

[89] DC 94-352 of 18 January 1995 on videosurveillance, recueil, p. 170, and DC 97-389 of 22 April 1997 on immigration, recueil, p. 45.

[90] DC 93-325 of 13 August 1993 on aliens, recueil, p. 224.

attaches constitutional status to the "right to lead a normal family life",[91] drawn from the Preamble to the Constitution of 1946, by reference to decisions from Strasbourg. Like the Constitutional Council, the Strasbourg Court recognises this right, particularly in relation to immigrants wishing to have their family join them in their country of residence.[92] As for the principle of the dignity of the human person, recognised as a constitutional principal in 1994 in the decision on the bioethics legislation, it is inconceivable that the Constitutional Council could have affirmed this without being mindful of decisions of the European Human Rights Court[93] and of decisions of other constitutional courts such as the German Constitutional Court in Karlsruhe.[94]

Without actually defining new rights, the Constitutional Council can also review traditional principles in the light of decisions from Strasbourg. It did so in a case concerning the freedom of expression, one of the fundamental principles of the French Revolution. Opposition to censorship in the Ancien Régime was extremely important for the philosophers of the Enlightenment and censorship was one of the grounds for rejecting the power of the King, so it is hardly surprising article 11 of the Declaration of 1789, which lays down the principle of "freedom to share ideas and opinions", declares this to be one of the most precious rights of Man. But the way in which freedom of expression is protected has had to evolve as modern media have emerged. For many people, freedom of expression now seems to rest on access to pluralist sources of information, the only means whereby the ability of individuals to form their own conclusions can be preserved. This idea is reflected in decisions of the Constitutional Council that hold pluralism to be a "condition of democracy".[95] This concept directly echoes a series of decisions by the European Human Rights Court describing freedom of expression as an "essential foundation of a democratic society".[96] Since the *Handyside* judgment in 1976,[97] the Strasbourg Court has repeatedly held that freedom of expression applies not only to information or ideas received and welcomed or considered to be inoffensive or indifferent but also to those that "shock or worry the State or any portion of public opinion, [since] that is inherent in pluralism, tolerance and open-mindedness without which there cannot be a democratic society". The Council's concept of freedom of expression is less extensive, but it is very close.

One of the areas where the influence of Strasbourg has been strongest is without doubt the criminal law and criminal procedure. On two occasions the

---

[91] DC 93-325 of 13 August 1993 on aliens, recueil, p. 224.

[92] For example, order of 29 May 1985, series A, No 94.

[93] *Ribitsch* v. *Austria*, Series A 336.

[94] Federal Constitutional Court, 24 April 1986, BverfGE, vol. 72, p. 105; and 24 February 1971, BverfGE, vol. 30, p. 103, cited in *Constitution et Ethique biomédicale*, eds. Noëlle Lenoir, Didier Maus and Bertrand Mathieu, (La Documentation Française, Actes du colloque international de 1997, Paris 1998), p. 111.

[95] DC 86-217 of 18 September 1986 and DC 93-333 of 21 January 1994 on audiovisual communication.

[96] See *Observer and Guardian* of 26 November 1991, Series A, Volume 216, § 59.

[97] Judgment of 29 April 1976. Series A, volume 24.

Council has made reference to "fair trial" implying "equal rights for both sides", seeking inspiration directly in decisions of the European Human Rights Court. It did so in the first instance in relation to the Stock Exchange Commission (COB) when it took court action to have violations of the Companies Acts penalised. The Council, relying on the principle of respect for natural justice, held that "in criminal matters, it [the principle] implies that there must be a fair procedure securing equal rights for both sides".[98]

Likewise, in the 1999 decision on the International Criminal Court the Council held that the procedure before that Court met the conditions required of a fair trial. The Strasbourg Court, meanwhile, has held that the right to a fair trial secured by article 6(1) of the European Human Rights Convention means that every party to a civil action and *a fortiori* to a criminal action must have a reasonable possibility of presenting his case to the court in such conditions that he is not placed at a disadvantage in relation to the other party.[99] Again, although it was proceeding on the basis of article 16 of the Declaration of 1789, the Constitutional Council had the European Court's decisions in mind when repeatedly asserting the right of every person to "an effective remedy".[100] Applying this principle, the Constitutional Council has, for example, held that aliens must have the right to contest decisions refusing them admission to France;[101] it has held that the right to be heard in a court of law must be maintained even if the possibilities of pleading the illegality of town-plans by way of an objection procedure must be regulated; and when reviewing the statute defining a new offence of driving at very high speed[102] in the Road Traffic Code, it examined the statute to see whether it actually secured "respect for natural justice and for the right to redress" for the offender.[103]

A few points by way of conclusion:

The Constitutional Council is more and more open to European law.

It does not itself review statutes for conformity with treaties in the course of its constitutional review procedure, but its statements regarding fundamental rights and freedoms are more and more inspired by the decisions of the Strasbourg Court.

The influence of the two courts—the Constitutional Council and the European Human Rights Court—works in both directions

On the one side the Constitutional Council is most attentive to decisions from Strasbourg; on the other, the Strasbourg Court is beginning to refer explicitly to

---

[98] DC 89-260 of 28 July 1989 on the security and transparency of the finance market, recueil, p. 71.

[99] See Gérard Cohen-Jonathan, 'La Convention Européenne des Droits de l'Homme' coll. *Droit public positif*,(Economica et Presses Universitaires d'Aix-Marseille, 1989), p. 431.

[100] By article 16 of the Declaration of 1789, "A society in which rights are not guaranteed and the separation of powers is not determined has no Constitution."

[101] DC 93-325 of 13 August 1993, *supra*.

[102] DC 93-335 of 21 January 1994, recueil p. 40, on a statute relating to town planning. The Council assets the principle that: "there can be no question of substantially depriving interested parties of their right to seek redress in the courts".

[103] DC 99-411 of 16 June 1999 on road safety.

decisions of the Constitutional Council[104] and even to take over certain expressions used in the grounds for decisions of the Constitutional Council.[105]

Any comparison between the positions of the Constitutional Council and of other constitutional or supreme courts is unreliable, as situations vary so widely between different European countries

By not directly securing the primacy of treaties over statutes but leaving it to other courts to achieve that result, is the Constitutional Council setting itself apart from other supreme or constitutional courts in Europe? The question is not easy to answer. So far the Austrian Court is the only one that has officially ranked the European Human Rights Convention among its constitutional norms.[106] The Council of Europe Convention ranks high in other European countries too, *de facto* or *de jure*. It ranks above statutes in countries which like France, are unitary (Belgium, Greece, Luxembourg, Portugal). It even ranks above the Constitution. Even though in the dualist countries (Germany, Denmark, Finland, Italy, United Kingdom and Sweden) it ranks simply on the same level as statutes, the practice is that it prevails over statutes by means of the legislative interpretation technique known as "interprétation conforme".[107] In France, while there are no doubts as to its supra-legislative status, it still remains for the Constitutional Council to remove the persisting ambiguity as to its status in the body of constitutional law.

The relationship between domestic constitutional law and Community law is distinguished in many ways from the relationship between national law and the European Human Rights Convention

First, the Court at Luxembourg has a monopoly of the interpretation and review of the European Treaties as a matter of principle, whereas the Court at Strasbourg plays a role that is theoretically secondary to that of the national courts. This may be the reason why constitutional courts are reluctant to submit to the Luxembourg Court's authority by referring questions for preliminary

---

[104] Judgment of 25 June 1996, *Amuur* v. *France*, RUDH, 1996, p. 144. The European Human Rights Court twice takes over the terms used in the Constitutional Council decision of 25 February 1992 on transit areas for aliens refused entry in French territory. The Luxembourg Court of Justice has defined "the constitutional traditions common to the Member States" as a source of general principles of Community law which it has jurisdiction to define.

[105] In *Zélinski et Pradal—Gonzalez and others* v. *France* (judgment given on 28 October 1998), the European Human Rights Court held that a validating legislative provision retroactively interpreting contracts giving social security staff in Alsace Moselle a bonus if they agreed to speak Alsatian when dealing with their users was contrary to the requirement of fair process. The administration did not wish to raise the bonus and, to avert the risk of litigation, persuaded the Government to insert a provision in a statute to remove the obligation to raise it. France was condemned by the Strasbourg Court, which held that there was no sufficient point of general interest allowing the administration to act in this way and deprive those concerned of their right to access to the courts. Even so, it is worth noting that the grounds given by the Strasbourg Court for its decision reflect the criteria used by the Constitutional Council, though it came to a radically different conclusion.

[106] Joël Rideau, *Le rôle de l'Union Européenne en matière de protection des droits de l'Homme*, (Martinus Nijhoff Publishers, The Hague, Boston, London, 1998), p. 268.

[107] 'Les droits fondamentaux en Europe entre justice constitutionnelle "transfrontière" de la CEDH et justice constitutional national : les lignes incertaines d'une relation structurée', in *Revue française de Droit constitutional (RFDC)*, 1996, p. 706.

rulings under article 177 of the Treaty of Rome. In 1991 the Spanish Constitutional Court refused to refer a case involving Community law to Luxembourg.[108] But the wind of change seems to be blowing, as other constitutional courts do not always share these objections. In 1997, the Luxembourg Court received references from a court in one of the German federal states and from the Belgian Court of Arbitration.[109] In France, the question is trickier as the time allowed for a ruling by the Constitutional Council is too short to be compatible with the European Court of Justice's preliminary ruling procedure.

In coming years we are likely to see a proliferation of conflicts between European courts and national constitutional courts, whose approaches to the same issues can be very different

At Community level, there is already a divergence between the Constitutional Council[110] and the Community authorities regarding the nature of the "general social contribution". In the Council of Europe context, the Strasbourg Court recently declared that the Verdeille Act on hunting and shooting was contrary to the European Human Rights Convention.[111] Admittedly, the Act dates from 1964 and was never referred to the Constitutional Council; but it is by no means certain that the Council, had it received a reference, would have held it unconstitutional. But surely these divergences are inherent in the very life of any Community. In this case they are living evidence of a growing europeanisation of the law in the countries that belong to the integrated regional entities—the Council of Europe and the European Union. Where there is conflict, there is also the need for a dispute-settlement procedure. This is the proper constructive way of looking at the relationship between legal systems in Europe.

In general terms, the relationship between domestic law and international law is the motive force for a dynamic linked to the transformation of the relationship between the Nation State and the rest of the world

In Europe, the relationship depends on progress in European integration. How is equilibrium to be achieved between preservation of national identities embodied in the actions of the national supreme and constitutional courts—and the political, and therefore legal, dynamic of the international community? That is one of the great issues facing the next century.

---

[108] Judgment 28/1991 of 14 February 1991, cited in ed. Joël Rideau, *Les Etats membres de l'Union European : adaptations, mutations, existences*, (Paris, LGDJ, 1997), p. 135.

[109] Judgment No 6/97 of 19 February 1997 of the Belgian Court of Arbitration (Case C 93/97 in the ECJ) and, regarding the Constitutional Court of a German Land, European Court of Justice Case C 158/97. Judgments cited in Jöel Rideau, *Le rôle de l'Union Européenne en matière de protection des droits de l'homme*, (Martinus Nihoff Publishers, The Hague-Boston, London, 1997), p. 336.

[110] In decision DC 91-302 of 30 December 1991 on the Finance Act for 1991, recueil p. 137, the Constitutional Council held the general social contribution to be a form of income tax, whereas the Community authorities treated it as a social security contribution, particularly as it fed the revenue of a sickness insurance scheme.

[111] See G. Charollois, 'La loi dite Verdeille relative à l'organisation des associations de chasseurs à l'épreuve de la Convention European de sauvegarde des droits de l'homme et des libertés fondamentales', in Dalloz,(16th Cahier, chronique, 1998) p. 175.

11

Judicial Protection of the Citizen under European Law

GIL CARLOS RODRIGUEZ IGLESIAS[1]

INTRODUCTION

The European Communities and the European Union are an important economic, political and legal phenomenon of the historic period spanning the second and third millennia of the Christian Age. From a legal point of view, one of the most striking features of this phenomenon is how important they have been in the widening and strengthening of the judicial protection of the rights of the citizen.

This paper tries to provide a global, yet summary, view of the system of judicial protection in the European Union, in particular through cases selected from the case law of the Court of Justice of the European Communities which has played a decisive role in shaping the European Community as a Community of law and as a Community of peoples and of citizens who are each holders of a set of rights to be protected.

THE JUDICIAL ORGANISATION OF THE EUROPEAN COMMUNITY AND THE LIMITED COMPETENCES OF THE EUROPEAN COURTS FOR THE DIRECT PROTECTION OF THE RIGHTS OF THE CITIZENS

Long before the principle of subsidiarity was expressly provided for in the Maastricht Treaty in 1992, the judicial organisation of the European Communities was worked out on the basis of this principle. From the outset the Court of Justice, to which a Court of First Instance has been attached since 1989, was only given the judicial functions which could not be exercised efficiently by the national courts. The national courts remained the ordinary judges for the application of Community law. In such a decentralised judicial system the direct protection of the rights of the citizen under Community law is basically a matter for the national courts.

The Court of Justice and since its establishment the Court of First Instance

---

[1] I am indebted to Elizabeth H. Willocks who assisted me in the preparation of this paper.

are only entrusted with the direct protection of the rights of the citizens *vis à vis* the actions of the European Institutions, not of the Member states. Moreover individuals can only challenge those acts of the Institutions which are addressed to them or which concern them directly and individually. The question whether these conditions on *locus standi* as provided for in Article 230 (ex-Article 173)[2] of the EC Treaty are sufficient is highly controversial. In my view the Court's case law shows that the interpretation of these conditions has taken account of the need to ensure the effective judicial protection of the rights of the individual and in this respect I shall recall some significant judgments.

In the case of *Calpak*[3] from 1980 the Court held that individuals could not be barred on grounds of standing from challenging Community regulations (which are general legislative acts) *per se* since the objective of Article 173 of the EC Treaty (now Article 230) is in particular to prevent the Community institutions from being in a position, merely by choosing the form of a regulation, to exclude an application by an individual against a decision which concerns him directly and individually.

In the case of *Weddell*[4] from 1990 the Court held that the regulation in question was in fact a "bundle of individual decisions" taken by the Commission in the guise of a regulation, each of those decisions affecting the legal position of each applicant. The application contesting that regulation was therefore admissible.

In the *Extramet*[5] judgment of 1991 the Court found that although regulations imposing anti-dumping duties are in fact, as regards their nature and scope, of a legislative character, inasmuch as they apply to all the traders concerned, taken as a whole, their provisions may none the less be of individual concern to certain traders[6] and therefore that measures imposing anti-dumping duties may, without losing their character as regulations, be of individual concern in certain circumstances to certain traders who therefore have standing to bring an action for annulment[7].

Recent judgments have especially underlined the importance of effective judicial protection. The *Codorníu*[8] judgment of 1994 is particularly important, although the reasoning is not very explicit.

In that case the applicant Codorníu, was a producer of quality sparkling wine in Spain for which he had a registered graphic trademark for the name "Gran crémant de Codorníu". The company had been using the mark since 1924 to designate one of its quality sparkling wines. In 1985 the Council passed a regulation which *inter alia* limited the use of the word "crémant" to producers in

---

[2] Pursuant to the Treaty of Amsterdam which entered into force on 1 May 1999 the Articles of the Treaty on European Union and on the European Community were renumbered.
[3] Joined cases 789 and 790/79 *Calpak SpA* [1980] ECR 1949, point 7 of the judgment.
[4] Case C-354/87 *Weddell/Commission* [1990] ECR I-3847, point 23 of the judgment.
[5] Case C-358/89 *Extramet* [1991] ECR 2501
[6] Point 13 of the judgment.
[7] Point 14 of the judgment.
[8] Case C-309/89 *Codorníu* [1994] ECR I-1853

Luxembourg and France. Codorníu raised an action before the Court challenging the regulation.

The Court considered that the regulation in question was a general legislative measure. However the Court found that since the regulation prevented Codorníu from relying on its registered graphic trademark it placed Codorníu in a situation which differentiated it from all other traders. It thus held that the action brought by Codorníu was admissible.

In the Court's judgment in the *Greenpeace*[9] case, which was heard on appeal from the Court of First Instance, the Court expressed the relevance of the principle of effective judicial protection with regard to the interpretation of the conditions on *locus standi* for the first time. This case concerned an action brought by Greenpeace on the basis of the rights it derived under the Environmental impact assessment Directive to challenge the Commission's decision to finance the construction of two power stations on the Canary Islands. Whilst the outcome of this case was not favourable to Greenpeace, the Court's judgment makes the point that the rights relied upon by Greenpeace under the Directive were fully protected by the national courts which could, if need be, refer a question to the Court for a preliminary ruling[10].

RECOGNISING AND UPHOLDING THE INDIVIDUAL'S RIGHTS IN THE NATIONAL COURTS

The role of the national judge in upholding and protecting the rights of the individual is extremely important in the Community judicial system. In developing the principles of direct effect, supremacy, and state liability for damage caused as a consequence of a breach of Community law in its case law, the Court of Justice has strengthened this role.

Whilst the principle of direct effect has been considerably developed and refined by the Court since the judgment in *Van Gend en Loos*[11] in 1963, its essence as identified in that case lies in the fact that individuals can directly invoke the rights conferred upon them under Community law before the national courts without any complementary element of domestic law being necessary—provided that the provisions in question are sufficiently precise and unconditional.

The reasoning in the judgment is as follows:

> "The objective of the EEC Treaty, which is to establish a Common Market, the functioning of which is of direct concern to interested parties in the Community, implies that this Treaty is more than an agreement which merely creates mutual obligations between the contracting states. This view is confirmed by the preamble to the Treaty which refers not only to governments but to peoples. It is also confirmed more

---

[9] Case C-321/95 P, *Greenpeace Council/Commission*, [1998] ECR I-1651
[10] Points 32 and 33 of the judgment.
[11] Case 26/62 *Van Gend en Loos* [1963] ECR 1

specifically by the establishment of institutions endowed with sovereign rights, the exercise of which affects Member states and also their citizens. . . . In addition the task assigned to the Court of Justice under Article 177[12], the object of which is to secure uniform interpretation of the Treaty by national courts and tribunals, confirms that the states have acknowledged that Community law has an authority which can be invoked by their nationals before those courts and tribunals.

The conclusion to be drawn from this is that the Community constitutes a new legal order of international law for the benefit of which the states have limited their sovereign rights, albeit within limited fields and the subjects of which comprise not only Member states but also their nationals. Independently of the legislation of Member states, Community law therefore not only imposes obligations on individuals but is also intended to confer upon them rights which become part of their legal heritage. These rights arise not only where they are expressly granted in the Treaty, but also by reason of obligations which the Treaty imposes in a clearly defined way upon individuals as well as upon Member states and upon the institutions of the Community."[13]

The direct effect of Community law is not therefore, a mere device to insert it into the domestic legal order, but rather the expression of the concept of Community law as a legal order whose subjects are not only states but also individuals, in a position of holding individual legal rights and obligations created directly by the Community legal order. In expressing this concept the Court made a very clear choice of interpretation which was decisive in the future development of the Community legal system. The concept underlies the current case law on direct effect, which the Court usually refers to as the rules which produce an effect such that they "create individual rights which the national courts and tribunals must protect".

The coexistence in one and the same territorial jurisdiction of the Community legal system and the legal system of the respective Member states can give rise to conflict between the laws of each system. The Court's case law has provided that these conflicts are to be resolved in accordance with the principle whereby Community law prevails over national law, the principle of supremacy as first defined in the *Costa/Enel*[14] judgment and then clarified in the case of *Simmenthal*[15].

In upholding the supremacy of Community law, the Court relied upon the following arguments: first the nature and purpose of the European Communities to which the Member states have transferred real powers which have entailed the consequent limitation of sovereign rights or powers exercised by the state; second in the binding and directly applicable nature of Community regulations as provided for in Article 249 (ex-Article 189) of the Treaty and the fact that this provision which is subject to no reservation, would be quite meaningless if a state could unilaterally nullify its effects by means of a legislative mea-

---

[12] Now Article 234 of the EC Treaty.
[13] Page 12 of the case report.
[14] Case 6/64 *Costa/ENEL* [1964] ECR 585
[15] Case 106/77 *Simmenthal* [1978] ECR 629

sure which could prevail over Community law; and third the obligation on the Member states to abstain from taking any new national legislative measure which could jeopardise the realisation of Community objectives. The Court deduced from the principle of supremacy the obligation on every national court in a case within its own jurisdiction to apply Community law in its entirety and to protect the rights which the latter confers on individuals and to set aside any provision of national law which may conflict with it, whether prior or subsequent to the Community rule[16]. And accordingly "any provision of a national legal system and any legislative, administrative or judicial practice which might impair the effectiveness of Community law by withholding from the national court having jurisdiction to apply such law the power to do everything necessary at the moment of its application to set aside national legislative provisions which might prevent Community rules from having full force and effect are incompatible with those requirements which are at the very essence of Community law."[17]

Of course the effectiveness of the principle of supremacy as set out by the Court depends on its being put into practice by the national jurisdictions, before which the real problems of conflict between domestic and Community laws are raised. On the whole it can be said that the national courts have respected the criteria laid down by the Court. Certainly there have been some notorious exceptions but most of the cases involving conflict between the case law of a national court and that of the Court of Justice have been resolved on the basis of aligning the former with the latter and more recently there has been a marked increase in the convergence of national case law with the case law of the Court.

As a corollary to the traditional principles of direct effect and supremacy the most recent cases have set out the principle of state liability for damage caused to individuals as a consequence of a breach of Community law.

This principle was clearly stated in the *Francovich*[18] judgment of 1991. The ruling was in answer to preliminary references by two Italian courts in proceedings involving the fact that Italy had not adopted the legislation necessary to implement the Community directive providing guarantees for workers in the event of insolvency of their employer. The Court, having concluded that the provisions of the Directive which provided for the workers' rights could not be considered as having direct effect, examined the question whether in these conditions the state could be obliged to make good the loss and damage which the workers had suffered as a result of the failure to transpose the Directive. The Court affirmed the existence of a general principle of state liability on the basis of the argument which highlighted in particular the fact that the full effectiveness of Community rules would be impaired and the protection of the rights which they grant would be weakened if individuals were unable to obtain redress when their rights are infringed by a breach of Community law for which

---

[16] Case 106/77 *Simmenthal* cited above at point 21 of the judgment.
[17] Point 22 of the judgment.
[18] Joined cases C-6/90 and C-9/90 *Francovich and Bonifaci* [1991] ECR I-5357

a Member state can be held responsible[19] and moreover the obligation of Member states to take all appropriate measures, whether general or particular, to ensure fulfilment of their obligations under Community law under Article 10 (ex-Article 5) of the Treaty which includes the obligation to nullify the unlawful consequences of a breach of Community law.[20]

This principle has since been developed in later judgments and in particular in the judgment in the joined cases of *Brasserie du pêcheur* and *Factortame III*[21]. In that judgment the Court specifically recognised that the principle of state liability is based upon the full effectiveness of Community rules and the effective protection of the rights which they confer, a principle inherent to the Community legal order and that the conditions giving rise to a right to reparation also derive from that principle.

The judgment also confirmed that a state incurs liability for breaches of Community law which are attributable to the national legislature where they are "sufficiently serious". In order that the breach should be "sufficiently serious", the decisive criterion is whether the state in question manifestly and gravely disregarded the limits of its discretion. The factors which the national court may take into consideration include *inter alia* the clarity and precision of the rule breached, the measure of discretion left by that rule, whether the infringement and the damage caused was involuntary or voluntary as well as whether any error of law was excusable or inexcusable[22].

The Factortame case, which was referred to the Court by the High Court of Justice Queen's Bench Division (Divisional Court), was then brought before the House of Lords on appeal on the question whether the breach of Community law by the UK legislature in that case was "sufficiently serious" so as to incur liability in damages. The House of Lords' judgment which upheld the Divisional Court's judgment[23] is a striking example of how the national courts relying on a ruling on the interpretation of Community law by the Court of Justice protect the rights of the individual.

The principle of state liability has been a decisive factor in the strengthening of the protection of the rights conferred on individuals by Community law. Indeed both this principle and the principle of direct effect are derived from the concept of Community law as an order whose subjects are also individuals. And whilst these developments come from the case law of the Court of Justice, the cases themselves are on reference from national courts further to actions brought by individuals claiming their rights under Community law. The result of these individual actions has brought about the progress in the process of construction of the Community as one of law and the process of European integra-

---

[19] Point 33 of the judgment.
[20] Point 36 of the judgment.
[21] Joined Cases C-46/93 and C-48/93 *Brasserie du pêcheur and Factortame* [1996] ECR I-1029
[22] Points 55 and 56 of the judgment.
[23] Judgment of the House of Lords of 28 October 1999 in *R v. Secretary of State for Transport ex parte Factortame Ltd.*

tion as we know it today. Moreover the scope of application of the freedoms of the internal market has been widened and Community law has been removed little by little from its purely economical component. I will return to this point below.

EFFECTIVE JUDICIAL PROTECTION IN THE NATIONAL COURTS OF THE RIGHTS CONFERRED BY COMMUNITY LAW

The application of Community law by national courts is governed by the principle of national institutional and procedural autonomy. This principle was formulated in connection with the application of procedural time limits under national law in the *Rewe*[24] judgment of 1976. The Court ruled that in the absence of Community rules, it is for the domestic legal system of each Member state to designate the courts having jurisdiction and to determine the procedural conditions governing actions at law intended to ensure the protection of the rights which citizens have from the direct effect of Community law, it being understood that such conditions cannot be less favourable than those relating to similar actions of a domestic nature and cannot make the exercise of those rights impossible[25]. In the *San Giorgio*[26] judgment of 1983 the Court added that the exercise of those rights should not be made "virtually impossible or excessively difficult".

The principle of Member state institutional and procedural autonomy has suffered some erosion in the sense that Community law has limited the scope of national procedural autonomy progressively so as to accommodate the requirements deriving from the principle of effective judicial protection.

One consequence has been that any national decision which applies Community law has to be reviewable and subject to judicial control. This right to a judicial remedy is a fundamental principle inherent to Community law. The main judgments on this point are those of *Johnston*[27] in 1986 and *Heylens*[28] in 1987.

In those judgments the Court defined this aspect of judicial protection as reflecting a general principle of law which underlies the constitutional traditions common to the Member states and which has been enshrined in Articles 6 and 13 of the European Convention for the Protection of Human Rights and Fundamental Freedoms[29].

In the *Heylens* judgment the Court extended the protection of such a fundamental right to the obligation to notify the reasons for every administrative decision upon which the effectiveness of judicial control depends[30].

The Court emphasised this fundamental right again in its judgment in

---

[24] Case 33/76 *Rewe* [1976] ECR 1989
[25] Point 5 of the judgment.
[26] Case 199/82 *San Giorgio* [1983] ECR 3595
[27] Case 222/84 *Johnston* [1986] ECR 1651
[28] Case 222/86 *Heylens* [1987] ECR 4097
[29] Point 18 of the *Johnston* judgment and point 14 of the *Heylens* judgment.
[30] Point 15 of the judgment.

Oleificio Borelli[31] which implies a more far-reaching interference with national procedural autonomy. In that case the Court held that it was for the national courts to rule on the lawfulness of a national measure which was submitted as a preparatory measure to the Commission even though under national law such preparatory measures were not subject to review and actions challenging those measures were not admissible under the national rules of procedure. The Court held that this review had to be conducted on the same terms as the national courts would review any final measure which, taken by the same national authority, might adversely affect third parties.

Another aspect of effective judicial protection has been that national procedural time limits cannot bar an effective remedy. In the case of *Emmott*[32] from 1991 the Court held that since individuals are unable to ascertain the full extent of their rights until such time as a directive has been properly transposed into national law, a period laid down by national law within which proceedings must be initiated in order to protect the rights conferred by the directive cannot begin to run before the directive has been properly transposed. The scope of this judgment has been restricted by further case law[33] which has made clear that Emmott can only be understood on its facts. But even with this limited scope, the judgment remains a striking manifestation of the requirements of effective judicial protection and effective remedies.

The most illustrative example of effective judicial protection is that of interim measures. In the *Factortame I*[34] judgment of 1990 the Court recognised that the national courts have jurisdiction to grant interim relief from the effects of a rule of national law which is allegedly contrary to Community law, pending a ruling on the corresponding preliminary question from the Court. The Court could not have been more explicit in holding that the effectiveness of the preliminary reference procedure would be weakened and "the full effectiveness of Community law would be just as much impaired if a rule of national law could prevent a court seised of a dispute governed by Community law from granting interim relief in order to ensure the full effectiveness of the judgment to be given on the existence of the rights claimed under Community law."[35]

Moreover in the *Zückerfabrik*[36] judgment in 1991 the Court recognised that national courts may order the provisional suspension of the effect of a piece of domestic legislation adopted in application of a Community rule where that rule is presumed invalid pending a ruling on the question of validity of that rule referred to the Court of Justice by the national court. The Court emphasised that the interim legal protection which Community law ensures for individuals

---

[31] Case C-97/91 *Borelli* [1992] ECR I-6313
[32] Case C-208/90 *Emmott* [1991] ECR I-4269
[33] Examples of the further case law on national time limits include the judgments in C-338/91 *Steenhorst Neerings* [1993] ECR I-5475, C-312/93 *Peterbroeck* [1995] ECR I-2195, C-188/95 *Fantask* [1997] ECR I-6783, C-231/96 *Edis* [1998] ECR I-4951 and C-326/96 *Levez* [1998] ECR I-7853
[34] C-213/89 *Factortame I* [1990] ECR I-2433
[35] Points 21 and 22 of the judgment.
[36] Joined cases C-143/88 and C-92/89 *Zückerfabrik* [1991] ECR I-415

before national courts must remain the same, irrespective of whether they contest the compatibility of national legal provisions with Community law or the validity of secondary Community law, in view of the fact that the dispute in both cases is based on Community law itself[37].

This judgment shows that the requirements of effective judicial protection must prevail, at least temporarily over the Court's exclusive jurisdiction to rule on the validity of Community acts[38].

Finally the case of *Atlanta*[39] of 1995 resulted in the Court holding that national courts have jurisdiction to order any necessary interim measures including the making of a positive legal order provisionally disapplying a rule of Community law.

The most interesting aspect of the case law on interim relief is that it has resulted in empowering national judges to grant relief which they would not necessarily have had jurisdiction to do under national law and even requires them to grant relief under Community law which they would not be allowed to do under national law[40].

The fact that the principle of effective judicial protection, which has deep roots in the legal systems of all the Member states, gives rise to conflict with procedural rules of national law might, at first sight, appear paradoxical. But given that national procedural rules are drafted for the protection of rights conferred by national law it is not surprising that they may prove to be inadequate in situations arising out of the coexistence of Community rules and national rules and may lead to a denial of justice. This high level of judicial control is the necessary corollary of the rule of law and the fundamental right to judicial review of administrative and legislative acts, which is without doubt one of the characteristic principles of Community law. It was this concept which led the Court to conclude in the *Les Verts*[41] judgment that the European Community is also a Community of law.

---

[37] Point 20 of the judgment.
[38] Case 314/85 *Foto Frost* [1987] ECR 4199
[39] Case C-466/93 *Atlanta* [1995] ECR I-3761
[40] This development has in turn had an effect on the development of national law. For example in Spain the Supreme Court further to the judgment in *Factortame I* initiated a new line of case law on interim measures bringing the protection as regards interim relief in respect of national laws up to the same high level of protection as that afforded regarding Community laws. This approach has since been upheld by the Spanish Constitutional court. See Eduardo Garcia de Enterria/Luis Ortega, *Spanish Report* in "*Le droit administratif sous l'influence de l'Europe*" 1996 p. 695. This publication also contains reports on the laws of most of the other Member states and the influence the Court's case law has had on them.
[41] Case C-294/83 *Les Verts* [1986] ECR 1339

FUNDAMENTAL ECONOMIC FREEDOMS AND THE PRINCIPLE OF
NON-DISCRIMINATION, EUROPEAN CITIZENSHIP

Although the drafters of the Treaty of Rome clearly described the main features of the common market: the free movement of goods, labour, services and capital as well as the freedom to establish business operations in each of Member states, the question as to whether those principles should entail the creation of individual rights for traders and workers was left unanswered.

As early as in the *Van Gend en Loos*[42] judgment the Court stated that those common market rules constituted much more than a political programme to be implemented at the discretion of the Member states, but rather a body of legal rules designed to create genuine individual rights. In the *Van Binsbergen* and *Reyners*[43] cases of 1974 the Court held that those common market rules had indeed become individual rights capable of being invoked against restrictive State measures. More recently the Court has also recognised that those common market rights might even be infringed by Community legislation[44], thereby also exposing actions of Community institutions to the scrutiny of the Court with regard to those rights. In recognising the wide scope of application of the freedoms of the internal market the Court has *inter alia* emphasised the paramount importance of the fundamental principle of non-discrimination on grounds of nationality. In so doing the Court has removed Community law little by little from its purely economic component extending the application of the Treaty *ratione materiae* as well as *ratione personae* and often developing the law "before the letter of the law". Indeed, the Court defined the common market as an area which should operate as an internal market long before the term "internal market" was introduced by the Single European Act.

By way of example, as regards the free movement of goods, the Court established in the *"Cassis de Dijon"*[45] judgment that any product lawfully marketed in one Member state must be able to circulate without hindrance throughout the common market, without having to fulfil the requirements laid down by each national legal system, unless a state is able to rely on overriding reasons justifying the specific conditions laid down in its national legislation. This judgment introduced the principle of mutual recognition and marked a major development in the law governing the internal market. About one year later the Commission issued a Communication[46] in which it announced a new policy further to that judgment whereby it would monitor more strictly the application of the Treaty rules on the free movement of goods as interpreted by the Court and

---

[42] Cited above.
[43] Cases 33/74 *Van Binsbergen* [1974] ECR 1299 and 2/74 *Reyners* [1974] ECR 631
[44] For a recent example see case C-114/96 *Kieffer and Thill* [1997] ECR I-3629
[45] Case 120/78, *Rewe-Zentral AG "Cassis de Dijon"* [1979] ECR 649
[46] Commission Communication concerning the consequences of the judgment given by the Court of Justice on 20 February 1979 in case 120/78 ("Cassis de Dijon") OJ C 256 of 3 October 1980, pp. 2–3

that it would be more selective in its work of harmonisation concentrating mainly on those national laws which have an impact on the functioning of the common market. In other words, one could say that the "*Cassis de Dijon*" judgment implied an extension of the scope of Article 30 and thus of its direct effect. This led to a concomitant reduction of the need to harmonise divergent commercial and technical rules of the Member states, since such harmonisation was not a prerequisite for the free movement of goods.

In the field of freedom to provide *services* in other Member states the Court held in the *Luisi and Carbone*[47] judgment of 1984 that the freedom to *provide* services also includes the freedom, for the *recipients* of services to go to another Member state in order to receive a service there, without being obstructed by restrictions and that tourists, persons receiving medical treatment and persons travelling for the purposes of education or business are to be regarded as recipients of services.[48]

And then in the *Cowan*[49] judgment of 1989 the Court stated in very clear terms that when Community law guarantees a natural person the freedom to go to another Member state the protection of that person from harm in the Member state in question, on the same basis as that of nationals and persons residing there, is a corollary of that freedom of movement[50].

The Court has also interpreted the principle of freedom to *establish* business operations in other Member states broadly to include for example in the *Kraus*[51] case of 1993 the right to use a postgraduate academic title in a Member state other than where the title was awarded. The Court emphasised that Article 52 (now Article 43) lays down a precise obligation of result which did not authorise a Member state, on the grounds of the fact that there was no secondary legislation yet in place, to deny to a person subject to Community law the practical benefits of the freedoms guaranteed by the Treaty[52].

In the case of *Gebhard*[53] the Court confirmed that the concept of establishment within the meaning of the Treaty is a very broad one, allowing a Community national to participate, on a stable and continuous basis, in the economic life of a Member state other than his State of origin and to profit therefrom, so contributing to economic and social interpenetration within the Community in the sphere of activities as self employed persons[54].

In the same judgment the Court then said something very important regarding its broad interpretative approach to all of the freedoms provided for in the Treaty:

[47] Joined cases 286/82 and 26/83 *Luisi and Carbone* [1984] ECR 377
[48] Point 16 of the judgment.
[49] Case 186/87 *Cowan* [1989] ECR 195
[50] Point 17 of the judgment.
[51] Case C-9/92 *Kraus* [1993] ECR 1663
[52] Points 27 to 30 of the judgment which refer to the Court's judgments in cases 222/86 *Heylens* [1987] ECR 4097, paragraphs 8 and 11; 118/75 *Watson and Behlmann* [1976] ECR 1185, paragraph 16 and C-370/90 *Singh* [1992] ECR I-426
[53] Case C-55/94 *Gebhard* [1995] ECR I-4165
[54] Point 25 of the judgment.

"national measures liable to hinder or make less attractive the exercise of fundamental freedoms guaranteed by the Treaty must fulfil four conditions: they must be applied in a non-discriminatory manner; they must be justified by imperative requirements in the general interest; they must be suitable for securing the attainment of the objective which they pursue; and they must not go beyond what is necessary in order to attain it[55].

It is probably with regard to the principle of the free movement of *labour and of workers* that the Court has been most ready to protect the rights of the citizen on the basis of the general treaty freedom without the adoption of specific secondary legislation. The Court has consistently rejected any argument on the basis of the fact that the free movement of workers is merely an aspect of economic integration, human labour as just a factor of production, a type of merchandise[56].

In the *Gravier*[57] judgment of 1985 the Court interpreted the full effect of this fundamental principle. This case concerned an action brought by a student in vocational training on grounds of discrimination since because he was from another Member state he had had to pay a special fee for that training. The Court's reasoning in upholding the broad interpretation of the Treaty to include the right to non-discrimination in vocational training is worth recalling. The Court held first that although educational organisation and policy were not as such included in the spheres which the Treaty has entrusted to the Community institutions, access to and participation in courses of instruction and apprenticeship, in particular vocational training were not unconnected with Community law[58]; second that the common vocational training policy referred to in one of the articles of the Treaty was gradually being established and that it constituted an indispensable element of the activities of the Community, whose objectives include *inter alia* the free movement of persons, the mobility of labour and the improvement of living standards of workers[59]; and that third, access to vocational training is in particular likely to promote free movement of persons throughout the Community, by enabling them to obtain a qualification in the Member state where they intend to work and by enabling them to complete their training and develop their particular talents in the Member state whose vocational training programmes include the special subject desired[60].

This development by the Court in its case law was later followed by the adoption of the three 1990 Directives recognising the right of free movement and abode within the Community independently of the exercise of any economic

---

[55] Point 39 of the judgment.
[56] See on this point in particular Melchior Wathelet "*European Citizenship and freedom of movement in the case law*" (Brussels conference "30 ans de libre circulation des travailleurs en Europe" 16 December 1998, not yet published)
[57] Case 293/83 *Gravier* [1985] ECR 593
[58] Point 19 of the judgment.
[59] Point 23 of the judgment.
[60] Point 24 of the judgment.

activity, for any national of a Member state with adequate resources and an all risks health insurance policy[61].

This short summary of the cases shows that the Court has ensured that free movement is no longer the reserve of workers, nor of providers of services nor of those companies seeking to establish their business abroad and has "humanised" these freedoms and opened them up to any individual who falls within the scope of the Treaty *ratione materiae* and *ratione personae* as interpreted by the Court.

Since the entry into force of the Maastricht Treaty on 1 November 1993 one of the Parts of the Treaty is now devoted to the "Citizenship of the Union" which constitutes a constitutional acknowledgment by the Member states of the importance of the individual. Whilst the rights conferred in this part of the Treaty are rather limited, the Court has shown in its case law that the provisions on European citizenship are not purely rhetorical declarations as some had thought.

In 1998 the Court was asked about the legal status of a Community national (a Spanish woman) who was not working but residing legally in Germany. She had claimed for a child allowance which the German authorities refused to grant without prior production of a residence permit, a permit which she did not have. In the judgment of *Martínez Sala*[62], the Court interpreted paragraph 2 of Article 8 (now Article 17, paragraph 2)[63] of the Treaty as meaning that such a Community national can rely on that provision in order to exercise her right as a Union citizen to non-discriminatory treatment on grounds of nationality even if she is not a worker and her right of residence derives only from national law and not from Community law as in the case at issue.

And in the judgment of *Wijsenbeek*[64] of September 1999 the Court interpreted Article 8a (now Article 18) which provides that "every citizen of the Union shall have the right to move and reside freely within the territory of the Member states, subject to the limitations and conditions laid down in the Treaty and by the measures adopted to give it effect" as meaning that a citizen entering a Member state from another Member state who is not exercising an economic activity can rely on that provision in so far as any penalty imposed upon him at the point of entry should not be discriminatory as compared to similar national infringements, nor disproportionate so as to create an obstacle to the free movement of persons.

This summary review shows a significant evolution of the position of the individual, who was first recognised as a subject of functional economic rights, what

---

[61] Directive 90/364/EEC on rights of residence (1990 OJ L180/26)

Directive 90/365/EEC in rights of residence for employees and self employed persons (OJ L180/28). Directive 90/366/EEC on rights of residence for students (1990 OJ L180/30)

[62] Case C-85/96 *Martínez Sala* [1998] ECR I-2691

[63] This provision provides that "Citizens of the Union shall enjoy the rights conferred by this Treaty and shall be subject to the duties imposed thereby".

[64] Case C-378/97 *Wijsenbeek*, judgment of 21 September 1999.

Professor Ipsen as early as 1963 characterised as a "Marktbürger"[65]—a "citizen of the (common) market". The case law of the Court has prompted a shift to the status of European citizen, which is now constitutionally enshrined in the Maastricht Treaty.

PROTECTION OF FUNDAMENTAL RIGHTS IN THE COMMUNITY LEGAL ORDER

There are two reasons why the protection of fundamental rights in the Community system is so important and which place the Court of Justice in a position of special responsibility in this area. The first is because there is no Bill of rights which has a constitutional or legislative status[66] in the Community legal order and the second is that respect for fundamental rights forms a constituent part of the common heritage upon which the very foundations of the Community lie constituting an indispensable prerequisite for any state wishing to accede to it.

In 1974 the Court held in the *Nold*[67] judgment that:

> "fundamental rights form an integral part of the general principles of law, the observance of which [the Court] ensures.
>
> In safeguarding these rights, the Court is bound to draw inspiration from constitutional traditions common to the Member states, and it cannot therefore uphold measures which are incompatible with fundamental rights recognized and protected by the Constitutions of those states.
>
> Similarly, international treaties for the protection of human rights on which the Member states have collaborated or of which they are signatories can supply guidelines which should be followed within the framework of Community law"[68].

This meant that every time a breach of such a right was alleged the Court sought to determine whether there was sufficient ground to establish on the basis of those constitutional traditions and international conventions whether the right in question should be recognized and incorporated into the Community legal order. According to the Court the constitutional law of a par-

---

[65] It seems that Professor Ipsen created this expression in his report for the *Second Conference on the Law of the European Communities* held at the Hague in 1963 *Neue Juristische Wochenschrift* 1964, 339, 340 (footnote 2).

[66] There have been some developments in this area. The European Council meeting in Cologne in June 1999 decided that a Charter of fundamental rights guaranteed in the Union should be established in order to make their overriding importance and relevance more visible. In this context a report of the Expert Group on Fundamental Rights commissioned by the European Commission was published in February 1999. This document concludes for the inclusion of a Bill of rights in the Treaty. At the Tampere Summit on 15 and 16 October 1999 the European Council decided to set up a body to draw up the draft Charter of fundamental rights for the European Union. This body is to be made up of 62 representatives of the heads of state of government, of each of the Member States, the Community institutions and the national parliaments (62 persons in all) with observers from the Court of Justice, the Council of Europe and the Court of Human Rights. At the time of writing it is understood that discussions will begin in December 1999.

[67] Case 4/73 *Nold* [1974] ECR 491

[68] Point 13 of the judgment.

ticular Member state cannot be taken in isolation in order to define the protection of fundamental rights in the Community system; rather, all the legal systems of the Member states and, in particular, their constitutional rules, must be taken into account so as to determine the common standard of protection.

The Court described its judicial task in the *Hauer*[69] case as follows:

". . . the question of a possible infringement of fundamental rights by a measure of the Community institutions can only be judged in the light of Community law itself. The introduction of special criteria for assessment stemming from the legislation or constitutional law of a particular Member state would, by damaging the substantive unity and efficacy of Community law, lead inevitably to the destruction of the unity of the Common Market and the jeopardising of the cohesion of the Community"[70]

As a result, the Court examines the "constitutional rules and practice" of the Member states for the purpose of Community law.

In the *Hoechst*[71] case on the scope and limits of the Commission's investigative powers in competition proceedings, the applicant argued on the basis of comparative law and in particular US anti-trust law. The Advocate General in that case also gave a thorough overview of the law in each of the Member states in order to show to what extent legal persons can rely on the right to the inviolability of the home.

In the judgment the Court found that there was no fundamental right to the inviolability of business premises on the ground that "there are not inconsiderable divergences between the legal systems of the Member states in regard to the nature and degree of protection afforded to those premises against intervention by the public authorities[72]". However, the Court stressed that:

"in all the legal systems of the Member states, any intervention by the public authorities in the sphere of private activities of any person, whether natural or legal, must have a legal basis and be justified on the grounds laid down by law, and, consequently, those systems provide, albeit in different forms, protection against arbitrary or disproportionate intervention"[73].

In the light of that principle, the Court recognized the right of companies not to be subject to arbitrary or disproportionate intervention.

The Court has sometimes defined as "fundamental rights" under Community law specific rights which only have their fundamental character under a particular national constitution[74]. This shows that the common standard of protection guaranteed by the Court is not the minimum common standard.

Among the international rules which form part of the common general principles of law which the Court draws upon to build the Community regime for

---

[69] Case 44/79 *Hauer* [1979] ECR 3727
[70] Point 14 of the judgment.
[71] Joined cases C-46/87 and C-227/88 *Hoechst/Commission* [1989] ECR 2895
[72] Point 17 of the judgment.
[73] Point 19 of the judgment.
[74] For instance the freedom to pursue a trade or profession which is a fundamental right under German Constitutional law. See case C-280/93 *Germany/Council* [1994] ECR I-4973, point 78.

the protection of fundamental rights, the European Convention for the Protection of Human Rights and Fundamental Freedoms is of particular relevance. The provisions of the Convention are not formally applied by the Court as international provisions as such, but are taken into consideration as a source for the identification of the general principles common to the legal systems of the Member states.

Examination of the many cases, which since the judgment in the *Rutili*[75] case, refer to the European Convention on Human Rights illustrates that, independently of the theoretical importance of the legal value of the Convention as a source of general principles, the Court in fact applies its provisions as an integral part of Community law. There are even aspects of the Court's case law which can be interpreted as a recognition in the Community context of the authority of the interpretation of the Convention by the specific judicial body specifically set up to interpret it, the European Court of Human Rights[76]. Thus in practice in the Court of Justice's case law the Convention performs a function equivalent to that of a basic charter of formally recognised fundamental rights.

The case law on due process of rights is a good example. Those rights are generally described as "rights of the defence". They have been recognized by the Court as a fundamental principle of Community law which must be observed by all Community institutions in their administrative procedures. The case law of the Court was developed mainly in the field of competition proceedings. Those rights, which are not defined in any of the procedural regulations that govern those proceedings, have different dimensions. They relate for example to the privilege against self-incrimination, the legal basis for search and seizure in business premises, the right to be heard, the lawyer-client privilege and the obligation on authorities to give reasons for their decisions.

In the *Orkem*[77] case from 1989, the self-incrimination privilege was invoked in response to a request for information that the Commission had addressed to companies in the course of competition proceedings. These requests called for the disclosure of information regarding alleged price and volume control initiatives that the Commission was investigating. The Court found that the Commission was not entitled to call for a general disclosure of unspecified acts or measures in support of the alleged infringements, although, in the view of the Court, a general right to remain silent does not exist. According to the Court, the recognition of the right to remain silent in only two Member states was not sufficient to make such a right a general principle of Community law. The Court also analyzed Article 6 of the European Convention on Human Rights which contains a general provision of what one would call the due process of law and found that it does not expressly guarantee a right not to give evidence against

---

[75] Case 36/75 *Rutili* [1975] ECR 1219

[76] See for instance case C-13/94 P. [1996] ECR I-2143, point 16; joined cases C-74/95 and C-129/95 X. [1996] ECR I-6609, point 25; cases C-368/95 *Familiapress* [1997] ECR I-3689, point 24 and C-185/95 P *Baustahlgewebe* [1998] ECR I-8417 point 29.

[77] Case 374/87 *Orkem* [1989] ECR 3283

oneself and, at least at the date of the Court's judgment in 1989, had not been interpreted by the European Court of Human Rights. However, the Court stated that the applicant's objection to certain questions of the Commission could be based on the principle of the protection of the rights of the defence in the sense that it was the Commission which had to submit and prove certain facts.

In the *Baustahlgewebe*[78] judgment of 1998 the Court applied the principle that judicial proceedings must be disposed of within a reasonable time as developed by the European Court of Human Rights on the basis of Article 6 of the Convention[79]. In particular it held that the reasonableness of such a period must be appraised in the light of the circumstances specific to each case and, in particular, the importance of the case for the person concerned, its complexity and the conduct of the applicant and the competent authorities[80].

Fundamental rights are also to be respected by Community institutions and by national authorities whenever they act in the sphere of Community law. Member state authorities act within that sphere when they implement Community measures, when they take measures that impinge upon rights protected by Community law or when they take action in areas regulated specifically by Community law.

In 1991 the Court emphasized in the *ERT*[81] case that national laws which are based upon Community provisions which authorise derogations to the fundamental freedoms of the Treaty must conform with the fundamental rights recognized in the Community legal order. In particular, where a Member state relies on Treaty provisions in order to justify rules which are likely to obstruct the exercise of a common market freedom, such justification, provided for by Community law, must be interpreted in the light of the general principles of law and in particular of fundamental rights. Thus national rules falling under the exceptions provided for by the Treaty must be compatible with the fundamental rights the observance of which is ensured by the Court[82].

It is significant that Article F, paragraph 2 of the Maastricht Treaty (the Treaty on European Union) expressly recognized the Court's case law on fundamental rights. It stated that "The Union shall respect fundamental rights, as

---

[78] Case C-185/95 P *Baustahlgewebe/Commission*, [1998] ECR I-8417

[79] In the judgment the Court referred to the following cases of the European Court of Human Rights: *Erkner and Hofner* 23 April 1987, Series A No 117, 66; *Kemmache* of 27 November 1991, Series A No 218, 60; *Phocas v France* of 23 April 1996, *Recueil des arrêts et décisions* 1996-II, p. 546, 71, and *Garyfallou AEBE v Greece* of 27 September 1997, *Recueil des arrêts et décisions* 1997-V, p. 1821, 39

[80] Point 29 of the judgment.

[81] Case C-260/89 *ERT* [1991] ECR I-2925

[82] The Court emphasised this point again in the *Familiapress* case (C-368/95 *Vereinigte Familiapress* [1997] ECR I-3689) where it said that those fundamental rights include freedom of expression, as enshrined in the European Convention on Human Rights. However whilst stating that a prohibition on selling publications may detract from the freedom of expression the Court took note of the fact that Article 10 does permit derogations from the freedom for the purposes of maintaining press diversity in so far as they are prescribed by law and are necessary in a democratic society.

guaranteed by the European Convention for the Protection of Human Rights and Fundamental Freedoms signed in Rome on 4 November 1950 and as they result from the constitutional traditions common to the Member states, as general principles of Community law." There could not be a clearer confirmation by the Member states of the constitutional significance of the Court's case law on the point.

The strange thing was that Article L of that Treaty paradoxically excluded the provision on fundamental rights from the Court's jurisdiction as regards in particular the second and third pillars. The Amsterdam Treaty has gone some way to rectifying the situation in so far as Article L (now Article 46) of the Treaty on European Union has been amended and confirms that the Court has the power to interpret Article 6 (2) (formerly Article F (2)) with regard to acts of the Institutions. In other words the Court has the power to test acts of the Institutions against the requirement to respect fundamental rights in so far as the Court has been given jurisdiction to review the legality of those acts. Member state action which could be contrary to Article 6(2) is still not explicitly subject to judicial control. But it is clear that the Court's jurisdiction under Community law remains intact and that therefore Member state action which falls under the scope of Community law remains subject to the Court's jurisdiction.

The Amsterdam Treaty has also incorporated the provisions on asylum, immigration and visas which were previously under the third pillar of the Treaty on European Union into the Community Treaty and thus into the fold of the Court's jurisdiction.

The Amsterdam Treaty also provides for sanctions for a serious and persistent breach of those rights by the Member states. Whereas the provision giving power to the European Council to impose these sanctions under Article 7 of the *Treaty on European Union* is not subject to judicial control, the measures taken by the Council of Ministers under the scope of *Community* law under Article 309 of the EC Treaty remain subject to judicial review.

Finally pursuant to Article 13 of the EC Treaty as amended by the Amsterdam Treaty, the Community is now empowered to take action to combat discrimination based on sex, racial or ethnic origin, religion or belief, disability, age or sexual orientation[83].

As the past forty years of legal developments in Europe have shown, the protection of fundamental rights is not a frozen legal field but rather a dynamic area of law which has to take account of the evolution in our societies. Indeed, the law is bound to respond to concerns shared by citizens even though such con-

---

[83] The Commission has recently put forward its proposals for a communication and three measures: a directive prohibiting discrimination on the grounds of racial or ethnic origin, religion or belief, disability, age or sexual orientation in employment; a directive prohibiting discrimination on the grounds of racial or ethnic origin in employment, education, the provision of goods and services and social protection; and an action programme designed to support and complement implementation of the directives through the exchange of information and experience and the dissemination of best practices in both legislative and non legislative areas.

cerns might not have been addressed by the constitutional frameworks governing our societies. As the history of the Community shows, political objectives formulated at a given moment may later become legal rules that might be enforced against public authorities as well as other private individuals.

The preservation of the environment, the protection of individual data, the accountability of public authorities and the transparency of administrative and legislative action are only a few examples of those emerging new fields. I would particularly like to emphasize the growing importance of the issue of transparency and the question of access to information held by Community institutions on which the Court of Justice and the Court of First Instance have already made a significant contribution to the recognition of such right of access to information[84].

FINAL REMARKS

The sole force of the European Community is the force of law. Respect for the rule of law and protection of the rights of the citizens are fundamental values common to the Member states of the European Union.

The overview provided in this paper has attempted to show the significance of effective judicial protection of the rights of the citizen in the European legal system. Indeed the principle of effective judicial protection underlies the most basic and characteristic legal principles of European Community law.

It is submitted that European Community law as interpreted by the European Court of Justice has had the effect of expanding the scope of judicial protection of individual rights throughout the Member states of the European Union— even beyond the scope of Community law.

---

[84] For example cases T-194/94 *Carvel and Guardian Newspapers/ Council* [1995] ECR II-2765, T-174/95 *Svenska Jornalistförbundet/Council* [1998] ECR II-2289, T-188/97 *Rothmans/ Commission* judgment of 19 July 1999, C-58/94 Netherlands/Council [1996] ECR I-2169 and most recently C-174/98P and C-189/98P *Netherlands and van der Wal/Commission* announced for 11 January 2000.

12

Some reflections on the First Year of Operation of the "New" European Court of Human Rights

LUZIUS WILDHABER

On 1 November 1998 Protocol No 11 to the European Convention on Human Rights entered into force, forty-eight years after the Convention was opened for signature. The Protocol aimed to streamline the Convention enforcement machinery by replacing the part-time Commission and Court of Human Rights by a single Court sitting on a full-time basis. It also strengthened the judicial character of the system by making acceptance of the Court's jurisdiction and of the right of individual petition compulsory, whereas it had previously been optional.

However, the driving force behind the reform of the system was the need to cope with an ever-increasing case-load as a result of a heightened awareness of the Convention in the older Contracting States and the growing membership of the Council of Europe. At the beginning of 1988 there were 21 member States of the Council of Europe. Eleven years on there are 41, all of which have ratified the European Convention. The Court's jurisdiction covers a geographical area with a population of some 800,000,000 potential applicants who have direct access to the Court and who ultimately, whatever the merit of their complaint, are entitled under the present system to a judicial decision. Let us dwell on that figure for a moment. Will a single Court be capable of providing relief for individuals on such a scale? Is it surprising that that the Court's case-load continues to rise steadily? The system is of course a subsidiary one, by which is meant that primary responsibility for human rights protection falls to the national authorities. Applicants are required to exhaust domestic remedies. Even so the task is enormous. At the same time the importance of the Convention and its enforcement machinery has never been greater. If the Council of Europe has expanded so rapidly over the last decade it was with the aim of consolidating democracy and the rule of law in the countries of Eastern and Central Europe. The Convention is a cornerstone of that policy. The twin principles of democracy and the rule of law that underlie all the Convention guarantees are the cement that will eventually bind Europe together in peace and stability. The

Convention is a formidable tool in pursuing that objective. Particularly in the light of recent discussion in the European Union context, it is timely to warn against any moves that would undermine the Convention's effectiveness and its credibility and in particular moves towards establishing a two-speed Europe of human rights.

This then is the background against which any examination of the "new" Court's first year in office should be seen. I should like to consider firstly the practical question to which I referred to above, namely how is the Court coping. Is it coping? Secondly, I will consider two specific problems facing the Court with reference to judgments delivered this year. Finally, I will mention briefly one or two of the decisions that have marked this first year of operation.

On the first question the main answer has to be statistical. The figures are impressive. The year has seen a 25% increase in incoming business compared with 1998, a year in which the case-load had already risen 25% in relation to 1997.

The Court has a "backlog" of some 12,000 (at 1.11.99) pending registered applications, over half of which were inherited from the old system. In response the Court has delivered 134 judgments and around 3,600 decisions. It has to be said that the start-up period was difficult. With the benefit of hindsight some of the transitional provisions appear unfortunate. The continuation of the Commission's activities for twelve months[1] deprived the Court of the full support of its workforce for much of this period. The requirement that cases from the old Court be examined by a Grand Chamber of seventeen judges placed an additional burden on the Court in its running-in period[2]. These problems compounded the difficulties that any new institution would have faced, and particularly one which, on day one, had a docket of nearly 7,000 registered applications. These factors mean that, on a practical level, it is perhaps premature to draw any firm conclusions. The Court came out of the transitional phase at the end of October 1999 and it is only from then onwards that we will really be able to see to what extent the system can cope.

However, it is already clear that if the case-load continues to rise—and all the indications are that it will—the machinery will be rapidly and severely stretched. What are the solutions? A first and most obvious one is that over a period of time the Court will need more resources. It appears that the gains in productivity resulting from the reform will not be sufficient to meet the increase in case-load. Why is this? After all, so one response goes, the main purpose of the reform was to make the enforcement machinery more effective and with 41 judges permanently present in Strasbourg, productivity should surely increase.

There are some fundamental misconceptions underlying that response. Firstly, the reform was nearly ten years in gestation and therefore did not and could not fully anticipate the impact of the growth of membership of the

---

[1] Article 5 § 3 of Protocol No. 11.
[2] Article 5 § 5 of Protocol No. 11.

Council of Europe. Secondly, the reform effectively removed one stage in the proceedings, that is the merits stage before the Commission. Yet the real problem for the Court arises in the early stages of the proceedings. In this respect the requirement of the exhaustion of domestic remedies can never be entirely effective in reducing case-load, because an applicant who has not exhausted his local remedies can still contact the Court, can still send a mass of documentation which has to be examined, can still, under present Rules, insist that his application be registered. And all this is going on in 37 different languages. Up to the decision on admissibility, applicants are allowed to use any of the official languages of the Contracting States. That last point is one of the reasons why the presence of full-time Judges makes little difference at this stage of the proceedings. Only a limited number of Judges can read a long letter, often with endless annexes, in, say, Polish, Turkish or Moldovan. It is also to some extent a waste of judicial time for Judges to become too "bogged down" at the early stage. We need judges to "*dire le droit*", to concentrate on the cases that raise real Convention issues, cases that will come to form part of the body of law making up the European "*ordre public*".

However, extra resources, additional lawyers to work on the early stages of the procedure are not the only answer. The Court has also to look critically at all its working methods. It is currently doing this with a working party with broad terms of reference. Here again I would hope to see recommendations that would allow for a more flexible approach in the earlier stages.

The Court has, I believe, to be prepared to innovate, but of course it can only do so within the framework of the Convention. For instance an inadmissibility decision even in a worthless case still requires a Committee of three Judges. It may be that ultimately further reform of the Convention will prove necessary if the Court is to survive well into the next century. That is too broad a question to deal with in this paper, but it is something that we should not lose sight of. Indeed we should be keenly aware that it is an issue that may soon become urgent.

So I come back to my question. How is the Court coping? Is the Court coping? My answer would be that it is, with some difficulty. The Court will nevertheless rise to the challenge. In doing so, it will need the support of the Contracting States and in particular its success will depend largely on the effectiveness of human rights protection at national level.

That brings me to examine two problems that the Court encounters in relation to the effectiveness of national systems.

One particular difficulty which confronts the Court, as it did its predecessor institutions, is that of repetitive violations. Where the Court has to consider large numbers of applications alleging virtually identical breaches and invariably finds that the applications are well-founded, two problems arise. One is practical and the other goes to the long-term credibility of the Convention system. On the practical level, a disproportionately large number of cases from one country on an issue that has to all intents and purposes already been determined ties down resources and heavily handicaps a body which is in any case overburdened. As to the credibility of the system, where over a period of time the Court repeatedly finds the same violation in respect of the same State, the fundamental obligation to abide by the Court's judgments is not being complied with. Execution of the Court's judgments, even if they are said to be declaratory, entails for the respondent State an obligation to remove the causes of the violation so as to ensure that it does not recur.

Those familiar with the Court will be aware that just such a problem arises in relation to the situation in Italy. As the Court noted in judgments in four Italian cases, *Bottazzi, A.P., Di Mauro* and *Ferrari*,[3] delivered in July of this year, since 1987 65 judgments have been delivered finding a violation of Article 6 § 1 in proceedings exceeding a "reasonable time" in the civil courts of the various regions of Italy. Similarly under the former Articles 31 and 32 of the Convention, more that 1,400 reports of the Commission have resulted in resolutions of the Committee of Ministers of the Council of Europe finding Italy to be in breach of Article 6 for the same reason.

In the *Bottazzi* judgment, the Court observed that such breaches reflected a continuing situation that had not yet been remedied and in respect of which litigants had no domestic remedy. The accumulation of breaches accordingly constituted a practice incompatible with the Convention. The implications of this finding are two-fold. Firstly, when dealing with the length of Italian civil proceedings, Chambers will in future be able to refer back to this Grand Chamber judgment and examine the facts of the case before them in the light of the practice found by the Grand Chamber. There will in other words be a presumption in favour of the applicant once the proceedings have exceeded a certain time and this should enable the Court to deal with these cases more rapidly. The second effect relates to execution. As long as the Court confined its finding of a breach to the particular facts before it, it could be argued that the Government's obligation to take general remedial action was limited. This argument is no longer open to the Italian authorities and responsibility is placed squarely with them and the Committee of Ministers which supervises the execution of the Court's judgments[4].

Another disturbing feature of some recent cases is illustrated by two Turkish cases, *Çakici* and *Tanrikulu*[5]. Both cases involved very serious allegations of violations in particular of Article 2 (right to life) and Article 3 (prohibition of inhuman and degrading treatment)

These cases are naturally a matter of grave concern, not least because the most fundamental rights protected by the Convention are involved. It is worrying that, whereas the Court did not make its first finding of a violation of Article 2 until 1995[6], thirty-six years after it was set up, it has now had to make such a

---

[3] Judgments of 28.7.1999
[4] Article 46 § 2 of the Convention.
[5] Judgments of 8.7.1999
[6] *McCann v. the United Kingdom*, judgment of 27 September 1995, Series A no.324.

finding on several occasions. However, I would like to concentrate on another aspect of the two cases, one which has serious long-term implications for the Court and the Convention system. In both cases the Commission had carried out a fact-finding exercise involving taking evidence in Turkey. That such investigations were necessary points to a breakdown in the subsidiary structure of the Convention system. As I stressed earlier, the primary responsibility under the Convention of guaranteeing the rights and freedoms which it protects falls to the national authorities. As is reflected in the rule requiring the exhaustion of domestic remedies, the notion of margin of appreciation and the so-called fourth instance doctrine, it is not the role of the Convention control mechanism to substitute itself for the national judicial authorities.

But that assumes that proceedings are in fact conducted and properly conducted at national level. The problem in these two Turkish cases is that the Strasbourg machinery was effectively acting as a court of first instance. In such circumstances the Court has little choice but to conclude that there has been no adequate investigation of the applicant's allegations at national level. This means firstly that any preliminary objection based on the non-exhaustion of domestic remedies is likely to fail as whatever remedies are available can hardly be exploited if no official investigation has been conducted. Secondly, irrespective of the finding of fact as to the direct involvement of the authorities in the alleged death or disappearance, the Court will find a violation of Article 2 on the ground that the authorities have failed to comply with the positive obligation under that Article, which requires by implication that when individuals have been killed by the use of force, there should be some form of official investigation[7]. There may in addition be a violation of Article 13 deriving directly from the lack of an investigation in so far as the effectiveness of any remedies will be undermined by the absence of an adequate investigation.

The consequences of failing to carry out an investigation are therefore far-reaching in terms of the Court's finding as to breaches of the Convention. At the same time on a practical level the Court is simply not in a position to carry out a significant number of investigations, which are particularly time and resource consuming. It is therefore in everyone's interest that the national authorities, who are in a much better position to make accurate assessments of the facts, should effect proper investigations themselves. I repeat that under the Convention system the first assessment as to whether there has been a violation should be made at national level. Consistent failure to do so entails a double risk: firstly that the additional workload will paralyse the system and secondly that the subsidiary character of the Convention system will be seriously weakened with potentially disastrous consequences for its long term success.

I now turn to some of the other cases the Court has dealt with this year. The first lesson to be drawn is one of continuity. The Court relies heavily on the case-law of its predecessor institutions, notably the old Court. Thus for example in a

---

[7] *Ya a* v. *Turkey*, judgment of 2 September 1998, *Reports* 1998-VI, p. 2438, § 98.

number of Article 10 cases the Court has clearly reaffirmed, with reference to earlier case-law, the importance of freedom of expression in a democratic society and the limited scope for national authorities to interfere with that freedom where the expression concerns a matter of general interest aired in the press.

The new Court's first judgment, delivered on 21 January 1999, was in the case of *Fressoz and Roire v. France*[8], concerning freedom of expression under Article 10 of the Convention. The applicants had reproduced, in the well-known French satirical weekly, *"Le Canard Enchainé"*, photocopies of the tax assessment of the managing director of the Peugeot car company, to illustrate an article drawing attention to a 45% salary increase awarded to the managing director, against a background of a pay dispute in the company. They were convicted of handling photocopies obtained through a breach of professional confidentiality and were fined. As in the large majority of Article 10 cases the Court accepted that the interference had been "prescribed by law" and pursued a legitimate aim. Its examination thus focussed on the issue whether it had been "necessary in a democratic society". The Court found first that the press article had contributed to a public debate on a matter of general interest. In those circumstances interference with the exercise of freedom of the press could not be compatible with Article 10 unless it was justified by an overriding requirement in the public interest. In view of the fact that the information contained in the photocopies was itself not confidential, there was no such overriding requirement here. The Court also considered whether the interest in the public's being informed outweighed the "duties and responsibilities" that the journalists had, in particular as a result of the suspect origin of the document. In this context Article 10 protected journalists' rights to divulge information on issues of general interest provided they were acting in good faith and on an accurate factual basis and gave "reliable and precise" information in accordance with the ethics of journalism.

To summarise, in assessing whether the interference fell within the national authorities'—in this context—rather narrow margin of appreciation, the Court asked three questions:

1. Is there a public debate on the issue which is the subject-matter of the contested expression?
2. Is there a competing interest sufficiently strong to outweigh the right of the public to be informed? and
3. Did the journalists act in good faith?

In the case of *Bladet Tromsø and Stensaas v. Norway*[9], the applicants had reproduced the controversial report of a seal hunting inspector alleging breaches of the seal hunting regulations by the crew of a seal hunting vessel. In the defamation proceedings brought against the applicants certain of the statements were declared null and void, and damages were awarded to the crew members.

---

[8] Judgment of 21.1.1999
[9] Judgment of 20.5.1999

The inspector's report had been withheld from publication by the Ministry of Fisheries in order among other things to give persons implicated an opportunity to explain and defend themselves.

Once again the Court was confronted with the issue of press freedom. Once again it asserted the crucial importance of a free press in a democratic society. Citing earlier case-law, it emphasised the vital role of the press as a public watchdog and once again it observed that the national margin of appreciation was consequently circumscribed. The three questions identified in the French case could be answered as follows: Firstly there was no dispute that there was a matter of public concern involved, that the report was published in the context of an extensive and vigorous public debate. Secondly, did the competing interest outweigh the public's right to be informed? In this case the competing interest was the right of others to protection of their reputation. This was a more difficult issue. The Court had regard to the nature and degree of the defamation and came to the conclusion that some of the allegations were not particularly serious and those that were serious had been expressed in rather broad terms and could be understood by readers as having been presented with a degree of exaggeration. In addition the criticism had not been an attack on all the crew members or on any specific crew member. In short the Court considered that the potential adverse effect of the impugned statements on each individual seal hunter's reputation was significantly attenuated. The competing interest could thus not outweigh the public's right to be informed.

The third matter to be determined was the good faith of the journalists concerned, or in other words the extent to which they had acted properly in accordance with journalistic ethics. Here the Court relied on the fact that the report had been drawn up by an inspector appointed by the Ministry of Fisheries. It considered that the press should normally be entitled to rely on the contents of official reports without undertaking independent research.

The Court was not unanimous in this decision. In the delicate balancing exercise that has to be carried out in these cases there are bound to be disagreements as to the side to which the scales tilt. In this case the distinctions were further blurred by subsequent revelations as to the reliability of the information published. However, the Court has to place itself in the position of journalists at the material time of publication and assess the justification of publishing in the light of what they then knew or should have known. It is on this basis that it will assess the proportionality of the interference with the legitimate aim pursued. It is true to say that the scales are and, I would argue, have to be heavily weighted in favour of the freedom of the press, as this case has shown. It is the essential role of a free press in a democratic society which limits the margin of appreciation or area of discretion available to national authorities in this field. If the justification of the judicial self-restraint which that margin implies is the democratic legitimacy of measures taken by democratic institutions, then the closer the form of expression comes to the core of democracy, logically the smaller the area of discretion, as for example in the context of normal political debate.

The case of *Rekvényi* v. *Hungary*[10] concerned an amendment to the Hungarian Constitution of 1994 prohibiting, among others, members of the police from engaging in political activities and joining a political party. The Court found that the restriction (which was somewhat narrowed by the case-law of the Constitutional Court and statute) was prescribed by law and pursued the legitimate aims of the protection of national security and public safety and the prevention of disorder. It concluded further that, especially seen against Hungary's historical background, measures taken in that country in order to protect the police force from the direct influence of party politics could be seen as answering a "pressing social need" in a democratic society. Here measures which on the face of it might be considered anti-democratic were aimed at protecting democracy in particular by ensuring that the police force was politically neutral, in contrast to the situation that had existed under the one-party communist State. It remains to be seen whether the judgment is to be taken as implying recognition that the transition from an undemocratic to a democratic regime may require special measures safeguarding democracy and human rights in the transitional period or whether the Court would consider restrictions on the political activities of policemen as generally acceptable even outside that context.

In the context of democracy another case of great interest is that of *Matthews* v. *the United Kingdom*[11], concerning the right of a British national resident in Gibraltar to vote in elections of the European Parliament. Without going into what was a lengthy and quite complex judgment, the case was significant for two reasons. Firstly it strongly reaffirmed the fundamental importance of effective political democracy as one of the underlying principles of the Convention and as the best means of maintaining those fundamental freedoms which are the foundation of justice and peace in the world, to quote the Convention preamble. Secondly it went a step further in defining the relationship between the Strasbourg Convention and the institutions and the legislation of the European Union. The Court recognised that acts of the European Community as such could not be challenged before the Court because the EC is not a Contracting Party and, moreover, that the Convention did not exclude the transfer of competences to international organisations. However, the obligation to secure Convention rights under Article 1 subsisted even after such a transfer and Contracting States might therefore be held responsible for a failure to do so. This would suggest that a State's responsibility may in certain situations be engaged not only in respect of national implementing legislation but also in relation to primary and directly applicable Community legislation.

In the two cases of *Lustig-Prean and Beckett* v *the United Kingdom* and *Smith and Grady* v. *the United Kingdom*[12], the Court sitting as a Chamber of seven Judges found a breach of Article 8 of the Convention. These cases concerned

[10] Judgment of 20.5.1999
[11] Judgment of 18.2.1999
[12] Judgments of 27.9.1999

service personnel who had been administratively discharged on the sole ground of their homosexuality in pursuance of a policy operating a blanket legal ban on homosexuals in the armed forces. The applicants had been subjected to investigations into their sexual orientation which were continued even after they had admitted their homosexuality, investigations which the Court subsequently described as having been of an exceptionally intrusive character.

The Court found that neither the investigation conducted into the applicants' sexual orientation nor their discharge on the ground of their homosexuality could be justified under Article 8 § 2 of the Convention and that there had consequently been a violation. The decision was unanimous and can have surprised few Strasbourg observers. While agreeing that the measures in question had been "in accordance with the law" and pursued a legitimate aim, the Court was unable to accept that convincing and weighty reasons had been offered by the Government to justify the ban on homosexuals. Among other things it noted the material before the domestic courts indicating that European countries operating such a ban were in a small minority. It also pointed to the lack of concrete evidence to substantiate the alleged damage to morale and fighting power. The interference in the applicants' private life was not therefore, in Convention terms, necessary in a democratic society; it did not answer a pressing social need and it was not proportionate to the legitimate aim pursued. Notwithstanding the margin of appreciation enjoyed by States in relation to the need to secure the operational effectiveness of the armed forces, insufficient protection had been afforded to the individual rights in issue.

One of the most interesting aspects of these cases was the approach taken by the national courts. In dismissing the application for judicial review in the High Court Lord Justice Simon Brown[13] applied the conventional Wednesbury principles, well known to the Strasbourg Court which has had in the past to assess the effectiveness of judicial review proceedings for the purposes of Article 13[14]. Under these principles the test was one of "irrationality". Justification would have to have been such as "outrageously defies logic or accepted moral standards for the court to be able to strike down the Minister's decision". As the learned Lord Justice stated: " if the Convention . . . were part of our law and we were accordingly entitled to ask whether the policy answers a pressing social need and whether the restriction on human rights involved can be shown to be proportionate to the benefits, then clearly the primary judgment would be for us and not others: the constitutional balance would shift".

In the Court of Appeal the Master of the Rolls noted the "very considerable cogency" of the applicant's arguments, but again the threshold of irrationality had not been crossed. The fact that a decision-maker had failed to take account

---

[13] R. v. *Ministry of Defence, ex parte Smith and Others* [1995] 2 Weekly Law Reports 305.

[14] See, for example, *Vilvarajah and Others* v. *the United Kingdom*, judgment of 30 October 1991, Series A no. 215, pp. 38–40, §§ 118–126; *Chahal* v. *the United Kingdom*, judgment of 15 November 1996, *Reports* 1996-V, 1832, at pp. 1868–1871, §§ 140–155.

of Convention obligations when exercising an administrative discretion was not of itself a ground for impugning the exercise of that discretion.

In other words, both in the High Court and in the Court of Appeal it was recognised at least implicitly that, had it been possible to apply the Convention test, the policy might well have been struck down. The failings of the policy were noted; it was, in Lord Justice Thorpe's words in the Court of Appeal, "ripe for review", but it was not irrational.

With the entry into force in 2000 of the Human Rights Act, the shift in constitutional balance to which Lord Justice Simon Brown referred will surely occur. I suspect that if it had already been in force, these cases might never have reached Strasbourg. British judges are evidently familiar with Convention standards and are ready to apply them once that competence is finally entrusted to them. That is good news for Strasbourg from every point of view. Cases more properly dealt with at local level will be less likely to reach Strasbourg. At the same time I am confident that, given the esteem in which the British judiciary is held, their decisions on Convention issues will be closely studied in Strasbourg and will influence jurisprudential development here. This is indeed how a subsidiary system should function.

How can I sum up the first twelve months of the "new" Court? As I have said they have not been without problems. Some are soluble, others are more intractable. Next year we will be celebrating the 50th anniversary of the Convention and I remain convinced, as I have said, that its importance has never been greater. But that should not stop us asking questions and even of the most fundamental kind. What is the purpose of the Convention, what are we trying to achieve when we apply and enforce it? Are we seeking to cure individual ills for as many European citizens as possible or are we trying to establish a Europe-wide constitutional order of fundamental rights in which the citizen can obtain relief from his or her domestic system? The answers to these questions should guide us in our reflection on how to approach the practical problems that confront the Convention system.

13

Preliminary Reflections on Fundamental Rights as the Basis of a Common European Law

CESARE MIRABELLI

The modern legal world has seen a growing recognition of fundamental human rights and the creation of new tools for their protection.

The tragic consequences of totalitarianism, in all of its embodiments throughout this century, give ample warning of the need to effectively protect human freedom and dignity against encroachment by all outside powers, including one's own state.

The violation of basic personal rights, as well as those of minority groups, has all too often gone so far as to deprive individuals of their very life, and to exterminate entire communities. This sobering fact requires us to recognize and safeguard a body of personal and collective rights that are inherently possessed by all people, in order to protect both individuals and the groups in which they live. Fundamental rights are more than simply a set of absolute legal entitlements that an individual can invoke; they are also a point of intersection among numerous legal systems, increasingly recognized and protected by different sources of law.

The notion that inalienable human rights must always be recognized and protected can trace its roots far back into the past. Yet it is only after the second world war that this idea has been recognized as universally valid on an international plane, with practical legal effect.

Since then, the need to safeguard human rights has found positive expression and explicit recognition in international law, with a resultant impact on domestic legal systems as well. Indeed, international protection of fundamental rights necessarily focuses on the condition of individuals within their community, so that these rights must be given effect in national law as a primary matter.

Furthermore, once international law recognizes that individuals enjoy rights that are intimately tied to human dignity, these rights must also (and perhaps most importantly) be protected vis-à-vis their own state.

RECOGNITION AND PROTECTION OF HUMAN RIGHTS IN THE UNITED NATIONS

This movement towards the recognition and international protection of human rights is seen quite clearly in the Charter of the United Nations. In the wake of the tragic experiences of the second world war, the San Francisco Conference of 1945 set out "to reaffirm faith in fundamental human rights, in the dignity and worth of the human person, in the equal rights of men and women" through an organization designed "to save succeeding generations from the scourge of war, which twice in our lifetime has brought untold sorrow to mankind." As part of its efforts to preserve international peace and security, the United Nations counts among its goals that of "promoting and encouraging respect for human rights and for fundamental freedoms for all without distinction as to race, sex, language, or religion." (art. 1).

These programmatic statements are fleshed out in other provisions of the Charter, which commits member states as well as the United Nations to promote the effective observance of fundamental rights (arts. 55, 56, and 76). Yet the Charter neither lists these rights nor indicates their content. This gap was filled in 1948 when the U.N. General Assembly approved the Universal Declaration of Human Rights in New York, positing that the "recognition of the inherent dignity and of the equal and inalienable rights of all members of the human family is the foundation of freedom, justice and peace in the world." It was accordingly "essential, if man is not to be compelled to have recourse, as a last resort, to rebellion against tyranny and oppression, that human rights should be protected by the rule of law." This document gave an international justification for safeguarding human rights through appropriate legal rules, partially in international law itself.

The Declaration is the first document, both chronologically and logically, to universally catalog and protect fundamental rights. It has more than merely moral and programmatic value, despite the fact that it was never designed to be a treaty opened for ratification by those states that approved its proclamation. In any event, the Declaration can be said to have legal value, in that it both complements and completes the commitments undertaken by member states of the United Nations to respect human rights—in other words, those rights identified by the Declaration. In this regard, the Declaration can be said to authoritatively interpret the obligations taken on by states that belong to the United Nations. Moreover, the Declaration defines the pursuit of human rights as one of the goals of the organization and establishes rules for the conduct of United Nations components.

Apart from these considerations, there is another basis for recognizing the binding legal effect of the human rights listed in the Universal Declaration: If these rights are essential to human dignity and rest on universally acknowledged values, one could say that they represent generally accepted principles of international law.

The question of the binding legal effect of those human rights enshrined in the Universal Declaration seems to be largely obviated by the positive recognition of such rights in international treaties that draw their inspiration from that document. In particular, efforts within the United Nations further articulated the scope and context of human rights in the International Covenant on Economic, Social, and Cultural Rights and the International Covenant on Civil and Political Rights (New York, 1966).

These conventions are subject to normal procedures for state ratification and enjoy binding effect as international treaty law.

THE EUROPEAN CONVENTION ON THE PROTECTION OF HUMAN RIGHTS AND FUNDAMENTAL FREEDOMS

The movement towards recognizing and effectively protecting fundamental rights internationally through conventions that bind states by means of normal treaty rules has also seen progress at the regional level.

Under the auspices of the Council of Europe, the Convention for the Protection of Human Rights and Fundamental Freedoms (Rome, 1950) expressly draws on the principles announced in the Universal Declaration and sets forth a legally binding list of fundamental individual rights and freedoms.

The European Convention is remarkable not so much because of the rights it protects, given that it defines rights much as other documents do, but rather because of the enforcement mechanisms it establishes. For the first time, individuals have recourse to an international body to seek declaratory relief or even reparations against states that have violated their rights. This innovation raises the possibility of a profound change in the individual's status in international law. This has important consequences for the weight and importance of fundamental rights, which not only bind states but also assume a directly international character.

As originally written, the Convention provided for individual protection through claims brought before the European Commission of Human Rights. This body was given the task of ascertaining violations of rights recognized by the Convention and, where the parties cannot reach a settlement, to seek a decision of the European Court of Human Rights. This procedure was limited, however, by the condition that states must consent to this supranational jurisdiction.

The protection of individual rights gained ground upon the adoption of Protocol 11 of 1994, which was directly aimed at bolstering the effectiveness of safeguards for human rights and fundamental freedoms. Individuals can now directly bring before the European Court claims that a contracting state has violated their rights guaranteed by the Convention. In bypassing the intermediate step foreseen by the original Convention, individuals gain an immediate right to an action for the protection of their own fundamental rights vis-à-vis an offending state.

FUNDAMENTAL RIGHTS GUARANTEED BY THE EUROPEAN CONVENTION AND NATIONAL LAWS

The rights and liberties guaranteed by the European Convention are designed to be recognized and applied in the domestic law of signatory states.

As a formal matter, the European Convention is much like other international agreements whose rules must be incorporated into national law according to the constitutional procedures of each state.

The Italian Constitution, unlike that of some other countries, does not provide for the automatic incorporation of treaty rules into domestic law. Nor does it grant treaty rules any particular status within the hierarchy of sources of law.

According to article 10 of the Constitution, the Italian legal system conforms to generally recognized rules of international law. This provision is most widely interpreted as referring only to general international law, not to treaty law. One could read this invocation of general international law as incorporating the principle of "*pacta sunt servanda*" and therefore, by extension, rules contained in treaties ratified by states. Yet even so, such rules would not assume a position superior to the ordinary laws that implement these treaties for purposes of domestic law. As a result, conflicts between these different sources of law would be resolved by reference to normal standards, such as the supremacy of the more recent law or by the relative level of specificity of each law. In domestic law, a new law would enjoy full validity and effectiveness even if it conflicted with a prior law implementing a treaty. The only consequence would be that a state might incur international responsibility for not observing its international obligations.

The question might be answered differently if one regarded the European Convention as reflecting universally recognized rules, which are merely memorialized in treaty form. In this view, human rights would consist of generally recognized principles of international law, and conventions announcing these rights would simply codify their content.

In any event, even if one cannot say that the rules derived from the European Convention are superior to ordinary legislation within the hierarchy of domestic law, one must nevertheless recognize a hierarchy of values in which human rights are paramount.

Among the most basic principles of the Italian Constitution is the recognition and protection of the inalienable rights of human beings in article 2, both as individuals and as members of social groups which give expression to their identity.

These rights are recognized, not granted, by the state. As such, they serve as the foundation of the constitutional system and enjoy a practical superiority over other sources of law.

According to one interpretation, article 2 of the Constitution draws on a conception of fundamental personal rights based on principles of natural law. Regardless of whether one agrees with this characterization, the provision is clearly an open-ended recognition of fundamental rights that is capable of embracing all human rights, whether cataloged in other constitutional provisions or proclaimed and protected by international instruments.

In line with this interpretive approach, the rules of the European Convention acquire significance through article 2 of the Constitution. The Convention's principles do not themselves possess constitutional status, in that the legislature must implement them by statute. Yet these rules flesh out the Constitution's catalog of fundamental rights. Even if one adopts a different interpretive approach, it must be admitted that the articulation of fundamental rights at the international level contributes to their fuller definition in the domestic context. The various formulations of these rights contribute to their gradual evolution and development, leading not only to a shared legal experience but also to a greater level of detail for those called upon to interpret these rights.

Disparate sources of law from various legal systems converge to safeguard human dignity. Each source helps to define the content of these rights, in a system that contains multiple and complementary levels and forums for enforcement, each of which mutually influences the others in terms of interpretation and the fostering of a common legal experience.

THE EUROPEAN COMMUNITY EXPERIENCE: FROM THE EXCLUSIVITY OF LEGAL SYSTEMS TO THEIR INTEGRATION.

One of the elements that characterize the evolution of European legal systems has been the creation of European Union law and its integration with that of member states.

The second half of this century has seen the creation of supranational institutions to which member states have ceded powers. The initial phase of this development virtually coincided with the drafting of the European Convention on the Protection of Human Rights and Fundamental Freedoms, and drew its inspiration from the same ideals: democracy, respect for fundamental rights, and the unity of all European peoples while recognizing the identity of each. This process began in 1951 with the formation of specialized communities: first the European Coal and Steel Community (ECSC), which created supranational institutions, and then the European Atomic Energy Community (Euratom). In 1957, six states gave birth to the European Economic Community, which received increasingly wide-ranging authority. Integration of member states, whose number has continued to grow, has progressively deepened. The goal of creating an area free of internal borders and an ever-closer union among European peoples led to the formation of the European Union. The overall process has involved more than simple cooperation among states, though cooperation is certainly one of the community's goals. The process that transformed a common European market into a single European market is deeper and broader, prefiguring further goals of political and institutional integration. The evolution connected with this process is far from over, both in the development of European institutions as well as in the extension of the Community to other European states.

Undeniably, the movement towards integration has been driven most obviously by economic factors, which determined the Community's first goals and led to the free movement of goods, people, services, and capital. Yet the unified market presupposes a common set of rules which, to achieve these economic objectives, must be uniformly applied throughout the community. At first glance, one might think that the law has a secondary, instrumental role in this process. Not so. Rather, one can justifiably claim that law is the cornerstone of the Community, and has helped to create the conditions that have allowed the Community's extraordinary development.

Above all, the very design of community institutions is grounded in the law. The law furthermore shapes in a completely original way the relationship between the legal systems of the community and of member states.

The special relationship between community law and national law moves beyond the traditional ideas that law emanates from the state and that legal systems are mutually exclusive, with each possessing separate jurisdiction to govern all activity with its own laws or with rules that it imports from other legal systems—imports which the state must incorporate into domestic law to give them legal effect.

The relationship between state law and community law is based on a different idea: the integration of legal systems, which are mutually complementary rather than exclusive. Community law is applicable in those areas assigned to Community jurisdiction, without any need for states to formally incorporate it or transform it into domestic law. The European Community has thus acquired law-making power in certain areas, which have been taken from member states. By using this law-making power, the Community creates rules that bind states as well as individuals and corporate actors in both social and economic fields.

The European Community is therefore a legal community, based on the principles and practice of legal integration.

State law and community law remain formally distinct, yet complementary. In the context of integration, these sources of law do not stand in a hierarchical relationship with one another. Instead, each draws on a separate source of authority. There is no superior source of law against which one can judge the legitimacy of other, hierarchically inferior sources of law. The principle of divided authority rather than that of hierarchy characterizes this approach to integration: one must apply the rule created by the legal system with authority in a given area. Thus, in areas of community authority, state law applies only to the extent it is compatible with community law. This presupposes the uniform interpretation of community law, which is ensured by the European Court of Justice. That Court authoritatively interprets community treaties, and decides on the legitimacy and proper interpretation of community acts. Its decisions bind national courts.

All of this encourages the harmonization of national law, a goal that the founding treaty of the European Community endorses as necessary for the functioning of a common market. But integration is qualitatively different from the harmonization of national law, a concept which still reflects the exclusive nature of domestic legal systems, or from the unification of law, which challenges the existence of multiple sources of law at its very roots.

COMMUNITY AND NATIONAL LAW: MOVING FROM A HIERARCHICAL RELATIONSHIP AMONG SOURCES OF LAW TO DIVISION OF AUTHORITY

Such a significant transfer to a supranational organization of legislative, administrative, and judicial powers that were once reserved to sovereign states must have a constitutional foundation.

In Italian law, the attribution of sovereign powers to the European Community finds its authorization in article 11 of the Constitution. This constitutional provision permits, on a basis of parity with other states, "limitations on sovereignty that are necessary for a legal system that ensures peace and justice among nations." This formula was not adopted by the Constituent Assembly with the idea of a supranational organization for economic integration in mind, of the type later embodied in the European Community. Wartime experiences instead raised thoughts of an international organization like the United Nations, aimed at maintaining peace at an international level, and granting the power to intervene to an organization founded for that purpose and which could compel state obedience. The wording adopted by article 11 of the Constitution instead left room for an unforeseen result: it justified the transfer of state authority to a supranational organization and provided constitutional grounding for permitting the limitations on sovereignty created by the founding treaties of the European Community.

This approach is by now well-settled; it has been repeatedly reaffirmed by the decisions of the Constitutional Court.

The Court has upheld limitations on the state's legislative, executive, and judicial powers which are necessary for the creation of a Community among European states. The Community has been considered a supranational interstate organization, designed as a tool for integration among member states: in areas assigned to community authority, states have transferred part of their own sovereignty to community institutions. In its judgment no. 183 of 1973, the Constitutional Court held that community organs can adopt acts with general normative authority, which need not be incorporated in domestic rules but have binding effect equal to that of state laws. In this way, community rules have direct application within states without any need for their incorporation or implementation.

The decisions of the Constitutional Court have also reiterated that the legal systems of community law and domestic law are separate and autonomous, yet coordinated. Community laws (which are neither international law nor foreign law nor domestic law), though not derived from an internal source, are immediately applicable without any need for incorporation, in the areas assigned to the jurisdiction of community institutions. Community and international legal systems remain distinct and independent; but the relationship between the two is one of coordination and integration, meaning that in areas of community authority, community law is directly applicable and conflicting state laws are not applicable. (Judgment no. 170 of 1984).

Accordingly, community laws and state laws, though arising from different sources of authority, co-exist and combine to govern areas in which both legal systems have law-making authority. The sources of both laws, community and domestic, are not ranked in a hierarchy but are distinguished according to areas of competence. In the event of conflict between domestic and community law, national judges are obliged to ignore the conflicting state law in favor of community law, which prevails without any need for a declaration of illegitimacy. Any conflict is resolved simply by declining to apply the law created by the source which lacks authority. (Judgment no. 389 of 1989).

THE ROLE OF FUNDAMENTAL RIGHTS IN THE RELATIONSHIP BETWEEN COMMUNITY AND NATIONAL LAW

Fundamental rights play an essential role in the relationship between community law and domestic law.

Community law recognizes and protects fundamental human rights, interpreting them much as in the law of member states. Decisions of the European Court of Justice have treated fundamental rights as an integral part of general principles of law, which the Court must enforce. Fundamental rights are identified and defined in accordance with the common constitutional traditions of member states. Likewise, the Court of Justice considers international human rights treaties drafted or ratified by member states when interpreting community law.

This judicial approach has found further expression in positive law. Fundamental rights are not only recognized in accordance with constitutional traditions shared by member states, but Article F of the Maastricht Treaty states that the European Union respects those rights guaranteed by the European Convention on the Protection of Human Rights and Fundamental Freedoms. The Convention therefore serves the role of a veritable Bill of Rights underlying the European Union.

The recognition and protection of fundamental individual rights in European Community law is both a condition of and a limit on the effectiveness of community law within the state. Limitations on state sovereignty, which permit the effectiveness of community law and its direct application by national judges, are compatible with the Constitution only to the extent that community law protects those fundamental rights guaranteed by the Constitution and assures that the European Court of Justice offers judicial protection against community acts that violate these rights.

In this way, the protection of fundamental rights constitutes one of the foundations for the legitimacy of transferring portions of state sovereignty to community institutions. On the other hand, these same fundamental rights guaranteed by the Constitution impose limits on the applicability of community law. Indeed, constitutional decisions recognize that fundamental rights form an integral and essential part of community law, while also holding that the Constitutional Court retains full authority to determine whether any law interpreted and applied by community institutions conflicts with the fundamental principles of the Italian Constitution or violates inalienable human rights. (Judgment no. 232 of 1989). In such a case, the Court would not be directly reviewing the constitutionality of a community law, but rather the national law ratifying the treaty to the extent that it permits application of a community law that conflicts with fundamental rights. This is more than a purely hypothetical possibility, and such an approach is designed to retain some way in exceptional circumstances to effectively protect citizens' fundamental rights from being irreparably harmed by community laws.

FUNDAMENTAL RIGHTS AND THE MULTIPLICITY OF SOURCES OF LAW AND PROTECTIVE MECHANISMS: CONSTITUTIONAL, COMMUNITY, AND INTERNATIONAL

Fundamental human rights are recognized, though formulated in different ways, by several sources of law: constitutional, community, and international.

Although legal systems and viewpoints may differ, the values protected are essentially the same: rights that are at the core of personhood, inherent to human dignity.

Fundamental rights are often described, in accordance with long-established tradition, as natural, inviolable, or inalienable, or using other expressions that seek to capture their core meaning as well as the ways in which they differ from other rights. One can therefore describe fundamental rights as "metapositive," in the sense that their source is beyond that of positive law. Such rights must be affirmed and protected in legal systems that do not explicitly recognize them and even in systems that expressly reject them. Any other course would deny their very nature and thus the reasons that justify their universal recognition. This approach emphasizes the important position claimed by fundamental rights, which demand recognition and protection even against authorities that deny their validity.

The enjoyment of fundamental rights is essential for assuring each individual the chance to maintain and express his own identity and dignity, as well as to express and develop his own personhood. Suppression or limitation of rights would suppress or limit not only the liberty and dignity of the victim of such a violation, but would also endanger the liberty and dignity of all, in that it would call into question the very notion of inviolability which is an intrinsic aspect of fundamental rights.

Human rights can be grouped around several essential cores, which sometimes reflect the traditional lists of venerable bills of rights, and other times express the protection of fundamental values in connection with new situations that arise in modern experience—particularly in light of the evolution of technology, such as computing and biotechnology.

The first core of fundamental rights relates to life, health, and bodily integrity: the human being's physical identity is protected, including against genetic manipulation. A second core regards the person's non-physical side, his dignity and liberty. According to now-classic formulations, such values include freedom of conscience, of religion, of thought and speech, and now reach systems and means of information. Another core group of rights regards a person's relationships: the integrity of the home and privacy, which must now be protected against potentially invasive computerized tools for probing into a person's life; the choice of lifestyle, the freedom to marry and start a family, to raise one's children; and relations with others, which implies the freedom to communicate, to meet, and to associate.

Yet another core area regards safeguards against power: personal liberty, respect for the law in establishing and applying punishments, and the right to fair procedures, in which the rights of defending oneself are assured.

Other essential rights include those of citizenship and political participation, as well as social rights, aimed at ensuring dignified living conditions.

This summary is not meant to exhaustively catalog fundamental rights. Nor is it necessary to specify the content of each right or to survey their formulations in various legal systems, since the goal here is simply to emphasize some of the factors that distinguish the structure of fundamental rights.

These rights differ according to their substance. Certain freedoms can be enjoyed by protecting individuals from outside interference. In such cases, it is enough to place limits on government or other actors in order to protect an individual's sphere of liberty. More often, fundamental rights guarantee people the right to do something, to undertake actions that concretely represent an exercise of their fundamental rights. Sometimes these acts are regulated by other laws that must conform to principles imposed by fundamental rights. Other times, the effective exercise of fundamental rights requires the cooperation of government or other actors; this cooperation is necessary so that the interests of the person, guaranteed by a fundamental right, can be effectively realized.

It is therefore not uncommon that fundamental rights must be affirmatively developed in other rights, which base themselves on "fundamental" rights and in turn allow their fulfillment.

Fundamental rights also embody principles, which guide the rules necessary for their implementation. These guide the construction of the legal system and constitute an essential factor in its interpretation.

Rules that govern specific legal situations may differ, yet still respond to the principles expressed in fundamental rights. Indeed, these rights underlie numerous legal systems. In light of their universal nature, fundamental rights can and should be applied in systems that inevitably differ for reasons of history, culture, and legal tradition. In this way, fundamental rights represent a common element in varying legal systems, all of which must ensure the enjoyment of these rights.

The importance of fundamental rights is accordingly clear in this context, in that they serve as a common foundation for both common law and civil law systems, especially in light of the fact that both systems draw on the same legal culture. The same principles and goals of protecting identical values can be achieved using different models and rules, all of which respond to the need to protect the same fundamental rights. The identity of values and principles does not necessarily require uniformity of rules and regulations.

FUNDAMENTAL RIGHTS AS ELEMENTS OF UNIFICATION AMONG LEGAL SYSTEMS;
THEIR PROTECTION BY NATIONAL, COMMUNITY, AND INTERNATIONAL COURTS

Fundamental human rights are at the center of numerous legal systems and, in a sense, serve as a unifying element. This means that fundamental rights must be protected in all legal systems (national, community, and international), with each system using its own particular methods.

Fundamental rights are thus subject to multiple forms of protection. Their safeguard is reinforced by the different levels and tools available to protect them and to ensure their effective enjoyment. In addition to protection by the state, which finds its highest expression in constitutional law, there must also be protection against the state, offered in international law through judicial and other channels to which individuals can seek direct access. Protection in the European Community rounds out the picture.

In this way, fundamental rights are recognized and protected through a network of legal systems, thereby influencing the inclusion and definition of each right in each system. The recognition and definition of each right must be accomplished while keeping in mind that fundamental rights are uniform, and that the distinct formulas that give them expression in particular legal systems must fit with one another. The existence of different tools for judicially protecting fundamental rights (national, community, and international) does not lead to formal interference among the various bodies endowed with relevant authority, each of which operates in the legal system to which it belongs. As a procedural matter, no judicial body is above another, nor is there any conflict between different judicial bodies, given the differences between the nature of each, the formal object of its judgment, the actors at which its judgment is aimed, and the effects of its decisions.

Constitutional, community, and international courts both differ and complement one another, and are not related in terms of supremacy or subordination.

Constitutional courts ensure the protection of fundamental rights in domestic law by eliminating rules that lead to violations of rights.

In legal systems based on the formal hierarchy of sources of law and on centralized judicial review, specialized courts can be asked to review the constitutionality of laws. In some legal systems, constitutional review of laws can be concrete and focus not on a law, in its abstract legal meaning and with decisions that have general effect, but on an act that caused a violation of a constitutional right and which can be declared, in the particular case, unconstitutional.

The European Court of Justice can decide upon the legitimacy of community acts and invalidate them to eliminate their potential to violate rights, and it can enjoin the application of national laws that conflict with community law, all within areas of Community authority. Through certified questions, which every national judge must submit when he entertains doubts about the interpretation of community law, the Court of Justice issues judgments that bind national courts, which themselves must apply community law.

The jurisdiction of the European Court of Human Rights ensures the protection of the same rights, compelling respect of those rights when states fail to concretely provide for their effective protection. This power does not depend on the type of law or action, nor on the person or government body, that caused the violation. States are called upon in each case to respond to the judgment, and to eliminate the violation using instruments available within its own legal system, or to rectify the damage, for which it may be forced to pay compensation.

These different judicial forums (national, community, and international) co-exist, and together they protect different situations, with different tools, each appropriate to the nature and character of the legal system in which it operates.

These numerous courts thus share the same goal of guaranteeing fundamental rights. This reveals the desirability of paying attention to these wide-ranging experiences when defining the substance of these rights.

FUNDAMENTAL RIGHTS AND COMPARATIVE LAW

To conclude this brief overview, one should emphasize that fundamental rights lie at the heart of an intersecting network of legal systems that recognizes and protects such rights. A multiplicity of different sources of law (national, community, and international) lists such rights and defines their substance. A multiplicity of tools is available for safeguarding them. National, community, and international courts work together, within their respective jurisdictions, to ensure their effective protection.

Common fundamental values not only inspire all of these legal systems, but also dictate the existence of laws that give effect to these rights in every area of the law.

All of this offers fertile ground for comparative law, which can be pursued with varying goals in mind, all of which are equally useful and important.

The first area of comparison regards the identification and definition of fundamental rights. In this area, comparison would look not only at sources of law, but also at judicial interpretations and developments.

Comparative law acquires particular relevance here given that fundamental rights are essentially unified, yet are subject to many forms of protection. The different formulations of rights in legal provisions and judicial decisions therefore mesh with each other, so that a gap in one can be plugged with the other. Comparative analysis is therefore justified not only by a cultural and academic curiosity, but also by the interpretive role it can play.

A second area in which comparative law can operate regards the concrete rules designed to give effect to and derived from fundamental rights.

In this regard, comparative law serves traditional goals. Comparative methods can be used to understand similarities and differences between different legal models, improving comprehension of each of these and the reasons behind different legislative solutions. Furthermore, comparisons allow one to judge the effectiveness of the models under consideration in relation to fundamental rights, which represent both foundations and goals that are shared by different legal systems. Comparative analysis can, finally, contribute to the design of new laws and to legal harmonization.

Fundamental rights and comparative law are therefore two elements, thematic and methodological, which invite further study. Through them we can appreciate the value of both unity in things that are essential, and diversity in things that distinguish without dividing.

14

Coming Together—the Future

LORD GOFF OF CHIEVELEY

A great, and undeserved, honour has been conferred upon me by an invitation to deliver the closing address at this remarkable Conference. A more doubtful honour has however been conferred upon me by an invitation to provide the text of my closing address several months in advance of the Conference, so that it can be published, with the other contributions, immediately after the event. A closing address is, after all, customarily intended to draw together the threads of the debate, or at least to have some connection with what has been said during the Conference. My first instinct was therefore to decline the invitation; but I realised that this would to some extent sabotage the proposed publication and so would not be fair to the publishers. I propose therefore now to dwell upon one or two of the themes which I expect to be central to our discussion.

The theme of the Conference is, as we must not forget, the Coming Together of the Common Law and the Civil Law. We will have heard contributions from speakers of great distinction on the subject of a new common law for Europe, with special reference to commercial law and public law, and the part which the common law of this country might play in this great venture; and I have had the opportunity of reading in advance papers of great interest presented by Lord Bingham and Lord Steyn, Professor Walter van Gerven and Professor Klaus Hopt, Professor Christian von Bar and Professor Basil Markesinis.

We start from the position that, in the various countries of Europe, past centuries have seen the development of the most extraordinary diversity and depth of culture that the world has ever known. This is true not only of philosophy and science, and of literature, music and the arts, but also of law. We have today in Europe a whole range of legal cultures, some owing their origin to Roman law and others not, some essentially codified and others not, some subscribing to an academic ideal and others not, and so on. Some of these systems have moreover spread to other parts of the world, the greater part of which has received institutions and legal systems of European origin, sometimes of civil law and sometimes of common law ancestry.

We should be profoundly grateful for this diversity. We can learn far more from these diverse systems than we could ever have derived from a single monolithic regime. It is of course from them that there has emerged the study of comparative law. Born around the turn of the century the subject has, for a variety of reasons, been the subject of a great explosion since the Second World War. We can now truly be said to live in the age of comparative law[1]. How fortunate we are to live and work in such a time as this!

Comparative law has so far been primarily concerned with substantive law. This is very understandable, because comparative law has been the creation of scholars, working in universities. Now, however, it is beginning to spread to other aspects of our legal systems—a point to which I shall turn in a moment, though I wish now to acknowledge the paper of absorbing interest prepared by Professor Klaus Hopt for this Conference, which provides an admirable example of this development. Much admirable work has been done in the area of comparative law, a substantial part of it in Germany. The *Introduction* by Zweigert and Kötz[2] has become the gateway to the subject, used everywhere and not only by students. And nowadays distinguished scholars are looking at the possibility of producing, through an almost Darwinian process of comparison and selection, a synthesis with the aim of creating a truly European law, consisting of what are seen to be the most acceptable legal principles derived from our several legal systems. Of the many works of this kind which have appeared in recent years, I wish to refer in particular to one—the Casebook Series[3] inspired by the indefatigable efforts of Professor Walter van Gerven who, with unique authority, has contributed to this Conference an account of his recent work on the Commission of the European Union.

How are we to regard this great new movement? Are we to welcome it as a great unifying force in Europe? Or are we to fear it as the potential destroyer of the different legal systems which we know well, which we understand, and which in truth form part of our national heritage and culture? If the planned outcome was to create a European Civil Code, binding in all countries of the European Union, this would displace our own systems of substantive law, and so to a significant extent mark their demise except where they have been exported overseas. However some of the projects presently envisaged relate only to a limited area of the law such as a European law of obligations, a subject to which I shall return in due course.

Here is a great question for us all. I would answer it as follows. First of all, I welcome unreservedly the study of comparative law. In my own work, I have done and continue to do my limited best to promote it, in every possible way. I have no doubt that many of us at the Conference do the same. We encourage the study of other systems of law in our universities and in independent institutes; we promote exchanges of professors and students between universities in dif-

---

[1] This was a point which I stressed in my Child's Lecture delivered in Oxford in 1986 (see (1988) 2 *Denning Law Journal* 79 at p.92). Developments since then, both in this country and elsewhere in the continent of Europe, have fulfilled my expectations.

[2] *An Introduction to Comparative Law*, 3rd revised edition (1998). English translation by Tony Weir.

[3] The first volume of the van Gerven Casebook Series is entitled *Tort Law*, and was co-authored with Jeremy Lever, Pierre Larouche, Christian von Bar and Genevieve Viney and published by Hart Publishing in 1998.

ferent European countries; we hold meetings between senior judges from our own and other European countries; we even attempt to take advantage of principles from other systems of law in our judgments, though I have learned from experience that nobody should underestimate the difficulties facing such an enterprise. Those of us who are professors write books on the subject, some of them of great distinction. It is surely right that this laudable work should not be limited to description and analysis of the law applicable in a number of European states—though this is a difficult enough task in itself—but should embrace attempts to distil from the different national laws an ideal set of legal principles applicable in particular subjects, as is being done by, for example, the Commission on European Contract Law.

We now know from Professor Christian von Bar's paper that, not content with his great achievement in producing his remarkable book on the Common European Law of Torts[4] he is establishing a study group of lawyers from different countries with the purpose of identifying the most desirable principles in the whole law of obligations. I respectfully applaud this great enterprise; though may I be forgiven for expressing my regret that the study group is called "Study Group on a European Code", a title which, despite Professor von Bar's disclaimer in his paper, is likely to provoke an adverse reaction among lawyers in some national jurisdictions.

Of course there will be some who, believing that uniformity of our private law is in itself a desirable objective, will see this as an opportunity to promote a binding European Code of Obligations. It is not indeed beyond the bounds of possibility that such a development will one day occur; but I believe that if the members of this school of thought rush their fences, this will prove to be counter-productive. Uniformity as an end in itself is an ideal which is not shared by all. It must not be forgotten that, in the United States which is, as we all know, a federal state, variations in the private laws of the 50 States of the Union are tolerated[5], the most notable example being the laws of the State of Louisiana which have their origins in the civil law. The American Law Institute's Restatement of the Law is designed to do no more than influence the States to move in the direction of a more unified system. Moreover in the United Kingdom, which has for nearly three hundred years been a unified country, Scotland and the Channel Islands, and to a lesser extent Northern Ireland, have separate systems of law which are distinct from that applicable in England and Wales. There is no move to unify them; indeed, any attempt to do so would provoke, and would always have provoked, the strongest reaction from the Scottish lawyers. The European Union is not yet even a federation; and the precedents I have cited appear to indicate that, even if it was, there would, at least at the

---

[4] Oxford, OUP, 1998.

[5] Though, arguably, made more tolerable because (a) all the States of the Union share a common language, and (b) the major law schools of the country do not teach the law of one particular State but a methodology and a set of basic rules applicable to all.

present time, be no compelling need for a common Civil Code, or even a common Code of Obligations.

In fact I believe it to be unlikely, at least in the foreseeable future, that a binding European Code of Obligations will see the light of day. The practical and political obstacles in the way of such a development are enormous. The problems facing the creation of a European Civil Code have been admirably described by Professor Markesinis in a paper published in the *European Review of Private Law* of 1998[6]. A European Code of Obligations is, of course, a more limited enterprise; but similar difficulties, on a lesser scale, would face those trying to create, and to persuade all European states to accept, such a Code. The formulation, and drafting, of such a Code is of itself a major task, far transcending the formulation of the principles of a single topic such as the sale of goods or arbitration; and we all know how long was the gestation period for the Vienna Convention and the Uncitral Model Law, not to mention the new Dutch Civil Code which in many respects is, itself, the product of a lengthy comparative exercise conducted by judges, academics and civil servants[7]. Moreover the adoption of a binding European Civil Code would surely call for the establishment of a European Supreme Court, with jurisdiction to hear appeals or references from the Supreme Courts of all the member states of an expanded European Union, to ensure a consistent application and, where necessary, development of the provisions of the Code; it is difficult to see how our present European Court of Justice, grappling with an existing case load which is likely to grow rather than diminish in size, could cope in addition with the supervision of a binding European private law. The powers of such a court might well be regarded by member states as more invasive than those invested in the European Court of Justice. I wonder how many of them would at present be prepared to contemplate so great a departure from the present state of affairs.

However this cautious assessment does not, in my opinion, diminish in any way the value of Professor von Bar's enterprise, as described by him in his paper. The influence it could bring to bear on national courts in the development of their own systems of law could surely be very great. The common law, with its uncodifed law of obligations and its judicial method of incremental development of the law, could well be more open to such an influence than other national systems; though I have been most interested to read of attempts to

---

[6] "Why a Code is not the best way to advance the cause of European legal unity" in *European Review of Private Law* 519–524 (1997). 1 note, incidentally, that many Continental European lawyers are also sceptical towards the idea of a Code and believe that at the very least the ground must first be prepared by that at the very least the ground must first be prepared by sustained academic work. Professor Reinhard Zimmermann is one of the most notable proponents of this school of thought: see his excellent "Savigny's Legacy. Legal History, Comparative Law and the Emergence of a European Legal Science" (1996) 112 *L.Q.R.* 576ff .

[7] English readers can find an interesting account in Advocate-General Arthur Hartkamp's essay "Interplay between Judges, Legislators and Academics, the Case of the New Civil Code of the Netherlands" in *Law Making, Law Finding and Law Shaping: the Diverse Influences* (ed. Basil S. Markesinis) (1997) 91–112.

reform the German law relating to breach of contract or, as it is described in Germany, irregularities of performance.[8]

Even so we have to recognise that no enterprise of this kind can produce perfection, or even attract universal agreement. There is no hidden treasure, no crock of gold, no Holy Grail, awaiting discovery; what will emerge is a series of preferred solutions. Academic lawyers, when they produce blueprints of this kind, cannot hope to command immediate or universal acceptance. They can only cast their bread upon the waters. In this connection, it has to be appreciated that the academic ideal has never been embraced in this country. Academic doctrine has never been a source of law. Of course, the judges of this country have the greatest respect for distinguished scholars, and for academic work of high quality. They mine their work ruthlessly for assistance. But they know that academic work, like every other form of legal activity, has its limitations. Views expressed in a substantial textbook cannot all be the subject of deep analysis, nor can the author have subjected every aspect of his subject to the minute investigation which is inherent in the judicial process[9]; indeed the greater the scope of the work, the greater the likelihood that parts of it will consist of untested, or inadequately tested, assumptions. Judges tend therefore to find themselves treating academic treatises as a starting point, but usually no more, in their work. As I myself was driven to say in a recent opinion in the House of Lords, "A crumb of analysis is worth a whole loaf of opinion"[10].

Professor von Bar has expressed the view that commercial and consumer-related law will not be able to continue in their current multiplicity, although other areas may remain in disharmony, thereby implying that a European codification will in due course be required in these two areas. This observation has considerable force in the case of consumer-related law, which has already been the subject of European directives; and in the case of commercial law he can derive some support from the Uniform Commercial Code of the United States. It must not however be forgotten that, in the case of commercial contracts, parties can and commonly do select the governing law. Moreover they frequently adopt one of the numerous standard forms, devised for the particular subject, which provide an applicable code governing the characteristic problems which tend to arise in the relevant trade, and which are frequently designed with reference to a particular system of law. There are numerous standard

---

[8] See, inter alia, Professor Lorenz's illuminating piece "Reform of the German Law of Breach of Contract" *E.L.R.* vol I, pp.317–344.

[9] The former Vice-Chancellor, Sir Robert Megarry, himself a distinguished author of textbooks, expressed this difference in the following passage: "The process of authorship is entirely different from that of a judicial decision. The author, no doubt, has the benefit of a broad and comprehensive survey of his chosen subject as a whole, together with a lengthy period of gestation, and intermittent opportunities for reconsideration. But he is exposed to the peril of yielding to preconceptions, and he lacks the advantage of that impact and sharpening of focus which the detailed facts of a particular case bring to the judge. Above all, he has to form his ideas without the aid of the purifying ordeal of skilled argument on the specific facts of the contested case. Argued law is tough law." *Cordell* v. *Second Claufield Properties* [1969] 2 Ch. 9 at p.16.

[10] *Hunter and Others* v. *Canary Wharf Ltd.* [1997] AC 655, 694.

forms used in the case of the many thousands of contracts negotiated each year in the City of London—in shipping and insurance, in banking and financial services, in the various commodity trades, and so on—many of them framed on the assumption that English law is the governing law, the most remarkable example perhaps being found in the case of contracts of marine insurance. None of this however detracts from the desirability that we should all keep our national laws of contract under review. Here once again, I welcome Professor von Bar's enterprise, and the beneficial influence it may well have upon national laws; indeed privately drafted "model laws", such as the comparative- inspired Lando Project on Contract Law, offer the benefits of a code shorn of the textual rigidity which usually accompanies codification[11]. But I very respectfully wonder whether codification of European commercial law is so obviously desirable as he suggests, or whether the history of the U.S. Commercial Code in fact provides an appropriate or useful analogy. In fact, it appears that the concept of a commercial contract is different in English and in German law. For example Zweigert and Kötz tell us that, in English law, the characteristic commercial contract is a contract for the carriage of goods by sea, whereas in German law it is a contract for the sale of land.

I turn now to a different subject, which I first raised in my Wilberforce Lecture[12]. We must remind ourselves that a legal system does not consist only of its substantive law. It embraces in addition its judicial system, and its judicial procedure seen in its widest sense. In a remarkable Lecture given to mark the 40th anniversary of the founding of the British Institute of International and Comparative Law[13], Jeremy Lever Q. C., a distinguished lawyer specialising in European law, argued forcefully that procedure is more important than substantive law. Of course, this all depends on what you mean by important. Moreover an equally persuasive argument could be advanced that our judicial systems themselves are more important than the procedure which provides the framework for proceedings in court. At all events, in considering the coming together of the common law and the civil law, it is surely right that we should not restrict ourselves to substantive law but ask ourselves whether, in these two areas, such a coming together is taking place. 1 am glad to be able to inform you that particular attention is now being paid to these subjects by the British Institute.

I turn first to procedure. Although it is relevant to consider criminal as well as civil procedure, and in particular the mode of trial in criminal proceedings, I shall for present purposes restrict myself to civil procedure.

Germany has taught us the importance of comparative civil procedure. In most, if not all, of their universities the law faculty includes a professor of civil

---

[11] See, e.g., *Principles of European Contract Law Part I, Performance, Non-Performance and Remedies*, ed. by Ole Lando and Hugh Beale (1995).

[12] An Introduction to Comparative Law, op. cit.

[13] [1999] 48 I.C.L.Q. 285 ff..

procedure, and there has inevitably developed an interest in the civil procedure of other countries, perhaps especially of this country. The same may well be happening nowadays in some other continental European countries. In contrast, this country has failed altogether to treat civil procedure as an academic discipline. This is a lamentable gap. A few individual law teachers are, very creditably, beginning to fill this gap; but without the necessary funding, they can achieve very little, and it is most unlikely that that funding will be made available.

It is a remarkable fact that, in the absence of any such academic support, there have recently been introduced in this country the most far-reaching reforms in our civil procedure since the nineteenth century. These have been largely the work of one senior judge—Lord Woolf, the Master of the Rolls (who presides over the Civil Division of the Court of Appeal), who is one of the Conference's keynote speakers and to whom we in this country owe a great debt. They are designed to streamline the civil process by placing greater powers in the hands of the presiding judge, and so to reduce the cost and delay of litigation. It is notorious that legal costs are very high in this country; but it has to be recognised that the delay is less, sometimes far less, than that which occurs in some other countries.

It is of some interest to record the origin of these reforms. Our old system of civil procedure reflected the fact that, until the middle of the present century, many substantial civil actions, were, like substantial criminal prosecutions, tried by juries. About 50 years ago, however, the role of the jury in civil actions was drastically curtailed by judicial decisions which had the effect that, in practical terms, the only civil actions now tried by juries are defamation cases. But we failed to notice that this change really undermined our old system of civil procedure which places the initiative in the hands of the advocates; and everything went on as before, as it usually does. However substantial changes were introduced in our Commercial Court. This court is primarily concerned with disputes arising out of contracts negotiated in the City of London, to which I have already referred. Of course, the vast majority of disputes under these contracts go to arbitration; but a significant number still come to court, and in these cases it is very common for one party, and not unusual for both parties, to come from overseas. In a sense, therefore, the Commercial Court is in competition with international arbitration; the Commercial Judges are well aware of this, all of them having appeared as advocates, and sat as arbitrators, in such arbitrations when they were practising barristers. In those arbitrations lawyers from both civil law countries and common law countries may appear in the same arbitration; and for this and other reasons there has naturally developed a sort of consensus about the applicable procedure, involving attributes drawn from both common law and civil law systems. The resulting procedure has included a simplification and exclusion of formality in the preliminary stages, coupled with a more "hands on" approach by the arbitrators. Inspired by this development, the Commercial Judges themselves introduced radical procedural reforms along the same lines in cases in the Commercial List. These have had the effect of reducing the time occupied by such cases by about 50 per cent. It was these reforms which, in their turn, inspired Lord Woolf when formulating his more far-reaching reforms applicable in the whole field of civil proceedings—changes which are in their turn inspiring similar developments elsewhere in the common law world. Indeed, I am reliably informed that the Woolf reforms have generated considerable interest even in civil law countries such as Germany and France. This is possibly the most important coming together of the common law and the civil law which has yet occurred, and one which is especially worthy of note since it is in the area of court procedure and practice that lawyers are at their most protective of the system in which they have been brought up. There are however other procedural topics which merit attention. One is the question whether the common law principle of *forum non conveniens* might be invoked to mitigate the rigidities inherent in the application of the rules of jurisdiction embodied in the Brussels Convention—a possibility which is perhaps becoming more attractive to continental European lawyers specialising in civil procedure than it has been in the past.

There is however another subject, so far even more neglected than civil procedure, which is surely awaiting exposure to comparative methodology. I speak of our different judicial systems, including our different judicial methods.

Here the contrast between the common law and civil law systems is perhaps at its most striking. We can see this in its most extreme form by comparing the English and German systems. Practically everything seems to be different—the English system being the product of history, having developed naturally over the centuries in a country where violent revolution has for a long time been unknown, and the German system having been devised by man. These differences are to be found in legal education; in the appointment of judges—the stress in England being on court experience as an advocate, and in Germany being on education and training with the effect that German judges embark on their judicial careers at a much younger age than their English counterparts; in the system of courts, with (among other things) a number of Courts of Appeal in Germany and just one in England; in the manning of the courts, the single judge being the norm at first instance in England (an inheritance, no doubt, from the jury) and three judges being the norm at first instance in Germany; in the number of professional judges, there being a much greater number in Germany than in England and Wales (though the numbers themselves are misleading since some functions performed by professional judges in Germany are performed by Masters of the Supreme Court, "commissioners" or lay magistrates in this country); and in the system of appeals—most, if not all, appeals being as of right in Germany, whereas in England most are only with leave, leading to great differences in the number of appeals heard and therefore in the size of appellate courts. For example, there are 12 Law Lords in the Supreme Court (the House of Lords) of this country (who also sit in the Privy Council hearing appeals from other countries overseas), and over 120 judges in the Bundesgerichtshof who (with the help of a substantial number of judicial assistants—the Law Lords at present have none, though this may change) have to consider a far greater number of appeals than the Law Lords dispose of in the House of Lords (about 70–80 each year). In this area, comparison would surely be of great interest, and perhaps of great benefit. There are many questions worthy of serious consideration which a common lawyer would be inclined to pose, but it is unnecessary for me to identify them in this paper.

We find similar contrasts when we turn to judicial method. These are particularly marked in the appellate process. In Germany, appeals are processed in a manner which, to a citizen of this country, appears more like the bureaucratic method of a civil servant than a court hearing; in England, the greatest emphasis is on the oral argument by barristers in open court. Both methods may be regarded as open to criticism. The German approach, to the eyes of a common lawyer, lacks the openness of an oral hearing in court, which may be thought to be more desirable in modern times when the stress is on open government; though the same criticism can be levelled at the system of dealing with petitions for leave to appeal to the House of Lords, most of which are disposed of on paper alone. In England, however, the time spent on the oral hearing has been recognised to be too long, having regard in particular to the increasing number and complexity of appeals and the steep rise in legal costs. Measures have therefore been taken recently in the Court of Appeal (involving the use of legal assistants) to reduce the length of oral argument, and the same is likely to happen in the House of Lords, when space is available to accommodate legal assistants. The aim is, however, not so much to reduce the importance of oral argument, as to curtail its length.

The most striking distinction between common law and civil law appellate systems is however to be found in the common law institution of the dissenting judgment. This is regarded as being of fundamental importance in common law countries. I have never heard any criticism of it in this country; it is however sometimes excluded on policy grounds, as in the Criminal Division of the English Court of Appeal. The common law experience proves that the dissenting judgment does not undermine the authority of the court, though this still appears to be the main objection advanced in civil law countries. It seems more probable that the real objection is that it is inconsistent with the character of the appellate process in force in those countries, which is designed to accommodate the large number of appeals generated in their systems. Certainly, there can be no question of the dissenting judgement being abandoned in the common law world. For example, I cannot imagine myself having been prevented from delivering my dissenting opinion in the *Pinochet*[14] case. Plainly it had no influence on the outcome of the case. It was really a public statement, and as such was available to the Foreign Offices of the world; I only hope that their Legal Advisers

---

[14] Reg. v. Bow Street Metropolitan Stipendiary Magistrate *Ex parte* Pinochet Ugarte [1999] 2 WLR 827, 849.

have read it. To have prevented me from delivering it would have appeared to me, and indeed to other lawyers in common law countries, as an unacceptable form of censorship, contrary to the public interest not only in England but also, in this particular case, in other countries overseas. The dissenting judgment, which has been a feature of the common law for centuries, is regarded by common lawyers as part of the natural order of things, and indeed as an institution of great value in the future development of the law. It is perhaps of some significance that dissents are permitted in some European courts of great importance, such as the European Court of Human Rights and the German Constitutional Court.

In truth, both the common law and the civilian judicial methods are the fruit of long tradition. The common law method is the product of an oral tradition and a collaboration between the judges and the barristers which find their origin in the ancient societies of judges, barristers and students called the Inns of Court, in the premises of one of which (Lincoln's Inn) our Conference will be held. The civilian method, I understand, finds its origin in the adoption of the Romano-Canonical mode of trial of the 13th and 14th centuries, which gave large managerial powers to the educated judge. Each of these two methods has its own inner strength and coherence and its own integrity; and each has its own advantages. In these circumstances, we cannot expect either the common law or the civilian judges to abandon the system in which they have been brought up. But in the twenty-first century we can surely expect the judges of both traditions to learn as much as they can from their counterparts, searching for inspiration and for material from which they can improve their own system. Evidence that this exchange of ideas is in fact beginning to take place may be found not only in Lord Woolf's reforms, but in meetings between senior judges of both systems. The Anglo-German Conferences which have already taken place have proved to be so successful that more are planned for the future. Meetings between senior British judges and judges of other European courts are planned and will, I trust and believe, also prove to be most productive.

I realise that, in the short time available to me at the Conference, it will not be possible for me to do more than touch upon the various topics which I have outlined in this written version of my closing address. I have nevertheless felt the need to place them on record; and I am fortified in my resolve to do so by the substantial nature of the contributions which I have been given the opportunity to read in advance. Comparative law is a subject of such extraordinary importance, and the coming together of the common law and the civil law is such a momentous event, that it is, I feel, inappropriate for me to abbreviate my contribution to this Conference.

I wish to conclude by saying that my many meetings with European lawyers, both judges and professors, have provided me with some of the happiest experiences of my life. I have learned that, in this work, much in the end depends on personal relationships; and that, once these are established on a satisfactory basis, everything else follows, in particular the trust and confidence that enable us to discuss even the most sensitive problems without restraint. It will be a great privilege for me to attend this Conference, and to enjoy the company and profit from the wisdom and experience of lawyers of the highest distinction from all over Europe whom we are most fortunate to have in our midst. For how much better could we hope for than to have as keynote speakers not only Lords Steyn and Bingham, but also Professor Klaus Hopt, one of Germany's leading experts in the field and Co-Director of the celebrated Max Planck Institute in Hamburg. The background of these colleagues is as diverse as their learning is undoubted. And these features of learning, cultural breadth and long experience are also evident in the case of our public law panellists. For I confess that in my entire life I can hardly remember listening to such a panel of eminent judges. To have brought together the Presidents of the European Court of Justice, the German Constitutional Court and the Italian Constitutional Court, together with the first woman member of the French Constitutional Court, and to have them share the platform with our own Lord Chief Justice and the Master of the Rolls, is not merely a remarkable achievement by the organisers of this Conference; it is also a clear sign that the common law and the civil law are coming together. Indeed, how could it be otherwise. For our interests do not only converge in matters of private law and judicial procedure, but also in matters of public law where, in the light of significant recent constitutional changes in this country, I can foresee our lawyers developing a great interest in the public law jurisdiction of courts elsewhere in the continent of Europe.

We in this country will all be greatly honoured that our most distinguished visitors should have spared the time to attend. I only hope that they will derive as much pleasure and profit from the occasion as I have no doubt that I myself will do.

Appendix

Millennium Conference Delegates
(as of December 30th 1999)

The Rt. Hon, the Lord Alexander, Under Treasurer, Middle Temple
Professor Dr Guido Alpa, Rome, Italy
H.E. Sr Ammaducci, Italian Ambassador at the Court of St. James
Professor Mads Andenas, British Institute of Intern. & Comp. Law
Mr David Anderson QC, Brick Court Chambers
The Rt. Hon Dame Mary Arden, Royal Courts of Justice
Professor Jean-Bernard Auby, Paris, France
The Rt. Hon Lord Justice Auld,
Sir Philip Bailhache, Bailiff of Jersey
Christopher Baker, Arden Chambers, London
Professor Christian von Bar, Osnabrück, Germany
Chris Bates, Clifford Chance, London
Miss Presley Baxendale QC, 2 Hare Court, London
Mr. Bruce W. Bean, Clifford Chance, London
Professor Jack Beatson QC, University of Cambridge
Professor John Bell FBA, University of Leeds
Martin Berkin, One Paper Buildings, London
Marcel Berlins, The Guardian
Sir Franklin Berman KCMG, Foreign & Commonwealth Office
The Rt. Hon the Lord Bingham of Cornhill, Lord Chief Justice of England and Wales
Professor Peter Birks QC, DCL, FBA, University of Oxford
William Blair Esq QC, 3 Gray's Inn Place, London
The Rt. Hon the Lord Borrie,1 Plowden Buildings, London
Chris Bright Esq., BCL, Clifford Chance
Stanley Brodie Esq QC, Treasurer, Inner Temple
The Rt. Hon Lord Justice Brown
The Rt. Hon the Lord Browne-Wilkinson, Senior Law Lord
Professor Marcel Brus, Leiden, The Netherlands
The Rt. Hon Dame Elizabeth Butler-Sloss
Excmo Sr Don Luis Martínez Calcerrada, President, Spanish Supreme Court
HE President Guy Canivet, Cour de Cassation, Paris, France
The Rt. Hon. The Lord Carlile of Berriew QC, Bell Yard
The Rt. Hon. Sir Robert Carswell, Lord Chief Justice of N. Ireland
Jeremy Carver Esq, CBE, Clifford Chance, London
Mr Armel C Cates, Clifford Chance, London
The Rt. Hon Lord Justice Chadwick
Nicholas Chambers Esq QC
Keith Clark Esq, Chairman, Clifford Chance
Professor Malcolm Clarke, University of Cambridge

Professor Dr. Michael Coester, University of Munich, Germany
Professor Dr. Dagmar Coester-Waltjen, University of Munich, Germany
His Honour Judge Laurence Collins QC, FBA, Herbert Smith
Mr John Collins, Treasury Solicitor's Department
The Hon. Sir Antony Colman,
Madame Justice Fernanda Contri, Corte Costituzionale, Italy
Professor Jeremy Cooper, Southampton Institute
Mr Ross Cranston QC MP, DCL, Solicitor General
Professor Paul Davies, London School of Economics
Simon Davis Esq, Clifford Chance, London
Peter Deegan Esq, Clifford Chance, Madrid
Conrad Dehn Esq QC, Fountain Court
Professor Thanassis Diamantopoulos, Athens, Greece
His Honour Judge Anthony Diamond QC, Essex Court Chambers
Mr Rainer Dobblestein, Legal Affairs Counsellor, German Embassy, London
Ms Clare Dyer, Legal Affairs Editor, The Guardian
Ms Jean Eaglesham, The Financial Times
Mr Michael Elland-Goldsmith, Clifford Chance, Paris
The Rt. Hon Lord Elles
Dr. Stefan Enchelmaier, Lady Margaret Hall, Oxford
Mr Justice Roger Errera, Conseil d' Etat, Paris, France
The Rt. Hon. Sir Anthony Evans, Treasurer, Gray's Inn
Duncan Fairgrieve, The Queen's College, Oxford
The Rt. Hon. The Lord Falconer of Thoroton, Cabinet Office
Ms Amanda Finlay, Lord Chancellor's Department
Dr. Sebastian Fohrbeck, Director DAAD, London
Professor Galli Fonseca, Emeritus President of the Corte di Cassazione, Italy.
Lady Fox QC, 4/5 Gray's Inn Square
Professor Dr. Hans Franken, Leiden, The Netherlands
Edward Garnier Esq., MP, Shaddow Attorney General
Professor Hazel Genn, University College London
Professor van Gerven. Former Advocate General, Court of the European Communities
The Rt. Hon. Lord Justice Peter Gibson
The Rt. Hon. Sir Iain Glidewell
The Rt. Hon the Lord Goff of Chieveley, PC, DCL, FBA, former Senior Law Lord
Binnie Goh, Treasury Solicitor's Department, London
Professor Sir Roy Goode, CBE, QC, FBA, University of Oxford
The Rt. Hon the Lord Goodhart QC, 11 Clarence Terrace
James Goudie QC, 11 King's Bench Walk, London
Mr Justice Dieter Grimm, Bundesverfassungsgericht, Germany
Miss Elisabeth-Anne Gumbel QC, Strand
Dr Richard J Haas CBE, London
A. H. Hammond, Treasury Solicitor
Mrs Pamela Harries
Mr Richard Hart, Hart Publishing
Gary Hart, Lord Chancellor's Department
Professor Robert Hazell, University College London
Miss Hilary Heilbron QC, Brick Court Chambers

Jonathan Hirst QC,
Professor M van Hoecke, Brussels, Belgium
Professor Klaus Hopt, Director Max Plank Institute, Hambrug
Michael Hutchings Esq, Sandhayes, Corsley, Warminster
The Rt Hon the Lord Hutton
HE President Rodriguez Iglesias, Court of the European Communities
The Rt Hon the Lord Irvine of Lairg. Lord Chancellor of Great Britain
Mr Justice Jackson, Royal Courts of Justice
Professor Francis Jacobs QC. Advocate General, Court of the European Communities
Mr Simon James, Clifford Chance, London
John Jarvis QC, Gray's Inn Place
The Hon. Mr Justice Keene
Mr Christopher Kellett, Clifford Chance, Madrid
The Rt. Hon. Lord Justice Kennedy
The Rt. Hon. The Baroness Kennedy of the Shaws
Tim Kerr, Esq., 4–5 Gray's Inn Square, London
Chris Kerse, Esq., EC Committee, House of Lords
Mr Justice Hans-Peter Kirchhoff, Bundesgerichtof, Germany
Professor Tim Koopmans, formerly a Justice at the European Court and Advocate
    General at the Netherlands Supreme Court
Madame Justice Noëlle Lenoir, Conseil Constitutionnel, Paris, France
Mark Leonard, Esq., Foreign Policy Centre
The Rt. Hon the Lord Lester of Herne Hill
Mr Jeremy Lever QC, All Souls College, Oxford
Allan Levy QC, Bedford Row
HE Professor Jutta Limbach, President of the Bundesverfassungsgerichtshof, Germany
David Lock, Parliamentary Secretary, Lord Chancellor's Department
HE Giovanni Longo, Vice President of the Corte de Cassazione, Rome Italy
Professor Dr. Dr. H.C. Marcus Lutter, University of Bonn, Germany
The Rt. Hon Sir Nicholas Lyell QC, MP, former Attorney General
His Honour Judge Machin,
Mr David Machin, Under Treasurer, Gray's Inn
The Rt. Hon Robert MacLennan MP, House of Commons
Ms Rache Magrill, Treasury Solititor's Department
Mr Alec Malek QC, 3 Verulam Buildings, London
The Rt. Hon Lord Justice Mance, Royal Courts of Justice
HE President Marchall, Cour de Cassation, Belgium
Mr Ivan Marisin, Clifford Chance, Moscow
Professor B. S. Markesinis QC, DCL, FBA, University of Oxford
Spyro, George Markesinis, Esq., Clifford Chance, London
Graham Mather, Esq.,European Policy Forum
Mr Martin Matthews, University College, Oxford
Michael Maunsell, British Institute of International & Comparative Law
The Rt. Hon Lord Justice May, Royal Courts of Justice
Mr Patrick Milmo Esq., QC,
Mrs Marina Milmo, Sweet and Maxwell, London
Professor C. Mirabelli, Corte Costitutionale, Rome, Italy
Ms Nuala Mole, The AIRE Centre

HE Ambassador, Count G von Moltke

Tim Morris Esq, Clifford Chance, London

Professor Dr. E Moustaira, University of Athens

Professor Dr. Horatia Muir-Watt, University of Paris I, France

The Rt. Hon. the Lord Mummery, Royal Courts of Justice

The Rt. Hon. the Lord Mustill,

Michael Nathanson Esq, Radcliffes

The Rt. Hon. the Lord Neill of Bladen QC, 1 Hare Court

The Rt. Hon. the Lord Nicholls of Birkenhead

HE Professor Dr. Walter Odersky, Emeritus President of the Bundesgerichtshof, Germany

The Rt. Hon Lord Justice Otton, Royal Courts of Justice, London

Vice-President Elizabeth Palm, Court of Human Rights, Strasbourg

Professor Dr. Charalambos Pampoukis, Secretary General, Greek Foreign Ministry

Nello Pasquini Esq, Radcliffe's London

Jacques Pelletier, Clifford Chance, Paris

Chris Perrin Esq. Clifford Chance, London

The Rt. Hon the Lord Phillips of Worth Matravers

Sir Hayden Phillips, Lord Chancellor's Department

H.E. Dr. Hans von Ploetz, German Ambassador to the Court of St. James

The Rt. Hon Lord Justice Potter

Professor Peter Quint, University of Maryland, USA

Professor Giorgi Rebuffa, University of Genoa, Italy

Errol Robathan, Esq., The College of Law, London

Professor Dr. Stefano Rodotta, Member of the Italian Parliament; Professor at the University of Rome, Italy

Kenneth Stuart Rokison Esq QC, Temple

Professor Christos Rozakis, Vice President of the Court of Human Rights, Strasbourg; former Minister of Foreign Affairs, Greece.

Yetunde Ruban, Treasury Solicitor's Department

The Rt. Hon the Lord Saville

The Rt. Hon Lord Justice Schiemann

Professor Dr Peter Schlechtriem, University of Freiburg, Germany

David Scorey, Esq., Essex Court Chambers, London

The Rt. Hon Lord Justice Sedley

Nick Segal Esq, Allen & Overy

Julian Shellard, Esq., Treasury Solicitor's Department

Stephen Robert Silber Esq QC, Conquest House

Marion Adele Simmons QC, South Square

Charles Sparrow Esq DL, QC, 13 Old Square, Lincoln's Inn

Professor Dean Spielmann, Luxembourg

George Staple Esq, QC, Clifford Chance, London

The Rt. Hon the Lord Steyn

Professor Marcel Storme, University of Gent, Royal Belgian Academy

William Swadling Esq., Brasenose College, Oxford

Mr Richard Thomas, Clifford Chance, London

Professor G Tremonti. Member of the Italian parliament and former Minister of Finance, Italy

Madame Justice Athanassia Tsambassi, Council of State, Athens, Greece
Augustus Ullstein Esq Esq., QC, 29 Bedford Row
Hannes Unberath, Esq., Worcester College, Oxford
Mr David Vaughan QC, Brick Court Chambers
John Veeder QC, Essex Court Chambers, London
Mr Anthony Voyiatzis, Attorney at Law, Athens, Greece
Professor Stephen Weatherill, Associate Director, Oxford Institute of European and Comparative Law
The Rt. Hon the Lord Wilberforce,
HE President Luzius Wildhaber, Court of Human Rights, Strasbourg
The Rt. Hon the Lord Williams of Mostyn QC, Attorney General
The Rt. Hon the Lord Windlesham, Principal of Brasenose College, Oxford
The Rt. Hon the Lord Woolf of Barnes, Master of the Rolls
Mr John Youdell, Treasury Solicitor's Department
Mr Raymond Youngs, Southampton Institute
Professor Dr. Zeno-Zenkovitch, University of Rome, Italy